The Veil Is Torn

*He yielded up the ghost, and behold
the veil of the Temple was rent in twain
from the top to the bottom.*

Matthew 27:50,51

The Veil Is Torn

In a holocaust of flame the Temple is destroyed

In September A.D. 70, after a bitter five-month siege, the future Roman emperor Titus and his legions breach the inner walls of Jerusalem and reduce most of the old city to a smoldering ruin. What seemed impossible had come to pass. The triumphant Romans enter the Temple and stand in the Holy of Holies. That night the Temple is put to the torch and destroyed. The old order is gone.

A.D. 30 to 70

FROM PENTECOST TO THE FALL OF JERUSALEM

The .
Christians

THEIR FIRST TWO THOUSAND YEARS

First Volume

CHP

CHRISTIAN HISTORY PROJECT

EDITOR

Ted Byfield has been a journalist for fifty-five years and a western Canadian magazine publisher since 1973, the founder of *Alberta Report* and *British Columbia Report* weekly news magazines and founding editor of *Alberta in the Twentieth Century*, a twelve-volume history of his province. A columnist for Canada's *Sun* newspapers and sometime contributor to the *National Post* and *Globe and Mail* national newspapers, he is active in evangelical journalistic outreach. He was one of the founders of St. John's School of Alberta, an Anglican school for boys where he developed a new method of teaching history.

ASSOCIATE EDITOR

Calvin Demmon of Marina, California, is a former editor of *Alberta Report* news magazine and former long-time columnist and city editor for the *Monterey County Herald*.

COVER

Standing near Jerusalem, this cross is a reconstruction of the type upon which Jesus died.
Photo: © Zev Radovan (Land of the Bible Photo Archive).

CHRISTIAN HISTORY PROJECT LIMITED PARTNERSHIP

President and CEO	Robert W. Doull
Controller	Terry White
Marketing Manager	Leanne Nash
Contact Center Manager	Kathy Therrien
Contact Center Administrators	Brian Lehr, Bheko Dube, Larry Hill
Credit Manager	Keith Bennett
Customer Service Manager	Lori Arndt
Customer Service	Grace de Guzman, Katrina Soetaert
Information Systems Manager	Michael Keast

The Veil Is Torn, A.D. 30 to 70, Pentecost to the Destruction of Jerusalem

Art Director and Designer	Denton Pendergast
Academic Consultants	Dr. William S. Barker, Dr. Kyril Holden, Dr. Dennis Martin
Series Planner	Barrett Pashak
Assistant Planner	Louise Henein
Director of Research	Moira Calder
Researchers	Rev. David Edwards, Glen Friesen, Micah Friesen, Louise Henein, Jon Hokanson, Alexei Krieger, Leanne Nash
Illustration and Photo Editor	Jack Keaschuk
Maps	Leanne Nash, illustrated by Mike Grant
Writers	Charlotte Allen, Ted Byfield, Calvin Demmon, Mark Galli, Steve Hopkins, Frederica Mathewes-Green, Allen North, Denyse O'Leary, Barrett Pashak, Gary Thomas
Illustrators	John Collier, Bob Crofut, Michael Dudash, Matt Frey, Jamie Holloway, Greg Harlin, Glenn Harrington, Richard Sparks, Shannon Stirnweis, Rob Wood
Art Director	Jack Keaschuk
Design Director	Dean Pickup
Production Editor	Rev. David Edwards
Proofreaders	P. A. Colwell, Faith Farthing
Special thanks to	Micha Ashkenazi: Israel Pilgrims Travel, Jerusalem

THE CHRISTIANS: Their First Two Thousand Years

First Printed 2002

Reprinted with revisions 2003

© 2003 Christian History Project Inc.

© 2003 Christian History Project Limited Partnership.

Chairman	Gerald J. Maier

NATIONAL LIBRARY OF CANADA CATALOGUING IN PUBLICATION DATA

Main entry under title:

The Veil Is Torn

(The Christians : the first two thousand years of our journey ; 1)
Includes bibliographical references and index.

ISBN 0-9689873-0-3

1. Church history–Primitive and early church, ca. 30-600. 2. Paul, the Apostle, Saint. 3. Persecution–History–Early church, ca. 30-600. I. Christian Millennial History Project. II. Series: Christians : the first two thousand years of our journey ; 1.

BR162.3.V44 2002   270.1   C2001-911625-X

PRINTED IN CANADA BY FRIESENS CORPORATION

CONTENTS

ILLUSTRATIONS

MAPS

CHP

For additional copies of this book or information on others in the series,
please contact us at:

The Christian History Project
10333 178 Street
Edmonton AB, Canada, T5S 1R5
www.christianhistoryproject.com

1-800-853-5402

FOREWORD

THE MOST DANGEROUS PEOPLE, said the twentieth-century Christian essayist G. K. Chesterton, are those who have been cut off from their cultural roots. Had he lived long enough, he would have seen his observation hideously fulfilled. At the time of his death in 1936, Germany, one of the greatest of the Christian nations, had been amputated from its Christian origins and was embracing instead wild doctrines founded on sheer nonsense. Thus deluded, the Germans set off the world's worst-ever war. People who don't believe in something, Chesterton also said, can be persuaded to believe in anything. How right he was.

Today, we are just such a people. That America, indeed the whole Western world, is being wrenched away from its cultural origins has become a self-evident fact. For half a century, our literature, our popular music and drama, the visual arts, Hollywood and much of the film industry have been disseminating a genre of nihilism that debases almost every form of human virtue and exalts sensual gratification beyond anything the senses could possibly fulfill. Meanwhile, the liberal arts faculties of our universities work zealously to cut off the branch they are sitting on, diligently destroying the very foundations upon which the whole concept of higher education rests. The result of all this is a culturally dispossessed people, the very situation in which Chesterton saw such mortal danger.

What are our foundations? Though it has of late become intellectually unfashionable to even think it, let alone say it, the fact is that our cultural origins are almost wholly Christian. Our founding educational institutions, our medical system, our commitment to the care of the aged and infirm, our concept of individual rights and responsibilities, all came to us through Christianity. Our best literature, our most enduring music, our finest sculptural masterpieces and many of the greatest paintings in every age are those of professed and dedicated Christians. Finally, our concept of democracy came to us from the Greeks through Christianity. Is it by mere coincidence that all those nations that have best instituted and preserved democratic government emerged from Christian origins? I don't think so.

The purpose of this series is to describe these foundations, to say who we are and how we got here. That is, to establish our real roots. It has been a long journey, two thousand years, and neither it nor we have been uniformly benevolent. But this is our past, this is our family, and knowing who it is and what it has done is the first step in finding our way home.

Ted Byfield

CHAPTER 1

Madman or God?

'Who are you?' the high priest demanded,
and Jesus' answer led him to the cross

T o any respectable and devout Jew, that mid-morning exhibition in the late spring of the year 3791 on the Jewish calendar—a date believed by the devout to be three thousand, seven hundred and ninety-one years after the creation of the world—would have been at once predictable, astonishing and outrageous. Predictable because it seemed likely these people were planning some new show to capture attention, astonishing because they rather specialized in the bizarre, and outrageous because everything they did was outrageous.

So now, there they were, these men, three dozen or more, mostly in their twenties, streaming from that house into the street, babbling like lunatics, and yelling out something about "the Coming of the Holy Spirit." They were drunk, obviously. A drunken debauch, and it was not even yet noon. Was this any way to celebrate Pentecost, the Jewish feast that welcomed the first harvest?

For the participants in that unusual event, all of whom were Jews, and for those who followed them for the next twenty centuries, it would mark the birth of the Christian church, the institutional embodiment of the world's numerically greatest religion. But for those sincere and God-fearing Jews who looked on from without at the time, it would have occasioned only dismay and disgust. They would no doubt be asking: What will it be next?

What indeed! What had it been already? The leader of these people, the man Jesus, of Nazareth, the one the authorities called "The Blasphemer," had been dead for six Sabbaths. Crucified, a hideous fate, after he was found guilty of blasphemy, of calling himself by the unmentionable name of God. Such a death was unfortunate, but necessary and deserved. Moreover, or so the authorities fondly thought, it would put an end to what was plainly a one-man movement.

Unhappily, they were wrong. His followers, now dancing around the street and babbling about "the Holy Spirit," somehow became persuaded he had returned from the dead. "Risen" was the word they used. Indeed, they insisted upon it, telling others they had repeatedly seen and talked to him and convincing them to join their celebration. So rather than quietly fade as had been hoped, the movement was now more alive than ever, and what had previously been an irritant was now becoming a first-class problem.

A problem for several reasons. The Romans, under whose imperial yoke Jewry had been suffering for more than a hundred years, viewed all novel Jewish religious movements as implicitly seditious, and they put them down with a

ferocity that could see thousands perish horribly, including the innocent. Worse still, the man Jesus and his movement came from Galilee, a hotbed of anti-Roman insurrection and intrigue, a province whose southern limits lay about sixty-five miles north of Jerusalem. Then too, the Blasphemer himself had repeatedly compromised the Law. And as every good Jew knew, the whole mission of the Jewish people, their very unity and integrity, consisted of and depended on the preservation of the Law. To compromise the Law was to challenge in particular the Pharisees, the party which saw the observance of the Law as the central responsibility of the Jewish people. Finally, the man was plainly anti-Temple as well. He said the imperishable building itself, indeed the whole ecclesiastical struc-ture that supported it and fulfilled the ritual animal sacrifice it had been consecrated to perform, was doomed. That made him equally offensive to

the high priests whose job was operating and preserving the Temple, and their party, the Sadducees.

So he was stopped, convicted of blasphemy in a Jewish trial and at the request of the Jewish leaders crucified by the Romans—God knows, the most ghastly death human ingenuity had ever contrived. Cruel, yes. But what was the alternative? Another religious movement, another insurrection, more hundreds slaughtered by the dreaded Twelfth Legion, the "Syrian Legion," as they called it, two of whose cohorts were stationed in Jerusalem. Both were under the orders of the Jew-hating Roman governor, Pilate. So as Caiaphas, the high priest, said at the time: "Better one man should suffer than the whole people." Harsh, certainly. But could you argue with his reasoning?

So the body was entombed, a huge boulder rolled against the entrance, and a guard posted by the Temple police. Toward dawn two days later, something happened. That seems conclusive enough. But what? The guard fled, the stone was moved, and the body disappeared. How this occurred, the authorities simply did not adequately explain. Clearly, they said, his followers must have bribed the guard, somehow rolled away the great stone and stolen the corpse. The obvious solution—to produce the man's body and have done with this nonsense—failed.

HARRINGTON

Passersby logically assume that the disciples, pouring out of the house from which a puzzling din is issuing, are nothing more than early-morning drunkards. But then each pilgrim to Jerusalem recognizes that this band of babblers is actually speaking in the language of his homeland. Peter excitedly calls out: "Let me explain this to you; listen carefully to what I say." People do listen, and three thousand are reported to join the fellowship of Jesus' disciples.

In first-century Judea, a round millstone-like rock was often rolled into place to seal a grave. Jesus' tomb was probably similar to this one, traditionally known as "Herod's Tomb" for Herod the Great. Archaeologists consider this more probably the burial site, not of Herod, but of his wife Mariamne. Herod himself was probably entombed in the Herodium (southeast of Bethlehem), one of the many fortresses and palaces he built throughout Judea.

The fact is, search though they certainly did, they couldn't find it.

So what could they do? Some no doubt suggested the Temple officials find another body, any body, and claim it was his. But then would they crucify it first? Where, how, and under what circumstances would you do the crucifying? And suppose the ruse were discovered! Better to just stay with the truth, some said. But then, what was the truth? No one knew—unless of course you were prepared to accept the preposterous fantasies of Jesus' followers. Such, for officialdom, was the imponderable problem the case posed.

But was this not in character? As they saw it, imponderables such as this had attended everything about the man since his initial appearance in Galilee some three years before.

His origins, like the origins of everything else in Galilee, were obscure. His widowed mother, now resident in Jerusalem with one of his faithful, told stories of curious manifestations in the heavens at the time of his birth, of angels appearing, of astrologers from the East, probably Zoroastrians, bringing gifts to the child. All patently ludicrous to those who had done away with him.

In any event, it had been disclosed during his trial that this man Jesus was not, in fact, Galilean-born. His mother, a direct descendant of King David, incidentally, and her husband had traveled south to Judea, specifically to the town of Bethlehem, six miles south of Jerusalem, to conform to one of the census schemes devised by Quirinius, governor of Syria at the time, who had jurisdiction over Judea.[1] You can't properly govern without assessing taxes, the Romans knew. To create a reliable tax roll, everyone had to be named, recorded, and

---

1. The precise year of Jesus Christ's birth, like the birth date of many great figures in the ancient world, is not known, and is confused by an apparent incompatibility between Matthew's account in the First Gospel and Luke's in the Third. Matthew has Jesus born before the death of Herod the Great, which occurred in 4 B.C. Luke ties the birth date to a census made in connection with a taxation scheme devised by Publius Sulpicius Quirinius, a Roman general and bureaucrat much mentioned by Roman historians, who became governor of Syria between A.D. 6 and 7. This, of course, would have Jesus born about a dozen years later. Some biblical historians hold that Luke erred. They say there had been earlier taxation censuses before Quirinius's, and Luke tied the birth to the wrong one. Other biblical historians see Luke as referring to an earlier census, when Quirinius was an administrator in the Middle East ca. 10–7 B.C.

counted. And the most efficient means of assuring accuracy, the Romans decided, was to require everyone to go back to the town of his birth.

This brought Jesus' heavily pregnant mother and her husband to Bethlehem, impossibly overcrowded because of the census. There, in the only space available, an animal stall behind a hotel, the child was born. Eight days later he was circumcised in the Temple at Jerusalem and given the name Joshua, or Jesus.[2]

The name, though historic, was not distinguished. There could easily have been a dozen or more Jesuses in every Judean village. However, the venue of his birth had definite theological implications. Jesus' adherents claimed him as the Messiah, the promised Savior of Israel. According to one widely held theory, the Messiah must be born in Bethlehem, of one of David's descendants. In addition, as a child in the Temple, so the story went, two ancients, both of them revered as prophets, had recognized the child as the future "Anointed One," which is what "messiah" means.

---

2. The names Joshua and Jesus are in fact the same name. The Jewish version would be spelled in the English alphabet as Jehoshua; the Greek equivalent would be Iesous.

Pilate's Fate

Some say he killed himself, some that he became Christian

Probably the most-mentioned Roman name in modern history is neither Julius Caesar nor Augustus, but rather that of a relatively minor Roman provincial governor called Pontius Pilate. The assertion that Jesus suffered under Pontius Pilate is recited in hundreds of languages all over the world in Christian creeds.

Nearly two millennia have passed since the death of this otherwise unremarkable bureaucrat, and little is known of his life except the details provided in the Gospels. The Jewish historian Josephus reports that Pilate ordered construction of an aqueduct to bring water into Jerusalem, and that the Jews were outraged—either because he used sacred funds for the project, or because he ran the aqueduct through a cemetery, making the water ceremonially undrinkable.

Josephus and the historian Philo both describe one or more incidents in which Pilate ordered images of the emperor Tiberius erected in Jerusalem. When the Jews vigorously protested, Pilate backed down. After his dramatic appearance in the New Testament, he slips into obscurity again.

For reasons that are unclear, Pilate was suspended from office in A.D. 37. Tradition holds that he committed suicide in 39. According to some early Christian writers, he killed himself in remorse over his part in the Crucifixion. Others say he recognized Jesus' divinity and became a believer himself. Over the centuries, that line of thought brought Pilate quite an honor: In the Ethiopic and Coptic churches, he is venerated as a saint. ■

Critics who were dubious about the historicity of Pontius Pilate were silenced by the twentieth-century discovery of a partially effaced stone inscription in seaside Caesarea. ". . . NTIUS PILATUS . . . ECTUS IUDAE . . ." it reads, identifying him as prefect of Judea. After the original was removed to a museum, this replica was placed at the discovery site near the ancient amphitheater of the city.

How preposterous, many genuinely pious Jews would respond. Was Israel's Messiah to be born in a stall and die on a Roman cross—a death as universally recognized for its shame as it was for its excruciating pain? The concept of the coming Messiah, the real Messiah, was the only sure hope of the Jewish people, they would say. For nearly ten centuries they had struggled to survive and preserve the Law and the sacrificial rituals in the Temple with which God had entrusted them. And survive they had, as a recurrently battered and beleaguered buffer state between the superpowers of East and West.

Once, more than a thousand years ago, under King David and his son Solomon, they had become

something of a superpower themselves, but this hegemony was brief, and throughout most of those centuries they had suffered recurrent invasion, siege, slaughter, captivity, deportation into slavery, cultural genocide, every conceivable mode of human misery. Once even the Temple itself had been destroyed and most of the people dragged away captive.[3] But God had soon seen to it that their captors were themselves overthrown, the people returned to their homeland, and their Temple restored.

Though the Messiah was merely a vision, a promise, the scholarly unanimously perceived this as a promise of the Scriptures. Every devout Jew believed implicitly in that promise. Messiah would come as the Scriptures foretold. He would be a conquering avenger who would right all wrongs, establish justice, and destroy forever the oppressor, whoever Israel's oppressor might be at the time.

There was, it is true, another very different view of the Messiah, implicit in some of the prophets. Isaiah in particular had foreseen the Anointed One not as a conqueror but as a suffering servant "despised for our transgressions, bruised for our iniquities" and "numbered with the transgressors." Yet, said Isaiah, with every lash stroke upon him, "we are healed. . . . For the Lord has laid on him the iniquity of us all." All this was linked to the words of the suffering figure portrayed in the

3. Two temples were to stand atop the Temple Mount in Jerusalem. The original was built by Solomon about 960 B.C., and destroyed by the Babylonians in 586 B.C. The second was built in 515 B.C., and vastly expanded by Herod the Great in the first century before Christ.

Underneath the main Church of the Nativity in Bethlehem, Greek Orthodox monks (right) clean the Grotto chapel, honored for centuries as the cave in which Jesus was born. At the left a Palestinian Christian venerates the spot (marked by a silver star) believed to be the actual spot where he lay.

Twenty-Second Psalm, who cries: "My God, my God, why hast thou forsaken me?"—words this Jesus would repeat from the cross. However, this doleful view of the prospective Messiah was for obvious reasons not very popular, and it was discounted by the more optimistic as reflecting merely the continued suffering of the Jewish people as a whole.

The current oppressor was imperial Rome. Its general, Pompey, had conquered Jerusalem more than a hundred years before. He spared the Temple, but defiantly strode into its "Holy of Holies," that sacred space that only the high priest could enter, then sneered that he had found in there nothing whatever. After that, Rome had lumped Judea, Galilee and a dozen other neighboring peoples in with Syria to the north, under a prefect appointed by the emperor. Sometimes the chosen method of government for Judea was a Roman proconsul or governor who usually reported to the prefect at Antioch. At other times, Rome would install a client king, preferably a Jew, to provide a veneer of Jewish independence.

Such a king had been Herod the Great, who took power fifty-nine years after the Roman conquest, and who was regarded by many as a sort of fake Jew. He was in fact an Idumean, from Judea's neighboring people to the south whom the Jews, in a moment of ascendancy a century earlier, had coerced into Judaism. Herod, succeeding his father, a sycophant of Rome, had parlayed this modest opportunity skillfully, and had made himself Rome's indispensable and reliable cat's-paw over much of the Middle East.

He ruled with fierce consistency, bringing peace to the area for the whole forty-one years of his reign by ruthlessly exterminating the slightest manifestations of anti-Roman nationalism. At the same time, he tried to ingratiate himself with the Jews by creating architectural wonders whose scale and grandeur would astonish archaeologists twenty centuries later.

He built for himself numerous palaces, four of them within thirty miles of Jerusalem. Nothing could equal these for lavish summer luxury. But by far the greatest and most magnificent of his palaces, named to honor his patron, the emperor Augustus, and his great general Marcus Agrippa, stood on the western edge of Jerusalem's Upper City. Its two vast reception halls enabled Herod to entertain hundreds of guests, while its opulent bedrooms and colonnaded courtyards, gardens and fountains brought renown even in faraway Rome. Peering from above it all were its three stout towers, 110 to 140 feet high, named for his brother Phasael, his friend Hippicus, and his beloved Mariamne, the wife he adored but whom he was forced through palace intrigue into executing, leaving him in a grief from which he would never recover.[4]

In Jerusalem also, he rebuilt and strengthened the city's walls, and erected a Roman amphitheater, something many Jews did not appreciate, since it smacked of Hellenism, the hated culture of the Greeks which, since its insinuation into Palestine with Alexander the Great three hundred years before, the Jews had persistently though hopelessly resisted. At Caesarea, fifty miles northwest of Jerusalem, Herod had pushed breakwaters out from the Mediterranean beaches to create and enclose a superb harbor, its entrance adorned with six spectacular monuments. Beside the

Nothing could equal Herod's palaces for lavish summer luxury. Their opulent bedrooms, colonnaded courtyards, gardens and fountains brought renown even in Rome.

harbor he built a model Roman city, with its amphitheater and hippodrome, its underground sewer system and its crafted streets meeting at precise right angles.

Finally he erected—as possible refuges for himself in case of insurrection, it was said—a system of desert fortresses, chief among them Machaerus east of the Dead Sea, Hyrcanaia west of it, and most impregnable of all, Masada, overlooking the Dead Sea from a mountaintop so precipitous and treacherous that few conquerors would be determined enough to scale it in sufficient strength to take the fortress itself. But most prized by the Jews was his reconstruction of the Temple at Jerusalem into a building of such awesome scale that it seemed to be as physically permanent as the spiritual strength it represented.

There was, it is true, at least one connective between Jesus and Herod. The former was born in or about the year that the latter died. In the tradition of Jesus' followers there was another link. Herod, once made aware that the celestial occurrences which ostensibly attended the child's birth, had set off rumors that Jesus was the expected Messiah, had reacted characteristically and butchered every infant in the vicinity.

---

4. Mariamne's mother, Alexandra, was an irrepressible conspirator in the court of Herod the Great, according to Josephus. At one point she tried secretly to lure the Roman general Marc Antony into Mariamne's bed, though her daughter was Herod's wife. Herod finally pretended to acquiesce in another of Alexandra's ambitions, to have her son made high priest. He made the appointment, then had the son drowned in one of his swimming pools. Mother and daughter grieved so wildly that Herod feared for his own life and concluded he had to put both to death. Thereafter he was stricken with depression, with visions of his beloved Mariamne awakening him in the night.

Harsh perhaps, but then, which was worse? The liquidation of a few score infants, or yet another "religious" movement, which would rapidly become yet another Jewish independence crusade, occasioning yet another crackdown by Rome, resulting in yet another slaughter of thousands? Where possible, you nipped such weeds in the bud. That was Rome's way, and under Herod the policy had one indisputable thing going for it. For the most part, it worked. It preserved peace.

In this instance, however, it didn't quite work. In some way warned of what was coming—by an angel, in the view of his followers—Jesus' parents took the child south through the Negev Desert into Egypt, returning later to take up residence at the town of Nazareth in Galilee.

Thereafter, and for the next twenty-seven or so years, little was heard of him. Far more was heard and known of his cousin John. Here was a prophet in the true ascetic tradition. A wild fellow who lived off the land in the semi-desert country east of Jerusalem, he would emerge and preach on the banks of the Jordan River. Great crowds would come from the countryside, even from Jerusalem itself, to hear him.

John's message was straight to the point. People—and by this he meant all the Jewish people—were living sinfully. God was enduring this, but God wouldn't do so much longer. The day of the Messiah was at hand, John said, and a great and terrible judgment was about to occur. Many believed him. What could they do? they asked. For this, he had two answers: repent and be baptized. Hundreds answered his call and were baptized in the waters of the Jordan River. Even the current Herod Antipas, son of the old tyrant and serving as tetrarch of Galilee, was said to have been strongly influenced by John.

One day this Jesus came from Nazareth and was himself baptized by John. There were reports of seemingly divine manifestations—of rumblings in the skies taken to be the voice of God, calling attention to this baptism. In any event, from that point on things began to change radically—for both Jesus and John.

Herod's magnificent palace, located west of the Temple precincts, comprised two mirrored wings surrounding a spacious courtyard. To the north (upper left in the photo) was the citadel with its great towers. All that remain of the palace and its precincts are the enormous foundation blocks of one of these towers, the Phasael, named after the king's brother. This model, built on the grounds of the Holyland Hotel in Jerusalem, is a reconstruction designed by Prof. M. Avi-Yonah.

Soon after, Jesus appeared as a visiting rabbi in the synagogue at his hometown of Nazareth. There he read a passage from the prophet Isaiah:

> The Spirit of the Lord God is upon me, because the Lord has anointed me to bring good tidings to the afflicted; he has sent me to bind up the broken-hearted, to proclaim liberty to the captives, and the opening of the prison to those who are bound; to proclaim the year of the Lord's favor (Isaiah 61:1–2a RSV).

Then, rolling up the scroll, he said: "This day is that scripture fulfilled in your ears." And he sat down while the congregation looked on astonished.

The upper Jordan (left) courses from Mount Hermon and winds its way south toward Lake Tiberias, the biblical Sea of Galilee. One of the points on the river claimed to be the scene of Jesus' baptism is Qasr el Yahud (top), five miles east of Jericho and the same distance upstream from the Dead Sea. Here, faithful of the Eastern Orthodox Churches, bearing the icon of Christ's baptism, observe the Feast of Jordan in January. A cross towers over the baptismal site at Qasr el Yahud (above). A Christian pilgrim (opposite page, left), like millions of others, funnels the waters of the Jordan into a bottle to take home.

The Jordan

River of history, river of God

The Jordan River, a stream storied in the roots of Judaism and Christianity, spans the one hundred direct miles between Mount Hermon, on the Syria-Lebanon-Israel border and the Dead Sea, but its serpentine twists and turns give it a riverbed distance of some 225 miles. About halfway down its course it widens to create Lake Tiberias, the biblical Sea of Galilee, in whose bordering villages the ministry of Jesus unfolded.

It is not always a gentle river, sometimes crashing down through steep rapids as it descends 689 feet from its source in northeast Israel's Lake Huleh to Lake Tiberias, and another 610 feet from the lake to the Dead Sea. Much of this happens at some of the lowest elevations on earth. At Lake Tiberias the Jordan is 695 feet below sea level, at the Dead Sea 1,315 feet below.

In a farewell address to the Israelites, Moses, whom God forbade to cross the river himself, promised, "Hear, O Israel, thou art to pass over Jordan this day" (Deut. 9:1). His successor, Joshua, was said to have led the Israelites dry-shod across the Jordan near Jericho into the Promised Land (Josh. 3:14–17). The prophet Elijah walked across the river with his anointed successor, Elisha, then ascended to heaven in a fiery chariot (2 Kings 2:11). Elisha healed Naaman, the Syrian general, by commanding him to wash in the Jordan (2 Kings 5:10).

John the Baptist, of course, brings the Jordan into the Christian story. It is he who baptizes Jesus at the outset of his ministry. Two sites where John conducted his baptisms are observed, one near Jericho called in Arabic al-Maghtas, the other near the point where the Jordan leaves Lake Tiberias. Here, Christians over the centuries have come to be rebaptized.

The river itself is little more than a stream, ninety to one hundred feet wide, three to ten feet deep. The name Jordan (in Arabic al-Urdunn, in Hebrew Iha-Yarden) means "flowing downward" or "the descending." And descend it does, not only geographically but also through history, a phenomenon of nature focusing the attention of man on realities that lie beyond nature. ■

About ten miles downstream from Lake Tiberias is the second site on the Jordan claimed as the place where John baptized Jesus. Special facilities have been provided for the droves of visitors such as these American pilgrims (top and above), clad in white robes, who have lined up for baptism, often rebaptism, in the hallowed waters of the River Jordan.

He was proclaiming himself the Messiah. Now this was not all that unusual. There had been at least three claimant messiahs thirty-some years earlier after the death of Herod the Great, all of whom had led uprisings that were suppressed with fire and sword. But from his beginning in Nazareth, this Jesus was fundamentally different. Like his cousin, he shunned the political. Unlike his cousin, he did not choose to dwell in the desert. He lived with his followers and seemed to enjoy the company of people, sometimes a very disreputable company. The incident in Nazareth began a three-year ministry that aroused hundreds, possibly several thousand, usually to support him, occasionally to oppose or abandon him. His ministry had ended six weeks earlier on a cross outside Jerusalem. So, anyway, the authorities hoped.

The explanation for his success was not mysterious. The man had shocking powers. At first, the authorities very much questioned the recurring reports of the miraculous. But the evidence for these strange events was so overwhelming that by continually challenging their authenticity, officialdom began casting doubt upon its own credibility.

The most common among the miracles were the healing of diseases. Lepers were "cleansed," paralytics were cured, fevers assumed to be fatal disappeared, a woman's unstanchable "issue of blood" (probably caused by what would come to be known as fibroids) vanished, chronic edema went away, the deaf acquired hearing, a withered hand was made whole. On at least four occasions the blind recovered their sight. It went on and on. There were three

instances—one at Nain about eighteen miles southwest of the Galilean Sea (which the Romans called Lake Tiberias), one somewhere on the west shore of the lake and one at the village of Bethany on the very outskirts of Jerusalem—in which people who were presumed dead were restored to life. In two instances they were children. The Bethany case understandably alarmed the Temple officials. With many more exhibitions like this, they knew, his movement would become irresistible.

There were also repeated stories of exorcism. Mute people were made to speak, a demon-possessed little girl was suddenly rendered tranquilly sane; so was a young boy. One demoniac was cured in the middle of a synagogue service.

In addition, he seemed to exert some uncanny control over the natural elements. There were stories, understandably significant to commercial fishermen, in which he told them to put their nets down at a given spot and they promptly dragged in a huge haul of fish. In at least one instance, he commanded a bad storm to stop and it instantly ceased. In another, he actually walked over the water. He cursed a tree and it immediately withered and died; he somehow fed an enormous crowd of people out of a couple of baskets of bread and fish; and at a wedding reception in Cana, ten miles west of Lake Tiberias, where they ran out of wine and the hostess was no doubt frantic, he obliged by converting several vases of water into (they say) an extremely good vintage.

To those who opposed him, therefore, it became inescapable that this man's power, if it were not from God (a possibility they viewed as absurd), must have

The fertile valleys and plains of Galilee were welltrodden by Jesus and his disciples during his brief ministry. The regions just west and north of the Sea of Galilee and the great pass of the Horns of Hittim (center) would have been especially familiar territory.

diabolical origins. The authorities logically concluded his miracles to be black magic and the man himself the agent of the devil. On this, both the high priestly party of the Sadducees and the party of the Pharisees agreed, though they agreed on little else.

And yet even they knew that the miracles, or magic, or whatever it was, could not alone account for his astonishing influence over the most improbable people. It was undeniable that he had been a beneficial influence in some ways. One of his followers, for instance, a man named Zaccheus, was a former tax collector. That is, he was one of those loathsome of the loathsome, a little quisling servant of the Romans who collected Caesar's taxes for him, overcharging and keeping whatever extra he could rake off for himself. It was a vicious system. But this Zaccheus suddenly up and gave half his goods to the poor and repaid the victims of his unfair assessments. With another tax collector, a certain Levi, whom they called Matthew, it was the same story.

Who's to blame?
The Jews or the Romans?

It was neither, said Dorothy Sayers, but just ordinary people behaving as we ordinarily do, and Plato foresaw it all

Who was to blame for killing Jesus Christ? Down through the centuries that question was destined to arise, often with persecution and bloodshed. Was it the Jews? Was it the Romans? Was it both of them?

Christian theology has never, in fact, attributed the Crucifixion to either one. Rather it places the blame on what it calls in Latin peccata mundi, "the sins of the world." And, oddly, the first man to explain the Christian answer to the question did so about four hundred years before Christ.

It was the Greek philosopher Plato who, in his foundational work on human government, *The Republic*, posed a hypothetical question. Suppose, he said, that a perfectly just man came into the world. He must not merely seem just, but be just.

However, it's important that he not be viewed as just. If he were, he would be honored and rewarded, "and then we shall not know whether he is just for the sake of justice, or for the sake of honors and rewards.

"Therefore let him be clothed in justice only, and have no other covering. . . . Let him be the best of men, and let him be thought the worst. Then he will have been put to the proof, and we shall see whether he will be affected by the fear of infamy. And let him continue thus to the hour of his death, being just and seeming unjust."

Plato asked what the fate of such a man would be, and he answered his own question: "He will be scourged, racked, bound. He will have his eyes burned

out. And at last, after suffering every kind of evil, he will be impaled."

In short, Plato already saw the inevitable fate of perfection in our imperfect world. Whether a perfectly just man met that fate in Athens in the fifth century B.C., or in Jerusalem in the first century A.D., or in New York City in the twenty-first century A.D., the outcome was foreordained: torture and death. That is, Plato placed the blame on human nature.

A twentieth-century Christian dramatist, the English classicist and detective story writer Dorothy L. Sayers, makes the same point. In the introduction to *The Man Born to Be King*, her series of radio plays on the life of Christ, she writes:

"The Christian affirmation is that a number of quite common-place human beings, in an obscure province of the Roman Empire, killed and murdered God Almighty—quite casually, almost as a matter of routine, and certainly with no notion that they were doing anything out of the way.

"Their motives, on the whole, were defensible, and in some respects praiseworthy. There was some malice, some weakness, and no doubt some wresting of the law—but no more than we are accustomed to find in human affairs.

"By no jugglings of fate, by no unforeseeable coincidence, by no supernatural machinations, but by that destiny which is character, and by the unimaginative following of their ordinary standards of behavior, they

There were loose women, like the notorious Mary, who hailed from that cesspool of sin on the west shore of Lake Tiberias, Magdala, so foul that it even appalled the Romans. Mary, however, had totally reformed, so it was said, through his influence upon her. There had been highly placed people as well—like Nicodemus, and Joseph who came from Arimathea (a town whose location is lost to history), both of them respected members of the Sanhedrin.

But most of his followers were simple people—commercial fishermen, like this Simon whom he called "The Rock," to whom he was said to have bequeathed the leadership of his cult. The rest were mostly the sons of shepherds, or they were small businessmen and the like from the villages of Galilee, a prosperous enough region, heaven knows, peopled not only by radical Jews seething for an insurrection, but also by the whole polyglot multiracial mix that first the Greeks and then the Romans had permitted to settle there. Religiously it was a backwater, a swamp,

were led, with a ghastly inevitability, to the commission of the crime of crimes.

"We, looking back, know what they were doing; the whole point and poignancy of the tragedy is lost unless we realize that they did not. . . . We are so much accustomed to seeing the whole story from a post-Resurrection, and indeed from a post-Nicene point of view, that we are apt, without realizing it, to attribute to all the New Testament characters the same theological awareness that we have ourselves.

"We judge their behavior as if all of them—disciples, Pharisees, Romans, and men in the street—had known with whom they were dealing, and what the meaning of all the events actually was. But they did not know it. The disciples had only the foggiest inkling of it, and nobody else came anywhere near grasping what it was all about.

"If the chief priests and the Roman governor had been aware they were engaged in crucifying God—if Herod the Great had ordered his famous massacre of the children at Bethlehem with the express purpose of doing away with God—then they would have been quite exceptionally wicked people.

"And indeed, we like to think that they were. It gives us a reassuring sensation that it can't happen here. . . .

"Unhappily, if we think about it at all, we must think otherwise. God was executed by people painfully like us, in a society very similar to our own—in the over-ripeness of the most splendid and sophisticated empire the world has ever seen. In a nation famous for its religious genius, and under a government renowned for its efficiency, he was executed by a corrupt church, a timid politician, and a fickle proletariat led by professional agitators. His executioners made vulgar jokes about him, called him filthy names, taunted him, smacked him in the face, flogged him with the lash, and hanged Him on the common gallows—a bloody, dusty, sweaty and sordid business.

"Show people that and they are shocked. So they should be. If that does not shock them, nothing can." ■

For British author and playwright Dorothy Sayers, Jesus died at the hands of people with no more malice than others in history, whose motives were defensible and even sometimes praiseworthy.

with every manner of heresy thriving—the very sort of place, senior Temple people concluded, that a man like this could gain a following.

But he was clever, oh so clever. His knowledge of the Law was overwhelming, and he had an uncanny ability to see through it and beyond it. This made him a holy terror in debate. Again and again they would try to corner him. Always it was a disaster, because he could run circles around the best professional disputants. "Who shall be greatest in your kingdom?" they asked him. It was a trap and he knew it. If he said the best man was he who best obeyed the Law, the Pharisees would back him but the Sadducees would boil over. If he said it was the man who most faithfully fulfilled the sacrifices required by Moses, the Pharisees would run him down. If he said it was he himself, they'd all pile on him. Instead, he took up a little child and held it high above his head. Whoever

Spotting the trap in the tax question, Jesus gave an ingenious answer. 'Give Caesar what belongs to Caesar,' he said, 'and give to God what belongs to God.'

receives the Word of God with the honesty, integrity and simplicity of a child, he said, will be greatest in the Kingdom of Heaven. They were all floored, and the women swarmed around him asking him to bless their children.

Then there was the case of the tax money. Should free Jews be paying taxes to Caesar, he was asked—a point that had been debated ever since the Romans arrived. Again, he saw the trap. If he said yes, he'd be called a traitor to Jewry and a coward. If he said no, the Romans could arrest him for sedition. "Show me the tribute money," he declared, and they passed him a coin. "Whose head's on it?" he demanded. "Caesar's!" they all shouted. "Then give Caesar what belongs to Caesar, and give God what belongs to God." It's an ingenious answer. For what is it that belongs to God? We do, of course. What he was pointing out is that God doesn't want our money, our time, our thought. He wants us! Every part of us. It was a complete answer, and it left them speechless.

All this, his critics would admit, must be placed on the man's plus side. But then there was his negative side. His followers could be accused of showing a certain contempt for respectable ecclesiastical office. They were impatient, that is, with hypocrisy hiding under the guise of established authority, and they had no use at all for those who abused such power.

A case that clearly exemplifies this had occurred right in Jerusalem. A certain man, blind from birth, who for years had begged for alms with others on the Temple steps, apparently pleaded with this Jesus for his eyesight. Now this was the Sabbath, and the proper response would have been for Jesus to attend to the man the following day. Instead, he put some mud on the man's eyes and told him to wash it off. When the man did so, he found he could see. So, anyway, the story went. Now since this beggar was well known, and since such a work of healing would represent a clear Sabbath violation, the case very soon came to the attention of the local synagogue, whose council summoned the formerly blind man to appear.

The ensuing conduct of this man was simply outrageous. His parents were called and refused to testify on his behalf. Then, as he was questioned, he began to point out the inconsistencies in the thinking of the council itself. Did the devil cure the sick? he demanded. Had ever a man born blind been cured before? Did God answer the prayers of bad men? Why was the council so interested in Jesus? Were its members thinking of becoming his disciples themselves? That kind of thing. In the end they shunned the man, expelled him from the synagogue, which of course cut him off from the whole community. He doubtless joined with Jesus' other followers.

Fresh from the pool of Siloam and reveling in the wonder of his new-found sight, the "man born blind" is more blind still to the fierce interrogation of the Pharisees gathered around him. Why did they want to hear the story of his healing again? he asks them. Were they thinking of becoming Jesus' disciples too? This brings upon him a torrent of abuse. "You were steeped in sin at birth," they say. "How dare you lecture us!"

Meanwhile, the same criticism of abusive authority finally put an end to Jesus' cousin John. After Herod Antipas's brother died, Herod married his brother's widow, Herodias. Since that represented a violation of the Law, John denounced him for it, and was arrested and imprisoned in the Machaerus. Herodias, by a cunning trick, forced Herod to execute him. Herod was much upset by this, because he admired John. But, like Jesus, John had simply gone too far.

Jesus, however, went a great deal farther than that. The most glaring and absolutely unspeakable element in his whole work and ministry lay in his theology. His pronouncements about his own identity rendered him absolutely unacceptable, a lunatic, a monster, or worse, perhaps the devil himself in human form.

The fact is, he consistently talked and acted—and it smacks of blasphemy to even repeat this—as though he were God himself. Not a servant of God. Not a prophet of God. Not even a mirror of God. But literally, the "Son of God." God, as it were, in the person of a man, like the disgusting fables of the Romans and Greeks whose so-called gods walked the earth as humans in disguise.

HARRINGTON

The whole tradition of Jewry, the whole mission of the people, was to deny the very possibility of such an abomination. God is one, and God is other. Between God and the natural world there can exist no direct connection, only the connection of creator to creature, artist to painting, author to story. The one is fundamentally distinct from the other.

Yet this assertion of divinity, sometimes implicit, sometimes explicit, ran through almost everything Jesus taught and said. "Your sins," he repeatedly told those whom he cured, "are forgiven." An obvious blasphemy. If one man cheats another, the victim can forgive the cheater. But then along comes this fellow who wasn't there when the offense took place and who had nothing whatever to do with it, and announces that he forgives the offender. It's as though he himself were the party chiefly offended.

Does he not know that only God can forgive sins? What does he think the whole ritual of the Temple is about? The animal is sacrificed, as God directed, to

No prophet ever spoke as he did. Not the Greeks, not even Buddha. 'I am the Way. I am the Truth. I am the Life,' Jesus said. What sane person could talk like this?

atone for the sins of the individual and of the people as a whole. He apparently substitutes himself for the whole Temple process.

"Why," he is asked, "do your followers not fast?" Fasting, denying one's appetites to honor God, has always been a requirement under the Law. "The wedding guests," he replies, "do not fast when the bridegroom is with them." Pardon? Fasting is decreed by the Law. Only God, who gave the Law, could suspend the Law. The implication is indisputable. He's saying he's God.

He looked out on Jerusalem. How often, he observed, have I sent you prophets. So, he implies, it has been he who all along has been sending the prophets! Later came a repulsive invitation to some sort of cannibalism. "Whoever eats my flesh and drinks my blood," he proclaimed, "has eternal life." What on earth could that mean? Small wonder that sensible people vowed to have nothing more to do with him after that sort of proclamation.

No prophet ever spoke as he spoke. Nor did even the great teachers of the Greeks, nor the prophet they call Buddha. They all said, "This is the way you should live. This is the Truth about God. This is the life you should lead." This man said, "I am the Way. I am the Truth. I am the Life." What sane person could talk like this?

And then came his outrageous pronouncement within the precinct of the Temple itself. "Before Abraham was," he announces, "I AM." It's the very name of God, the name the mere mention of which calls for the death penalty, and he applied it to himself. But he always cleverly relies on the element of shock. By the time his hearers recovered from this ghastly assertion and quite properly took up stones to rid themselves of him, he had slipped through the crowd and gone.

From what his intimate followers say, it got worse. "Show us God and we shall be satisfied," said one of them, and the man replied: "Have I been with you all this time, and you don't know who I am? The man who has seen me has seen God!" Totally deranged, obviously. Utterly possessed. Servant of Satan. But fortunately, these assertions had by now become so commonplace that the high priest Caiaphas was able to use them to put a swift end to the problem. Or so he thought.

Arresting Jesus wasn't simple. He had by now a huge following in the countryside, and hundreds of his followers had come to Jerusalem for Passover. If he had been arrested publicly a riot was almost certain. And the high priests emphatically did not want that. Forty years before, a riot that broke out at Passover had led to a further outbreak at Pentecost fifty days later, during which the Romans rounded up two thousand people and skewered them to crosses all over the city. Caiaphas didn't want something like that on his conscience. The man had to be arrested, tried, convicted and put down before most people knew what was going on.

Jesus' followers were uncommonly loyal. Except, that is, for one, a fellow named Iscariot who, as the high priests doubtless saw it, had finally perceived the essential fraudulence of this Nazarene and was willing to tell them where he could be quietly arrested without trouble—in the Gethsemane Garden up on the Mount of Olives, where he and his lieutenants would be spending the night.

The arrest came off with only a minor altercation—predictably caused by the designated favorite Simon who, as so often happens with such people, subsequently denied even knowing this Jesus (Some Rock!). But the trial that followed went badly. To convict the accused, under the Jewish system, at least two witnesses had to agree. No two could be found who did.

That's when Caiaphas played his trump card. Knowing the man's bizarre theology, he first put the prisoner under oath—a questionable expedient, since he proposed to convict the witness out of his own mouth, but there were precedents for it. He then simply asked the man who he was. Jesus replied, as Caiaphas had plainly foreseen, with the name of God, and he quietly added that he would return as judge of the world. Now this must be either a staggering truth or a patently obvious blasphemy. Since to Caiaphas the former was ridiculous, he assumed the latter, declared it blasphemy, ritually ripped his high priestly robe, and pronounced the death penalty.

Such a sentence required Roman approval because the Romans would have to carry it out. This meant taking the case to Pilate who, seeing the Jewish

It was death for the Jews to speak the name of God. When they wrote it, it was called the Tetragrammaton for the four Hebrew letters of the name, YHWH (read in Hebrew from right to left). Its written form, however, became an object of devotion and was placed on the Shiviti, a decorative plaque usually hung on the eastern wall of synagogues to indicate the proper direction of prayer. This Shiviti is a nineteenth-century folk-art version from Persia.

Confronting a crowd of followers
and detractors, Jesus horrifies both.
He not only speaks the unutterable
name of God—I AM—but applies it
to himself. "At this," records John,
"they picked up stones to stone him,
but Jesus hid himself, slipping away
from the Temple grounds."

authorities wanted the man dead, instantly decided to try keeping him alive. He stalled, sending the case to Herod Antipas because the man was a Galilean, not a Judean, and therefore the matter was not within his jurisdiction. But Herod bounced it back after discovering the man had been born at Bethlehem in Judea after all, and was therefore Pilate's problem.

Now Pilate, whatever else might be said about him, was a Roman. And the Romans, for all their brutality, had a powerful sense of justice. There seemed to be a miscarriage of it here. Furthermore, Jesus, standing calm, silent, utterly controlled, impressed him. Here was a Jew behaving like a Roman. Then, too, there was that curious story of Pilate's wife dreaming about the man and sending a note warning her husband to have nothing to do with the case.

So Pilate's next move was to offer Jesus as "Passover Prisoner"—it was a tradition that one condemned man be liberated every year on the national holiday. But this move had been foreseen, and the crowd was coached into demanding someone else. "Ecce homo!" cried Pilate to the crowd—"Behold the man!" But, stirred up by the high priests and elders, they cried for his blood: "Let him be crucified!"

And in the end, Pilate caved in. Caiaphas apparently knew him well. Pilate had already been on the carpet at Rome for his treatment of the Jews. Jesus was talking of establishing a "kingdom." That would have to be deemed sedition. If Pilate let him go, said Caiaphas, he would demonstrate himself "not Caesar's friend." That ploy was all it took. Pilate symbolically washed his hands to absolve himself of what he considered an unjust verdict, then ordered the crucifixion to proceed. That meant first the lash, and then the cross.

Jesus unquestionably died well. None of the usual cursing and screaming. Even the duty centurion commanding the execution squad was impressed, calling him "Truly, the Son of God." Not that it proved much. This Jesus seemed to have had what people would consider an unhealthy respect for the Roman army. He had actually once cured the servant of a centurion and announced the man had greater faith than anything he had encountered among the Jews. Something about their discipline, no doubt. In any event what did it matter that a Roman called someone "Son of God"? Roman gods constantly haunted the earth, even breeding with mortals to beget hybrid children.

By that night, the prisoner was declared dead, and the Passover Feast had still not begun. The whole business was over and done with in little more than a day—all told, a very efficient piece of work by Caiaphas, considering the problems he faced. Understandably, therefore, by that Passover eve it seemed certain that this would spell the end of the "Jesus" movement, or whatever they called it.

There had been, or so it was rumored, a curious incident, however. When the man died, the veil of the curtain covering the Holy of Holies, the most sacred precinct in the Temple, had suddenly split in two from the top to the bottom. If true this was a most ominous sign. Then, two days later the whole thing began blowing up. His followers, who it was assumed would rapidly disperse, instead were all over the city and countryside. "Jesus is alive," they proclaimed. "He is

Archaeological proof of the existence of the high priest Caiaphas, this forty-inch-long ossuary found in a Jerusalem tomb, held his bones. After a body disintegrated, the bones were often deposited in an ossuary to preserve scarce burial sites for future members of the family.

HARRINGTON

Only when the resurrected Jesus addresses her by name does Mary Magdalene recognize the man she had assumed to be a gardener as the resurrected Jesus. "Mary," he says softly. "Rabonni!" she replies ecstatically in Aramaic, meaning "my teacher," probably the term by which his disciples affectionately knew him.

risen." They seemed absolutely convinced of it—convinced enough, anyway, to risk arrest for saying so. For the high priests, the thing was getting completely out of hand, and now came this drunken extravaganza in the streets.

Messiah is come, said the Nazarene's followers. They will convert Jewry. They will convert the world. "Some hope!" the high priests no doubt scoffed. A ragged mob of fishermen, ex-tax collectors, shopkeepers and sheepherders. Human gullibility seems boundless. They have no leaders, no money, no sound scholarship, no credibility, and no official status. And what was all this babbling about the coming of the Holy Spirit?

Do they not understand that the faith is as permanent and secure as the Temple itself? And firm the Temple would stand, the high priests said, until the real Messiah finally arrives. ■

Crucifixion: No death more hideous

Rome's awful experts made certain it was painful, humiliating—and slow

The "most extreme form of punishment," wrote the Roman senator and lawyer Cicero about seventy-five years before the birth of Christ, is crucifixion. He called it "atrociously cruel," not only in the physical pain it inflicts, but equally in the humiliation it brings to the man crucified.

"The very word 'cross' should be far removed," he said, "not only from the person of a Roman citizen, but from his thoughts, his eyes and his ears. For it is not merely the actual occurrence of these things but the very mention of them that is unworthy of a Roman citizen or a free man."

To Romans, both the cross and the executioner who tied the prisoner's hands, veiled his head and crucified him, were realities not mentioned in polite company. Only rarely were Roman citizens crucified, usually on a charge of high treason in wartime.

For slaves, however, or for rebellious Roman troops, or cities resisting siege, or brigands and highway robbers, it was the acceptable form of punishment, and its usage goes back long before the Romans to the Phoenicians, Persians, and Egyptians. The Phoenicians had tried other forms of execution—spearing, boiling in oil, strangulation, stoning, drowning, burning—but had rejected them all as too quick. Crucifixion, especially in its early usage, was rarely quick.

It was also much-used by the Greeks. Writing in the fifth century B.C., Plato describes the fate of a conspirator who had sought to establish himself as a tyrant: "He is put on a rack and

In 1968, construction crews uncovered the tomb of "Jehohanan the son of HGQWL," who had been crucified in the first century A.D. The right heel bone was pierced laterally by a four and a half inch spike, and remains of olive wood were found between the nail and the bone. This suggests that the nail had first been driven through a wooden plaque to hold the victim more securely to the main upright of the cross.

mutilated, forced to watch his wife and children subjected to many other signal outrages, then finally crucified or burned on a coat of pitch." Herodotus, Plato's contemporary, describes the execution of the ruler Atayctes: "They nailed him to a plank and left him there, then stoned to death his son before his eyes."

But it was the ever-efficient Romans who made the most use of crucifixion. Of their three common forms of execution, decapitation by sword was the least severe, burning next, and crucifixion the worst. In its early Roman form, it was reserved entirely for slaves who would hear the dread words from the sentencing magistrate: "*Pone crucem servo*"— "Put the cross on the slave." In the Spartacus rebellion of 73 B.C., six thousand slaves were crucified on a single day.

Even death in the arena, where the victims were torn to pieces by wild animals, was not as severe as crucifixion, if only because it came more quickly. But death by wild beasts was costly and cumbersome. Crucifixion, on the other hand, was cheap and could be arranged almost anywhere.

In the Roman practice, the prisoner was always flogged first. The Romans saw this beating as "half death," because it must stop short of actually killing the prisoner. A man, called a *lictor*, was trained

in the use of the *flagellum,* which consisted of a wooden handle and several long thongs of leather at the end of which were sewn pieces of bone or chain. The number of strokes was never specified, nor was the part of the body upon which the prisoner could be beaten. As the strokes followed one after the other, however, the prisoner must be checked carefully, because a man could die under a Roman flogging, and if he did, the *lictor* would be held responsible.

Sometimes the cross consisted solely of a six-foot vertical stake (they called it the *stipes crucis*), but more frequently this was combined with a crosspiece (*patibulum*) in the form of a T or an X. Sometimes (as with Jesus)

A reconstruction near Jerusalem of the type of cross likely employed by the Romans in first-century Judea shows the sedecula, a plank fastened to the upright below the main crossbeam. It provided the victim, whose torso had been twisted to the side, sufficient support to prolong the agony of his death.

HARRINGTON

"My God, my God, why hast thou forsaken me?
. . . a company of evildoers encircle me; they have pierced my hands and feet . . .
they divide my garments among them, and for my raiment they cast lots.
But thou, O LORD, be not far off! O thou my help, hasten to my aid!
. . . I will tell of thy name to my brethren;
. . . men shall tell of the LORD to the coming generation, and proclaim
his deliverance to a people yet unborn, that he has wrought it."

Psalm 22 (RSV), written a thousand years before that day on Golgotha

the crosspiece was lowered slightly below the top of the upright to make room for a placard proclaiming the man's crime.

The assembled cross they called the *crux humilis*, if it was for a common slave or brigand. For a distinguished prisoner—an enemy leader or a celebrated rebel—a *crux sublimis* was used, raising the victim much higher off the ground.

The victim carried either the whole cross or the crosspiece to the scene of his execution. The Romans made a practice of conducting crucifixions beside the most crowded roads, so that as many people as possible would be paralyzed with horror and fear.

Once at the site, the victim was stripped naked, save for a cloth that covered his genital area and was folded behind his back. His near nakedness was not only intended to add to his humiliation, but more pertinently to expose him to the constant torment of insects.

The soldiers first tied his shoulders to the upright beam, then held one arm flat against the crosspiece. A five-inch spike was then hammered through the tender gap between the bones in the middle of the wrist. After the other wrist was impaled, the legs were then stretched out, one foot placed over the other, and a single spike driven through both feet.

At this point, kind women would sometimes approach the victim and give him a mixture of wine and an herb intended to relieve pain by rendering the accused groggy. This was in fact against the Law. Usually, however, the soldiers allowed it. In Jesus' case, he refused to take it, apparently convinced that he had to remain fully conscious throughout the whole ordeal.

When the cross was raised, the ultimate torment assailed the prisoner. His shoulders were tied back to the upright beam, and by hoisting himself upward he could relieve, to a degree, the excruciating pain in his feet, which were carrying most of his weight. But in this position, he could not properly breathe. He would gasp for air, and in so doing let his weight fall back onto his feet. Sometimes a small plank called a *sedecula*, or seat, was fastened to provide support and thereby prolong the agony.

Since no vital organs were injured, death usually came very slowly, perhaps over several days. The worst aspect of it, said one witness, was the screaming. Sometimes, out of pity, their own boredom, or some other consideration, the soldiers would break the prisoner's legs. This prevented him from resting his weight on his feet, and he would suffocate. Such a "humanitarian" measure, however, was not common among Romans. If from no other cause, the victim would eventually die from hunger or thirst.

The actual posture of the victim on the cross depended on the sadistic whim of the executioner. The Roman philosopher, statesman, and actor Seneca notes: "I see crosses there, not just of one kind, but made in many different ways; some of their victims with head down to the ground; some impale their private parts; others stretch out their arms on the gibbet." Sometimes, writes the Jewish historian Josephus, "the soldiers themselves in rage and bitterness nailed up their victims in different postures as a grim joke."

It was slaves, however, far more than enemies, who suffered crucifixion under the Romans. The satirical poet Juvenal, born about the mid-first century, tells of a Roman matron who wanted a slave crucified. To her husband's objection, she replied: "This is my will and my command. If you are looking for a reason it is simply that I want it." The poet Horace tells of a slave whose master caught him tasting the soup as he brought it from the kitchen. The master had him crucified.

Horace, with gallows humor, speaks of "feeding the crows while on the cross." Plautus, in 184 B.C., writes of the "horrible cross of slaves," and he quotes one slave's fatalistic pessimism: "I know the cross will be my grave, that is where my ancestors are, my father, grandfathers, great-grandfathers and great-great-grandfathers."

The usual Jewish form of execution was stoning. However, the idea of exhibiting bodies as a warning to others was required by the Jewish Law. The corpses of convicted blasphemers and idolaters must be hanged on a tree to show that they were cursed by God.

Jews, too, occasionally imposed crucifixion. Josephus recalls that during the Hasmonian-Hellenistic period, the high priest Alexander Janneus (103–76 BC) had eight hundred Pharisees crucified, and ordered their wives and children to be slaughtered before their eyes as they hung dying.

Like the Romans, Jews regarded crucifixion as shameful. A crucified person was regarded as cursed by God. The sheer dishonor of such a death, many said, argued incontestably against Jesus being the Messiah.

Crucifixion remained the standard method of Roman execution until the emperor Constantine legalized Christianity in the fourth century A.D., and formally abolished it.

Not for another two hundred years did "naturalistic" crucifixes, showing the body of a human Christ nailed to the cross, appear in Christian devotions, and not until the thirteenth century did they regularly appear over the altars of Christian churches. By then, the hideous reality of the act itself was something few human beings would ever have to see. ■

CHAPTER 2

The unpromising Peter takes over

The man who denied Christ three times becomes his fearless witness before officialdom and the people

On a quiet stone-paved alley just outside the Zion Gate in Jerusalem's Old City stands an unadorned, two-story stone building, dwarfed by the tower and dome of the adjacent Dormition Abbey. From the doorway on the alley, a set of steps leads to the second floor of the building. Passing a guard reading his Hebrew newspaper, the visitor proceeds into a renovated room, twenty-five by twenty-five feet, whose Gothic arches and stained-glass windows testify to its origins as a twelfth-century Crusader church. Arabic inscriptions on the walls evidence its subsequent history as a mosque. Visitors shuffle through, some stopping to pray aloud or sing with others in their tour groups.

Almost no archaeologist would unreservedly agree with twelfth-century pilgrims and twenty-first-century visitors, however, that the building stands on the site of "the Upper Room," scene of the Last Supper, the place where fifty days later the Holy Spirit descended and empowered the Christian Church to spread the message of Jesus Christ to the world.

Still, whether at this very place or at another not far from it, something powerful and strange certainly occurred on that Jewish feast called Pentecost, on or about the year A.D. 31. Those who were present told a gripping story. First they heard a terrific rushing sound, like a mighty wind, filling the whole house. As they looked around in astonishment, each could see what they would later describe to the best of their abilities as something that was essentially indescribable. It was as though tiny "tongues of fire" rested over the head of each man, they said. And when they tried to speak, words from languages none of them knew fell from their lips.

Some people later scoffed, saying the whole bunch must be drunk. But others who heard them—Parthians and Medes and Elamites and Asians and visitors from many other nations who were present for the feast—recognized the languages as their own and were astonished to hear and understand, in the fluent outbursts from these ordinary Galileans, praises of the works of God. As for the speakers, they found the experience eerie and wonderful—the most exciting thing that had happened to them, ever.

Whatever it was that took place in that room that day, it completely transformed the tiny circle of very frightened men and women who had cowered there after the crucifixion of their leader, the Nazarene, Jesus, who they now said was not only the Messiah, but a Messiah risen from death: alive. Intellectually, scholastically, socially and above all ecclesiastically, they were a collection of nobodies. And not even Jerusalem nobodies; most of them came from Galilee, a rustic backwater. Now, out of their hideout on that future quiet alley they poured, advancing upon the Temple—fearless, fervid, and imbued with a message that most of the Temple's officialdom definitely did not anticipate and would not want to hear.

Why Peter?

He was undependable and cowardly, and he lied. Why not John?

Artist Richard Sparks envisioned Peter (above), with the face of a fisherman, focused on the laying of the nets, eyes squinted as the sun glints off the water.

Why Jesus conferred a position of leadership on the uncertain person of the apostle Peter has puzzled Christians for two thousand years.

In her play *The Zeal of Thy House*, the twentieth-century detective story writer and Christian apologist Dorothy L. Sayers tackles the puzzle head-on. She puts into the mouth of the fictional abbot of the twelfth-century Catholic cathedral at Canterbury, the following lines:

God founded his church, not upon John,
The loved disciple, that lay so close to his heart
And knew his mind—not upon John, but Peter,
Peter the liar, Peter the coward, Peter
The rock, the common man. John was all gold,
And gold is rare; the work might wait while God
Ransacked the corners of the earth to find
Another John; but Peter is the stone
Whereof the world is made. So stands the Church,
Stone upon stone, and Christ the corner-stone,
Carved of the same stuff, common flesh and blood,
With you, and me, and Peter; and he can,
Being the alchemist's stone, the stone of Solomon,
Turn stone to gold, and purge the gold itself
From dross, till all is gold. ∎

Even the Temple itself failed to intimidate them, though the mere bulk and soaring stone of its walls, the grandeur of its decor, was obviously calculated to intimidate everybody. Chief among its integrities was its sheer permanence. It had stood for 545 years. No one could conceive that in another thirty-nine, at the hands of the overwhelming forces of Rome, it would be utterly destroyed.

The Temple site, holiest area in the holy city of Jerusalem, had been chosen by King Solomon himself when in about 960 B.C. he built the first Temple there, as a home for the cherished Ark of the Covenant and a center for Jewish worship. Solomon's Temple was demolished around 586 B.C. by King Nebuchadnezzar, who razed the entire city of Jerusalem as well and carried the Jews off to his own land, Babylon. When the Jews were allowed to return to Jerusalem in 538, they began building the second Temple on the desolate site of the first, and though the new Temple was declared complete in 515 B.C., it endured the successive waves of non-Jewish domination that followed the surrender of Jerusalem to the great

Herod's spectacular redevelopment program changed the face of the Holy Land. But nowhere was his achievement more magnificent and astonishing than at the Temple in Jerusalem.

Macedonian general Alexander. Jewish rebels seized Jerusalem again in 167 B.C. and once more dedicated the Temple for worship.

Then came Herod the Great, appointed king of Judea in 37 B.C., twenty-five years after Rome conquered the Holy Land and declared it a "client state." Herod, a half-Jew, won his position by serving as adviser, mentor and confidant to Julius Caesar and his imperial successor Octavius Augustus, founders of what had by now become the greatest empire the world had ever known. On their behalf Herod ordered unflinchingly whatever slaughter or carnage the preservation of peace and good order seemed to require. The massacre of the infants at Bethlehem, marked and mourned as villainy by Christians for the next two thousand years, was an undistinguished incident in his sanguinary record.

Not for nothing, however, is he known to history as Herod "the Great." Once he was installed by the Romans as puppet king of the Jews, his spectacular redevelopment program changed the face of the Holy Land. But his mightiest achievement was his magnificent expansion and adornment of the Temple at Jerusalem, an architectural triumph that would astonish the world.

With huge cut stones weighing as much as fifty tons, he bent the rule that the Temple area could not be broadened, creating a massive stone platform that buried the form of the mountain upon which it sat. A section of Herod's platform would survive into the twenty-first century.[1]

All of this history was known, of course, to Peter and the others as they

---

1. The Western Wall of the vast platform which Herod the Great built atop Temple Mount in Jerusalem survives as the Wailing Wall, a Jewish shrine that became the dead-center of bloody territorial disputes between Israel and the Palestinian Arabs in the twentieth century.

approached the Temple, still deeply stirred within by what had happened to them in the Upper Room, their conviction strengthened by Peter's strong confidence and impulsive resolve. Recognized by the group as their senior spokesman (and by Catholic Christians as the church's first pope), Peter was certainly one of the two central figures in the tumultuous events that were about to unfold. To future generations, especially those with twenty-first-century sensibilities, he would seem an unlikely leader. He was a fisherman when he joined Jesus, and the Gospel accounts make clear that he was impetuous and hot-tempered, quick to assert his opinions and just as quick to recant them when rebuked. Worst of all, shortly after Jesus' arrest, a badly frightened Peter had flatly and repeatedly denied any connection with him, pretending to know nothing whatever about him. Even after the Resurrection, Jesus' last words on earth to Peter were an admonition.[2]

Despite these flaws, Peter also had his strengths. He had spent his life as a commercial fisherman, and no one who has seen a commercial fisherman at work would be surprised at Peter's taking this leadership role. Even with the technology of the twenty-first century, commercial fishing is no job for the faint of heart. Demanding and dangerous, it requires steady nerves, raw

Peter's vocation as a commercial fisherman required steady nerves, raw courage, great physical strength, and an ability to act decisively and instantly when conditions demanded.

courage, great physical strength, and an ability to act decisively and instantly when conditions demand. And those conditions were far worse in the first century. Much of Peter's life had been spent on the open water in tiny boats, dwarfed by the elements, spray-drenched, sails flapping wildly in wind, waves convulsing his vessel. His home town, Capernaum, like every fishing village in the world, ancient or modern, mourned with tragic frequency the drowned, the maimed and those who went to work and were never seen again. Such was fishing and such was Peter, the improbable spokesman for this most improbable group of men. (See sidebar.)

His voice, so often in the past raised above the roar of wind and crashing water, now resounded over the throng of curious spectators surrounding and following the apostles. "Jews and all you who live in Jerusalem, understand this," he cried. "Give me your attention!" Puzzled, the crowd fell silent. "These men are not drunk, as you assume—it is only the third hour of the day!"

Carefully, methodically, the big fisherman, his hands callused, laid before his listeners a version of biblical prophecy. Had they read, he asked, the prophet Joel?

---

2. Having been challenged and commanded three times by the risen Jesus to "Feed my sheep," Peter was finally commanded, "Follow me." Yes, says Peter, but he then notes that another disciple, John, had also been so instructed, and it was said John would live until Jesus returns. "What is that to thee?" Jesus replied sharply. "Follow me!"

From a sea that is a lake came the men who changed a world

Out of the tiny villages around Galilee's sometimes stormy waters, unassuming men and women became the founders of Christianity

The ministry of Jesus focuses strongly on events that occurred on and around the Sea of Galilee (called Yam Kinneret today), a forty-thousand-acre freshwater lake fed out of and flowing into the Jordan River, and the only significant body of water in the landlocked tetrarchy of Galilee. (The shoreline of the Mediterranean Sea to the west of Galilee was part of the Roman province of Syria).

The "sea," or lake, was the economic center of Galilee, an agriculturally rich but culturally provincial district. It was also an administrative center: Herod Antipas, a son of Herod the Great who ruled Galilee from Jesus' boyhood to a few years after his death, had his palace in Tiberias, a city he built on the lake's southwestern shore. Major roads linked the sea to Damascus in Syria and to ports along the Mediterranean. But the lake itself was primarily known for its abundance of fish, which supplied the local inhabitants with food and was a major export commodity, consumed as far away as Rome by some accounts. Sardines, tilapia (also known as St. Peter's fish), and a large kind of carp called the barbel were the most common. They in turn fed on smaller fish and on the mollusks that proliferated on the bottom of the sea. According to Jewish tradition, the general Joshua gave fishing rights on the lake to the tribe of Naphtali in about 1,300 B.C., and it had probably been fished by others for many millennia before that.

In Jesus' day, the lake was ringed by fishing boats, fishing villages, and sixteen harbors, with the important fishing centers the prosperous towns of Capernaum at the lake's northwestern tip, and Bethsaida-Julias, about five miles east on the other side of the Jordan. The Jordan River marked Galilee's eastern boundary, and Bethsaida-Julias lay within a territory called Gaulanitis (roughly contiguous to today's Golan Heights) belonging to Antipas's half brother Philip. Jesus knew both towns well. His own home town,

Fishermen still harvest the depths of the Sea of Galilee, known today as Lake Tiberias or Lake Kinneret. Not a "sea" but, in reality, a small lake (fourteen by eight miles), it lies 686 feet below the level of the Mediterranean and has a maximum depth of 157 feet. Fishing for sardines and tilapia still affords a livelihood for some, but of the thriving market towns that circled the lake in Peter's day, only Tiberias on the western shore still exists.

hilly and landlocked Nazareth, was about twenty-five miles southwest of Capernaum, not far from another major city, Sepphoris. In Capernaum lived four of Jesus' chief disciples among the Twelve, fishermen all—the brothers Peter and Andrew and the brothers James and John. Another of the Twelve, Philip, was from Bethsaida-Julias, where Jesus visited often.

Peter, who had a wife and mother-in-law in Capernaum, and his brother Andrew were partner-owners of a commercial fishing boat with Zebedee, the father of James and John. As such, recent archaeological excavations have revealed, these disciples would have been relatively prosperous men. A large first-century fisherman's house containing a sail needle, net weights, and a fisherman's seal recently uncovered in Bethsaida-Julias also contained many animal bones, indicating that its inhabitants ate well. The five disciples who came from these towns undoubtedly gave up comfortable, if physically strenuous, lives to follow Jesus.

In 1986, members of an Israeli kibbutz on Yam Kinneret, walking on the lake bottom after a drought, discovered a twenty-seven-foot-long first-century fishing boat that was probably much like the ones Jesus' disciples used in their trade. The boat, now carefully preserved, together with a first-century mosaic depicting a fishing boat found at the site of another ancient village, Magdala, has given us a clear picture of what these craft were like: They typically had a single mast, a square sail (supplemented by oars), a curved stern, and decks fore and aft on top of which the fishermen could cook if they wished, and under which they could sleep, as Jesus did on at least one occasion. They held crews of at least five, together with a skipper-helmsman.

Fishing was accomplished by using a parachute-like throw net, cast by someone standing on the boat, a dragnet pulled across the sea bottom by the crew, or a trammel, a kind of stationary net-trap set up at night. The fisherman also used hooks and lines, spears, and wicker traps, and frequented small ponds in the marshes on the shoreline. Most of the fish caught were shipped straight to a processing center for salting, smoking, or pickling and thence for export. Magdala, about eight miles down the Galilean coast from Capernaum, and the home of Jesus' female follower Mary Magdalene, was a major fish-processing town with a reputation for boisterous

and decadent living. Its Hebrew name, Migdal Nunia, means "tower of fish."

There are forty-five references in the Gospels to boats or fishing in connection with Jesus' activities. He preaches to a crowd on the beach as he sits in a boat. He instigates a miraculously large catch of fish for his disciples. He slips off in a boat to pray in a deserted place along the shoreline. Once, as his disciples are on a boat battling a sudden storm, he walks upon the waters of the Sea of Galilee to calm them. And when he sees the brothers Peter (Simon) and Andrew casting a net into the Sea of Galilee, he offers to make them fishers of men. ∎

In 1986, low water levels on the Sea of Galilee exposed the remains of a first-century cedar-and-oak boat of the sort with which Jesus and his disciples would have been familiar. It measured twenty-seven by seven and a half feet. Used for both fishing and transportation, it was large enough to hold more than a dozen people.

"And it shall happen in the last days, says God,
I will pour out my Spirit upon all flesh,
so that your sons and your daughters shall prophesy,
so that your young men shall see visions,
so that your old men shall dream dreams....
And I will cause wonders to happen in the heaven above,
and signs on the earth below." (Acts 2:17–19)[3]

What they had seen and heard in and around the Upper Room, Peter said, had nothing to do with drunkenness. Rather, he boldly declared, it was unmistakable evidence that the ancient prophecies were coming to pass—in their own time, before their very eyes. And what it meant was this: Jesus, the man whom they had seen crucified and whose death some among them had cheered, was in fact alive, "both Lord and Messiah."

Instead of reacting in rage, hooting him down or pelting him with stones, the crowd responded to Peter's explanation in a curious manner. After all, with their own eyes and ears they had witnessed something unusual and powerful. "They felt a deep grief in their hearts," the writer Luke says in describing the emotion that swept through the crowd at Peter's words. "They said to Peter and the other

What they had heard in the Upper Room, Peter said, had nothing to do with drunkenness. What it meant was that the man they had seen crucified and killed was alive.

apostles: 'What shall we do, brothers?'" Peter's answer was simple and direct. "Repent and let each of you be baptized, calling on the name of Jesus, the Messiah, that your sins may be forgiven, and then you will receive the gift of the Holy Spirit."

And on that day, about three thousand followed Peter's instruction, were baptized, and joined the apostles' fellowship. Their faith, based as it was upon what they had seen happen in their city and in and around the Upper Room, spread rapidly. They were well liked by the people in Jerusalem, Luke reports, and their numbers continued to increase. And for their meetings of instruction and worship, they naturally gathered where their religious assemblies had always been held: in the great Temple. Though Gentiles were barred from all but the Temple's outer court—indeed, violations of that rule were punishable by death— these followers of Jesus and Peter were Jews, and therefore entitled to use the Temple for the worship of God.

Inside the Temple walls were a series of courtyards, each more restrictive than the last. Like the Gentiles, women had their own area or court, outside the Court of Israelites and the Court of Priests. The main sacrificial altar loomed before the entrance to the holy central shrine, which was divided inside into two sections separated by a curtain. In the first section, the priests made preparations twice

---

3. In most instances, the scriptural quotes in this chapter are from the *Anchor Bible* translated by Johannes Munck. (Doubleday, Garden City, NY, 1964.)

The vestments (right) worn by the high priest during the rituals of the High Holy Days in the Temple were prescribed in detail in the twenty-eighth chapter of the Book of Exodus. Included in the garments was a breast-plate embedded with twelve precious and semiprecious stones (below) representing the tribes of Israel.

daily, for the morning and evening sacrifices. Beyond the veil and the curtain, in the room known as the Holy of Holies, the Ark of the Covenant was believed by some to be present still. Only the high priest was permitted to pass through the veil separating the Holy of Holies from the anteroom, only once a year, and always aware that a misstep could result in his death.

The Temple bustled with activity from dawn to nightfall, and not just religious activity. Every adult male among the eighty thousand Jews who lived in Jerusalem year-round was required, under the ancient laws, to pay a yearly Temple tax of one-half shekel each. (The value of a shekel remains obscure, but according to the Old Testament book of Exodus, thirty shekels was the price of a slave.) There were also freewill offerings, publicly applauded bequests and gifts, wood offerings for the sacrifices, and periodic fund-raising drives for special needs. In the Temple treasury sat trumpet-shaped containers into which worshipers could drop coins. (One such worshiper was the widow celebrated in Mark's Gospel, who gave just two small coins—the "widow's mite." Jesus, seeing what she had done, remarked that by giving all that she had, she had contributed far more than the wealthiest donor.) The annual cash flow, supporting the work of thousands of priests and other personnel and funding the rest of the staggering overhead costs, had long before made the Temple an important commercial center. Bankers kept monies on deposit in the Temple—the fourth book of Maccabees speaks of private fortunes held there for safekeeping.

Much of the Temple's commerce arose in support of religious ceremonies, in particular the unending rounds of animal sacrifices that occurred there each day. Bulls, calves, sheep, goats, and birds were sold on the premises. So many animals were brought to the Temple for sacrifice that the entire livestock industry in the area around Jerusalem was said to be devoted to that purpose.

Thousands of priests, along with their Levite guards and assistants and hosts of others, were required to keep all of this going. Each priest served a week's duty in the Temple, at the rate of about seven hundred priests a week on a twenty-four-week rotating schedule, with as many as eighteen thousand priests from Jerusalem included in the rotation. During their one or two weeks of service each year, they were entitled to keep some of what remained of the sacrificial animals, particularly hides, which could be sold to boost a priest's income. Under ancient law they were also entitled to offerings specifically collected for their income, but many priests lived in poverty. Although the taxes and offerings were scripturally required, not all were paid, and there were huge expenses to meet besides the priests' salaries.

The sacrifices began at dawn, with the solemn killing and butchering of a lamb by priests bedecked in white linen and sashes decorated with flowers of crimson, purple and blue. Sacrificial ceremonies continued throughout the day,

The Temple sacrifices began at dawn with the solemn killing and butchering of a lamb by priests dressed in white linen, and continued through the day as the sewers filled with blood.

accompanied by singing and cymbal-crashing. In addition to the communal rituals, there were privately funded sacrifices, paid for by individuals or families grateful for spiritual favors, seeking benefits, or fulfilling religious vows. A second lamb would be sacrificed on behalf of the community as a whole each evening, just before conclusion of the daily service.

Though ceremonies were conducted with reverence, the din raised by hundreds of men at work and hosts of animals in captivity and distress was deafening. Smoke rose from the burnt offerings, the sweet odor of wood flames and roasting flesh mingling with the stench of incinerated bones and hair, settling heavily over the city. An unending river of blood, coursing from the beasts' carefully slit throats, flowed away through an elaborate system of sewers and sluices, above and below ground.

Despite the slaughterhouse motif, or perhaps because of it, the atmosphere in and around the Temple was lively, charged with excitement, even joyful. Excited and exhausted pilgrims of all ages and descriptions arrived on foot, meeting other travelers, reuniting with family members, setting up camp around the city, singing and praying and weeping happily. During the great pilgrimage festivals—Passover and the Feast of Unleavened Bread in the spring, the Feast of Pentecost seven weeks later, and the Feast of Tabernacles in autumn—as many

The Temple:
Herod's legacy in gold and stone

The redevelopment of the Temple in Jerusalem employed armies of workers for more than a lifetime to create a monument for a man who would never see its gleaming completion

During the reign of Herod the Great, construction of ornate structures by a multitude of talented artisans boomed in Judea. Their skills—carpentry, tapestry, sculpture, goldsmithing and stonemasonry—blended seamlessly in the rebuilding of the Temple of Jerusalem, the religious, cultural and economic center of the kingdom.

Although Herod the Great began it in 20 B.C., Temple construction continued well past his death in 4 B.C. and was finally completed by the governor Albinus about A.D. 62. According to some accounts, as many as ten thousand lay workers and one thousand priest-managers were employed in creating a structure standing 100 cubits (170 feet) at its highest point (the Temple House) and made from materials ranging from Lebanese cedar to Italian marble.

The intricacy and craftsmanship were apparent in such features as the detailed capitals for the 162 columns, the stone latticework that separated the courts, and the solemn inscriptions warning Gentiles not to venture beyond their restricted areas on pain of death.

Although prone to exaggeration, the Jewish historian Josephus describes the exterior of the Temple as gleaming with gold. The Talmud says Herod was advised against this ostentation by wise men who said to him, "Leave it alone, for it is more beautiful as it is, having the appearance of waves of the sea." All but one of the ten gates, however, were gilded, and there was lavish golden accenting throughout, especially on the Temple House itself, where 150 square feet of the exterior was covered in gilt the thickness of a coin. The interior of the Holy of Holies was awash with gold.

After the sack of Jerusalem in A.D. 70, so much plundered gold saturated the Syrian market—most of it from the Temple—that the value of the metal fell by half. ■

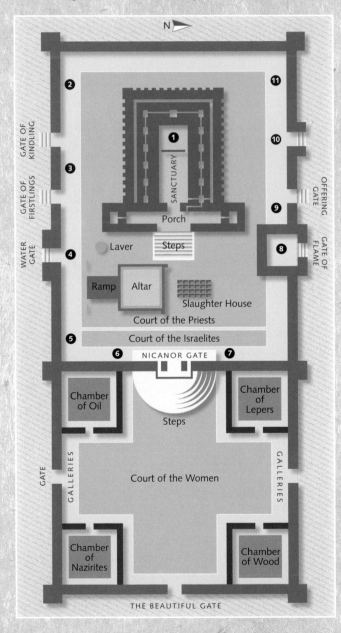

Plan of the Second Temple (labeled): N; Gate of Kindling; Gate of Firstlings; Water Gate; Sanctuary; Porch; Steps; Laver; Ramp; Altar; Slaughter House; Court of the Priests; Court of the Israelites; Nicanor Gate; Offering Gate; Gate of Flame; Chamber of Oil; Chamber of Lepers; Steps; Galleries; Court of the Women; Chamber of Nazirites; Chamber of Wood; Gate; The Beautiful Gate

Plan of the Second Temple

1 Holy of Holies
2 Chamber of Kindling
3 Golah Chamber
4 House of Abtinos
5 Chamber of Hewn Stone
6 Chamber of Makers of Baked Cakes
7 Chamber of Pinehas, the Keeper of Vestments
8 Chamber of Hearth
9 Porwah Chamber
10 Rinsing Chamber
11 Salt Chamber

4

3

Western ("Wailing") Wall

Royal
Portico

Temple

Antonia
Fortress

Court
of the
Gentiles

Solomon's Colonnade

N ▷

YARDS   METERS
0   100   0   100

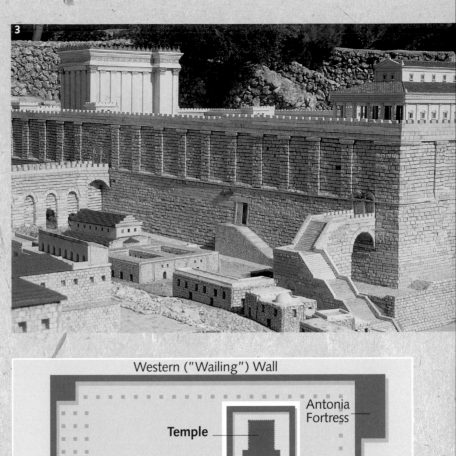

1

2

*Photos on these two pages: (1) The main
sanctuary of Herod the Great's Temple (seen
from the east in this model at the Holyland
Hotel in Jerusalem) likely rose to an imposing
ninety feet above the rest of the various courts
that surrounded it. To its left in the model (the
south) is the Royal Portico, the main point of
entry for the throngs that crowded the Temple
daily. (2) Just below the Royal Portico were
the double Hulda Gates, now sealed and
partially obscured by an addition to the wall
but with intact stairs. Jesus would have
trudged up these stairs to an interior ramp that
led up to the Royal Portico. (3) The reconstructed model clearly shows the location of
the grand exterior staircase on the southwest
corner of the Temple mount. (4) The remnants
of the supporting ledge for these stairs are
known now as Robinson's Arch, after the
archaeologist who discovered them.*

as two hundred and fifty thousand visitors would descend upon Jerusalem, all under holy obligation to offer Temple sacrifices, as singers sang and pipers played. Drawn by the bustle and commotion, and eager to see or be seen by the swarms of worshipers, were scholars, soldiers, merchants, beggars, tourists, prophets and pickpockets, jostling each other daily on the Temple platform, in what one modern scholar described as a Judean version of London's Hyde Park Corner.

In mid-afternoon, Peter and John and the others—not yet known as "Christians," and not yet feared or despised by the Temple hierarchy— approached the thirty-five-acre Temple complex, intending to worship with the other Jews. Surrounded by fellow beggars at the entrance known as the Beautiful Gate was a crippled man who called out to them, appealing for alms, a handout. Much of the population of Jerusalem was dependent upon charity, and the Temple was the center of various formal and informal means of aiding the poor. Peter studied this particular beggar intently, recognizing him as a familiar figure—a man who, aged about forty and unable to walk, was carried daily to the gate by his friends. But there was something unusual about his fierce, desperate appeal that day. John, too, stopped and looked at the man. Suddenly, Peter spoke: "Look at us!"

The man struggled eagerly to sit up, hoping that he was about to receive a good-sized donation. Instead, Peter said something quite remarkable: "I have no silver or gold, but what I do have I give you. In the name of Jesus Christ the Nazarene, walk!" And with that, he reached down, took the man by his right hand, and pulled him up.

The writer Luke, trained as a physician, describes what happened to the man next: "Immediately his feet and ankles were strengthened." He leapt to his feet, testing them cautiously at first, walking about tentatively, and then he began "walking and leaping and praising God." All of this happened in full view of the crowds in the Temple area. The man, who had spent much of his life begging at the gate, was well known to the Temple's faithful who now saw him leaping about like a child. It was astounding.

A limestone sundial found during Temple Mount excavations may have been used by the priests to time the ongoing cycle of services. It appears to be the only artifact linked directly to Herod's Temple, so thorough was the Roman destruction of the holy mountain.

Overcome with emotion, the man clung to Peter and John as they entered the Temple, its magnificent gold-covered facade glowing in the afternoon sun. Joining the crowd funneling into the area, the disciples and their new follower climbed a broad stairway up to the entrance gate, entering as others who had already completed their business in the Temple exited from a smaller gate,

slightly to the west. Peter and John had been intent on worship, but the excited company around them grew larger as word of what had happened spread. They reached an area known as Solomon's Colonnade before they were so surrounded by onlookers that they could go no farther.

Once again, Peter took matters into his own hands, addressing the astonished crowd. "Why do you marvel at this, or why do you stare at us as if we had by our own power or holiness enabled this man to walk? The God of Abraham, Isaac, and Jacob, the God of our fathers, has glorified his servant Jesus. . . . Through faith in his name, Jesus' name has given strength to this man, whom you see and know, and the faith that is called out by (Jesus) gave this man the full use of his limbs, as you can all see.

". . . Repent therefore, and turn, so that your sins may be wiped out."

The commotion soon attracted the attention of Temple officials. A group of priests, the Temple commander, and some of the Sadducees approached them aggressively, pushing through the mass of people, seizing Peter and John and pulling them out, placing them formally under arrest, and locking them up for the night. Still, what had happened that day could hardly be denied by those who had seen it. Peter's gripping explanation of the meaning of the man's healing, combined with his urging that they change their lives and follow in the

In an episode reminiscent of their Master's miracles, Peter and John healed a crippled beggar at the Temple gates. A crowd gathered quickly as news of the healing spread. Characteristically, Peter then took the opportunity to admonish the onlookers for their failure to have recognized the Messiah whom God had raised up "to bless you in turning every one of you from your wickedness." At once furious and alarmed, the Temple authorities arrest the two disciples. Here, they are led away.

way of Jesus, had a profound effect. Luke calculates that the number of men in the assembly of Peter grew to about five thousand that afternoon.

On the following day, the high priest Annas assembled the seventy-member council known as the Sanhedrin to consider what should be done about the growing disruption in their midst. The aristocratic Sanhedrin wielded power not only within the Temple and Judaism, but also in the general government; it was designated to administer both Jewish Law, for which it was the final court of appeal, but also, to some extent, civil and criminal law as well.

The Sanhedrin included a number of Sadducees—members of a party within Judaism that regarded any reference to bodily resurrection as blasphemously unacceptable under the traditions and beliefs handed down to them from Moses. They were strict in their Temple observances, and they enforced severe penalties on any who slipped. Also among the Sanhedrin was a strong force of Pharisees, Jerusalem's other major party. Though "pharisaical" would later come to mean strict, hypocritical, and straitlaced, the Pharisees of the early first century were far more lenient than the Sadducees, allowing the rules to be bent under certain circumstances rather than rigidly applied. The Pharisees therefore enjoyed much greater popular support. A third faction, the scribes, were scholars and theologians, guardians and interpreters of Jewish tradition. Because they were highly respected, scribes were often appointed to important offices, both religious and public. None of the factions represented in the Sanhedrin was inclined to take lightly a potential threat to the traditions and order observed in the Temple, and they were firmly resolved to find out what this sudden wave of mania meant and to determine how to deal with it.

Found in a Jerusalem house dating from Herod's era, these two plaster fragments bear one of the earliest known likenesses of the menorah (seven-branched candelabra) that stood in the Temple.

After spending the night in captivity, Peter and John were hauled before the Sanhedrin for questioning, and along with them, the guards brought the man who had been healed. The first question put the Sanhedrin's concern about the disciples succinctly: "By what power or by what name have you done this?"

Once again, it was Peter who rose boldly to the occasion. "If today, because of a kindness to a sick man, we are asked by what means he was cured, let it be known to all of you and to all the people of Israel, that it is through the name of Jesus Christ the Nazarene, whom you crucified, but whom God raised from the dead—it is through him that this man stands before you cured. . . . And there is no salvation through anyone else. For there is no other name under heaven given to men through which we must be saved."

The answer astonished the learned company. Peter and John were both mere fishermen from the backcountry, uncouth, unqualified, unlearned in the fine points of the Law. Did they not realize whom they were addressing in such brazen terms? They were also known to have been among the followers of Jesus before his execution. And here before them was another man, standing bolt upright, walking under his own power—the same man who had languished for years outside the Temple. Some, no doubt, had occasionally dropped a few coins in his palm.

They briefly dismissed the trio from the hearing and tried to figure out what to do. It was a delicate problem. Word of the miraculous healing had already spread far and wide, and there were many eyewitnesses. Issuing an official denial that the thing had ever happened was certainly not an option. The best they could hope to accomplish, they decided, was to threaten Peter and John severely, order them not to talk about any of this, and especially not to mention the name of Jesus, anymore.

Satisfied with this plan, they called Peter and John back and forbade them to preach about Jesus, to talk about him or even to mention him. Their pronounce-

The powerful earthquake that shook the ground and rattled the building meant just one thing to the apostles: God had heard their prayer and would answer it.

ment, however, singularly failed to impress the accused. They owed, they replied, a duty to God in regard to this incident, and that duty superseded their duty to obey the Sanhedrin. Put simply: "We cannot refrain from speaking of that which we have seen and heard."

This willful refusal to accept the Sanhedrin's authority amounted to open rebellion, but by the very nature of their positions, those who sat on the council were keenly attuned to political reality. They knew that all of Jerusalem was abuzz about what had happened, and that many had attributed it to God. Imposing punishment on those at the center of it would not sit well at all. Not for the moment anyway. The frustrated officials once again ordered John and Peter to keep quiet and, seeing no other choice, turned them loose.

After reuniting with the others, Peter and John related all that had happened, including the Sanhedrin's declaration that they were to stop talking about Jesus. They then led the group in prayer, the prayer recorded by Luke as the first communal prayer of the Christians, ending with this plea: "Now today, Lord, take notice of (the rulers') threats, and grant that your servants may speak your word with all boldness, in reaching out your hand in healing, and making signs and deeds take place through the name of your holy servant Jesus."

As they prayed, they remained uncertain about what all of this meant and whether they were on the right track. But they received confirmation in an unmistakable way. What seemed a powerful earthquake shook the ground and rattled the building, and to the apostles it could mean only one thing: God had heard their prayer, and would answer it.

As with any group of people that gathers for a common purpose, the apostles faced immediate, practical needs for organization. By this time, the vacancy created by Judas Iscariot's suicide had been filled. At the behest of Peter, the number of the Twelve had been restored, prior to Pentecost, by the simple expedient of narrowing the eligible candidates down to two and then drawing straws. Matthias was chosen to take Judas's place. (Partly because Matthias is mentioned only once in the New Testament—on this occasion—some would argue later that the apostles had jumped the gun and made the wrong choice, and that Christ had already chosen the real successor, whom he would reveal on the road to Damascus.)

Those who had come to believe wanted, naturally, to remain with others of like mind. That created the need for some kind of ongoing structure to take care of the basic, physical needs of the growing assembly. Glad to be part of the movement, many of those who owned land or other property sold it and gave the money to others who needed it. One man, Joseph Barnabas, set a particularly striking example, selling a field that he owned, bringing the money to the apostles, and laying it before them at their feet.

Meanwhile, the group had to contend with the usual foibles of humanity. There are always those who jockey for position and prestige, watching the others carefully for clues as to what they can do to gain attention and favor. Two such members of the infant church were Ananias and Sapphira, a married couple. Having jealously observed the warm regard in which Joseph was held after his sacrificial contribution of the proceeds of his land to the group, they determined to obtain the same status for themselves. After all, they, too, owned a field. They sold it, and they received quite a bit of money—too much money, really, to give it all away, they decided. They would keep some of it back, and the amount they gave to the apostles would still be impressive, would still exalt their standing, while they would not run the risk of having no funds for themselves should all of this collapse and throw them back on their own resources. Ananias, therefore, took only part of the money with him when he imitated Joseph and brought the cash to Peter, laying it at his feet.

Peter, however, had been watching Ananias, and he immediately became suspicious. Instead of praising the gift, he questioned Ananias sharply, asking him outright if, indeed, he had turned over all the profits from the sale as he claimed. When Ananias assured Peter that the entire sum was before him, Peter recognized it as a bald falsehood: "Why did Satan fill your heart so that you lied to the Holy Spirit and put some of the money for the land aside for yourself? Was it not yours as long as you owned it? After it was sold was not the money yours to dispose of? Why did you decide in your heart to act so? You have not lied to men, but to God." Under Peter's rebuke, Ananias suddenly collapsed, falling to the ground. When others rushed forward to help him, they found that he was dead, and they were gripped with fear. They quickly wrapped his body, took it out, and buried it.

Three hours later, Ananias's wife, Sapphira, came in, unaware of her husband's fate. Peter asked her the same questions: Had they sold the land for so much? Yes, she said. Had they brought all the money to the apostles, as they said? Yes. So Peter dashed Sapphira's hopes for acclaim and prominence as well: "How can you two have agreed to put the Spirit of the Lord to such a test?

Listen, you can hear the footsteps of the men who have just buried your husband coming back through the door, and they will carry you out as well." And, just as her husband had done, Sapphira collapsed before Peter and died. The men who had buried Ananias came in, took her out, and buried her beside her husband.

The stark fear experienced by those who witnessed the deaths of Ananias and Sapphira was rooted in a belief by some of the disciples that they would not die before Christ returned to earth and gathered up his people. Here, though, they had seen two members of the congregation fall dead before them—and that raised the possibility that others might die before the second coming as well. Besides having it impressed upon them that punishment follows disobedience to the Holy Spirit, the apostles found themselves wondering who if any of them would make it through to the end, and what would happen to those who did not.

In defiance of the Sanhedrin's orders, Peter and John continued to gather with the others at the Temple,

usually in Solomon's Colonnade as before. There they continued to attract attention, but by now other Jews had heard of the arrests and the strict instructions imposed by the Sanhedrin, and were wary of being associated with the energetic rebels. In general, though, Luke reports, the people held them in respect. And soon, once again, others were joining them, crowds of men and women, many bringing members of their families who were sick and placing them on beds and cots along the path that Peter customarily took, in the hope that his shadow, or just his presence, would heal. And healings took place, followed quickly by widespread reports of these miraculous events, so that Jerusalem was quickly awash in travelers from other towns, bringing their sick and afflicted for help.

All of this was observed by members of the Sanhedrin with a mixture of

Like other Followers of the Way, Ananias and Sapphira sold land to contribute funds to Jerusalem's fledgling church. But they secretly kept back some of the proceeds for themselves. Questioned by Peter, Ananias lies about it. Instantly, says the Acts of the Apostles, he drops dead. Unaware of this, Sapphira unwittingly tries to deceive Peter in the same way. "Listen!" says Peter. "You can hear the footsteps of the men who have just buried your husband. They will carry you out as well!" And so they do.

concern and disgust. These simpletons, mere peasantry, were creating a continual disturbance, upsetting respectable visitors, distracting the worship, becoming a veritable magnet for confusion and trouble. Talk was useless, a group of Sadducees decided. It was time to act. They suddenly seized all twelve apostles and arrested them publicly. That, they concluded, would be that.

It wasn't. That night, as the Twelve huddled behind bars, a strange thing occurred. A figure appeared among them—living, certainly, but not human. What they remembered most was its blinding brilliance. They concluded it was an angel. Powerfully, the figure pulled on the prison door that instantly swung open, the heavy bolts flying. Then the figure spoke. They were not to return to their homes. They were not to flee the city. They were to proceed forthwith to the Temple, and resume their witness to Christ. Thrilled, frightened, dumbfounded, they obeyed.

Meanwhile, the high priest had convened the Sanhedrin. The question before the council, he said, was the disposal of the prisoners. They were now at last in custody. Things had gone well. All twelve had been arrested without incident. It

Abruptly, the meeting of the Sanhedrin halted. Somehow all twelve apostles had escaped from prison and were in the Temple, brazenly telling people about Jesus again.

remained to decide. . . . Abruptly the meeting was stopped. A disturbing report had just come in from the prison. Somehow all twelve prisoners had escaped. No one knew where they were. It was simply inexplicable. Every precaution had been taken. Guards posted, doors bolted. There must be some explanation for this. But what?

Then, as the meeting dissolved into bewildered disorder and baffled members pressed for detail, another messenger burst into the chamber. Where the Twelve had gone was no longer a mystery, he announced. They were standing, brazen and defiant, as they always did, in the midst of the Temple, openly telling people about Jesus and urging them to follow the way of life he had proclaimed.

For the second time, the commander of the Temple and his deputies went out and escorted the apostles back before the Sanhedrin. Luke makes the point that they were brought by persuasion, not force, because the people were clearly on the apostles' side and the arresting officials feared that they themselves might be stoned. The high priest sternly rebuked the Twelve, reminding them that the Sanhedrin had expressly commanded them not to teach in Jesus' name. They had ignored that commandment, not only filling Jerusalem with their teaching, he said, but seeking "to bring this man's [Jesus'] blood upon our heads."

Replied Peter: "One must obey God rather than men." What he and the others were teaching, he said, they could not deny because they had witnessed it with their own eyes.

Thrown into an uproar by the apostles' intransigence, some members of the Sanhedrin wanted them executed immediately. One man, however, a well-respected Pharisee and teacher of the Law whose renown would live long in the future Judaism, took the floor. His name was Gamaliel. After sending the apostles out, he said to the other members of the council: "Beware of these men, whatever you intend to do." There had been other movements in which people claimed to be "somebody," he said. He cited two recent cases—that of a man named Theudas who had about four hundred followers, and that of another man named Judas of Galilee who also had a large following. After these men died, Theudas by execution, their flocks were scattered, and their teachings quickly lost all favor with the public. The Sanhedrin should therefore let Peter, John and the other apostles alone, the practical Gamaliel said, "for if this design or this work comes from men it will be destroyed, but if it comes from God you cannot destroy them."

The furnace of Herod's fortress, the Herodium, yielded up this terra-cotta disk. On it is the Aramaic alphabet written twice—probably by a student diligently practicing his skills.

Having seen the favor with which the public had received the apostles and their teachings, the Sanhedrin followed Gamaliel's advice, although they did order the men beaten and told them once again that they were not to speak in the name of Jesus.[4] Then they let them go.

Despite the beatings, the apostles were at least free. They were also, Luke says, "glad that they had been held worthy of disgrace for the sake of his name." And they continued to teach and talk about Jesus, proclaiming him the Messiah, in their homes and in the Temple.

Meanwhile, they must contend with their own growing pains as a group. In any movement, especially one experiencing rapid development, tensions and factions are inevitable, and there was no exception for the followers of Jesus' teachings. Two groups, identified by Luke as "Hellenists" and "Hebrews," emerged. The members of both groups were Jews, but they were divided by language and culture. The Hebrews spoke Aramaic,[5] which is thought to have been Jesus' primary language though he also used Greek and Hebrew. The Hellenists were Greek-speaking, and many of their customs drew from the Greek tradition as well. The Hebrews may have seen the Hellenists as too compromising and may have favored Aramaic as more patriotic or appropriate. Whatever the source of division, it became a sore point, and the Hellenists repeatedly complained that their widows were being shortchanged by the Hebrews in the daily division and distribution of food and property.

---

4. Luke does not elaborate on the severity of this beating. If it were the standard Jewish punishment for religious offenses, it would have been far from a light penalty. Such transgressions called for thirty-nine strokes of the lash, a punishment Paul the Apostle would recall receiving five times (2 Cor. 11:24). The thirty-nine "stripes" were one less than the maximum of forty decreed for "the wicked man" by the Book of Deuteronomy (25:3).

5. Aramaic was the international language of Middle Eastern countries at the time of Christ, spoken from Mesopotamia to the east coast of the Mediterranean. Throughout the late period of the Old Testament it gradually replaced Hebrew as the spoken language of Judea. Since it was the language spoken by Jesus to his disciples, this means even the Hellenistic Greek of the New Testament must represent a translation from Jesus' original words. Some scholars believe that at least two of the four Gospels were written originally in Aramaic and translated into Hellenistic Greek. In the twenty-first century, Aramaic was still being spoken in small isolated communities throughout the Middle East, most of them Christian.

SPARKS

The deacon Stephen had begun his defense before the Sanhedrin with a tranquility that even his foes discerned as angelic. Nevertheless, his message was more than they could endure. With ears covered and yelling to drown out his description of a heaven whose existence they could not concede, the council is about to drag him to his death.

Finding themselves so occupied in matters of internal politics that their mission of preaching Jesus' message was impaired, the apostles called a general meeting. They needed administrators, they said, to handle such disputes and thereby give them time to carry out their work of prayer and ministry. Seven "reputable men, filled with the Spirit and wisdom," would be appointed to that task. The community agreed with the proposal, and seven were selected to serve as "deacons," from the Greek word *diakon*, a servant or waiter. First among them was one named Stephen who fit the bill precisely: He was "filled with faith and the Holy Spirit." Named with him were Philip, who would become a noted evangelist to the non-Jewish world, along with Prochorus, Nicanor, Timon,

Parmenas, and Nicholas of Antioch—this last man a Syrian convert to Judaism. Their names suggest that all seven were Hellenists, and they may even have been the leaders of the Hellenist group. Having found a solution to the problem of the Hellenist widows, the apostles were able to pursue their evangelistic mission with even greater success, and the numbers of the faithful continued to increase.

Stephen, in particular, was a forceful and charismatic leader, "filled with grace and power," Luke says, and "working great wonders and signs among the people." Opponents of the movement, and doubters, attempted to debate with him, but "they could not withstand the wisdom and the spirit with which he spoke." Irritated and embarrassed, they decided to try to stop him. They did so by reporting to the Jewish leaders—falsely—that they had heard Stephen publicly blaspheming both God and Moses. They pressed this trumped-up case with such energy that they finally succeeded in having Stephen arrested and brought before the Sanhedrin.

At his hearing, witnesses came forward to swear under oath, while twisting and misrepresenting his words, that Stephen "never stops saying things against [this] holy place and the Law." They had even heard him claim, they said, that the dead Jesus whom he worshiped would soon destroy the Temple and change the very

Spending too much of their time in settling squabbles, the apostles called a general meeting. They needed administrators, they said, so seven 'deacons' were selected.

customs that had been handed down to them from Moses. Having heard the charges against him, the Sanhedrin allowed Stephen to speak in his own defense. He had already proven himself to be a compelling debater, and he rose to the challenge. As he began, his face shone with conviction, Luke says, "like the face of an angel."

Stephen's speech to the Sanhedrin marked a crucial turning point in the movement that would come to be known as Christianity. He drew a connection between the ancient rites of the Temple and the new order of things brought by Jesus, offering the new as the fulfillment of the old. While the rites of the Temple were in their time essential, it was absurd to suggest that God, the creator of the universe, would dwell solely in a building made by human hands. He quoted Isaiah: "What kind of house can you build for me? says the Lord, or what is to be my resting place? Did not my hand make all these things?" The Most High, Stephen declared with authority, "does not dwell in houses made by human hands." The assertion directly challenged a continuing role for the Temple as the center of God's power and the only proper place for worship to occur.

But Stephen did not stop there. Carefully summarizing crucial events in Jewish history from the time of Abraham and the patriarchs to the building of the first Temple by Solomon, he emphasized Israel's repeated rejections of men who would, after their deaths, be hailed as prophets. "You stiff-necked people," he said. ". . . You are just like your ancestors. Which of the prophets did your

At his stoning (left), Stephen's last words echo those of his Savior, "Lord, do not hold this sin against them." The dreaded Saul (above), fierce foe of the new faith and inflexible protector of the ancient Covenant, takes grim satisfaction in Stephen's brutal demise. The Acts of the Apostles records that "devout men buried Stephen, and made great lamentation over him." He was the first Christian martyr, a word that means "witness." Stephen would be the first of an army. In the twentieth century alone, its numbers would reach the millions.

SPARKS

ancestors not persecute? They put to death those who foretold the coming of the righteous one, whose betrayers and murderers you have now become. You received the Law as transmitted by angels, but you did not observe it."

This was more than enough for the infuriated members of the Sanhedrin.

This chapel, built in 1970 over a site where Stephen's stoning may have occurred, is an unprepossessing structure. It stands below the northeast corner of the ancient walls of Jerusalem.

"They ground their teeth at him," Luke writes, but Stephen went on, adding to the insult by staring upwards intently, his face still shining with absolute confidence, and declaring that he saw above him "the heavens opened and the Son of Man standing at the right hand of God."

At that, all pretense of a fair trial failed. Without reaching any formal decision or pronouncing a verdict, the angry officials rushed upon Stephen and ordered him carried out of the city, determined to stone him to death. Four methods of capital punishment had been prescribed, historically, in Jewish Law and custom: stoning, burning, strangulation, and beheading. Under the Romans, the Jewish administrators had lost most of their authority to determine and punish capital offenses, except for cases of blasphemy against the Temple. Though the outcome of his trial was unjust under Jewish Law, Stephen's attack on the continuing sanctity of the Temple could not have been clearer. Moreover, the Jewish people were under solemn obligation to stamp out evil in their midst by capital punishment when it was required—or to be punished for their failure to do so.

The Old Testament laid out in detail the procedure for stoning, and if Stephen's executioners followed it to the letter they would have taken him outside the city, as required, to forestall the pollution by a corpse within the walls. They would have stopped at an open field that was scattered with stones of the proper size and heft—not too large to throw, but heavy enough to inflict fatal injury. As Stephen's captors stripped him, a group of witnesses would have been appointed and charged with two duties. Understanding what they were about to do, they would have removed their cloaks and laid them aside, then approached Stephen, who was still standing, and laid their hands on his head. That symbolic action was followed by the witnesses' second obligation: They would be the first to throw stones, and therefore they would be held responsible if the execution later turned out to be wrong.

The remaining details of Stephen's execution can be inferred from Luke's record. He offered no resistance. His executioners picked up rocks from the ground and hurled them at him. As the first stones struck Stephen's body, he raised his arms involuntarily. Once the witnesses had completed the ceremonial stoning, the rest of the crowd joined in to finish the deed, pounding him with stones, opening cuts in his flesh and bruising his face and head. Bleeding heavily as the stoning continued, he cried out: "Lord Jesus, receive my spirit," and fell to his knees under the hail of rocks. The brutal pummeling went on. Then in a loud voice, he cried out, "Lord, do not hold this sin against them." With that, he lapsed into unconsciousness and died. Finally seeing no sign of movement in his battered body, those in the crowd let the last stones drop from their hands, and walked slowly back towards the city. The disciples recovered the corpse and buried it in great sorrow.

Stephen thus became the first Christian martyr. His unflinching sacrifice is still commemorated in the names of thousands of Christian churches, schools, cathedrals, monasteries and hospitals around the world.[6]

Standing beside the pile of cloaks shed by the witnesses, another young Jew had watched Stephen's execution with keen interest. His expression indicated a fierce hatred for this sect, a resolve to exterminate it and its threat to the whole mission of Israel and its people. The disciples knew little about him, except that his name was Saul. ∎

The amazing faith of 'Doubting Thomas'

India's Christians are sure the 'downer' disciple exceeded them all

Modern-day Christian churches on the Malabar Coast in India trace their origin to the evangelistic mission of Thomas, an apostle best known not for his faith but for his doubt. Curiously, however, if the traditions of the most ancient Christian churches of India are true, "Doubting Thomas" may have traveled farther with the gospel than any of the other apostles.

The character of Thomas portrayed in the New Testament, chiefly in the Gospel of John, is absolutely consistent. He is by nature the quintessential pessimist and skeptic.

Unless he sees the print of the nails in Jesus' hands, he says, he will not believe that he is alive. Jesus thereupon shows him the nail marks, and chides him for lack of faith. Similarly, when Jesus announces he's heading for Jerusalem and the other apostles urge caution, Thomas responds in character. "Let us go and die with him," he says, cheerlessly. When Jesus tells the disciples they know where he is going and the way he is going to take, Thomas protests: "We don't know where you're going and we don't know the way either" (John 14:5). "I am the Way," replies Jesus.

---

6. The day chosen to mark the death of the first Christian martyr, the Feast of Stephen—December 26 in the West and December 27 in the East—would call to the minds of English-speaking Christians the legend of a saintly tenth-century Christian king who on "the Feast of Stephen," right after Christmas, tramps through the snow in winter to bring help to a starving peasant. The popular carol was written by the Anglican hymnographer John Mason Neale. The King himself, however, is not legendary. Wenceslas of Bohemia (907–929) was murdered for his efforts to bring peace to the Christians of eastern and western Europe and is commemorated as saint, king, and martyr.

That such a crepehanger should take the gospel as far away as India seems, therefore, absurd. Yet the Gospel accounts subtly disclose another side to his nature. Thomas, after all, is prepared to go to Jerusalem, however gloomy the prospects. And once shown the print of the nails, Thomas responds: "My Lord and my God!" It's the only place in the Gospels where the term "God" is applied to Jesus without qualification.

In any event, the Indian church reveres the accounts of Thomas's exploits, uninhibited by historical qualms, though the only detailed account of it is a Gnostic miracle story written some time after A.D. 200. It also preserves a vital shred of Thomas's character as portrayed in John's Gospel. He was convinced, says the Gnostic story, that his mission to India would fail, but went anyway because Jesus in a vision insisted.

We are then told that Thomas Didymus (the second name means "twin," though no mention is made in the Gospel accounts of his sibling) went first to North India, to the kingdom of Gondophernes, who reigned from A.D. 19 to 45. It was a good choice, because Gondophernes was the most important king in north-western India, and his capital, Taxila, was a bustling cosmopolitan center. According to one story, Thomas, a builder, was asked to construct a palace for the king, but gave the money to the city's poor instead. When asked to account for the missing funds, Thomas explained that he was building the palace not on Earth but in heaven. Although Gondophernes reacted by throwing the evangelist into prison, we are told that the king later embraced Christianity and released him.

Thomas next turned his attention to southern India, where he labored in Chera on the Malabar Coast for many years and established a viable church, even converting a number of Brahmans (members of India's priestly caste). While the Malabar tradition of his ministry insists that he was a good debater, he is supposed to have won converts more by his example than by his arguments.

There is a persistent tradition that Thomas also visited China. He could certainly have found his way there because south Indian traders regularly sailed east, but there are only scattered hints of any such mission by Thomas. We are told that he set his sights on eastern India upon his return, and it proved to be the scene of his martyrdom.

The tradition says Thomas was martyred in July of A.D. 72 in Mylapore, the "city of peacocks" on the Coromandel coast in eastern India. He was passing a small hill that housed a temple of the destructive goddess Kali. The priests demanded that he worship her, but when they compelled him to enter the temple, the presence of the goddess seemed to vanish. The priests, outraged, killed him with a spear. One account says that the killing was actually carried out by four soldiers.

Thomas is said to be buried on a small hill at Mylapore. The tomb of the *sadhu* (holy man) from the West, as he came to be called, was revered not only among Eastern Christians but by Muslims and Hindus as well. It is also reported that some of his remains, regarded as holy relics, were moved to Edessa in Syria, where he had a following because he had sent disciples there.

Both Eusebius (ca. A.D. 260–340) and Jerome (A.D. 342–420) mention Thomas's apostolic work in India. There is no direct evidence, but that is not in itself surprising. Even Gondophernes's history was obliterated when his successors were overwhelmed

by the Kushana dynasty, about A.D. 78. For many centuries afterward, Gondophernes was considered legendary, because he was known only through Christian works relating Thomas's missionary journey. However, coins found during nineteenth-century excavation in the area have helped to reconstruct the history of Gondophernes's kingdom.

Thomas's visit to India, if it occurred, was timely. Navigators had recently discovered that ships that cooperated with the seasonal monsoon winds could cross the Arabian Sea and head directly for west Indian ports. The more ancient practice had required ships from the West to hug the coasts of Arabia, Persia, and Baluchistan, then the whole length of the Indian coast, returning laboriously by the same route. By Thomas's day, the voyage to India and back had been reduced from several years to only one.

Greeks and Romans, anxious to trade gold for pepper, spices, gems, and silk, swarmed into Indian ports. Indian kings assisted them by stationing trade agents in Rome and Alexandria. There was also a Roman garrison and temple at Musiris, where Thomas is said to have landed in A.D. 52. As a Christian missionary who needed contacts, he would easily have found people there who knew the languages, customs, and culture of the Middle East and the Roman Empire. The practice of the apostles was to evangelize Jewish communities first, and Thomas is said to have converted most of the resident Jews before starting on the Brahmans.

The apostle Bartholomew, whom many sources equate with Nathaniel, is also said to have preached in India some time after A.D. 35, in the coastal region of Western India and the Konkan coast (called "Citerior"—meaning "nearer"—India by the Romans). Both Jerome and Eusebius mention Bartholomew's evangelism in India, as does Rufinus, a contemporary of Jerome. His mission field included Bombay, which would one day become the commercial capital of India and the only gateway to the rich Deccan hinterland. The town of Kalyan, today a suburb of Bombay, had an established Jewish colony known as the Bene-Israel, to which he probably went first. After the Persian church established control over the Indian church, the history of the Bartholomew Christians became mingled with that of the Thomas Christians. Bartholomew himself is believed to have been martyred in Armenia.

Christians received a ready welcome on the Malabar Coast. The Chera king appointed Christian leaders to oversee trade and, when necessary, to provide security. Theologically, the Indian Christian communities came under control of the Persian church, primarily because their bishops were usually trained in Persia.

In A.D. 1290, Marco Polo saw Thomas's shrine at Mylapore and picked up a local story that Thomas had been killed accidentally by an archer shooting peacocks. Later repeating of this story may have been an attempt, in a pluralistic religious setting, to focus attention away from Thomas's martyrdom.

Significant European contact with the Thomas church began only when the Portuguese began to visit India in the sixteenth century. Expecting to find an untouched mission field, they found, to their surprise, an active church. In 1517, two Portuguese visited Thomas's shrine in Mylapore where, according to one report, his tomb was still venerated by Christians and non-Christians alike.

In the twenty-first century, the church remains strong in the southwestern state of Kerala, where Christians have long described themselves as "Christians of St. Thomas." A living tradition of folklore, songs, and dances among the Malabar Christians describes the apostle's work in south India. His feast day is celebrated on the first Sunday after Easter, the day Jesus asked the famously doubting apostle to believe in his eventual triumph.

Whatever the veracity of the Thomas stories, they at least demonstrate that there is room in Christianity for the natural pessimist, that all Christians are not expected to be instant enthusiasts and boosters. That no doubt is why C. S. Lewis delighted whole generations of children with the character Puddleglum in the Narnia stories.

Perhaps, indeed, some Thomas-type was the model for the doleful Puddleglum, the preeminent downer, for whom every sky looks like rain, every foreseeable problem looks inevitable, every prospect looks grim, and all futures look bleak. Yet when it actually does rain, when the problems do arise, when the future does turn out grim, and when everybody is ready to quit, it is Puddleglum, pessimistic as always, who nevertheless keeps right on going. No calamity can faze him because he expected nothing but calamity anyway. ■

CHAPTER 3

Exiled into victory

Saul's brutal campaign to 'cleanse' Jerusalem
backfires as the deported 'Followers'
carry the faith with them

S tephen's uncomplaining yet unrepentant death incited an even deeper resolve among the opponents of the new faith, particularly in the young man named Saul, who had found himself deeply angered as he watched Stephen die. Blasphemers and heretics who challenge centuries-old truths aren't supposed to die nobly. Yet in the hailstorm of rocks that killed him, Stephen had fallen with a face of unmistakable triumph and faith. It was unnerving.

Saul became even more determined to achieve the desired effect of Stephen's stoning—stark terror. His rationale can be surmised. Among these so-called "Followers of the Way," the Hellenists like Stephen were the radicals, the loudmouths, the ones who besmirched the Temple, the Law, and all they stood for. These posed the greatest threat, he no doubt reasoned. They were the ones who must be driven clear out of Jerusalem.

Arrests, yes. Pounding on the doors at night, yes. Men dragged off while their wives and children screamed, yes. In fact, why not take the wives as well, leaving the children to fend for themselves? Beatings? Of course. More executions, more public stonings, more terror, if need be. Whatever it takes.

Certainly all this was unpleasant. Particularly disturbing were the cries from the

children. But Saul knew that God sometimes required the unpleasant. Look at the past—the great deeds against the Philistines, the Canaanites—had Samson held back? Did Joshua show mercy? No. While these occurrences had been "unpleasant," they still happened. Not only did they happen, but God apparently approved of them. In fact, God became angry when his servants shrank from the unpleasant.

Thus Saul now saw it his clear duty to rid the holy city of these vermin.

With the first of the blasphemous Galileans dead, Saul's assault against the Christians takes to the streets. Women and men accused of harboring the heretical belief are dragged off to prison while Saul supervises the crackdown. God's service, he doubtless reasons, sometimes requires severity.

Jerusalem's soil must not be polluted with degeneracy and blasphemy. And to drive them out and keep them out, he must ensure that the effort against them was as unpleasant and painful as possible. They must not even think about returning. He would pursue them, drive them farther and farther away—into Samaria, north and south along the Mediterranean coast, even into Egypt, Syria, and Asia Minor, if need be.

True, that would leave their less radical element still living in Jerusalem. This group had also been deceived by the imposter known as Jesus. But they remained loyal to the faith, loyal to the Law, loyal to the Temple. Everything in its own time. . . .

Whatever the terrors of Saul, all twelve apostles stayed in Jerusalem, as did James (later called "The Just"), a kinsman of Jesus[1] named in the Gospels of Mark and Matthew. Like others close to Jesus during his early years, James was initially hostile toward Jesus' ministry. He thought Jesus was losing his mind. He had tried to restrain the man's embarrassing teaching and public appearances.

In the wake of the Crucifixion, however, all that changed. James had had an encounter with the resurrected Jesus that affected him so profoundly he put aside his skepticism and joined the early church, convincing his siblings to follow (all were present in the Upper Room at Pentecost).

Partly through his close ties to Jesus, partly because he had met him alive after his Crucifixion, partly because of his unreserved devotion to God, James embodied authority. Much of the weight of leadership began falling on him. He became known as a "pillar" of the church. As far as leadership in Jerusalem was concerned—and Jerusalem was the church's unquestioned center—James's

The ascetic James was said to spend so much time kneeling in prayer that he developed calluses. Out of this grew his affectionate nickname, 'Camel-Knees.'

authority there soon rivaled, if not overshadowed, that of any other apostle, including Peter, making James a virtual overseer, or bishop, in the holy city.

Though never numbered among the Twelve, James would eventually be included as an apostle in the writings of Paul. Later Christian writers describe him as an ascetic, possibly an adherent of the strict Nazirite sect. One writer records that James spent so much time in prayer "that his knees grew hard like a camel's from his continually bending them in worship of God and beseeching forgiveness for the people." Thus, the affectionate nickname, "Camel Knees." In addition to his personal adherence to all required observances of the Torah, James appears to have been the most sensitive of the early leaders of the church when it came to Jewish perceptions about the gospel, and he worked diligently to maintain a strong relationship with devout Jews. As a disciple of Jesus, James considered himself also a Jew and was committed to continue to live as a Jew. But fidelity to the Law was becoming a major issue. What exactly was the place of the Followers of the Way within Judaism? The Hellenist Jews spoke Greek,

---

1. James's actual blood relationship to Jesus is a matter of debate within various Christian traditions. As a rule, Protestants view James as Jesus' cousin or half brother, the son of Joseph and Mary, conceived after Jesus had been born. Roman Catholics and Eastern Orthodox view James as either a cousin or a step-brother—a child of Joseph from an earlier marriage (but not of Mary who, according to both Catholic and Orthodox teaching, remained a virgin throughout her life).

not Hebrew. They had their own Greek Bible. If there came to be Gentile Followers, what would their duty be? For such questions, there were no self-evident answers.

Meanwhile, astounding things were happening outside Jerusalem. The Hellenist Followers, driven out of the city by Saul, were rapidly spreading their contagious message among the Jews of what was known as the "Diaspora," or the "Dispersion." Throughout both the Roman Empire in the West and the Persian Empire in the East, prosperous and thriving Jewish communities could be found in most major cities. It was to these that the followers of Jesus carried what they called "the good news."

How these Jews had settled throughout the world is a fascinating story in itself. When the Babylonians conquered Judea in the sixth century B.C., most of the Jewish population was carried off into exile in the conquerors' land. Then Persia overwhelmed Babylon, and many Jews returned to their homeland. Others remained in Persia where strong and influential Jewish communities arose. But they did not entirely assimilate. They maintained their own culture and religion. From 335 to 323 B.C., Alexander the Great's irresistible army crushed Persia, and seeded the Greek language and culture throughout Asia Minor, around the Syrian coast into Palestine and Egypt, and eastward through Mesopotamia, as far as India. Though Alexander's military conquests would be challenged following his death, the imprint of his presence was left upon the ancient world for centuries to follow, providing it with a common tongue and a common set of cultural ideas—the perfect setting for the spread of a new religion. The name of that Greek culture was Hellenism.

"Synagogue" is Greek for "the place where people are led together" and the local synagogue was indeed such a place for most Jews who lived in lands at great distances from the Temple. Still, the reminders were always there, even in those synagogues relatively near the great sacred building—such as this first-century structure whose foundation was discovered at Gamla (in the lower Golan Heights east of the Sea of Galilee). It was so designed that when the faithful faced the Ark, they also faced toward the Temple.

After Alexander died, just four months shy of his thirty-third birthday, his empire was eventually divided among three competing successors. Of those, the one most kindly inclined toward the Jews was Seleucus I Nicator, who ruled Persia, Asia Minor, and Syria. Seleucus saw the Jews as a stabilizing force in what was then considered a "frontier" environment. So he offered them tax and land incentives, among other things, to move into Syrian cities, particularly Antioch. The Jews responded in large numbers, until eventually there were more Jews living in Syria than anywhere else in the Diaspora.

Jews were resident in Rome by the second century B.C. where by the time of Christ they numbered as many as fifty thousand. Alexandria in Egypt, founded by and named for the great conqueror, became the center of Hellenism, and boasted an even larger Jewish community. All told, by the first century A.D., there were close to one million Jews living in Egypt and as many as five or six million living in the Diaspora. Propagated by the very oppression that sought to destroy it, the Jewish faith had truly become a world religion.

They were separated, of course, from the Temple in Jerusalem, though tens of thousands made pilgrimage there for the great festivals. But at home, they were unable to carry out many of Judaism's ancient daily rituals and sacrifices. So for Jews in the Diaspora, their local synagogue became the center of their community life. The synagogues could never replace the Temple, but they did offer Jewish people a chance to worship and to hear the Scriptures being taught and read. They served as schools for children and as courts of law to settle disputes among Jews. The stories, songs, and prophecies of Scripture became deeply important to their identity as a unique people.

The rise of the Roman empire provided added legal protection, as Judaism was classified by Roman law as a "licensed religion," a status that allowed Jews

---

2. Legend has it that at the behest of Ptolemy II of Egypt (285–246 B.C.), Demetrius of Phalerum, the royal librarian of Alexandria, invited a group of Jewish scholars to come to his city and undertake the translation of the Hebrew Scriptures into Greek. The high priest Eleazar in Jerusalem agreed, and sent seventy-two translators, six from each tribe of Israel, along with a copy of the Torah written in gold lettering. The translators were shuttled out to an island where they completed their work in a miraculous seventy-two days. The version became known as the *Septuagint* from the Latin word for seventy. Later versions of this legend have the translators working either alone or in pairs and finding to everyone's astonishment, when they came together to share their work, that all their translations were exactly alike.

DUDASH

Assembled at the behest of Ptolemy II Philadelphus, who wanted a Greek version of the Jewish sacred books, seventy-two Jewish scholars (six from each of the twelve tribes) gather in Alexandria to carry out the painstaking translation. Three centuries later, 300 of the 350 Old Testament citations quoted in the New Testament would be drawn from what became known as the Septuagint, from the Latin word for seventy.

the freedom to gather together for worship, to collect money from fellow worshipers, and to set up their own court system. Since some aspects of the Jewish faith seemed scandalous to Gentile neighbors, the Jews' legal status became an important and vital defense.

Despite the binding influence of the synagogue, as succeeding generations of Jews made their homes outside Palestine and adopted Greek as their primary language, it was inevitable that the Hebrew Scriptures would have to be translated into Greek. Thus was born the Septuagint, meaning "seventy," from the number of translators it took to make it.[2] Few translations of Scripture have been so monumental and so revered. The only Christian equivalents would be

The numerous circumstances which resulted in ritual impurity for a Jew led to the proliferation of ritual baths (mikveh) like this first-century one at Jericho. About twelve feet deep, it is just one of several discovered in and near Herod's palace in that desert oasis.

the Latin Vulgate, translated by Jerome in the late-fourth century, which was the official Bible for much of the western world for a thousand years, and for its cultural impact, anyway, the King James Version, completed in 1611, which would remain the favored translation of many believers in North America and the British Empire into the twenty-first century. The Septuagint was ultimately presented to the king and Jewish community in Alexandria, and was pronounced so perfect a rendition of the Hebrew that further alterations were forbidden.

All this was to have a dynamic consequence. As Hellenist followers of Jesus came into Diaspora communities, they had a shared Greek version of the Old Testament Scriptures with which to discuss and debate the Jewish belief in a coming Messiah. The "good news" was that the Messiah had arrived.

For certain members of the synagogues, it was particularly good. These were people for whom the improbable pagan mythologies of the Roman world, with their vague and indistinct promises of an afterlife and their virtual indifference to the moral behavior of individuals, had long ago lost their appeal. Indeed, the gods were often more petty, more corrupt, and more debauched than were mere mortals. Hence, many Gentiles became fascinated by the Jewish faith, which presented a stark and promising contrast, offering a strong community life and emphasizing a personal communion with a single, all-powerful deity, whose own character formed the basis of ethical responsibility among his followers. This God was righteous and asked his creatures to become righteous.

The Jewish faith seemed to offer much that paganism lacked, and many Gentiles had converted to Judaism and became what were known as "God-fearers." But there were major problems, all arising from the Law, the Torah. The food laws, for example, made it impossible for converts to dine with their fellow Gentiles. Because social and business arrangements, then as later, were frequently concluded over the dinner table, this became an obstacle. A far more troublesome obstacle was the Torah's insistence upon circumcision. To the male mind in the Greco-Roman world, circumcision was a grotesque and offensive practice. While these men may have admired the Jewish God, they couldn't stomach his demands, at least as orthodox Jews presented them. Moreover, seething just below the surface in all this was the general anti-Semitism of the Hellenist world. (See sidebar page 78.)

Thus, the God-fearers found themselves isolated on the fringes of two societies. They weren't fully accepted as Jews because they stopped short of full adherence to the Torah; but they weren't entirely acceptable to their Gentile friends and families either because they recognized the Jewish God and his moral teachings. They were caught between two worlds, and the early followers of Jesus showed a way to unite them. The synagogues of the Diaspora created

The suffering of the chosen

Anti-Semitic massacres long predate Christianity as the gifted become the resented

The persecution of the Jews, a phenomenon that would darken some of the pages of Christian history for two thousand years, did not, however, begin with Christianity. Anti-Jewish pogroms occurred in the eastern Roman Empire while Christianity was itself a tiny Jewish sect, or before it existed at all.

Campaigns against Jews go back, in fact, to the mass deportations after the Babylonians captured and sacked Jerusalem in 586 B.C. and brought much of the Jewish population home as slaves.

Soon after their arrival in Babylon, the Jews won the confidence and respect of their captors. Thus, forty-eight years later, when Cyrus the Great of Persia had defeated the Babylonians and was allowing the Jews to return to their homeland, many opted to remain behind in Babylon. A major Jewish presence then developed outside the "Holy Land." This became known as the "Diaspora," from a Greek word meaning "dispersion."

When Alexander the Great defeated the Persians and marched on Judea in 332 B.C., the high priests surrendered the city unresistingly, and Judea fell under the control of Alexander and his Greek-speaking successors. So a further exodus of Jews began, to the Hellenistic cities around the Mediterranean, and particularly to Alexandria, the city that Alexander founded and named for himself. By the first century A.D., Alexandria's population was forty per cent Jewish, and the Diaspora consisted of five million people, four million of them in the Roman Empire.

However, the Jews of the Diaspora never could become completely assimilated with the people around them. The Torah taught that they had been set apart as God's chosen people (Deut. 7:6). To remain

This relief is just one of several from the palace of King Sennacherib at Nineveh in modern Iraq chronicling the capture of the Jews. It depicts Jewish families with their belongings on their way into exile following the Assyrian conquest of the fortified town of Lachish in 701 B.C. Little better than a century later, a rebuilt Lachish would again be subdued, this time by King Nebuchadnezzar of Babylon. In the various exiles they endured or after voluntary migrations to other lands, the Jews might become despised and persecuted aliens, or sometimes rise to prosperity as merchants and the advisers and tutors of kings, thereby evoking the jealousy of the local populace.

Jews, they had to be *different*. Their faith forbade them to marry Gentiles or eat with them. Their strict Sabbath laws prevented them from lifting so much as a finger to any work on Saturdays, even if their city were threatened. Their male children had to be circumcised. Their religion, their critics charged, caused them to look down on everyone else. All these factors made Alexandria a hotbed of anti-Semitism that frequently became violent.

By the year A.D. 38, the prefect of Egypt, by then a Roman province, could sneeringly ask Alexandria's Jews a dangerously loaded question: If there were a fire, earthquake, or flood on a Saturday, would they do nothing? Would they still walk determinedly down the street with their thumbs hidden in their clothing so as not to be tempted into helping meet the civic crisis? The prefect thought not. He was sure they would at least rescue their own families.

Making things worse, many of the Jews were clever, industrious, imaginative, and they soon became wealthy as a result. The satirical poets Juvenal and Horace jeered them and their exclusivist religion. The orator-philosopher Seneca called them "an evil nation," and the lawyer-statesman Cicero told a public hearing, "You know how large a group they are, how unanimously they stick together, how influential they are in politics. I will lower my voice and speak just loudly enough for the jury to hear me; for there are plenty of people to stir up those Jews against me."

Cicero died in 43 B.C. Apart from such snide comments, and recurring persecutions of the Jews in Alexandria, serious violence against the Diaspora anywhere else was infrequent. Then came the year A.D. 66, when the nationalistic Jewish Zealots gained control of Jerusalem, butchered the city's Roman garrison, defeated the Twelfth Legion and launched the Jewish War. (See chapter 9.) A wild slaughter of the local Jews broke out in cities around the eastern Mediterranean area.

The Jewish historian Josephus tells how on the same day and at the same hour when the Jerusalem garrison was destroyed, an anti-Jewish rampage broke out in the Roman garrison city of Caesarea, sixty miles to the northwest, in which twenty thousand men, women and children were slaughtered. This, he said, claimed every last living Jew in the coastal city. Though the number was certainly exaggerated, the scope of the slaughter was probably not.

In Syria to the north, a similar genocide went on for days because the Jews there were armed and pitched battles broke out. Josephus writes that in cities throughout the province the streets were "choked" with corpses, the bodies of the aged, children, and women stripped of their clothing. Again, he places the death toll at twenty thousand. Thirteen thousand Jews were murdered in the city of Scythopolis, fifty miles north of Jerusalem near the Upper Jordan. At Ascalon in Syria, he reports twenty-five hundred Jews slain, at Ptolemais two thousand, and at Hippos and Gadara more still. All this Josephus attributes to the "hate or fear" with which they regarded their Jewish neighbors.

But as might be expected, the worst holocaust occurred at Alexandria. With the example of the anti-Jewish outbreaks in other cities to spur them, a Greek mob assailed a big Jewish crowd assembled in the Alexandria amphitheater. Most of the Jews fled, but the rioters dragged three of them away to be burned alive.

Josephus records that the entire Jewish populace in the city arose to their defense, creating a far bigger mob than the Greek one. These rushed on the Greeks, hurling stones at them and threatening to burn them all to death. Standing above the melee, Tiberius Alexander, the Roman governor, pleaded with both sides to desist, but this met with jeers and abuse.

The Romans would not countenance defiance. The governor called into action two legions then stationed in the city, along with another two thousand troops that happened to be passing through from Libya. He sent these into the "Delta," the Jewish quarter, with authority to kill and loot. The Jews, who were themselves well armed, resisted stoutly, but they were no match for the highly disciplined and organized Roman units.

The result was wholesale carnage. Josephus writes of the Jews: "They were destroyed unmercifully, some being caught in the open field, and others forced into their houses, which were first plundered of what was in them, and then set on fire by the Romans. No mercy was shown to the infants and no regard for the aged, and the whole place overflowed with blood. Fifty thousand lay dead in heaps. Finally, those still alive pleaded to be spared. Having pity for them, Alexander gave the order for the troops to withdraw.

"Being accustomed to obeying orders, the Romans did so immediately. But the populace of Alexandria bore such a great hatred for the Jews that it was difficult to recall them. They hated to leave the dead bodies alone."

Behind each of these calamities lies the same factor, a pent-up hatred of Jews that gripped the Roman world when few in it had even heard of Christianity. The explanation lay almost wholly in the fact that the Jews divorced themselves from the general society around them.

But if they had not done so, noted the celebrated nineteenth-century Oxford historian Alfred Edersheim, the Jews would almost certainly have vanished into Hellenistic and Roman society and thereby lost the message that was delivered to the world. ■

fertile ground for the seed that the Hellenistic Followers of the Way had carried from Jerusalem, and since they were still considered to be members of a sect of Judaism, the early church benefited from the same legal protections given by the Roman state to the Jewish faith.

The Followers brought something else. Some of them seemed able to heal. In the first century, without antibiotics, vaccinations, or even aspirin, people were powerless against most forms of sickness. Whether it be indigestion or chronic headache, the usual recourse was simply to suffer. The wounded in battle could often expect to die. Appendicitis was usually fatal. Childbirth involved a high risk, for both the baby and the mother. There were no physiotherapies, and none but the simplest prosthetics to help the disabled, no eyeglasses to remedy the inevitable dimming of vision with age, nothing but superstitious incantations for the demonically possessed. Futility and frustration were the common currency of life. Nobody could help.

Nobody, perhaps, except one Philip, a Samaritan Jew who had gone up to Jerusalem and was now back in Samaria as the disciple of the man Jesus who was crucified. Philip was a deacon, chosen at the same time as the martyred Stephen. To the suffering in Samaria, he proclaimed that the Jewish Messiah was at hand, offering power, healing, and hope to all who would believe. Philip was a Hellenist not a Palestinian, and since the Palestinians had a troubled history with Samaria (see sidebar), he had a definite advantage.

When Philip would notice someone sick in the crowd, he did what Jesus had done: reached out his hand, prayed to his Father in heaven, and the poor victim would be instantly healed! So a stir would go through the Samaritan town. Did people actually see what they thought they saw? Could he do it again? He could, and he did. Again and again. Friends would bring the stricken. With grotesque outbursts, demons would leave the possessed. On and on Philip would go, the commanding voice never wavering, the relentless energy never failing.

Through Philip, Samaria became one of the first hotbeds of the new faith. When the Samaritan crowds saw Philip perform the miraculous, they started listening. When they personally witnessed demons sent screaming out of people's bodies upon Philip's command, when they saw paralytics and cripples walking, the Samaritans did more than listen. They started believing. Before long, Philip had a growing church on his hands.

Word of what was happening reached Jerusalem, and with James the Just firmly in charge of the believers there, the apostles decided to send Peter and John to assist Philip. This solidified James's standing in Jerusalem and marked one of the most significant milestones in the history of Christianity. The new faith began breaking away from its Jewish roots. Two of the original disciples were leaving Jerusalem to take it into foreign lands.

But Samaria, like the rest of the world, had its opportunists. One Simon Magus watched Philip's acts

"God's wine," in Greek, reads this bronze seal (appearing in reverse as a seal would) which identified the vintage set aside for use in the various religious rituals of first-century Judea. The use of Greek indicates the widespread Hellenization of at least the educated and influential segments of the Jewish population.

with something more than awe, astonishment, and thankfulness, notably with fear and envy. Before Philip arrived, he had been Samaria's authority on all things religious and miraculous. Calling himself a "divine emanation," a man in whom the power of God was strongly felt, Simon taught that he was the Messiah figure; that he was the true manifestation of the deity. But now here was this Philip, making no such claim—asserting, instead, that his authority and power had been given to him by a man who no longer lived. And Philip was doing things Simon could only dream of, things that made Simon's magic look like nothing more than parlor tricks.

Simon knew immediately when he was beaten. So he went to Philip, asking to be baptized into this great power. After declaring himself a believer, Simon became Philip's apprentice, as he would have thought of their relationship. He followed Philip wherever he went, still amazed at the things he saw Philip do.

Such was the situation Peter and John discovered when they arrived from

A 'good' Samaritan? Why that just couldn't be

Centuries of raw hatred lent a sharp edge to Christ's famous parable that escapes the modern reader

One of the parables Jesus Christ would bequeath to posterity was the "Good Samaritan," about a man from Samaria who rescued the victim of highway brigands after first a priest and then a Levite had passed him by and left him to die. Lost on many who would hear the story, however, would be its central irony. To the Jews of Jesus' day, a "good" Samaritan was an oxymoron. If the man were a Samaritan, he couldn't be good, and if he were good, he couldn't be a Samaritan.

First-century Jews viewed the people who occupied the 870 square miles of land that stretched from the Mediterranean to the Jordan River, separating Jewish Judea in the south from Jewish Galilee in the north (see map page 253), as frauds and impostors. They posed as the descendants of the lost Jewish tribes of Ephraim and Manasseh. This, said the Jews, was nonsense: Those tribes had vanished forever when the Assyrians conquered the northern kingdom of Israel in 722 B.C. The Samaritans were actually the whelps of a lot of immigrants the Assyrians imported into the area as replacement settlers, they said.

Not so, replied the Samaritans. The Assyrians had in fact left most of the populace behind after their conquest, and these were as validly Jewish as the Judeans in the south. And just as David on behalf of the tribe of Judah had established a sacred site on Temple Mount at Jerusalem, so their forefather Omri had established a sacred temple for his tribes on Mount Gerizim, near Shechem, about thirty miles north of Jerusalem. If there ever was a temple on Gerizim, archaeologists were never to discover it. What they have found in great measure, however, are the remnants of the Samaritan capital, itself known as Samaria, built by Omri in the ninth century B.C. (1 Kings 16:24).

During the successive realms that followed the Assyrian conquest, Samaria experienced several rebirths. After Alexander conquered the region in 330 B.C., he rebuilt it. When the Jews defeated Alexander's successors and regained control of the area, their king, Hyrcanus, reduced the city to ashes. In the Roman era, Herod the Great rebuilt it and named it Sebaste. From then it gradually declined to become the Arab village of Sibastiyeh.

Meanwhile, the faith of the Samaritans was to prove peculiarly durable. Bitter over the Jewish destruction of their capital by Hyrcanus, they hated the Jews by Jesus' day with a vehemence matched only by the Jewish hatred of them. The Romans at first inclined towards the Samaritans, an advantage they exploited to the full. In A.D. 6–9, for instance, they intruded into the Jerusalem temple at Passover,

Jerusalem. They commanded instant respect. They wore authority as those born to it. And while Philip was able to perform miracles of healing, Peter and John did something more. When they laid their hands on people who had been baptized, these people received what was said to be the gift of the Holy Spirit. Although the record in Acts doesn't describe exactly what physical manifestations marked the receiving of this gift, it is clear from Simon's reaction that the results were much like the occurrences at Pentecost. Some of those affected spoke in tongues; others began doing miraculous works themselves.

Simon was enthralled; he couldn't restrain himself; he must have this power. So he approached Peter with a bold request: "Here's some money," he said. "In return, give me the ability to pray for others as you do, so that when I lay my hands on them, they, too, may receive the Holy Spirit." Peter's response was characteristically volcanic. "May your silver perish with you, because you thought you could obtain God's gift with money!" he declared. His words revealed the state

thereby polluting it and successfully canceling the feast. By A.D. 52, they slaughtered a whole contingent of Jewish pilgrims near the Galilean-Samaritan border.

Fourteen years later, however, their alliance with the Romans had dissolved and they joined the Jews in their rebellion against Rome—joined ferociously, in fact, standing off Vespasian's legions for a full thirty days before their water ran out, and the Romans cut down ten thousand of them.

Some theologians, including Abram Spiro and S. Lowy, discern a pronounced Samaritan influence on Christianity. They note that Stephen, the first Christian martyr, may have been from Samaria, because his celebrated speech that led to his execution challenged the authority of the Temple. Some detect a Samaritan influence in the Epistle to the Hebrews, and a few even suggest St. John's Gospel was written for Samaritans.

After the fall of Jerusalem and the development of rabbinical Judaism, their conflict with the Jews declined, and the Samaritans spread throughout the empire. Samaritan synagogues once existed at Rome, Thessalonica, Cairo, and Constantinople. Byzantine Christians distinguished sharply between Jews and Samaritans and were very hard on the latter. When they twice rebelled in the sixth century against repressive Christian legislation they were slaughtered.

They fared better under the Muslim Arabs, and their faith began to pick up elements of Islam. Indeed, their assertion, "There is no God but God," derives directly from the Muslim. However, in medieval times, they worked together with the Jews and Christians to defend themselves against the Turks, who were also Muslims.

By the twenty-first century their numbers had receded to approximately four hundred souls, two hundred of them living in Nablus, forty miles north of Jerusalem, the rest in Tel Aviv. ■

Vested in festive white, modern-day Samaritans participate in a procession of the Torah during Shavuot prayers on Mount Gerizim. The festival which falls seven weeks after Passover was originally a barley harvest celebration. Later, under rabbinic influence, it was associated with the giving of the Law (Torah) on Mount Sinai.

of Simon's heart, and Peter warned that he was close to spiritual destruction.

Simon, mortified at Peter's commanding response, cowered before the apostle, begging him to pray to God on his behalf. After this encounter he disappears from the biblical record, but not entirely from history. Simon Magus would eventually combine the teachings of this new faith with elements of his former spiritual practices, helping create a religion called Gnosticism that would haunt the church for years to come. (Simon bequeathed something else to Christian posterity—the word "simony," the buying and selling of ecclesiastical offices, a practice widely used and widely condemned in later church history.)

From Samaria, Philip proceeded to the Mediterranean coast, then headed south toward Egypt. A chariot, from Jerusalem, clattered up behind him. The writer of Acts describes this pilgrim as "an Ethiopian eunuch, a court official of Candace, queen of the Ethiopians, in charge of her entire treasury." (The term "Candace" was a title, not a personal name for the queen of Ethiopia, who at this time may have been a woman known as Amanitere. "Ethiopia" here refers not to the twenty-first-century nation-state, but to the kingdom of

Seeing the wonders worked by the Holy Spirit and the rather rudimentary means for acquiring this Spirit, the laying on of hands, Simon Magus makes his pitch to Peter—along with a gratuity to encourage a positive response. The fiery apostle rebuffs the proposition with a short but frightening lecture, leaving Simon to beg that none of Peter's forebodings come true.

Meroe, which occupied the Upper Nile region south from Aswan to Khartoum where the Blue and White Nile Rivers converge.)

When Philip heard the eunuch reading aloud from the book of the prophet Isaiah, he went up to the man's chariot and asked him if he understood what he was reading. The eunuch invited Philip into his chariot, and Philip climbed up, seated himself, and began presenting Jesus as the Messiah that Isaiah was writing about. The eunuch soon became convinced, and demanded that Philip baptize him on the spot. This Philip did. That event signaled the beginning of the conversion of many influential and powerful people, says the book of Acts. After the eunuch's baptism, "the spirit of the Lord snatched Philip away" and deposited him in Azotus, on the coast directly west of Jerusalem. From there Philip continued up through the coastal cities until he reached Caesarea Maritima, the military and administrative capital of Palestine, where he remained. Twenty

The eunuch invited him into his chariot and Philip began presenting Jesus as the Messiah whom Isaiah had prophesied. Convinced, the eunuch asked to be baptized on the spot.

years later, he was still living in that city with his four unmarried daughters, each of whom had "the gift of prophecy."

Meanwhile, Peter's success in Samaria had encouraged him to travel and preach in other areas, particularly in the northwestern part of Judea, along the Mediterranean coast. Among the places he visited was Lydda, a city on the southern end of the Plain of Sharon. Though a community of believers was already present in Lydda when Peter arrived, its numbers greatly swelled after the healing of a man named Aeneas, who had been bedridden for eight years.

Twenty miles up the road from Lydda lay the port city of Joppa. The believers there soon heard of Peter's act in Lydda, and when a godly and popular woman named Tabitha died (her Greek name was Dorcas), they sent word to Peter in Lydda, begging him to come as soon as possible. When Peter arrived, he shunned the theatrics that would have delighted Simon Magus, and instead sent everyone out of the room. After a fervent session of prayer, he called out to Tabitha to open her eyes, and the woman came to life again. This, of course, created a sensation in Joppa, and Peter agreed to stay there "for some time."

Perhaps as astonishing as this miracle was Peter's growing legalistic flexibility. That a Palestinian Jew should stay, for example, with a tanner named Simon was considered amazing. Because of their constant contact with the bodies of dead animals, tanners were held to be ritually unclean, and they therefore occupied one of the lowest rungs of Jewish society. In agreeing to stay with Simon, Peter indicated he was already becoming less strict in his adherence to the Mosaic Law. This perhaps prepared him for what was about to happen.

As Peter worked in Joppa, thirty miles north on the coast at Caesarea, a God-fearing centurion named Cornelius was at afternoon prayer. The writer of the

Book of Acts states that Cornelius was attached to the "Italian cohort," a unit numbering roughly six hundred men. That, and his name, indicate that Cornelius was an Italian of Roman blood, an officer of no little prestige, living in the Roman provincial capital. Cornelius had come to believe in God, but had stopped short of becoming a Jewish proselyte.

During his prayers, Cornelius had a terrifying vision. He saw an angel of God, who addressed him by name. He listened in frightened awe as the angel confirmed that God had heard his prayers and seen his good deeds; now God wanted Cornelius to summon a Jewish man named Peter from Joppa. Cornelius immediately ordered three of his men—one soldier and two slaves—to invite Peter to come to Caesarea.

As Cornelius's men approached Joppa, Peter went up to the roof of Simon's house to pray. He was hungry, and in the midst of his prayers Peter fell into a trance, witnessing a startling vision, one that could only be vile or repellent for an observant Jew. Laid out in front of Peter, on top of a sheet, were a variety of wild beasts, reptiles and birds—all of them strictly forbidden as food by the Mosaic code. "Get up, Peter," a voice called out. "Kill and eat."

Peter was offended. Throughout his entire life he had been taught to avoid precisely these animals. Not a speck of meat from any of these creatures had ever passed his lips; now would he feast on several at once? The mere thought was repugnant, sickening, obscene. "Surely not, Lord!" Peter replied. "I have never eaten anything impure or unclean." But the voice admonished him: "Do not call anything impure that God has made clean." But Peter wasn't convinced. Twice more the same vision appeared and the same discussion took place. Finally, the sheet and the animals were raised back into heaven.

To a first-century Jew, such a vision would come as astonishing, perverse, vile and offensive. Yet it had come from heaven. How could this be? As Peter pondered the impact of this revelation, the voice spoke to him once more, telling him that he would soon be visited by three men and that he was to go with them, for God himself had sent them.

At that very moment, Cornelius's contingent arrived at Simon's house. When Peter went down to talk to them, they explained that they had come from a Gentile's home. He was righteous and God-fearing, respected by Jews—but still a Gentile, and it was forbidden by Jewish Law for a Jew to set foot inside a Gentile's house. Would Peter return with them to be Cornelius's guest?

However unthinkable the prospect, Peter was haunted by the vision. He welcomed Cornelius's contingent into Simon's house, then left with the three men the next day for Caesarea.

At Cornelius's house, he was given a warm and almost too enthusiastic welcome. "Stand up," Peter told the centurion abruptly. "I am only a man myself." Then, surrounded by Cornelius's friends and relatives, Peter set forth the theological issue. "You are well aware," he told the large gathering, "that it is against our Law for a Jew to associate with a Gentile or visit him. But God has shown me that I should not call any man impure or unclean."

DUDASH

As Peter recounted the story of Jesus, the gathered Gentiles began speaking in the same tongues that the Jewish believers had experienced during Pentecost. The Jews accompanying Peter could scarcely believe what they were seeing and hearing. Peter, never at a loss for words, matter-of-factly proclaimed: "Can anyone keep these people from being baptized with water? They have received the Holy Spirit just as we have."

Word quickly spread that Peter had visited the home of a Gentile and that, even worse, he had actually baptized a group of these uncircumcised people in the name of Jesus Christ. He barely had time to dust off his sandals upon returning to Palestine before the Palestinian believers began criticizing his actions. It was bad enough, they thought, that Peter had eaten with a Gentile and therefore made

At Gaza, a crossroads for travelers passing to and from Egypt, the deacon Philip meets a eunuch who is a senior minister and confidant of the queen of the Ethiopians. Philip leads the Ethiopian bureaucrat through an explanation of Isaiah's "Suffering Servant" passage. The conversion is sealed here with the baptism that the new convert insists upon. "See, here is water! What is to prevent my being baptized?" he had asked.

himself unclean. But baptizing Gentiles without circumcising them or requiring them first to become Jewish proselytes? That was going too far.

This was a crucial moment in Christendom. Whether the followers of Jesus would welcome non-Jewish adherents without imposing the onerous requirements of the Law would prove pivotal in the new faith's ability to convert the world. Peter's defense had an almost apologetic tone to it. "If God gave them the same gift as he gave us," he pleaded, "who was I to think that I could oppose God?" For the moment, he won over his critics, leading them to a crucial understanding. "So then," they said with a note of wonder, "God has granted even the Gentiles repentance unto life." This understanding was

DUDASH

Shortly after rebuking a divine voice that ordered him to eat "unclean" foods, Peter finds himself at table with a Gentile, and not just any Gentile, but a representative of the foreign power oppressing his people. As he listens to the centurion Cornelius's story, the plain-spoken fisherman concludes, "Truly I perceive that God shows no partiality, but in every nation anyone who fears him and does what is right is acceptable." Peter's resolve will later flag, however, creating an onerous problem for Paul.

about to be widely applied in a city called Antioch.

Antioch-on-the-Orontes, built by Seleucus I in 300 B.C., was then the third largest city in the Roman world, a center of Hellenistic civilization and home to one of the largest communities of the western Jewish Diaspora. Its population included Greeks, Syrians, Macedonians, and Jews, thrown together in one diverse, ethnically inclusive mix, while its location on the road between Asia Minor and Egypt helped ensure its prosperity. It boasted two immense fresh-water aqueducts, a forum, an amphitheater, a circus, an imperial palace, and a grand colonnade, making it a city favored by emperors. Though landlocked, it was idyllic with its lush river valley, a plain to the north and springs in the south.

Some of the believers who had fled Saul's persecutions made their way to Antioch and specifically targeted the Gentiles. A "great number" of Gentiles believed the message, says the Acts, and the apostles in Jerusalem sent other leaders to help establish the nascent church and build it into maturity. The willingness of the Antioch church to accept Gentiles as full brothers and sisters in Christ may have been what distinguished the followers of Jesus from other Jews in the eyes of the non-Jewish population. In fact imperial authorities in Antioch developed a name for them. They called them in Latin *christiani*, or "Christians."[3]

Just as the fervent attempts to stop Judaism four centuries before had hastened its spread, so Saul's reign of terror fueled the spread of Christianity. But persecution was like the tide; it rose wave upon wave, and the newest wave was about to break over the Christians in Jerusalem, this one more threatening than any before. It came under King Herod Agrippa I.

Agrippa was a pale shadow of his mighty and dreaded grandfather, Herod the Great. Old Herod had carried out other notable murders, apart from the celebrated slaughter of the children around Bethlehem. Before his own death he executed three of his sons, including Agrippa's father, Aristobulus. That left Agrippa to be raised in Rome by his mother Bernice. He became close friends with the future emperor Claudius, and with Drusus, son of the emperor Tiberius.

In another age, Agrippa would have been known as a playboy. His lavish living drove him into debt. After Drusus was assassinated, Agrippa no longer had a close friend at court and was forced to leave Rome. He returned as the crony of Tiberius's heir, Gaius Caligula, but his loose tongue, as uncontrolled as his spending, soon got him into trouble. Rashly, Agrippa spoke openly of his contempt for Tiberius, questioning the emperor's fitness to rule. Gossip carried his words to the emperor's ears and this carried Agrippa into prison. Fortunately for Agrippa, Tiberius died six months later. Gaius

Syrian Antioch (present-day Antakya in Turkey) once was home to over half a million citizens. Yet, the splendors of the city described as "the Queen of the East" were reduced over the centuries to such rubble that today little remains on the site. (Right) In the mid-1920s an American-led archaeological team unearths the massive paving stones which were used in the Square of Tiberius near the site of the Temple of Augustus. (Above) Tyche of Antioch sits atop a figure representing the Orontes River on which the city was located. The goddess of fortune and fertility, Tyche was an apt patroness for the prosperous and influential center. This third-century B.C. statue is displayed at the Vatican Museums.

succeeded Tiberius, liberated his friend from prison, and awarded Agrippa a symbolic gift, a gold chain equal in weight to the iron chain he had been forced to wear while in confinement.

This was followed by another award. In A.D. 37 Gaius appointed Agrippa to govern a region north of Judea with the title "king." Four years later, Gaius was assassinated and was succeeded by Agrippa's childhood friend, Claudius. Claudius ended Judea's provincial status, removing it from direct Roman rule, and added it to Agrippa's kingdom.

Though a friend of Gaius, Agrippa had won the goodwill of the Jewish people by obstructing Gaius's plans to install a statue of himself in the Temple in Jerusalem, an act that would surely have led to the open rebellion of the Jews. But even the most skilled of politicians would have difficulty keeping order and peace in Judea. As a consequence, Agrippa was always on the lookout for ways to maintain positive relations with the most powerful factions in the city, particularly the Temple authorities represented by the party of the Sadducees. They, in turn, saw one problem that the new king might relieve. He could help rid them of the pestilent followers of that Nazarene, Jesus.

Agrippa obliged. He arrested and ordered beheaded the apostle James Zebedee, one of the Twelve and brother of the apostle John (not to be confused with James the Just, kinsman of Jesus, now leading the church in Jerusalem). This was a monumental arrest.

James went back to the very roots of Jesus' ministry. He had been one of the trio of disciples who had been allowed to witness the raising of Jairus's little daughter. He had been present at the mysterious mountaintop transfiguration of Jesus. He had been there in the Garden of Gethsemane. If calling on the name of Jesus did not protect so favored a son, who, indeed, could be spared? According to the fourth-century church historian Eusebius (recording a tradition passed on by Clement of Alexandria some 150 years after James's death), one of the guards who arrested James was so moved by the apostle's steadfast and dynamic faith that he became a professing believer on the spot—and then took his place next to James when he was beheaded.

James's beheading so pleased the Temple authorities that Agrippa decided to go even one step higher—and arrested Peter. The panic that this attack sent through the community was sharp and understandable. They had barely weathered the merciless fury of Saul. Now they had become pawns in Agrippa's political game. Peter, whom some recalled as the rock upon which Christ's church was to be built, was bound and helpless in prison. But Peter had been arrested before and somehow escaped. So this time Agrippa ordered four squads of four soldiers—sixteen men in all—to stand guard. Once Passover was over, the trial of Peter was to begin.

---

3. Antioch became well known as the primary depository for relics said to have been connected with Christ. It is believed by some that the disciples of Jesus saved and maintained certain relics of his Passion. When Jewish authorities began persecuting the leaders of the new Church, these relics would have been transported out of Judea for their protection and preservation. Nicholas of Antioch served as one of the first seven deacons of the Jerusalem church, and Antioch provided the most logical and likely repository for these treasured objects.

But why such renewed animosity now, some doubtless asked then, and have asked ever since. What had changed? The probable answer lay in Peter's conversion of Cornelius and the Jerusalem church's support of that action. To those faithful to the Law, it must have appeared as a blatant desertion of the Law, thereby encouraging others to do the same. James the Just, though a prominent leader in the Jerusalem church, continued to honor the Temple, and thus was not seen as a major threat. But Peter, with the others more open to assimilation, was quickly becoming a danger. Peter had to go. He was arrested and imprisoned. That was on the Feast of Unleavened Bread, the ceremonial period leading up to the Passover. This was ominous timing. It was at precisely this point in the Jewish liturgical calendar that Jesus himself had been arrested. Unable to influence events, and clearly out of other options, the believers gathered in their house churches to pray.

What happened next Peter would later describe. He was imprisoned in the Antonia Fortress, beside the Temple to the north. As he lay sleeping in his cell a glowing angel appeared, awakened him, effortlessly removed his shackles, and simply led him out. Peter, in a disbelieving trance, passed the guards unobserved. The great iron door at the entrance to the fortress opened before them and they passed through. Then Peter found himself alone—and free.

The night air brought him to his senses. Fully awake now, he ran toward Mary's home, where a house church was meeting, and fervently knocked on the door. Rhoda, a servant girl sent to respond, asked who it was. She was afraid to open the door, sharing the growing fear of all the believers. A knock on the door was far more likely to be a harbinger of bad news than good.

When Peter identified himself, Rhoda was so excited that she closed the door and ran back into the house to announce the good news, leaving Peter standing alone, and no doubt baffled. Hearing her report, the gathered believers suspected Rhoda was out of her mind. When she persisted, they thought that perhaps Peter had been killed and was appearing to them as an angel. In the meantime, no one went to look. Left outside as these theories were expounded, Peter kept knocking. Finally, another believer heard the pounding, ran to the door, and opened it. There, in the flesh, very much alive and not an angel, stood Peter, the rock of Christendom.

"Saul, still breathing threats and murder against the disciples," Luke records in Acts, "went to the high priest and asked him for letters to the synagogues at Damascus, so that if he found any belonging to Jesus' flock, men or women, he might bring them bound to Jerusalem."

Shouts and exclamations rang in the air. Peter quickly motioned for them to be quiet—he was a fugitive facing a death sentence, after all. He told them of his miraculous escape, left instructions for them to "tell James and the brothers about this," and, in the interest of safety, fled. Hours later, Agrippa arose from his sleep and called for his prisoner, only to find an empty cell and sixteen sheepish and uncomprehending guards. Enraged, Agrippa ordered all sixteen executed.[4]

Meanwhile, very strange stories, unbelievable stories, were circulating about Saul. He had seen that his expulsion of the Hellenists from Jerusalem, far from solving the problem, had made it infinitely worse. This reversal might have defeated a lesser man. It had merely inflamed Saul. For his was the mind of the purist, the absolutist, the intractable ideologue. Nearly twenty centuries later, the Russian writer Boris Pasternak would adequately describe the Saul mindset with his portrait of the dreaded General Strelnikov in his novel *Doctor Zhivago*:

> He had two characteristic features, two passions: an unusual power of clear and logical reasoning, and a great moral purity and sense of justice; he was ardent and honorable. But he would not have made a scientist of the sort who break new ground. His intelligence lacked the capacity for bold leaps into the unknown, the sudden flashes of insight that transcend barren, logical deductions. And if he were really to do good, he would have needed, in addition to his principles, a heart capable of violating them—a heart which knows only of particular, not of general cases, and which achieves greatness in little actions.
> Filled with the loftiest aspirations from his childhood, he had looked upon the world as a vast arena where everyone competed for perfection, keeping scrupulously to the rules. When he found that this was not so, it did not occur to him that his conception of the world order might have been oversimplified. He nursed his grievance and with it the ambition to judge between life and the dark forces that distorted it, and to be life's champion and avenger.

Since the followers of this Jesus had taken their poisonous delusions into the Diaspora, then he, Saul, must follow them. He must redouble his efforts. He must emphasize to the high priests that the sect must be liquidated, not only in Jerusalem, but wherever it threatened the soul of Judaism. But he had needed their writ, their order for an arrest. True, the Romans would not honor it since the high priests carried no legal authority beyond Judea. But these simpletons would not know that. Or if they did, they would be incapable of mounting a successful protest. And once he had dragged them back into Jerusalem, he could dispose of them as necessity required.

Thus, with the writ securely in his possession, he had taken the best route north. It was the road to Damascus. ∎

---

4. Just three years later, Agrippa would face his own mortality. Having fallen into a heated dispute with the cities of Tyre and Sidon in Phoenicia, he sought the upper hand by halting all shipments of grain to those centers. Tyre and Sidon gave in, sending a delegation to Agrippa in order to regain his favor. At a festival being held in honor of the emperor Claudius, Agrippa arose at daybreak, brilliantly dressed in a silver robe that flashed like a star in the dawn light, to speak to the assembled crowd. At the end of his speech, the delegation from Tyre and Sidon led the crowd in praise of Agrippa: "This is the voice of a god," they shouted, "and not of a mortal!" Standing before the crowd, basking in its adulation, Agrippa suddenly collapsed. Because he did not "give praise to God," the book of Acts records, an angel of the Lord struck him down. After a painful five-day bout of suffering, Herod Agrippa I died in A.D. 44, at the age of fifty-four.

CHAPTER 4

The conversion that changed history

No longer the Christians' chief enemy,
Saul of Tarsus sets out with a new name
on an unimaginable adventure

The midday sun was almost directly overhead as the horsemen pounded north along the dusty road toward Damascus, now only a few miles away. At the head of the small band, the grim-faced Pharisee gritted his teeth and whipped his mount. Suddenly, blinding light stopped the riders in their tracks. Horses reared and bolted. Saul, the lead rider, was thrown. His companions also fell to the ground, where they lay trembling in fear, eyes squeezed shut against the overwhelming brightness. Slowly, they stood up. Each appeared to be listening to something.

Within moments, the scene reverted. All was again as it had been. But not so with Saul. Stunned and barely coherent, he was standing, staring ahead and stretching his arms out strangely. His eyes were open now, but uncomprehending. He could not see. Taking him by the hand, the others led him on foot the rest of the way into the city. They left him in a rented room, where he lay listless and seemingly dispirited.

What else could they do? They had been on a mission to harass and take prisoner the followers of the crucified Nazarene Jesus. But it was Saul's idea. Saul had gained authority for it. Saul had organized it, and Saul was carrying it out.

Now blind, stunned, and incoherent, Saul could no longer lead anything. There was nothing to do but return to Jerusalem and report to the high priests. Let them decide the next move. The adventure was over.

In fact, the adventure had scarcely begun. But it would be an unimaginably different adventure from the one on which they had embarked.

The above is, of course, an attempted reconstruction of events of that fateful incident on the Damascus road. The three surviving accounts of it in Acts 9, 22, and 26 do not fill in such detail. We don't know whether Saul rode a horse, or a camel, or a mule, though given the official nature of his mission it was more probably a horse. What we do know is that something very like this must assuredly have happened. For the vision Saul saw and spoke to, he said, was the very man Jesus whose movement he was so fervidly seeking to destroy. That man would change the life of Saul and lead Saul to change the course of human history.

He had embarked on this mission, Saul later recalled,

The old road to Damascus rises gently into the Golan Heights, past a largely rural landscape. Until the fourth-century Jewish revolt against the emperor Gallus, the area through which this once-important highway runs was densely populated.

"breathing out threats and slaughter against the disciples of the Lord." No doubt his passions were further inflamed along the way, as he rode across the Jordan, through Judea, through Galilee, the very countryside where Jesus had so stirred up the rabble with his infuriating public spectacles. If Saul himself had ever seen the man in those days, or heard him preach, he never said so. But he certainly knew the startling stories that the man's alleged resurrection were keeping alive—repulsive stuff, dangerous, poisonous to the whole accepted mission of his people. By the time he neared Damascus and his quarry, he was seething.

Then it happened. The road had left the desert and now ran through verdant, garden-filled countryside. The city walls were in sight. "A great light from the sky suddenly blazed around me and my fellow travelers," Saul recounted later:

> We all fell to the ground and I heard a voice saying to me in Hebrew: "Saul, Saul why are you persecuting me? It is hard for you to kick against your own conscience."
> "Who are you, Lord?" I said.
> And the Lord said to me, "I am Jesus whom you are persecuting."
> My companions naturally saw the light, but they did not hear the voice of the one who was talking to me.
> "What am I to do, Lord?" I asked.
> "I have shown myself to you for a reason—you are chosen to be my servant and a witness of what you have seen of me today, and of visions of me which you will see. I will rescue you both from your own people and from the Gentiles to whom I now send you. I send you to open their eyes, to turn them from darkness to light, from the power of Satan to God, so that they may know forgiveness of their sins, and take their place with all those who are made holy by their faith in me."
> And I said, "What shall I do, Lord?"
> And he said, "Get up and go into Damascus; and there you will be told everything which has been appointed for you to do" (Acts 22:7–10 and 26:14–18).

As Saul stumbled toward Damascus, the implications would have crashed into his mind. His whole world, his whole life, his whole crusade had been one calamitous mistake. He had been horribly, monstrously, catastrophically wrong. He was overcome by a searing, mind-numbing remorse. He had to rethink every-

The man Saul encountered on the road to Damascus was the same Jesus whose movement he had sought so fervently to destroy. Saul's vision would change the course of history.

thing he had assumed, everything he had believed, everything he had done, everything that mattered to him most. For three days he lay in this pool of guilt-ridden darkness. Blind, enervated, and unable to eat, he prayed for forgiveness, for the restoration of his sight, and for instruction from God.

Meanwhile, elsewhere in the city, a follower of Christ named Ananias had a vision. Jesus told him to go to the house of Judas in a street called Straight. There he would find a blind man called Saul of Tarsus. Lay your hands on him, Jesus said, and restore his sight.

Ananias was understandably aghast. Saul, the terror of Jerusalem, the man who had consented to the stoning of Stephen, the man who was dragging Jesus' followers into jail, the most feared human name they knew, this horror figure was now in Damascus. And he, poor, undistinguished Ananias, was to go and touch this monster and somehow restore his sight. Across the ages one can guess the plaintive thought, felt and spoken by so many Christians in so many circumstances: Why me?

Jesus' response was even more astounding: "Go and do it, for I have chosen Saul to carry my name to the Gentiles."

Fearful but obedient, Ananias found the ailing rabbi and nervously greeted him as "Brother Saul." Then, as directed, he placed his hands on him, something like scales fell from Saul's eyes, and instantly his vision was restored. Saul, Ananias said, Jesus has chosen you to bring his message to the Gentiles, and Saul the Pharisee was baptized. He would soon become Paul the Apostle, the Latin name he would shortly begin using.

Paul's conversion would be the most important event in the history of Christianity after the resurrection of Christ. The incident on the road to Damascus, probably about A.D. 33, was to set the faith on a new course, as the events of the next thirty-five to forty years would show. Explaining that remarkable incident, rather, explaining it away, would tax the imaginations of the skeptical over the ages. It was sunstroke, it was guilt-driven self-hypnosis, it was brain fever, it was a blood clot, it was epilepsy-induced hysteria. By the twentieth century, psychology came forth with a whole cornucopia of possibilities. Wholesale reversal of attitude is not all that unusual, said psychologist Carl Jung. Paul may have fought so passionately against the movement because he was secretly drawn to it and was subconsciously wracked by guilt, a guilt made much worse when he saw the courage and serenity of Stephen as he died.

The scales fell from his eyes and Saul was baptized. His name became Paul, his conversion the most important event in Christianity after Christ's resurrection.

Anglican Bishop Jeffrey Ellison thinks Paul had secretly envied the followers of Christ because he discerned in them a closeness to God that could not be achieved by even the most punctilious Pharisee.

What seems incontestable is the fact that Paul's heart was wholly transformed. The former persecutor would become a living example of the power of grace. His arrogantly narrow obsession with the Law vanished. He was filled with love and an overwhelming need to share the wonders of the Holy Spirit. In the coming years, both men and women in cities over much of the eastern Mediterranean world would quickly discern this and work tirelessly beside him. In so doing they would make the gospel of Christ, hitherto the exclusive, parochial property of a small sect of Jews, into a universal faith for men, women, and children of every race and nation in the world.

That was Paul's task. Across distant lands and raging seas, it would drive him onward, through emotional strife, heated conflict, and untold physical danger, until thirty-some years later, his life would end under the sword of a Roman executioner—a privileged death, as it happens. Roman citizens must not be crucified, and Paul was proud to have been born a Roman citizen, a birth that occurred about the same time as that of Jesus. Paul was born and grew up among other Diaspora Jews in a predominantly Greek culture. His family's Roman citizenship was probably won by an ancestor; possibly his father had rendered a critical service to the empire.

Tarsus, his birthplace, was a fortified city on the river Cydnus, ten miles from the Mediterranean coast of southeastern Asia Minor in what would become Turkey. It controlled the intersection of several major overland trading routes and was capital of the province of Cilicia, whose fertile plain produced cereals, grapes, and, most importantly, flax for a thriving linen industry. The area was also known for a woven goat-hair cloth called cilicium.

With a rich two-thousand-year cultural history shaped mainly by Persians, Phoenicians, and Greeks, Tarsus was also a center of sophisticated Hellenistic culture. It was a university town in which education was revered and schools of rhetoric flourished. The sensuous rhythms of Phoenician music were heard often, but women in public were expected to cover themselves completely and wear veils. Absorbed into the Roman system when Pompey reorganized Asia Minor in 66 B.C., Tarsus had opposed Cassius, the murderer of its patron, Julius Caesar. Antony rewarded the city's loyalty by granting a privilege of freedom, which Augustus renewed while exempting it from imperial taxation.

Paul's parents had probably emigrated from Judea. His father was perhaps a prosperous tent-maker in the import-export business. Paul studied the Greek Septuagint version of Jewish scriptures. His Roman citizenship was a lifelong point of pride, though Paul took the most pride in his Jewish heritage: "Circumcised on my eighth day, Israelite by race, of the tribe of Benjamin, a Hebrew born and bred," he would write proudly.

A superior student, Paul eventually went to Jerusalem to learn from the renowned Jewish teacher Gamaliel. There he was "taught according to the perfect manner of the law of the fathers, and was zealous toward God. . . . I was thoroughly trained in every point of our ancestral law," he later

After his traumatic experience on the road to Damascus left him blind, Saul took up residence on Straight Street, which to this day is a major market thoroughfare in Damascus (above). It is here that Ananias, following a vision from God, sought out Saul and restored the onetime persecutor's eyesight.

Long before it became known chiefly as the home town of St. Paul, Tarsus was famous for other celebrity residents. The Cleopatra Gate (below) on the western wall of the city dates from the time when the Egyptian queen and Marc Antony sojourned there, feasting lavishly while waiting for their ill-fated fleet to be assembled.

recalled. From his rabbinical studies, Paul acquired mental agility, subtlety of scriptural interpretation, and a sense of complete religious dedication to God. He became a rabbi, a Pharisee, and a rising star in the synagogue. "In the practice of our national religion, I was outstripping many of my Jewish contemporaries in my boundless devotion to the traditions of my ancestors."

And yet, just when Paul was proving his superiority as a Pharisee through his meticulous observance and detailed knowledge of the sacred Jewish Law, something most disturbing—something downright infuriating—had begun to happen. People in this Jesus phenomenon, whatever it was, were in effect saying that Paul was missing the point. Oh, they didn't mock him by name. But they seemed to question the sufficiency of the Law, to which Paul was devoting his life. They represented a sort of personal threat. After all, he was gaining elite status and recognition among Jews. He was a Roman citizen, he had a future in the larger world. These people were casting doubt on it all.

But mainly Paul's fury was fueled by a relentless spiritual zeal. He took his religion very seriously and his own performance of it more seriously still. God required that Jews live the most righteous life possible and the Law showed them

In his heart, though he hardly dared think it, Paul knew that the whole magnificent structure of Jewish Law stood as a hopeless barrier between man and God.

the way. He had spent years training himself to do this. In addition to his keen intelligence, he possessed extraordinary self-discipline and power of will. That, no doubt, is why he had broken with Gamaliel over the question of how best to contend with these Jesus people who called themselves the Followers of the Way. Just let them run their course, said his teacher. Time will reveal the truth. But the fiery Paul had dismissed this as foolhardy. These people posed a mortal threat. What they taught and what the Jewish tradition taught were utterly incompatible.

Of that he was positive. Wholeheartedly he believed in the Hebrews' sacred ancestral traditions, in the importance of ancient dietary rules, of ritual purifications, of tithing, of Sabbath restrictions and the whole magnificent structure, preserved through the ages. Genuine piety must be equated with knowledge of the Law and the meticulous observance of it.

Yet, in his heart of hearts something gnawed at him, something he could barely bring himself to face, but a reality that he could not escape either. The fact was—dare he even think it?—that the Law, instead of bringing man closer to God, was setting up a hopeless barrier. One might go a long way to meet its demands and requirements, but no one went the whole way, himself included. Giving it your best effort was fine but ultimately pointless. The Law was there to be obeyed. If you didn't obey it—all of it—you were doomed, Jewry was doomed, humanity was doomed. It was an ugly thought but irrepressible, and it pursued him, pursued him all the way down to the Damascus Road.

As his sight returned and he looked about Damascus, he saw the city for what it was, a beautiful place, in fact, the oldest continually inhabited city in the world. About 170 miles north of Jerusalem, it was a great crossroads where trade routes from Asia Minor and Mesopotamia joined before splitting to run across the plateau into Arabia or down the coast to Egypt. Flanked by foothills at the edge of the desert, for centuries the city had been encircled by lush, irrigated flower and vegetable gardens.

It was a place where Paul could feel at home—a former Greek city whose culture remained strongly Hellenized, despite periodic absorption by Assyrian, Babylonian, and Persian empires. In the first century B.C., Nabatean Arabs, who controlled the neighboring territory to the east, had seized it. But they lost it to the Armenians, who in 66 B.C. lost it to the Romans, who placed it under the control of the governor of Syria.

The language of the streets was Greek, but there was a large Jewish community of perhaps twenty thousand who spoke Aramaic, the language of the Semitic desert dwellers to the east. Paul had targeted Damascus in part because Jesus' followers had been coexisting too peacefully with other Jews in the Damascus

Advice to first-century travelers: Don't go alone

Roman highways are an engineering wonder—but bears, dogs, and bandits strike terror on the side road

From the outpost of Jerusalem, across North Africa and through the future Spain, France, Greece, Macedonia, Turkey, and Syria, there lay in Paul's day a vast network of paved highways. Along them, Roman civilization advanced. Wide enough for soldiers to march six abreast and so carefully constructed as to require no repairs for, in some cases, a thousand years, the roads from Rome, linked end to end, could have twice encircled the earth.

These were the highways that Paul and his companions often traveled, and as long as they stayed on them, they did so in relative security. More often, however, they were on the empire's secondary roads, where safety and even survival were very uncertain indeed.

In the world of the eastern Mediterranean the secondary roads were dependably passable only in the summer when streams were either dry or reduced to mere trickles. In the late winter and spring, they turned into raging torrents, crossed only at dangerous fords where travelers, up to their waist in swirling water, could be easily swept downstream. Bridges often consisted merely of logs thrown over the stream. The traveler, carrying his baggage, must delicately negotiate his way across.

Robbers and gangs of bandits were a much worse hazard. In the civil wars that ended less than a century before Paul's time, brigandage became chronic and remained so into the first century. The Roman army's policing activity was confined to the main roads. Once off them, the traveler, who had no option but to take his money with him, was fair game for robbery and possibly murder. That's why few traveled alone, and most were armed at least with a staff.

Gangs, often driven into brigandage by poverty, roved the countryside on constant lookout for prospective victims, sometimes marauding country houses, holding the occupants at sword-point while the premises were looted. To defend themselves against this, the householders usually kept vicious dogs.

"When we reached a small village, the inhabitants very naturally mistook us for a brigade of bandits," writes the philosopher and poet Apuleius who lived about a century after Paul. "They were in such alarm that they unchained a pack of large mastiffs, which they kept as watch dogs, very savage beasts, worse than any wolf or bear, and set them at us with shouts,

synagogues. "The Way," as they termed it, had taken root here even before Stephen's death, and membership had expanded with the influx of the refugees Paul had driven out of Jerusalem.

Now, amazingly, the man responsible for this had arrived to join them here in worship. At first they tolerated him only because of the enormous respect everyone held for Ananias. But Paul quickly emerged as a bright new force, eager to describe his astounding encounter and the "good news" of the risen Messiah. Penitent but proud, he preached in the synagogues, where congregations included numerous Gentile God-fearers. Soon thereafter he left Damascus on a one-man mission to the deserts of Arabia in the kingdom of Nabatea, which began almost at the walls of Damascus and extended east and south of the Dead Sea. How long Paul spent there is not recorded. However, the trip appears to have sparked a nasty ruckus.[1]

Tensions between Arabs and Jews always ran high in these parts due to a long history of territorial rivalry. But the immediate problem was Nabatean

Rome not only built and patrolled a vast network of roads throughout the empire, it aided both its armies and civilian travelers by marking the distances between cities. This milepost outside Capernaum dates from the first century.

recalls authorities warning travelers in central Greece against packs of enormous wolves that were attacking even houses. "We were told that the road we wished to take was strewn with half-eaten corpses, and clean-picked skeletons, and that we ought to proceed with all possible caution—the higher the sun the milder the wolves—and in a compact body with no stragglers."

But on the great highways built by the army, the traveler had safety and conveniences that would not be equaled in Europe for thirteen hundred years after the empire collapsed. Built on a firm rock foundation, overlaid by layers of stones in descending size, and finally topped with huge flat paving stones and crowned to drain off water, they enabled the legions to travel at twenty miles a day to any trouble spot. Five hundred army garrisons at intervals along the roads policed them.

They also served for commercial and civilian travel, whether on foot, donkey, camel, or horse, or in the creaking carts with wooden wheels that would be useless on the secondary roads. It was on these that most people risked life and limb. When Jesus tells the story of the man who "fell among thieves" in the parable of the Good Samaritan, nobody is recorded as having doubted its credibility. And when Paul writes to the church in Corinth of the hazards of travel—"in perils of waters, in perils of robbers . . . in perils in the city, in perils in the wilderness, in perils in the sea . . . in weariness and painfulness, in watchings often, in hunger and thirst . . . in cold and nakedness," nobody accused him of exaggeration. People knew all about such dangers. ∎

halloos and discordant cries." Staying at country inns was both essential and particularly dangerous. The wealthy might be able to pay for some privacy. Everyone else took his chances, sharing rooms and beds with they knew not whom, often having to keep their baggage beside them, lest their roommate pillage it during the night. And unless they dragged it all with them, every trip to the latrine or dining room risked robbery.

Wild animals were as great a danger as bandits. Bears, wild boars, and wolves are all mentioned by Apuleius, who says the lone journeyer lived in terror when the roads took him through a wooded area. He

King Aretas IV, who enjoyed his power at the sufferance of Rome and who feared the imperial wrath. The emperor Tiberius, like his predecessors and successors, was not pleased by popular enthusiasm for any religious novelty. A new religion meant new problems, especially one whose preachers spouted off about women, slaves, and all races of mankind being equal in the eyes of God. What kind of chaos might erupt if listeners took him seriously? Thus Paul probably had to run for his life as armed Nabateans chased him back behind the protective walls of Damascus. He returned to preaching in the local synagogues. At this point, he also

Paul may never have seen Petra, the capital of the Nabatean Arab kingdom, sixty miles south of the Dead Sea. But he spent time trying, unsuccessfully, to convert some of the citizens in the northern reaches of the kingdom. The splendid monuments, temples and tombs of Petra, carved from solid stone as is this one known as the Treasury, reflect the wealth of the Nabateans, who controlled trade routes between the Mediterranean and Asia for five centuries.

discovered that he would have to support himself because, some historians speculate, when word of his bizarre conversion reached Tarsus, his family disinherited him.

As a young rabbi of that time, Paul had not actually been expected to learn a trade (a tradition that was reversed after A.D. 70, when Jews fell on much harder times). So, even if his family were tent-makers, only now did he learn the skills of the family business. However, tent-making was a very practical trade for an itinerant missionary. Cities were filled with awnings, while tents, pavilions, and sails were in demand throughout the Mediterranean world. There were jobs along every road and by every sea. Usually the fabric was linen, sometimes leather. The trade brought contact with all levels of society and was entirely portable. Paul needed to carry only a moon-shaped knife, awl, needles, and waxed thread. Also, the business was quiet and sedentary, so he could preach and work at the same time. But there were two disadvantages: Both the pay and the social status were relatively low. (And Paul was not above mentioning this periodically for the rest of his life.)

Paul spent the next three years learning his trade and preaching—until his mission in Damascus came to an abrupt and dramatic end. The Nabateans regained control of the city and they still wanted to arrest him. Assuming, rightly, that he would try to flee, the Arabs decided to grab him when he passed through a city gate. So they set up guards at all seven of them. Then, in a daring scenario that became legend in the early church, Paul escaped. He simply climbed into a

1. Some historians have speculated that Paul went into the desert primarily to pray and meditate as he reordered his thinking. But others believe this unlikely. His references to the revealed gospel suggest he received his revelation all at once. Moreover, he aroused the hostile attention of Nabateans, an improbable development if he had gone into the desert simply to meditate.

After offending the Nabatean governor of Damascus, Paul beat a hasty retreat out of the city. As he recounts in his second letter to the Corinthians, he fled under cover of darkness, lowered from a "window" (perhaps this one) by means of a basket.

large wicker basket that friends lowered over the wall where the guards couldn't see it. Once safely outside, he headed to Jerusalem, where Jesus' apostles were still headquartered. He wanted to learn firsthand what Jesus did and said before the Crucifixion and what these men knew about the Resurrection. He also wanted to establish the legitimacy of his own ministry.

Although the news of Paul's improbable conversion had long since come to Jerusalem, Jesus' followers were naturally suspicious and fearful of him, especially because tensions with the Temple authorities were running so high. Once again, a trusted intermediary paved the way. In this case, it was the Cypriot Jew named Barnabas, the cousin of Mary, in whose house Peter's group met. Barnabas had made that generous contribution to the church's common fund for the needy after the first Pentecost. Highly regarded in Jerusalem, he was also active among the faithful at Damascus and Antioch. Paul "had preached boldly at Damascus in the name of Jesus," said Barnabas. This reassured them.

Not that Paul felt the obligation to reassure them. In no sense did he believe he had less authority than those disciples whom Jesus chose before the Crucifixion. But he was a practical man. He needed to establish bonds with Peter (whom he always called by his Aramaic name, Cephas) and James, the kinsman of Jesus, and he wanted them to endorse his work. He hungered for facts he could get nowhere else—an account of Christ's words and actions, and what had actually happened at the Last Supper.

Paul described how he had received his apostolic commission from the risen Jesus himself. The gospel he preached came down to two points, he said: Salvation comes only by God's grace; and by God's mercy you obtain that grace through an expression of faith. Peter and James agreed that Jesus also stressed these points. The three met for fourteen days, and Paul received their blessing for his mission to the Gentiles.[2]

But his visit came to a quick conclusion for what would soon become a familiar reason: His life was threatened. This time the danger came from his old

2. Peter's presence at this first conference with Paul and James in Jerusalem poses a problem of timing. If the conference occurred before Peter's arrest and miraculous escape, as detailed in the previous chapter, then the problem disappears. If after, then Peter would have had to be secretly in Jerusalem, risking rearrest and probable execution, to attend the conference. His presence at the Jerusalem council some years later would have entailed the same risk, though it is nowhere mentioned. One possible explanation lies in the conversion of Saul. If the chief pressure to eliminate Peter had been coming from the persecutor Saul, then the risk of rearrest would have been considerably diminished by Saul's conversion.

associates, who now saw him as a dangerous traitor. One day his proselytizing zeal and a streak of combativeness drove him to a reckless confrontation in a Jerusalem synagogue. There he attempted to convert the Hellenistic Jews in a debate. Arguments flew back and forth. Paul finally walked out with no converts. He went off to pray, fell into a trance, and was warned by Jesus to get out of the city fast, because the Jews were coming after him. He should resume his mission to the Gentiles forthwith.

Assisted by Peter and James, he escaped to Caesarea, then took a ship for Tarsus, where he began an independent, largely undocumented mission in Cilicia and Syria for the next eight or so years. Historians refer to this period as the "missing years" because details are sketchy and unrecorded. Paul was apparently a lone operator, preaching and teaching at the northeastern end of the Mediterranean.

Syria, on the east coast of the great sea, had served as the bridge between Egypt and Mesopotamia, the two major centers of civilization for thousands of

Once Christianity's most relentless persecutor, Paul was now its consummate promoter. Though his appearance was unprepossessing, his odd charisma endeared him to all.

years. Bounded by the sea on the west, Syria extended south to Palestine and east to the Arabian desert and the Euphrates River. Populated mainly by Semitic peoples, it comprised a coastal plain, a few mountain crags, and an interior tableland. It was separated from Cilicia to the west by the Amanus Mountains, where several passes, the Syrian Gates, permitted travel, though they were always dangerous due to cave-dwelling thieves.

Paul, some historians believe, spent three or four years founding churches in Tarsus, then expanded to the neighboring cities of Cilicia Pedias, and then into Syria and its chief city, Antioch. Congregations in Judea heard accounts of his evangelistic ardor, he later wrote, and praised God for it. Once Christianity's most relentless persecutor, he was now its most consummate promoter. His sincerity and single-mindedness enveloped everyone he met. For all his energy, passion, and charisma, however, he was not an imposing figure. No contemporary description of his appearance has ever been found. The earliest attempt, in the late-second-century *Acts of Paul and Thecla*,[3] is singularly unflattering, portraying him with somewhat bowed legs, thick, dark eyebrows that nearly met above his prominent nose, and a short, pointed beard. What is incontestable is

---

3. The apocryphal *Acts of Paul and Thecla*, which appeared about A.D. 180, records the Christian ministry of a woman named Thecla who heard Paul preach at Iconium and was so moved by him that she broke off an engagement to marry and dedicated her life to Christ as a virgin. She became a female apostle, preached the faith in the Galatian cities, was on several occasions miraculously saved from a martyr's death, and finally died in Seleucia. Historians regard the accounts as legendary, but many consider there may be a seed of truth behind them, that such a woman of Iconium did indeed assist Paul, may very well have been ordered executed, and somehow escaped.

that he radiated a warm, appealing aura. He endeared himself to both men and women, and many devoted their lives to the message he gave them.

He was as gregarious and engaging as he was earnest and strong-willed. He was also courageous, passionate, impulsive, bold, aggressive, argumentative, and determined. If he had a sense of humor, it was never noted. Neither is there evidence of any aesthetic sense. The "Isles of Greece" that so enchanted nineteenth-century poet and essayist Byron are lost on Paul. He passes through them for years, never once commenting on their mystical beauty. Yet, he had a deep understanding of human nature, a swift and intelligent mind, and a thorough knowledge of the Torah and its messianic prophecies. Although he claimed to be a lackluster orator, he was well schooled in rhetoric and moved listeners to conversion with his sermons.

The seriousness with which he approached spiritual matters was not changed on the Damascus road. But the transformation he underwent forever energized

Paul's revelations affirmed in him the notion that it was good to suffer insults, hardships and persecution in the name of Christ. 'When I am weak,' he wrote, 'I am strong.'

his ministry. The former arrogant, mechanistic, hairsplitting Pharisee who measured spirituality by legal degrees became an apostle of faith, a minister humbled by the power of grace, love, and the Holy Spirit, a missionary who lived only to share a divine gift that was available to anyone who would willingly embrace it. This ultimately made him a polarizing force. He attracted and retained converts in droves, but his enthusiasm, intensity, and exuberant conviction could also make people uncomfortable and spark opposition and even hatred.

Some time about A.D. 42 or 43, Paul was further inspired by a mysterious "ecstatic" revelation, which he recounts in his second letter to the Corinthians. What happened, he could not describe. "Whether in the body or out of the body," he writes, he was transported to "paradise" or "the third heaven." There he heard things impermissible to put into words. Though it elated him, the experience also left him with a humiliating physical disability. He termed it "a splinter in the flesh."[4] He prayed three times that it would go away. Instead, Christ told him, "My grace is sufficient for you, for my power is made perfect in weakness." Thus the experience deepened his sense of "life in the Spirit" as a life of committed action. It also affirmed the notion that it was good, even desirable, to endure suffering in the name of Christ. Thus Paul could write, "I will all the more gladly boast of my weaknesses, that the power of Christ may rest upon me.

---

4. Paul's mysterious disability has set off centuries of guesswork as to its identity. The early fathers alone offer sixteen possible physical maladies including epilepsy, ophthalmia, malaria, neurasthenia, and a speech impediment. Modern neuropsychology provided later speculators with a dozen or more further possibilities, none conclusive and none flattering. Whatever it was, Paul managed in spite of it.

For the sake of Christ, then, I am content with weaknesses, insults, hardships, persecutions and calamities; for when I am weak, I am strong" (2 Cor. 12:10).

At the end of the eight "missing years," Paul appears in Antioch, Syria, one of fifteen centers in that part of the world that bore the same name, all conferred by Seleucus I, Alexander the Great's general. In the first century, it was a highly competitive spiritual marketplace. The first Jewish Christians probably arrived there about the same time Paul returned to Tarsus, and by the early 40s, the place was attracting as many Followers of the Way as Jerusalem had. Often these new people were Gentiles and tensions grew between those and the Jewish Followers. Meanwhile, other far more lethal conflicts were building between Jews and Gentiles generally in Antioch. The anti-Roman nationalist movement in Jerusalem, always simmering, was threatening to come to a boil in open rebellion. This was provoking the usual anti-Jewish demonstrations all over the empire. At Antioch, synagogues were being burned and Jews massacred.

So the Jerusalem church dispatched Barnabas as a representative to the city. This has sometimes been described as a sort of reconnaissance mission to determine if Christians there were following the true gospel. However, it is more probable that Barnabas was sent to be a stabilizing force in these tense times. A big man, a sturdy, imposing figure, the Cyprus-born Levite spoke Greek and Aramaic. His name meant "Encourager" and it was appropriate. He knew how to give a pat on the back when it was most needed. The Antioch church welcomed him warmly and treated him like an apostle, a status he would never have enjoyed in Jerusalem.

By the winter of A.D. 45–46, Barnabas realized that he needed a knowledge-able partner. Taking the road around the end of the Mediterranean to Tarsus, only eighty miles away, he found his old friend Paul. He found that Paul, too, had gained enthusiasm for spreading the good news to more distant peoples. The pair formed a teaching-preaching team in the Syrian capital. Barnabas wanted to find more converts in his native Cyprus. So in A.D. 47, the pair launched what became Christianity's first-recorded missionary expedition. They did not seek authorization from the church in Jerusalem. With them when they embarked from Seleucia, the commercial port of Antioch, was a cousin whom Barnabas had invited named John Mark, who would best be remembered in Christian tradition as the author of the New Testament's second Gospel. He was a young man from Jerusalem, well known by the original apostles because Peter's group met in his mother's house.

The easternmost point of Cyprus lay only about eighty miles off the Syrian coast. The largest island in the eastern Mediterranean,

Paul and Barnabas may have stepped from this harbor wall at Seleucia when boarding the ship that was to take them to Cyprus. Because of silt deposited over the years by the Orontes River, the wall now stands some distance from water of any sort.

THE MISSION OF PAUL AND BARNABAS

In A.D. 47, Paul and Barnabas launched Christianity's first recorded missionary expedition, from Antioch in Syria to Cyprus and the cities of southern Asia Minor.

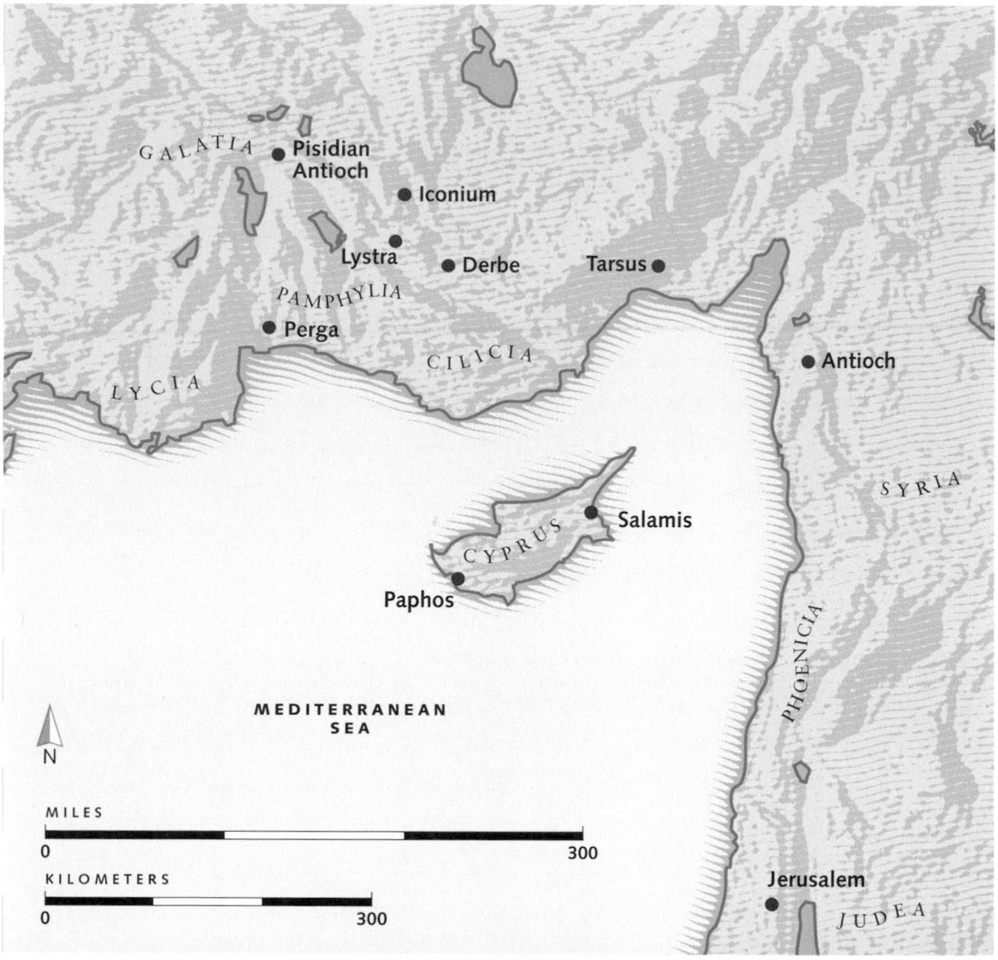
GALATIA
Pisidian Antioch
Iconium
Lystra
Derbe
Tarsus
PAMPHYLIA
Perga
CILICIA
LYCIA
Antioch
SYRIA
Salamis
CYPRUS
Paphos
PHOENICIA
MEDITERRANEAN SEA
N
MILES
0
300
KILOMETERS
0
300
Jerusalem
JUDEA

By the middle of the first century Antioch, the chief city of Syria, was home to a large number of Followers of the Way, many of whom were Gentiles. Paul and Barnabas established themselves as an effective teaching/preaching team in Antioch before embarking on their journey to spread the good news to the cities and towns around the eastern Mediterranean. Their first destination was Cyprus, where they caused a stir in the synagogue in the ancient island capital of Paphos. The ruins of the synagogue at Paphos (right) can still be seen today. At Antioch in Pisidia, a Roman army center in the highlands of southern Asia Minor, Paul and Barnabas were escorted from the town by angry local Jews, upset by the number of Gentiles drawn by Paul's message of forgiveness of sins. Today the ruins of the town's main street (far right) look out over the rolling hills of what is now south-central Turkey.

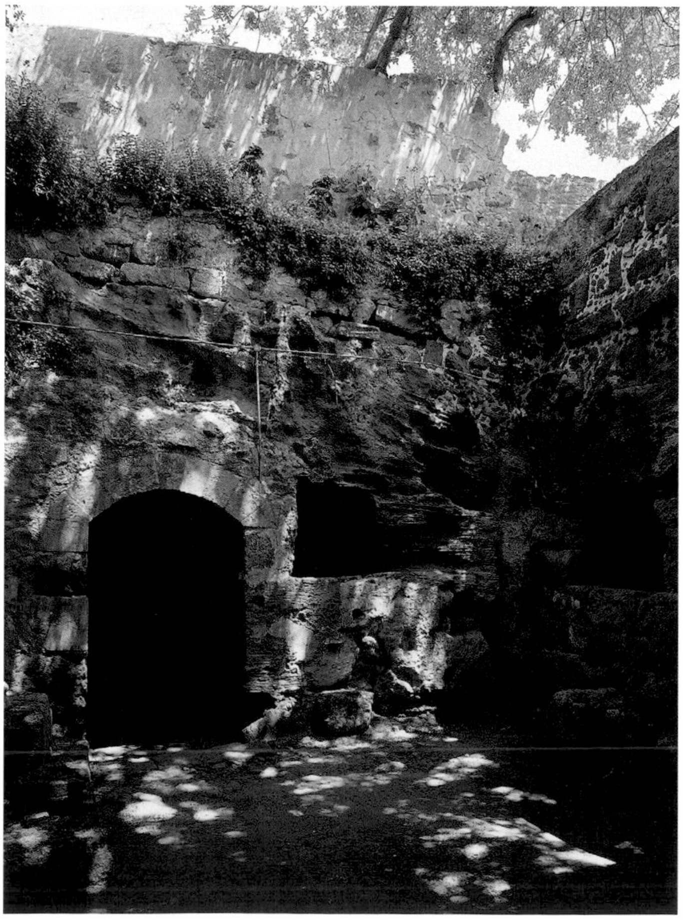

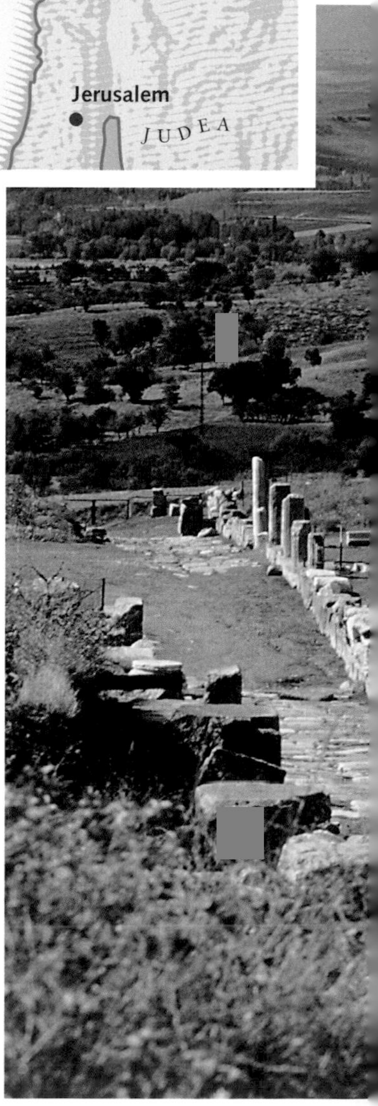

it was relatively arid and was known for its rich copper mines. After Herod the Great leased the mines, many Jews had moved there. Now Christian communities were also scattered across the island, settled by refugees from Jerusalem. Presumably the trio sailed about the second week of March to avoid the strong westerlies that blow later in the spring. Landing at Salamis in the southeast, they walked 160 winding miles to Paphos, the capital, on the west end.

The governor, a proconsul named Sergius Paulus, greeted the missionaries in person. Paul took charge and began to preach. The proconsul was enthralled. Others were not, among them a Jew named Elymas, who dabbled in the occult crafts associated with Simon Magus. Elymas, who had been ingratiating himself with the governor as an adviser, feared losing his influence if the governor became a Christian. So he tried to interrupt Paul's sermon. Paul was livid. "You son of the Devil!" he shouted. "Will you not stop making crooked the straight paths of the Lord? And now listen, the hand of the Lord is against you, and you will be blind for awhile." Immediately Elymas lost his sight, and Sergius Paulus was even more impressed. He became a convert—the highest official Paul had so far won over.[5]

From Paphos, the threesome now sailed to the coast of Asia Minor. But after they landed near Perga, some 220 miles west of Tarsus, John Mark

quit. Instead of heading inland with the others, he returned to Jerusalem, perhaps simply fearful of the wild, rugged interior of Asia Minor and the fierce people said to live there. Paul and Barnabas continued on foot without him to the southern part of Galatia, which had been declared an imperial province by Augustus in 25 B.C. About one hundred miles inland, they arrived at a city named Antioch in Pisidia (not to be confused with the Syrian capital). A Roman army center sitting at some 3,600 feet above sea level in the lofty tablelands and lake district, the place was highly cosmopolitan, filled with Galatians, Phrygians, Greeks, Jews, Celts, and also

5. Though Paul's name-change from Saul is usually linked to his conversion on the road to Damascus, the change does not actually take place until the conversion of Sergius Paulus, the Roman governor of Cyprus, when Paul himself begins using his Latin name. Why he made the change, he never explains. Was it possibly in honor of this distinguished convert?

Roman army veterans of the Alauda Legion, raised in Gaul by Julius Caesar and known as "the Lark whose regimental badge was a skylark."[6]

Paul and Barnabas promptly went to the synagogue and began preaching, always their modus operandi. The congregations included not only Jews, whom they would willingly convert, but also the God-fearers, who were open to his gospel and were a link to other Gentiles. In his sermon, Paul connected Jesus to scriptural prophecy and messianic descent from David. "Through this man, forgiveness of sins is proclaimed to you," he said. "By him every one of you that believes is justified from all things, from which you could not be justified by the Law of Moses."

His words caused a sensation. On the next Sabbath, it seemed as if the whole city turned out. Outnumbered by Gentiles, the local orthodox Jews challenged him and rejected his message. "It was necessary that the word of God first be spoken to you," he responded. "Since you reject it, and judge yourselves to be unworthy of eternal life, we are now turning to the Gentiles." He then echoed

In Lystra, Paul took the crowd by surprise by locking eyes with a crippled man and barking, 'Stand upright on your feet!' When the man got up and walked, the crowd went wild.

the prophet Isaiah, saying, "I have set you to be a light for the Gentiles, so that you may bring salvation to the ends of the earth." That was enough for the Jews, who angrily escorted Paul and Barnabas to the town limits and told them to stay out. By then, however, the pair had recruited enough Gentiles to organize a purely Gentile congregation, separate from the synagogue, the first of the churches in Galatia.

Now they walked southeast about sixty miles to Iconium, on a fertile grain-producing plain, where events followed a similar pattern—first a sermon to the Jews, followed by a near-riot, but attracting enough Gentile converts to form a congregation, so that by the time they were run out of town they had founded a church.

About twenty miles to the southwest in an unsophisticated country town called Lystra, however, things took a different turn. When he began preaching here, Paul took the crowd by surprise with a sign. Locking eyes with a crippled man sitting on the ground, he barked a command: "Stand upright on your feet!" When the fellow sprang up and began to walk, the crowd went wild. This was the best show the place had seen in a long time. Abandoning Greek, people started yelling in their native Lycaonian tongue: "The gods have come down to us in human form!" They called the taller Barnabas by the name Zeus, the father of the gods. Paul became Hermes, god of communication.

At first the two didn't grasp what all the commotion was about. But when

6. Paul and Barnabas may have chosen Pisidian Antioch on the recommendation of Sergius Paulus, because Sergius's family had ties there. There is also speculation that Paul had contracted malaria on the swampy coast after they arrived in Asia Minor and went to the highlands to recuperate. He subsequently claimed in a letter that it was "because of a bodily ailment" that he first came to the people.

After the miraculous healing of a cripple at Lystra, Paul and Barnabas become reluctant celebrities. With the crowd proclaiming, "The gods have come down to us in human form," Paul is hailed as Hermes and Barnabas as Zeus. Despite the two disciples' protests, the pagan priests and the citizenry attempt to offer sacrifices to them.

they saw the chief priest of Zeus heading toward his temple with oxen and garlands, they figured it out fast. They had been drawn into a pagan sacrifice, an outright blasphemy. Appalled, the two started ripping off their clothes to show they were human. "Why are you doing this? We are mortals just like you," shouted Paul, "and we bring you good news that you should turn away from these worthless things to the living God." His rebuke turned the fevered crowd against them. Angered, insulted, and egged on by Jews who had arrived from Pisidian Antioch, the mob grew violent. They stoned Paul unconscious, dragged him outside the town, and left him for dead. Later, as Barnabas and a few sympathizers were puzzling over what to do with his limp and apparently

The curious, controversial rite of circumcision

Arguments over an ancient practice divide Jesus' early followers, and the gulf remains for 2,000 years

The curious rite of male circumcision, in which the foreskin is surgically removed from the penis, usually in infancy, was the central issue that divided Jesus' first followers from other Jews two to three decades after the Crucifixion. It thereby played a pivotal role in the split that would separate Christianity from Judaism for the next two thousand years.

Jewish followers of Jesus, loyal to Jewish tradition, demanded that adult Gentile males wishing to become Christian be required to submit to circumcision, just as other Gentiles had done when they wanted to become attached to the synagogue as God-fearers. Paul opposed them. The disagreement began a split which, widened by other theological issues, soon created a gulf that was never in two millennia to be bridged.

To the Jew, circumcision was far more than a merely physical thing. It gave the Jewish people a sense of national identity. It sealed a covenant between them and God. Indeed, it made the individual Jew a fellow worker with God and a part of God's plan. Jews spoke of "the circumcised heart" or "circumcised lips," meaning a will devoted to the Law of God, and a mouth that drew people toward God. Even the physical aspects of the land itself were viewed as "circumcised." Devotional writers spoke of the "circumcised fruit trees" of Israel. Similarly the term "uncircumcised" came to mean unclean, profane or imperfect.

For the Jews, the practice had been instituted about seventeen hundred years before Christ by their patriarch Abraham, with the Law requiring circumcision of every Jewish male, customarily on the eighth day of

his life. The antecedents of the rite, however, go back further. The historian Herodotus, writing in the 400s B.C., traces it to the Egyptians, some of whose nobility observed a somewhat similar practice. They slit the foreskin and let it hang free.

As the practice spread up the eastern Mediterranean coast to the Semitic countries, it changed. The whole foreskin was removed. Artistic renderings of Syrian warriors dating back to the second millennium B.C. show them circumcised, and it was at about this point that the Hebrews adopted it.

However, John J. Tierney, writing in the *Catholic Encyclopedia*, reports the rite of circumcision among the Aztec and Mayan races in America, the Filipinos in East Asia, and native tribes in central Australia. In the South Pacific, he notes, the Samoans sometimes refer to the Europeans as "the uncircumcised." All this suggests an origin other than the Egyptians.

Because of its sacramental implications, the observation of the rite, or the failure to observe it, often enters into Jewish history. For example, Genesis 34:1–26 tells how Shechem, the impetuous son of Hamor the Hivite, raped Jacob's daughter, Dinah. Then he decided he wanted to marry her. Jacob's sons, infuriated, hatched a plan: They said they would not permit marriage between one of their own and Shechem and Hamor's people unless all the other men agreed to be circumcised. Urged by the infatuated Shechem, all of his male relatives agreed, and the dramatic and bloody mass operation took place. Two days later, while Shechem's men were still lying about

lifeless body, he slowly stirred and began to recover. The next day, Barnabas and Paul left for Derbe, the last town on their itinerary, about sixty miles southeast. Here they preached and "made many disciples"—and for the first time encountered no opposition.

At this point, it would have been most direct to return to Syrian Antioch by way of Tarsus. Instead, the pair retraced their entire journey, met again with the new Christians, and appointed elders in each community. As a result, they were able to establish permanent churches in all these places. They then sailed back to Antioch, ebullient over their mission's success.

The exuberance of the two returning missionaries was deflated as soon as

"in pain" and recuperating, a raiding party led by two of Jacob's sons attacked and killed them all. Shechem's people had asked for it, said their attackers. They had treated their sister "like a harlot."

Moses, for unexplained reasons, failed to circumcise his son. God would have killed Moses, says the book of Exodus (4:24–26), but his wife, Zipporah, took up a sharp stone and circumcised the child herself, thereby saving her husband's life from divine vengeance.

With the arrival in the Jewish lands of Alexander the Great, and the subsequent intrusion of Greek culture, the rite of circumcision fell into social disrepute. To the Greeks, and later the Romans, the male glans was a repugnant object, and some men pinned the foreskin to ensure that the glans remained covered and was not seen. Since male athletes often performed naked, circumcision rendered Jewish contestants physically disgusting to Greeks and Romans. To become a citizen, a man was required to undergo athletic training, so the effect of circumcision was to deny citizenship to Jews. Jewish men stirred similar revulsion in the public baths.

The result was that many Jews during the Greco-Roman period quietly abandoned the practice. In the succeeding Hasmonean era, after the Jews successfully revolted against their Greek overlords, things went ill for the backsliders—they were required to undergo circumcision, painfully, as adults.

After A.D. 70, when another Jewish revolt failed, this one against the Romans, the imperial government imposed a special tax on all circumcised subjects.

And after a further Jewish rebellion sixty-five years later, circumcision was prohibited by law. Though this ban was soon repealed, Rome never did fully restore the right to proselytize and to circumcise Gentile converts.

The Jewish philosopher Philo, defending circumcision against the jeers of Greek and Roman intellectuals, argued that it rendered a man less susceptible to disease, that by clearing away an obstruction it fostered fertility and that by deliberately sundering the flesh it promoted spiritual "cleanliness." Finally, he said, it excised the pleasures of sex, which have the power to "bewitch the mind." It thereby subjugated to the will of God the human member that begets children.

Not all Christians rejected this reasoning. Ethiopian Christianity, always heavily influenced by the Old Testament, retained the practice. So did many Egyptian Christians. But beyond the Jews, its greatest survival came in Islam. Muslim boys, aged seven to twelve, are routinely circumcised, though the Koran, the holy book of Islam, does not require it nor even mention it.

In the mid-twentieth century, many Gentile parents had their male infants medically circumcised on hygienic grounds, though this theory fell from wide acceptance toward the century's end. By then, too, children's rights advocates were opposing it as "invasive" and were urging the courts in western countries to follow the example of Rome and prohibit circumcision by law. ■

A circumcision is depicted on this eight-inch sixteenth-century silver plate, which was crafted for use in the ritual.

they arrived in Antioch. Big trouble greeted them. Hard-liners from Jerusalem had appeared in the city to insist that all converts adhere to Jewish Law and tradition—including, for males, the blood and pain of circumcision. Plainly, therefore, the evangelization of Gentiles had continued to raise both religious and political problems for the Jerusalem church. Most Jews held a low opinion of Gentile morality and the influx of these converts sullied a vision of the church as the ultimate "flowering of Judaism." Jewish converts resented Gentiles, who could join on what seemed too-easy terms. Zealots opposed anyone building bridges to non-Hebrew peoples. And persecution increased pressure to affirm

Many Jewish Christians believed the Gentiles were joining them on too-easy terms. They demanded the converts keep the Law of Moses—including, of course, circumcision.

Jewish identity and values wherever possible. Thus, many Jewish Christians wanted Gentile converts to comply with the same requirements as Jews: Be circumcised. Keep the Law of Moses.

The effect of such a severe requirement, broached to Paul's and Barnabas's new converts as a seeming "by-the-way" afterthought, would have been to destroy everything the two had accomplished. But the hard-liners right along had opposed what they considered casual conversions. Gentiles weren't the problem, they said. Lax church leaders had been too compromising. It had to stop.

This began an escalating crisis that unfolded like a three-act play. Act I took place immediately in Antioch. Barnabas confronted the "false brethren" who, Paul said, "slipped in to spy out our freedom which we have in Christ Jesus, that they might bring us into bondage" (Gal. 2:4). The Antioch church members decided to send the two missionaries to the elders in Jerusalem to straighten things out.

Act II began in Jerusalem, where the arrival of Paul and Barnabas became the occasion of a momentous event: the first official council in the history of the church. The historian Jerome Murphy-O'Connor in his book *Paul: A Critical Life*, points out that it is impossible to tell if just one large, stormy meeting took place or whether, as appears likely, there were smaller separate discussions between the Antioch emissaries and Peter, James, and John.

"I laid before them the gospel which I preach among the Gentiles, lest somehow I should be running or had run in vain," Paul later recalled, and the Jerusalem leaders endorsed his work (once again). "They saw that I had been entrusted with the gospel to the uncircumcised. . . . So, when they perceived that grace was given to me, James and Cephas [Peter] and John, the men of repute as pillars, gave to me and Barnabas the right hand of fellowship, that we should go to the Gentiles and the uncircumcised." In fact, the two had brought with them an uncircumcised Greek convert named Titus, as a living, breathing, walking test case. Nowhere during the meeting, Paul noted, was Titus "compelled to be circumcised" by these Jerusalem authorities.

The meeting began with Paul and Barnabas describing the success of their foray into southern Galatia. Surely, they contended, God would allow such wondrous results only if they preached the true gospel. The hard-liners ignored that point. They wanted to talk about laws and circumcision. Adherence to Jewish Law must be required of all converts, they argued. There must be no compromise. Finally, Peter took the floor. He reiterated his "anti-circumcision" position from the conversion of the centurion Cornelius. God "put no difference between them [Gentiles] and us [Jews], purifying their hearts by faith . . . through the grace of the Lord Jesus Christ we shall be saved, even as they."

In the end, James the Just settled the matter. He cited Hebrew prophets who said that God would rebuild the tabernacle of David so "that the residue of men might seek after the Lord, and all the Gentiles, upon whom my name is called." Therefore, he concluded, "Trouble them not, which from among Gentiles are turned to God."

He would place upon converts only minimal restrictions. These were carried to Antioch in the first written "apostolic decree" as follows: "It seemed good to the Holy Spirit and to us to lay upon you no greater burden than these necessary things: that you abstain from what has been sacrificed to idols, and from blood, and from what is strangled, and from fornication. If you keep yourselves from these, you will do well. Farewell" (Acts 15:28–29). Thus the official doctrine of the church was defined.

It was a huge victory for Paul and Barnabas and a startling defeat for the legalist faction, a purposeful and well-organized movement that insisted on the

When Peter and Barnabas abandoned the Gentile table to eat with the Jews, Paul was stunned. He found such behavior blatantly offensive to Gentile converts and to his own principles.

full burden of the Law for both Gentiles and Jews. They had counted on the legalistic sympathies of James, along with his political awareness of the need for Jewish solidarity. But James may well have felt that such shallowly formed Christian "Jews" would only weaken the new faith in the long run. In any case, Act II ended with the triumphant return of Paul and Barnabas to Antioch. The pair planned another mission further into Asia Minor. But since it was now November, they would spend the winter in the city before heading out. It was a trip they would never make together, however, because the curtain was about to rise on Act III.

This final drama took place some weeks later. Peter had been visiting Antioch and all was going smoothly until a Jerusalem delegation arrived, purportedly from James. Up until then, Peter had been eating with the church's Gentiles. But now, under pressure from this Jewish clique, he abandoned the Gentiles' table to sit only with his fellow Jews. Then Barnabas did the same.

Did being a Christian also mean being a Law-observing Jew?
The debate was settled at Jerusalem, where James judged the arguments made
by both sides. His solemn conclusion: "We should not make it difficult for the
Gentiles who are turning to God." Then the council of apostles and elders, led
by James, dictates its pastoral letter "To the Gentile believers in Antioch, Syria,
and Cilicia." Their brief message would fling open the doors of salvation.

Such table fellowship was no small matter. Throughout the Near East, formal meals were a prime social event. In house churches such as those in Antioch, this fellowship forged a vital link between the Jews and Gentiles.

Paul was stunned, furious, and bitterly disappointed at such a betrayal, and thoroughly disgusted by the apparent "fear of the circumcision party." Peter's behavior was blatantly offensive to Gentile converts and ran counter to his own recently re-avowed principles. "I said to Cephas in front of them all," Paul wrote later, "If you, Jew as you are, live in the Gentile and not the Jewish way, how is it you try to compel Gentiles to live like Jews?"

Here was indeed a spectacle to behold—one of the two greatest apostles in the history of the church publicly dressing down the other on a matter of moral principle! But Paul, possessed of the mission with which he was entrusted, was adamant. He simply would not tolerate any suggestion that Gentiles were second-class Christians. The Council of Jerusalem had officially demolished the partition between Jews and Gentiles. He did not want it rebuilt. And the only logical reason he saw for preserving the social barrier[7] was to keep it as a religious barrier.

The immediate outcome of this confrontation is lost to history, but some historians, not all, view the church at Antioch thereafter divided along Jewish-Gentile lines. Between Paul and Barnabas, another issue had arisen. Barnabas again wanted to bring along John Mark. "Are you serious?" Paul would have asked. "After he quit the last time?" This was too much.

With Barnabas opposing him in the matter of John Mark, Paul found himself almost alone and surrounded by opponents: by hard-line Temple Jews who saw him as a danger; by the Christian legalists, both Gentiles and Jews, ostensibly backed by the Church authorities in Jerusalem, who considered him reckless and misguided; by pagans, who regarded him as an unpleasant rival and annoying threat; by Greek intellectuals, who viewed him as unbalanced, if not deranged; and, increasingly, by Roman authorities, who viewed him as a disruptive nuisance.

Nevertheless, more resolved than ever in his faith and purpose, he embarked that spring on a new mission. And he was not quite alone. Beside him was a man named Silas. ■

---

7. Historian Murphy-O'Connor points out that James may actually have favored such social separation right along. In the apostolic decree, he was in effect agreeing with Paul that what mattered most in the church was faith in Christ. But to some Jewish Christian hard-liners, his message could have been, in effect: We'll let the Gentiles into the church, but we can still keep them separate socially. Other historians believe Paul's influence remained significant at Antioch, and his subsequent admonition to the Galatians on this subject probably did much to end the Jewish-Gentile segregation in Antioch's Christian community.

*At daybreak, the ship carrying Paul comes in sight of Neapolis,
and Europe. European soil would prove to be exceptionally fertile
for the seeds of faith that Paul and his companions brought.*

Westward to Europe and the world

Ignoring bandits, pagans, beatings, and imprisonment, Paul takes his message to new churches, and the Gentiles

Standing like a fortress wall along the south coast of Turkey, the Taurus Mountains glower down upon the Mediterranean. Steep, jagged, cut by deep, twisting ravines through which the waters of winter crash down in torrents, they are a formidable barrier to road builders, travelers, pilgrims, tourists and invaders. Toward the great sea's northeastern corner, however, the Tauruses retreat slightly from the coast, creating the Cilician Plain, in the midst of which stands the ancient city known as Tarsus, Turkey's seventieth city in terms of population.

Tarsus has known greater days. Probably its greatest came unspectacularly, in the spring of A.D. 50 or thereabouts. The Jew named Paul, destined to become Tarsus's greatest-ever son, took the road north, toward the ominously shadowed barrier of the Tauruses. About thirty miles ahead of him lay the single crack in the great mountain barrier. From here, the road ran west, a mere trail, barely wide enough for two men to walk abreast, through a series of narrow, hazardous defiles. Nearly two thousand years later, travelers would still call them the Cilician Gates.

The gates had seen much history. Through them in 401 B.C., the Greek survivors of the Battle of Cunaxa had fled for home after their leader, Cyrus the Younger, was slain. Through the tight passage, coming the other way sixty-eight years later, squeezed the mighty forces of Alexander on their way to conquer the known world. Now, through the same pass, the greatest conquest Europe would ever know was about to begin, and the force that would accomplish it was an army of two—Paul and, beside him, his companion Silas.

Silas was a Jerusalem Jew, his name probably derived from the Talmudic name *Shila*, and he clearly had the confidence of James, Peter, John, and the Jerusalem church leadership. They had entrusted him and a companion with the vital letter formally exempting Gentile Christians from circumcision. He had delivered it at Antioch and in the ensuing weeks had become persuaded it was Christ himself who had commissioned Paul as apostle to the Gentiles. Thus, when others abandoned Paul, Silas did not. He offered Paul something more. His Latin name, Silvanus, disclosed him as a Roman citizen, a distinct advantage in the tumultuous adventures that would follow. Hence, it was a party of two that crossed the Tauruses through the Cilician Gates and headed west to the Roman provinces of Galatia, Asia, Macedonia, and the world.

About ten days beyond the Gates, they reached the town of Lystra, which

Even today, the ramparts of the Taurus mountains are a formidable obstacle to travel from the coastal plains around Tarsus into the interior of Asia Minor. Paul, now accompanied by Silas, would likely have traversed the mountains through one of the few passes in the eastern reaches of the range. Still known as the Cilician Gates, it winds under the nearly twelve-thousand-foot peak of the Bey Dagh (in the background).

would become Zostera, near Hatunsary on the maps of the future Turkey. Here, they added a third member to the party—young Timothy, in Greek *Timotheos*, whose name was to be associated with Paul's in six of Paul's letters in the New Testament, two of which would be addressed directly to Timothy, whom Paul would call "my true-born son in the faith." Lystra held some bad memories for Paul. He had been stoned by a hostile crowd here and given up for dead. But he and Barnabas had escaped, leaving behind a durable Christian community. One member of it was a certain Eunice, a Jewess married to a Gentile. Timothy, their son, was therefore considered Jewish by birth,[1] but since he had never been circumcised he was, by Jewish Law, an apostate, a rebel against his own religion.

Timothy was highly recommended to Paul by his fellow believers, but he posed a problem. If Paul acquiesced in Timothy's apostasy, this would make Paul an apostate as well, thereby denying him access to any synagogue. Paul soon solved this. He circumcised Timothy, regularizing his status in the Jewish community.

All three now moved deeper into the province of Galatia, the locale that had held such dread for John Mark that he had abandoned Paul and Barnabas and gone home. But John Mark had good reason to be nervous. The Galatians had never become enamored with Greek civilization. They were, in fact, the race

Timothy posed a dilemma. If he remained a rebel against Judaism, Paul would be banned from the synagogues. Paul solved the problem by having Timothy circumcised.

known as the Celts, who made their first appearance in history in what would one day be north-central Germany, about four thousand years ago. From there, they moved west, becoming known in the future Spain as the Celtiberians, in Ireland as the Gaels, in Scotland as the Picts, in England as the Britons, in France as the Gauls, and in the Low Countries as the Belgae.

They struck south too, once actually sacking and burning Rome, though they were soon hurled out. They became such a problem to the Greeks, Macedonians, and Thracians that the king of Bithynia made a deal with them. They could have the whole pasture land of Asia Minor, he said, if they would stay there and leave Bithynia and its neighbors to the north alone. They agreed, and in 288–287 B.C., some twenty thousand of them—men, women, children, and baggage—crossed over from Europe and occupied the great, bleak, dry, rolling, treeless plateau that accounts for about twelve thousand square miles in the center of the future Turkey. There they became the Galatians.

They kept their promise and did not return to Europe. But for the next two centuries they made themselves the terror of Asia Minor, supplementing the meager income of their pastoral, drought-prone property by robbing, pillaging, and

---

1. According to the Law, Jewish descent is from the maternal line. "Your son by an Israelite woman is called your son, but your son by a heathen woman is not called your son" (Talmud 68b).

slaughtering their neighbors or, whenever the market was good, selling them into slavery. The civilized peoples of the coastal cities loathed and dreaded them. To the Greeks, writes the historian Jerome Murphy-O'Connor, they were "large, unpredictable simpletons, ferocious and highly dangerous when angry, but without stamina and easy to trick." They went into battle naked, and they drank too much.

However, they were also honest, truthful and oddly generous to visitors. "They invite strangers to their feasts," writes Diodorus Siculus (80–20 B.C.), "and do not inquire until after the meal who they are and of what things they are in need. And it is their custom, even during the course of the meal, to seize upon any trivial matter as an occasion for keen disputation, and then to challenge one another to single combat without any regard for their lives. . . . They are also boasters and threateners, and are fond of pompous language, and yet have sharp wits and are not without cleverness at learning. Among them are found lyric poets whom they call Bards."

In 88 B.C., a neighboring king summoned sixty of their leading men to a great banquet, where he massacred them all. The Romans helped them avenge this reversal. That made them permanent and dependable allies of Rome, and by Paul's time, Galatia was a Roman province. However disgusting to the Greeks, to Paul they were merely one more variety of Gentile human souls whom Christ had died for. He and Barnabas had founded churches in at least four Galatian centers.[2]

To the Greeks, the Galatians were boorish, stupid, ferocious drunkards who sometimes went into battle naked. To Paul, they were another variety of human soul.

When he returned to visit them, Paul did not like what he found. He discovered, as he had no doubt already heard, that he was not conducting the only mission to the Gentiles. Others, probably out of Antioch but claiming authority from Jerusalem, had actually reached the Galatian churches, spent considerable time with them and largely persuaded them that he, Paul, was a compromiser and a fraud. The Law, they argued, had been given to Abraham, and Jesus had now made it possible for all the peoples of the world to come under the Law. But like the Jews, all must submit themselves to the Law's commands and, among other things, be circumcised. Otherwise, in no sense could they be true followers of Christ.

The implications of such thinking had long been clear to Paul. For one thing, circumcision made no sense whatever to the Gentiles. The spiritual point of it was entirely lost on them, and many saw it as a weird eastern form of self-

---

2. There are two historical views on the nature of the Galatians among whom Paul worked and to whom he addressed the letter that would become a book in the New Testament. Under one view, the churches he and Barnabas founded at Lystra, Derbe, Iconium, and Pisidian Antioch were all in "South" Galatia, which was more civilized than "North" Galatia. The language Paul uses in his letter could scarcely have been addressed to primitive barbarians, they say. Other historians reply that this distinction between North and South is arbitrary, not historical. As to literary aptitude, they say, skill with language would always be an attested Celtic quality. Consider, for example, the descendants of the more western cousins of the Galatians, the Irish, who would provide many of Britain's greatest writers.

mutilation, like castration, something the Egyptians were given to. Worse still, the effect would be to render Christianity as simply another sect of Judaism. Worst of all, if faith in Christ were reduced to mere adherence to a number of moral, social, and dietary rules, the liberation from the Law that Jesus had come to bring, the freedom it was Paul's responsibility to preach, would be utterly lost. The Law, impossible by itself as a means of salvation, could be fulfilled because one could now live in Christ and, through him, in the very life of God. What mattered now, therefore, was the relationship of the individual to Jesus Christ. This was a war, in other words, a war that he must not lose.

How Paul replied on the spot to the Galatians, history does not record. How he replied to them in a subsequent letter was to become one of the books of the New Testament. The Epistle to the Galatians, addressed to wayward congregations in the lonely grasslands of central Asia Minor, would be read in homes and churches all around the world for centuries to come.

Paul knew the disputatious Galatians. To pick a fight with them, he realized, would accomplish nothing. He addresses them as "O you dear idiots of Galatia," and the tone is more affectionate than accusatory. He goes on to

The unique letter from James

Could this be the earliest book in the New Testament?

Most historians agree that the first-written book in the New Testament was Paul's Epistle to the Thessalonians. But not all. Some believe that the letter written by James, "the brother of the Lord" (Gal.1:19), could very well be the earliest book, and in fact may have been written within a dozen years of Jesus' death.

Certainly James's letter is unique in several respects. It is the least "doctrinal" of any of the letters in the New Testament. Moreover, it is exceedingly "Jewish," in that it echoes the language of the prophets and the Old Testament's book of Proverbs. Finally, it consists almost solely of advice on how Jesus' Jewish followers ought, and ought not, to live, a seeming manual for Christian conduct.

James takes a hard line, for instance, on the matter of suffering and adversity. When temptations enter your life, says James, "don't resent them as intruders, but welcome them as friends. Realize that they come to test your faith and produce in you a quality of endurance." Such troubles "will enable you to become men of mature character, men of integrity, with no weak spots" (James 1:2–4 JBP).

The disciple of Christ should not desire wealth, so that God can raise him to "true riches," while the man who is rich here "will wither away like the summer flowers," James warns. Disciples should also learn to distinguish between trials and temptation. Trials are sent by God to strengthen us, whereas "a man's temptation is due to the pull of his own inward desires which greatly attract him" (James 1:10–14).

"Don't merely hear the message, but put it into practice," says James. "If anyone appears to be religious, but cannot control his tongue, he deceives himself, and we may be sure that his religion is useless" (James 1:26). The tongue is like the rudder on a ship. Though it is a very small device, it can move the whole vessel. So the tongue, by what it does, "can poison our whole body, set the whole life ablaze and feed the fires of hell" (James 3:4–6).

"Religion that is pure and genuine in the sight of God the Father will show itself by such things as visiting orphans and widows in their distress and keeping oneself uncontaminated by the world" (James 1:27).

Neither should Jesus' disciples defer to mere wealth. The poor man in rags should be shown just as much consideration and respect as the rich man with fine jewelry and costly clothes. Had they not noticed, James asks, that God chooses poor men, not rich, to carry his message (James 2:1–5)?

It's also important that Christians not be given to making great plans, because God at any moment could call them to their deaths. They should be patient and honest, sharing their joys and concerns

strike two notes—heartbreak that they had been led astray and reasoned argument to lead them back.

He is "amazed," he says, that they had actually embraced "another gospel"—because there really is no such thing. Peter, James, and John, the "pillars" of the church in Jerusalem, had all agreed that Gentiles need not come under the Law. Titus, an uncircumcised Gentile, had actually been at the conference, and no one had proposed that he be circumcised. So why now the Gentiles of Galatia? But beyond that, did they not realize that salvation cannot be won by obeying a system of regulations? What matters is not the Law, but faith in Jesus Christ.

Abraham, they might recall, had two sons, one by a slave and one by a free woman. Those who descended from the slave were under the Law and therefore remained, spiritually speaking, slaves of the Law. But they, the Christians of Galatia, had come to God through faith in Jesus Christ. "So then, my brothers, we are not to look upon ourselves as the sons of the slave woman, but of the free, not sons of slavery under the Law, but sons of freedom under grace" (Gal. 4:30–31 JBP).

But this did not mean, Paul warned, that they could abuse their freedom by

with other believers and, above all, helping their brothers to keep the faith, for when they do so, this will "cover a multitude of sins."

James is certain that jealousy and conflict will arise among Christians. The question is, what should they do about these rivalries? "What do you suppose [such feuds] come from? Can't you see they arise from conflicting desires for pleasure within yourselves?" (James 4:1) The answer: "Come close to God and he will come close to you. . . . Humble yourselves in the sight of the Lord [and] he will lift you up" (James 4:7–10).

Christians have periodically argued over whether James's letter should be included in the New Testament at all. For one thing, it is much shorter than most of Paul's letters, other than the purely pastoral ones to Philemon, Timothy and Titus. For another, James was not of the original Twelve. And again, did James the Just actually write it, or was it another James, or did someone write it on his behalf?

Most important, however, as Martin Luther would argue in the sixteenth century, James's letter appears to be written in contradiction of Paul's teaching on faith. It raises the question: Which matters most? The depth of our faith and how loyally we believe? Or what we do as the result of what we believe, our "works"? Halfway through his letter, James discredits the validity of "faith" if it is not accompanied by "works." He asks, "So you believe there is one God? That's fine. So do all the devils in hell, and shudder in terror. For my dear, shortsighted man, can't you see far enough to realize that faith without right actions is dead and useless?"

Since this seems a clear contradiction of Paul's emphasis on faith, many have proposed that James wrote his letter to contradict Paul. However, if it was written earlier, say in the forties, this would place it before Paul's ministry, so it could hardly have been written to contradict Paul.

This became a major issue among some Christians when Luther, stoutly arguing that faith was ultimately what mattered, attacked James's letter as "an epistle of straw" and regarded its inclusion in the New Testament as a mistake. The British Evangelical theologian Donald Guthrie in his *New Testament Introduction*, argues that the epistle represents the thinking of many of Jesus' followers at a time the faith was being established. It is not at all clear that James wrote to correct Paul, he observes. Perhaps Paul wrote to correct James. We don't really know who wrote first.

Some, however, like the twentieth-century scholar C. S. Lewis, concluded that the argument of faith-versus-works was flawed, since one would not go far without the other. "It's like trying to decide which blade of a pair of scissors is the more important," said Lewis.

More recently, some theologians, such as New York Evangelical Spiros Zodhiates in *The Epistle of James and the Life of Faith*, have come to see Paul and James not as face-to-face in dispute with one another, but as back-to-back defending the same cause of Christ against different opponents—James against backsliders whose conduct belied their professed faith, Paul against legalists who saw conforming to the Jewish Law as that which would save their souls.

If any one demonstrated himself proof against both errors, it was James himself. In his heroically defiant death, he left an example that all Christians through all ages would admire. (See sidebar chapter 8 pages 234–235.) ■

yielding to their lower nature, by indulging in sexual immorality, impurity of mind, sensuality, worship of false gods, witchcraft, hatred, strife, jealousy, bad temper, rivalry, factions, party spirit, envy, drunkenness, orgies, and the like. Rather, they should see within themselves the product of the Spirit—love, joy, peace, patience, kindness, generosity, fidelity, tolerance, and self-control.

Whether the Galatian response was to return to Paul's "gospel" is not known. He would visit them again in a subsequent mission journey "to strengthen" them. That would be about four years later, and it was perhaps after that occasion that he wrote his letter to them. In the meantime, his next step was determined by a dream in which he saw a Macedonian man beckoning him to "come and help us." That seemed clear enough. The trio had already moved more than five hundred miles by the Roman roads to the port of Troas near the northwest corner of Asia Minor, jump-off point for the Macedonian ports on the north coast of the Aegean. In Troas, they had been joined by a fourth, a man who was

Although Paul addresses them as 'You dear idiots of Galatia,' his tone is more affectionate than disparaging. He realized it would accomplish nothing to pick a fight.

to become Paul's companion and the narrator of his struggles, a man whose polished Greek, eye for detail, and knack for storytelling would enable him to write approximately one quarter of the New Testament. His name was Luke.[3]

The voyage taken in response to Paul's dream went well. They made the 120-mile crossing to Macedonia in less than two days. (The same trip in the reverse direction some eight years later would take them more than a week.) This put them into Neapolis (modern Kavalla), port city for the Macedonian center of Philippi. It lay just fifteen miles ahead, along one of the best roads in the empire, the Via Egnatia, a masterpiece of construction by the Roman army that snaked across the mountains of Macedonia to connect the Adriatic and Aegean.

Philippi's claim to historical renown was fairly recent. Though it was founded four centuries earlier by Philip of Macedonia, father of Alexander the Great, as a town atop a hill, it was best known throughout the empire as the place where an army under Brutus and Cassius, two of Julius Caesar's assassins, was trounced in 42 B.C. by Caesar's avengers, Marc Antony and Octavius (later known as Augustus). Eleven years after the Battle of Philippi, Octavius defeated his erstwhile partner Antony and transferred Antony's defeated veterans out of Italy and into Macedonia, a safe distance from Rome. They settled alongside the veterans of the Brutus-Cassius force, who had already been planted in the place.

PAUL ON OUR REAL ADVERSARIES

"For we are not contending against flesh and blood, but against the principalities, against the powers, against the world rulers of this present darkness, against the spiritual hosts of wickedness in the heavenly places."

Ephesians 6:12 RSV

3. Luke announces his entry into Paul's ministry in an odd way. In his second book, the *Acts of the Apostles*, which from the thirteenth chapter onward is almost wholly a history of St. Paul, Luke makes a curious change when the narrative gets the reader as far as Troas. Suddenly the writer no longer talks about what "they" did, but about what "we" did. He will do this at two other points in the story, all three, for no discernible reason, involving sea voyages (Acts 16:10–17; 20:5–21; 27:1–28). When Luke writes of "they," of course, he is reporting like a journalist on events that others saw or experienced.

Typical of the rock-paved highways the Romans constructed throughout their empire, the Via Egnatia today (seen here near Philippi) seems only a slight improvement over barren soil. But to Paul and Silas and other first-century travelers, it gave evidence of civilization and the security of Roman rule.

As with other ancient Roman cities, the public latrine at Philippi is one of the best preserved of the city's ruins. Seating about thirty-six, it had no provision for separating the sexes.

Thus, these ex-legionaries and onetime enemies formed a Latin-speaking island in a sea of Greek. By now the city had sprawled down the hillside, encroaching upon the marshland that lay between it and the sea, but looking out also on the fertile and beautiful farmlands to the west.

Paul, as was his practice, first sought out the synagogue, only to discover there wasn't one, meaning that in all Philippi there were not even the requisite ten male Jews to form a congregation. However, he was told, a few devout women, some Jewish-born and some converts to Judaism, met on the Sabbath beside a little stream, about a mile from the town, to worship God, read the Scriptures, and sing. Paul and his companions joined them and told them of Jesus the Messiah, his death, his Resurrection, and the grace he conferred upon those who were baptized and believed in him. The women's enthusiasm seems to have been instant, deep, and durable. Philippi became the strongest and most problem-free of Paul's churches, backing him with words, deeds, and money. The Philippian church had one other idiosyncrasy. It began and remained in Paul's time a church mostly of women.

One in particular became a powerful supporter. Her real name is unknown. Luke records it as Lydia, which (says the historian F. F. Bruce) simply means "a woman from Lydia." She came, however, from Thyatira, a center over on the Asia side, where the people for centuries had extracted from the mollusks found along the shore porphyry, a purple dye that would not fade. Lydia had moved to Philippi and set up a business, importing the dye and selling it in Macedonia. At Thyatira, where there was a strong Jewish community, she had become a God-fearer, a convert to Judaism. Hearing Paul's message, she was baptized along with her whole household, which would include not only kinfolk, but slaves and freedmen. She gave her home over to Paul and his companions.

But there were other women active in the Philippian church on whom Paul relied. Two in particular—Euodi and Syntyche—are singled out in a letter Paul wrote to the Philippians about ten years later, after these two quarreled. "They worked hard for me in the gospel," he writes (Phil. 4:3), and exhorts the rest of the community to help them resolve their differences. But he also admonishes the two, with advice that would be cited to resolve the congregational and marital quarrels of Christians down through the ages: "Live together in harmony, live together in love, as though you had only one mind and one spirit between you. Never act from motives of rivalry or personal vanity, but in humility think more of each other than you do of yourselves. None of you should think only of his own affairs, but consider other people's interests also" (Phil. 2:3–4 JBP). It was good advice, observes Jerome Murphy-O'Connor, but Paul himself didn't always take it, as his fulminations against his own rivals would amply demonstrate.

Many historians note another, but more positive, inconsistency. Paul had an ambiguous attitude toward women. On the one hand, he was a product of the ancient synagogue. "Let women be silent in church," he decrees (1 Cor. 14:34–35 JBP). "They are not to be allowed to speak. They must submit to this regulation as the Law itself instructs. If they have questions to ask, they must ask their husbands at home, for there is something improper about a woman speaking in church." On the other hand, he conferred major responsibilities on women, not only at Philippi, but at Corinth, Ephesus, and elsewhere. And whatever his prejudices, women obviously admired, served, and trusted him.

Perhaps they had heard his assertion: "There is neither Jew nor Greek, there is neither bond nor free, there is neither male nor female: for you are all one in Christ Jesus" (Gal. 3:28 KJV). By the twenty-first century, those words would become a cliché. In the first century, they bespoke a revolution, and they were matched in Christian practice. The use of baptism as the central rite, says the historian Alan F. Segal in *Paul the Convert: The Apostolate and Apostasy of Saul the Pharisee*, made women full partners with men in Christian communities. Though women might actually have retained an inferior place in society, and though slaves, out of necessity, must have been returned to their masters, Paul felt that the distinctions between Jew and Gentile, which were based on ritual

Author unknown: The mysterious letter to the Hebrews

Did this early and extraordinary insight into the identity of Jesus come from Paul's scholarly helper, Apollos?

As Paul worked tirelessly during the decade of the 50s to establish Christian missions in Asia Minor, Macedonia, and Greece, he suddenly acquired a strong, loyal, scholarly, persuasive, and rather mysterious Jewish helper. About ten years later another mystery developed. A letter with an extraordinary insight into the identity of Jesus was written by an unknown Jew, probably from Rome. What is not known, though the question has provoked debate for centuries, is whether Paul's mystery helper wrote the mystery letter.

The man was named Apollonius, more familiarly Apollos. A product of the huge Jewish community in Alexandria, he appeared in the synagogue at Ephesus, speaking informatively of the teachings of Christ and was sufficiently knowledgeable of the Scriptures to handily refute arguments hurled at him by opponents. Two of his listeners were Paul's assistants, the tent-makers Priscilla and Aquila, who recruited him to Paul's work.

In this cause, Apollos was sent across the Aegean to Corinth, a city that was a constant source of problems for Paul, and he gained such success there that Paul, in a subsequent letter, mentions Apollos as developing the kind of personal following that Paul sought to discourage.

Christians should not consider themselves, Paul wrote, as disciples of Paul, or of Peter, or of Apollos. They should all regard themselves disciples of Christ, because it was Christ, not one of his disciples, who was crucified for them. Christ gives each Christian a particular job to do. He, Paul, planted the seed, Apollos watered it, and God made it grow. (1 Cor. 3:5–7). Apollos's work, in other words, was considered as furthering Paul's.

Apollos vanishes from the scriptural records at this point. Church tradition takes him from Greece to Rome, and it was there, about ten years later, that the strange letter was probably written. It was addressed to Jewish followers of Jesus, probably in Palestine, who were being tempted away from the faith. It is known to history as the Epistle to the Hebrews.

The theologian Tertullian, writing in the late second century, ascribed Hebrews to Barnabas. Martin Luther, writing in the sixteenth, concluded that Apollos wrote it; the nineteenth-century theologian Adolf von Harnack attributed it to Priscilla; and the twentieth-century British historian F. F. Bruce goes along with Luther and favors Apollos as author. Bruce puts the letter's date at A.D. 63.

status, could be erased by new rituals of unity.

Paul's appeal to women did not escape the attention of their husbands, notes F. F. Bruce in the book *Paul: Apostle of the Free Spirit*. At Thessalonica, he recruited into Christianity the wives of some of the foremost citizens. Gentile husbands did not object to their wives flirting with Judaism; it was becoming trendy. "But they would look quite differently on their wives' association with a very odd collection of enthusiasts who (as it seemed to them) were hypnotized by these strangers who had come to their city from goodness knows where and who (they might be sure) meant no good. It was their wealth that they were after, if not something more discreditable still."

Paul's ministry in Philippi lasted, by some estimates, about a year. It came to an end abruptly and violently. Paul and his company one day found themselves followed by a slave girl who incessantly shrieked out, "These men are servants of the most high God, and they are telling you the way of salvation!" This girl was

During the second and third centuries, the Christians at Alexandria came to believe it was written by Paul, though his name isn't on it or in it, and it was accepted into the New Testament as a Pauline letter. Nearly all later historians, however, consider this impossible. Neither the style nor the content is found anywhere in Paul. And though its teaching is compatible with Paul's, it is not the same and it introduces ideas that Paul nowhere mentions.

On one thing, however, all seem agreed. Since it assumes that the routine rituals of the animal sacrifices were continuing as they had for centuries at the Temple in Jerusalem, Hebrews must have been written before A.D. 70.

This matters. Its portrayal of Christ is that of a being who, while fully man, was also something far beyond the merely human. Paul, too, portrayed such a being, though in a different way. This meant that the earliest theories answering the question—Who was this man?—are depicting something for which no previous human experience had provided adequate language. Christ's "divinity," that is, is not a later Christian doctrine, but the earliest one.

In the Epistle to the Hebrews, Christ is the "Son." Through the Son, God made the world. By going through death, the Son destroyed the power of death and made it possible for mankind to be absolved of the sin that besets them.

The Book of Genesis (14:17–19) and the 110th Psalm (3–5), speak of a figure greater than Abraham, a man both king and high priest, named Melchizedek. Christ was greater than the angels and greater, too, than Melchizedek, says the letter, though of the same priestly order. Christ's sacrifice was not of bulls and goats, but of his own blood. Thus, the New Covenant would replace the Old, whose animal sacrifices are weak, out of date, and will be superseded.

Such a prophecy in the ears of any devout Jew, committed as nearly all were to the eternal rites of the Temple, would be understandably outrageous. Yet, a few years later, with sword, fire and slaughter, it would find grim and ghastly fulfillment. ∎

A portion of the mysterious Epistle to the Hebrews from a third-century copy on a papyrus scroll. The original letter is thought to have been written around A.D. 63. It has variously been ascribed to Paul, Barnabas, Priscilla and most often to Apollos, an Alexandrian Jew who aided Paul in establishing Christian missions in Asia Minor.

regarded locally as "possessed," but by a peculiar demon which enabled her, said her owners, to forecast the future. They offered her services at a price. To Paul, she was simply a nuisance. The endorsement of a reputed lunatic did little for his credibility, and besides, she made so much noise, people couldn't hear what he was saying. Finally exasperated, he turned on her fiercely, directing his voice not at the girl but at the demon within her: "I command you in the name of Jesus Christ to come out of her!" Instantly the intruder left her.[4]

Though Paul's attentions had undoubtedly cured the girl, her owners were far from grateful. By being recognizably rid of her demon, she had also been deprived of her supposed gift of prophecy, and everybody knew it. Paul had cost them their major asset. They pressed through the crowd, seized Paul and Silas, and dragged them to the town square, denouncing them as troublemaking,

The magistrates ordered Paul and Silas stripped and beaten with rods, a sentence carried out then and there. The crowd, which didn't like Jews, cheered the punishers.

property-destroying Jews. Then they called on the magistrates to punish the two for trying to convert Roman citizens. Such proselytizing, however, though officially discouraged, was not technically against the law.

The magistrates arrived in state array, preceded by their lictors in emulation of the consuls at Rome. The lictors bore before them the *fasces*, rods bundled around axes symbolizing the power of the Roman state to enforce laws and punish offenders. With neither a trial nor, for that matter, even the clear infraction of a law, the magistrates disregarded the protests of Paul and Silas and ordered them stripped and beaten with rods, a sentence the lictors carried out there and then. The crowd, which didn't like Jews, cheered them on, Luke reports.

Bruised and bloodied, the pair was then hauled off to the local jail, where their legs were clamped into stocks. As the night approached, they began to cheer themselves up by singing hymns and praying aloud. The historian Giuseppe Ricciotti in his book *Paul the Apostle*, imagines the hoarse voices, the cursing and swearing of the other prisoners. Near midnight, Luke reports, there was suddenly a deafening rumble. The building began to shake, the bars jangled free in the windows, the doors swung open, the fetters on their wrists and legs

---

4. Paul's exorcism of the slave girl is not described in the text. From exorcisms down through the ages, however, some concept of the kind of thing that could happen can be surmised. In *An Exorcist Tells His Story*, Father Gabriele Amorth, an exorcist of the diocese of Rome, describes a number of experiences with his mentor, another exorcist, Father Candido Amantini. One dramatic encounter: "Father Candido asked an eleven-year-old boy some tough questions after he became convinced of the presence of a demon. He asked, 'On earth there are many great scientists, some very fine intellects, who deny the existence of God and your existence. What do you say to that?' And the boy immediately answered, 'Those are not very fine intellects! They are very fine mediocrities. . . .' The exorcist continued, 'Explain to me what is the meaning of reclaiming your freedom before God, when you are nothing if you are separated from him, just as I am nothing. . . . Come on, speak!' The demon, full of anger and fear, would twist, drool, and sob in a horrible way, a way not possible for an eleven-year-old, and say, 'Do not test me like this! Do not test me like this!'" Whether the boy was eventually healed is not reported.

fell loose. The horrified jailer rushed to the scene, saw the open doors, and gave up all hope. If the prisoners were gone, he knew his life was as good as lost. Perhaps he'd even heard that King Agrippa, down in Judea, had put sixteen jail guards to death when another of these so-called Christians, a man named Peter, had under similarly dumbfounding circumstances escaped jail in Jerusalem. The jailer drew his sword and prepared to fall on it. Better death this way than under torture. Then he heard a voice shouting at him. It was that prisoner, Paul. Why had Paul not fled? What was going on?

"Stop!" shouted Paul. "Don't do that. We're all here."

The jailer was thunderstruck. He called for lights to be brought forward, and entered what was left of the jail. It was true. Paul and Silas were standing right there. He began trembling. Who were these people? He led them outside. Then it dawned on him. Just as the poor, wretched little slave girl had said, these men were in fact and in deed "servants of the Most High God." He led them from the jailhouse and fell at their feet. "Sirs," he said, still trembling, "what must I do to be saved?" Their answer was immediate: "Believe in the Lord Jesus Christ." He took them into his house, washed their wounds, fed them, and his whole household was baptized. He would be their last convert in Philippi. And this one was male.

But the story wasn't quite over. Constables arrived from the magistrates and ordered the two released. Not just yet, replied Paul; there was a little matter that remained to be resolved. They had been punished with no hearing, no evidence, no trial, and no law. The magistrates might like to know that both he and Silas were Roman citizens.

Consternation no doubt registered on the faces of the constables. Paul's ostensible offenses were nothing compared with the charges that now faced the magistrates. Roman law was very specific and very strict on this point. You don't convict a citizen without a trial. A hundred years before, the great jurist Cicero had said, "If a Roman citizen is bound, it is a misdeed; if he is struck it is a crime; and if he is killed it is almost parricide (murder of a kinsman)." Backing up Cicero was legislation that was half a millennium old. The *Lex Valeria* of 509 B.C., says Ricciotti, prohibited striking a citizen without a previous and explicit popular decision. The *Lex Portia* of 248 B.C. prohibited scourging a citizen for any reason whatever. The magistrates knew this. Worse still, they knew that Paul knew it. They also knew that in similar cases, whole cities had been penalized for the action of a single magistrate.

What could they do to right this dreadful wrong? They could apologize, said Paul. So they did. Profusely. But they had one more request of him. Would he and his party please get out of town? The people were angry. Controlling them

As in so many of the places he visited, Paul was arrested and held in Philippi's jail, this time for ostensibly depriving a local huckster of his living. A sign at the entrance to the ruins of the city's jail claims this to be the site of the apostle's incarceration.

would be difficult. Paul agreed, bade farewell to Lydia, and headed west with Timothy and Silas on the Via Egnatia, leaving Luke behind. But a church had been planted in Philippi that would be a joy to him for the rest of his life.

Something else had been accomplished that they could not realize at the time. Though there were already Christians at Rome (and how they got there nobody knows), the first formal Christian mission had been established beyond the Aegean, on the continent called Europe. For the Christians, Philippi would provide the gateway to Europe, just as Europe, fourteen hundred years later, would provide the gateway to the world.

Things would not work out nearly so well at their next destination, however. It was Macedonia's capital and largest city—Thessalonica, founded by Cassander, one of Alexander the Great's generals, in 315 B.C., and named for Cassander's wife, Thessalonica, who was Alexander's half sister. Construction of the Via Egnatia, coupled with the fact that its harbor was the best port on the Macedonian coast, gave it a thriving economy. But by Paul's day, it was not a happy place. Murphy-O'Connor portrays it as run by a dominant business and bureaucratic elite, closely tied to Rome. These saw to it that the working people did not share its prosperity. To make a bare living, they had to work twelve hours a day, seven days a week. Moreover, such solace as they were able to derive from their religion had, like everything else, been usurped by the wealthy, or so the story went. The god Cabirus had been their protector, but for reasons unexplained, Thessalonica's gentry took a fancy to Cabirus and incorporated him into the state religion as a god for the upper class. So now even spiritual sustenance was denied them.

Thessalonica's manifold business opportunities had attracted a large Jewish population, and it was to the synagogue congregation that Paul and Silas first

Besides jail time, riots were a constant consequence of Paul's missionary visits. His stop in Thessalonica (the old port area is shown here) was no exception. Some of the rioters complained to city officials, "These men who have caused trouble all over the world have now come here." Under cover of night, Paul was spirited out of Thessalonica and on to Boroea.

made their overtures. For three successive Sabbaths, they were heard gladly. But then critics gathered, and the controversial nature of their message got them expelled. Even so, a number of wealthy women and a prominent Jew named Jason continued loyal to them, while they turned their attention to the Gentiles, in particular to the hard-pressed working population. Paul got a job as a tent-maker, putting in the usual twelve-hour day.

To the poor, the message of a messiah with no material possessions whatever, who regarded the poor as favored by God, who said it was the wealthy who had to tremble at the divine judgment, came with especial meaning. The little congregation soon became a large congregation, and growing steadily. This success did not please the synagogue leaders. They went to the marketplace, organized a gang of bullyboys, and set out to drag Paul and company before the magistrates. Failing to find them, they grabbed Jason and some of the other local leaders instead. "These," they said, "are the people who are turning the world upside down."

F. F. Bruce makes a point: This description of the early Christian community—that they were upsetting the world—has provided a subject for countless sermons. Few of the preachers, however, realize how dangerous was this charge at the time. Jewish resistance to Rome was growing steadily in Judea and Galilee, and involving some Jews throughout the Diaspora as well. The authorities would take this "turning the world upside down" as evidence these were Jewish conspirators against Rome, being supported by a local man, Jason. However, they decided on a prudent course. They told Jason: Get these men out of town

PAUL ON WORRYING

"Have no anxiety about anything, but by prayer and supplication with thanksgiving let your requests be made known to God. And the peace of God, which passes all under-standing, will keep your hearts and your minds in Christ Jesus."

Philippians 4:6–7 RSV

He had planned to move west across Macedonia, then cross the Adriatic to Rome, but the hostility was so close on his heels that the trio took refuge in Boroea.

and the charges will be dropped. Paul had no option but to concur.

But he left in misery. His poor converts would now face the jeering, and perhaps violence, of Thessalonica. Bruce reconstructs what they would be saying: "A fine lot these Jewish propagandists are. They come here and entice you to leave the synagogue and follow them, but the moment trouble arises, off they go and leave their dupes to face the music." Cowardice was something of which Paul had never before been accused. But if he remained, then he, his companions, Jason, and his converts would all be jailed. So he departed—under cover of darkness. It was humiliating.

His plan, some say, had been to keep moving west across Macedonia to the Adriatic terminus of the Via Egnatia at Dyrrhachium, then to cross the Adriatic to Italy and Rome. But the hostility following so close now on his heels voided this plan, and instead, the trio moved south to Boroea, a quiet little place bypassed by the march of progress, since it lay about thirty miles off the Via Egnatia. There, the synagogue congregation again welcomed the visitors and listened intently to them. However, when the inevitable delegation arrived from Thessalonica, warning against these interlopers, Paul again had to leave town in a hurry, his new converts at Boroea advising him that because all the roads would be dangerous to him, his party should split up.

This made sense. It was Paul they were after. So Silas should remain at Boroea to foster the work there. Timothy—poor, shy, delicate Timothy—should return to the lions' den at Thessalonica and see what had happened. Had any of the Thessalonians remained faithful? Or when the retribution of the city's elite came down upon them, had they all abandoned the faith? The two could follow Paul later. Meanwhile, he would continue south. Not too far ahead lay a city that positively thrived on theological and philosophical controversy, relished it, and indulged in it day in and day out as an irresistible sport. All three would be safer there than anywhere. That city was, of course, Athens.

The name alone conveyed a whole catalogue of values—social, political, cultural, philosophical, and theological—everything that was meant by the word Hellenism, which Paul as a well-instructed Jew of the Diaspora had been trained from his childhood to both understand and resist. The armies of the great Alexander had burst out of Macedonia in the fourth century B.C. and had conquered the known world and much of the hitherto unknown. But those were merely military victories. The real conquest came behind them in the form of trade, books, art, music, drama, lifestyles and above all, language. To get anywhere in the Hellenistic world, you must be bilingual, speaking your native tongue along with a

Not far ahead lay a city that positively thrived on theological and philosophical controversy, relished it, indulged in it as an irresistible sport: the magnificent Athens.

peculiar Greek called *Koine*, the common Greek spoken at Athens.

By the first century A.D., however, the glory of Athens lay about four hundred years behind—frozen in time by the magnificent memorials the past had bequeathed to the present, chief among them the Parthenon, the temple dedicated to Athena, which presided over the city from the top of the Acropolis, so that, as the historian Paul Maier observed in his book *In the Fullness of Time*, it was difficult to decide, even twenty centuries after Paul, which view was the most magnificent—that of the Acropolis seen from the city below, or that of the city below, seen from the Acropolis.

Alexander's father had already conquered Athens too, of course, along with everything else, but he was sensible enough to leave it as an independent city. The Romans lived at peace with the city until the first century B.C., when Athens rose in an abortive revolt. The Romans stormed the place and took it back in 86 B.C., but soon restored the city's freedom. Now Athens was conquering Rome, as was its habit. Greek plays translated into Latin were all the rage in Roman society, as were Greek attitudes and sexual proclivities, much to the dismay of those who remembered, both accurately and nostalgically, the high morality of the old Roman republic before Caesar Augustus had converted it into an empire.

Paul walked through the teeming streets shuddering, the severe monotheism of his Jewish heritage, the sure knowledge that there could be only one God and one alone, deeply offended by nearly everything he saw. He had known paganism at Tarsus, of course, but on nothing like this scale. Here there were all manner of gods, hundreds of them, of every conceivable shape and identity. The place seemed a citadel of idolatry.

He went first, as usual, to the synagogue, where to his astonishment, the ocean of paganism around them apparently didn't alarm the Athenian Jews, who, of course, were accustomed to it. From there he moved unerringly to the *agora*, the marketplace, where the Athenians traded not only in goods, but also in ideas. The agora was, in fact, a kind of forum for the discussion of everything and anything, and Paul had a great deal to discuss.

Unfortunately, the reception was not encouraging. When he spoke of God, people no doubt wondered which god. When he spoke of the Law, people

Cities without street names, streets without addresses

Finding anyone's house in Paul's day could be a bewildering job

In the seemingly constant travel of first-century Christians between cities and within them, some of the difficulties of finding places and people then may escape modern readers—street names in ancient cities were often merely a matter of local usage. There was no such thing as an official or legal name, and the same street might have several different ones.

Streets simply grew, without surveys, without property lines, and without house numbers. Worst of all, they did not necessarily run in straight lines or meet at right angles.

The following dialogue is taken from *The Brothers* by playwright Terence, a former slave who adapted Greek comedies for a Roman, Latin-speaking audience. The scene is Athens, early in the second century B.C. Two hundred years later, city life was little changed, making the play a big hit with Roman audiences. The translation is by John Sargeaunt.

DEMEA: Tell me the place then.

SYRUS: Do you know the colonnade by the meat market down the way?

DEMEA: Of course I do.

SYRUS: Go that way straight up the street. When you get there the slope is right there in front of you; down it you go. At the end there is a chapel on this side. Just by the side of it there's an alley.

DEMEA: Which?

SYRUS: The one where the great wild fig-tree is.

DEMEA: I know it.

SYRUS: Take that way.

DEMEA: That's a blind alley.

SYRUS: So it is, by Jove. Tut, tut, you must think me a fool. I made a mistake. Come back to the colonnade. Yes, yes, there's a much nearer way, and much less chance of missing it. Do you know Cratinus's house, the millionaire man there?

DEMEA: Yes.

SYRUS: When you are past it, turn to your left, go straight along the street, and when you come to the Temple of Diana turn to the right. Before you come to the town-gate, close by the pool, there's a baker's shop and opposite is a workshop. That's where he is. ∎

would ask, which law? When he spoke of sin the term would have been at least comprehensible, since the Greeks fully understood moral failure. But the mention of salvation would have been devoid of any sense. He could not cite the Scriptures, the prophets, the patriarchs, because all these were meaningless. Moreover, the people were unkind, haughty, snobbish. "What is this bird-brain trying to say?" said some of the Stoic and Epicurean philosophers who frequented the agora. "He seems," replied others, "to be trying to proclaim some more gods to us, and foreign ones at that."

True, such problems were hardly new to Paul. While his hearers in the past had been mostly Jews or converts to Judaism, he had also brought Christ to pagans, who had no knowledge of either the Law or the Scriptures. So whatever their skepticism, Paul managed, at last, to pique the interest of the agora crowd. "May we know what this new teaching of yours really is?" said one. "You talk of matters which sound strange to our ears and we should like to know what they mean" (Acts 17:20). Would he perhaps address their council? It was named for the site on which it met, the Areopagus, or Mars Hill, just northwest of the Acropolis, in the very shadow of the Parthenon itself. Paul readily agreed.

Here surely was a heaven-sent opportunity. He could present the Christian case to the intellectual elite of the world's most intellectual city. Certainly, he would be

The Acropolis of Athens (right) serves as a backdrop for the Areopagus (hill of Ares, or Mars) in the foreground. The Athenian council addressed by Paul met on the summit of the hill and served as a judicial body and debating society.

regarded more as a curiosity than as a source of illumination, because Athens was notoriously fascinated by novelty. Worse yet, he must make sense to an audience upon whom most of the terminology essential to his message would be lost. Still, it was an opportunity.

Paul began his address to the assembled crowd diplomatically. Athens, he said, was certainly a religious city. (That was a compliment, not a sarcasm. It would please his listeners.) There were temples and altars to gods everywhere. But one in particular he had noted—it was dedicated "to the Unknown God." He was there today to talk about the Unknown God.

There was a murmur of interest. He had them; they were listening. He was

The Athenians and foreigners who gather at the Areopagus to hear Paul preach prove to be a tough audience. A particular sticking point for them is the notion of a bodily resurrection. Many sneer and ridicule the apostle, while others put him off with a polite "we must do this again." Only a few become believers.

there to speak, not of a god, but of *the* God, he
said, the God who made the world and everything
in it, the God who was Lord of heaven and earth,
the God who could not possibly live in a temple,
or be somehow waited on by human hands as
though he needed things that his creatures could
provide him with; he being the one who had given
breath itself to men and every other breathing
creature. From one ancestor, he had created every
human being. This was the God who would determine where each creature would live, and how
long, in the hope that during this lifetime, each
might search for God, feel for him, and find him.

But he was never far from any of us. In fact, we
live in him, move in him, and have our very being
in him. We ought not, therefore, to think of him in
terms of gold and silver, or picture him in shapes
that we ourselves can fashion.

There were nods of approval. After all, what
Paul had said was generally compatible with the
Stoic philosophy. All through the ages, he
continued, God had allowed men to live in
ignorance. But now this had changed. God was
commanding all men everywhere to repent from
the ways they had taken. He had fixed a day when he would judge all by the
standards of a man appointed to fulfill this function. A distinct chill became
discernible. And God, said Paul, had guaranteed the unique office of this man
by raising him from the dead.

That did it. Jeers, hoots and taunts broke out in the crowd. If the Athenians
were persuaded of anything, it was that people who died stayed dead. The
concept of a resurrected human being was to them utter nonsense, and they did
not shrink from letting Paul know. So his careful sermon ended in a disaster,
and he left the Areopagus humiliated. Yet, not quite a disaster. A certain
Dionysius, a member of the council, was won over by Paul's sermon and
became Christian. So did a woman named Damaris. Luke reports nothing
further about them, and they are not mentioned in any of Paul's subsequent
epistles. But the fourth-century church historian Eusebius records that
Dionysius became the first bishop of Athens.

Disgusted and discouraged, Paul himself was not impressed with his own
performance. He knew he must leave Athens. "We preach Christ crucified,"
he would later write. "To the Jews it's a stumbling block, and to the Greeks,
foolishness." Athens was to remain intransigently hostile to Christianity.
More than 250 years later, with the new faith proliferating all over the
empire, Athens stayed stubbornly pagan. The day would come, however,

The temple of Apollo stands as one of the last vestiges of ancient Corinth, the city that gave Paul a great missionary success and some grievous pastoral problems. The Acrocorinth can be seen behind the temple.

when the Parthenon would stand above the intersection of "St. Paul's Street" and "the Avenue of Dionysius the Areopagite," when a Greek Orthodox church would dominate the site of the agora that once saw a "babbler" named Paul ranting on about some crucified criminal who was humanity's savior, and when embedded in a bronze plaque at the foot of Mars Hill would be the text of Paul's sermon.

But the greatest dividend of all from Paul's endeavors at Athens lay well beyond even his perceptions. There was more to Athens than paganism and philosophical mind games. The city held within itself a treasure of which Paul was at best only vaguely aware. The philosopher and historian W. G. de Burgh sums it up in his great twentieth-century work, *The Legacy of the Ancient World*, "Among the peoples of the ancient world there are three," he writes, "who bequeathed a legacy that is a living power at the present day. These three peoples are the Hebrew, the Greek, and the Roman. The creations of their genius . . . constitute a heritage of lasting inspiration to mankind."

From the Hebrews, he explains, comes our knowledge of God, from the Romans our concept of equality before the law and the political organization essential to effect it, and from the Greeks, our concept of a representative republic. This means that every time a twenty-first-century man or woman casts a vote, or assumes a right to stand and speak at a public meeting, or asserts an opinion in challenge of established authority, he or she is exercising a prerogative invented and conferred upon us by the Greeks in general and by the Athenians in particular. And the Christian church, the instrument through which all three legacies would be combined, preserved and conveyed over the centuries from that era to this, had its Athenian birth that woebegone day when Paul the Apostle assumed he had failed miserably on Mars Hill.

Even so, as Paul saw himself at the time, almost everything was going wrong. Galatia was falling to the legalist faction, while Thessalonica, Boroea, and Athens had all, so far as the human eye could see, been cheerless failures. Only Philippi offered any hope. And there was no word from either Timothy or Silas, meaning perhaps that the worst had happened. Finally, look what now lay ahead. The next logical stop was Corinth. Could any place on the face of the earth be less promising than Corinth?

Corinth was the boomtown of the empire, rolling in wealth, swirling with every known human species, every known human sin, and every known human profession, especially the oldest one. By reputation, Corinth was one enormous brothel. Even its religion was sex. The Latin name of the Corinthian goddess was *Venus*, in Greek *Aphrodite* with the title *Pandemos* appended, meaning goddess of all the people. This was not an exaggeration. The temple of Aphrodite stood atop the Acrocorinth, where one thousand prostitutes were on duty around the clock, many of them beautiful. They had been purchased as slaves by wealthy men, bestowed upon Aphrodite as a benefaction, and were paid as civic employees. There were two other classes of prostitute—the *hetairai*, for the luxury trade, and the common tarts, who worked the bordellos lining streets emblazoned with lewd and suggestive advertising. In the center of the city cemetery stood a statue dedicated to Lais, a celebrated whore from the temple, memorialized by the figure of a lioness tearing apart and devouring its lunch. Thousands upon thousands streamed into Corinth from every corner of the empire, arriving with money and frequently leaving with syphilis, for which there was no known treatment. In Paul's day, it was called "the Corinthian Disease," while "playing the Corinthian" meant committing adultery, and a "Corinthian girl" was another name for a floozy. Into this cesspool of the Mediterranean would come Paul, with his message of bodily restraint and holy poverty.

Moreover, he was, frankly, broke. He must now trudge alone the fifty miles from Athens to Corinth with no money, no home, no friends to look forward to.[5] These reflections, observes Bruce, gave him a new resolve. No longer would he depend on rhetorical eloquence or intellectual brilliance. Henceforth he must rely on the only force he had found wholly dependable, Christ himself. Very truthfully, he would later write to the Corinthians: "My brothers, when I came to you . . . I did not come with any brilliance of speech or intellect. You may as well know now that it was my secret determination to concentrate entirely on Jesus Christ himself and the fact of his death upon the cross. As a matter of fact, in myself I was feeling far from strong; I was nervous and rather shaky. What I said and preached had none of the attractiveness of the clever mind, but was a demonstration of the power of the Spirit. Plainly, God's purpose was that your faith should

5. Discouraged as he was by his experience in Athens, Paul faced another problem in his walk from Athens to Corinth, notably, physical danger. The shore road skirted the north coast of the Gulf of Saronicos. At one point it was reduced to a narrow path along a high ledge, with a rock wall towering above him on the right and the sea raging far below him on the left. Bandits frequented the area, usually pitching their victims into the sea. Not until the emperor Hadrian's day, nearly seventy years after Paul, did the Romans finally build a road that bypassed this hazardous spot.

not rest upon man's cleverness, but upon the power of God" (1 Cor. 2:1–5 JBP). So much for snooty Athens, so much for the intellectual gurus of the Areopagus. It was a different Paul who prepared to leave for Corinth.

That's when the first good news arrived. Timothy and Silas showed up from Macedonia. The Thessalonians, said Timothy, had not broken. Neither the hostility of their former friends nor the threat of official harassment had discouraged them. Nor had they lost confidence in Paul when he left town by night. They could see the necessity for this. They had not only kept the faith, they were spreading it. The Spirit was visibly at work among them.

A buoyant Paul sent a letter to them at the first opportunity. "Although accepting our message meant serious trouble, you experienced the joy of the Holy Spirit," he said. "You thus became an example to all who believe, both in Macedonia and Achaia.[6] You have become a sort of sounding board from which the Word of the Lord has rung out, not only in Macedonia and Achaia, but everywhere that the story of your faith in God has become known. We find we do not have to tell people about it. They tell *us* the story of our coming to you; how you turned from idols to serve the true and living God, and how your whole lives now look forward to the coming of his Son from Heaven—the son Jesus, whom God raised from the dead, and who delivered us from the judgment which hung over our heads" (1 Thess. 1:6–10 JBP). Paul could not have known that his exuberant commendation to the tough, tenacious Christians at Thessalonica would conclude the opening chapter of the first book to be written in what would one day be called the New Testament.

When the trio reached Corinth, Paul looked for a job. In this boomtown, finding one wasn't hard, and now came his second bit of good news. He was

Stones that witnessed Paul's stay in Corinth: The bema (left) was a monumental public rostrum on which Paul was invited to speak. A Latin inscription on a section of limestone pavement (top) states that the city commissioner, Erastus, had the paving done at his own expense. This same Erastus became one of the stalwarts in the Corinthian church and is mentioned in the Acts and in two of Paul's letters. A marble slab (above) reads "[syn]agog hebra[aion]" (Synagogue of the Jews).

---

6. Achaia was the name of the Roman province that covered about two thirds of modern Greece, lying south of the province of Macedonia. Greece now extends north to include the city of Thessalonica, which in Roman times lay in Macedonia.

"directed," as Christians would see it, to the tent-making shop run by a husband-wife team. Oddly, however, in four out of six references in the New Testament, it is identified as a wife-husband team, with the wife's name first. That name was formally Prisca, informally Priscilla, indicating a noble Roman family of ancient origins. Her husband, Aquila, was a Jew from Pontus, a Roman province on the south shore of the Black Sea. They apparently met and married at Rome. Since Paul nowhere claims to have brought them into the faith, it's probable they were

The first Christian hymns

Some words from the New Testament were songs that still resound daily in the churches

Since the dawn of mankind, music has served to set the soul ringing with the love of God. Christ himself sang a hymn at the Last Supper, and on the cross cried out to his Father in the opening words of the Twenty-Second Psalm, written a thousand years before the Crucifixion, "My God, my God, why do you reject me?" The psalm ends with the promise that God will proclaim his deliverance "to a people yet unborn." It was in this spirit that the early Christians began to sing.

Thus in the Acts of the Apostles, Paul and Silas, imprisoned at Philippi, sing hymns as the other prisoners listen. The earliest church services included singing as a regular component, and in two of his letters Paul specifically exhorts the faithful to sing.

The first Christian songs consisted of the canticles of the New Testament. There are three, all from Luke's gospel: the *Magnificat*, the song of the Virgin Mary pregnant with the unborn Jesus (1:46–55); the *Benedictus*, proclaimed by Zacharias, father of John the Baptist (1:68–79); and the *Nunc Dimittis*, pronounced by the aged prophet Simeon after he beholds the baby Jesus (2:29–32). All three are still sung as part of the daily offices in Catholic, Orthodox, and Anglican churches.

Many scholars discern hymns in the texts of the New Testament epistles. In the historian Jerome Murphy-O'Connor's book *Paul: A Critical Life*, he reassembles Philippians 2:6–11 into a magnificent hymn, even after its translation into English. He believes it was written by someone in one of the churches that Paul founded:

Christ Jesus:
Who, being in the form of God
Did not claim godly treatment

But he emptied himself
Taking the form of a servant.
Being born in the likeness of men
And being found in shape as a man
He humbled himself
Becoming obedient unto death.
Therefore God super-exalted him
And gave him the supreme name
So that at Jesus' name
Every knee should bow
And every tongue confess
"Jesus Christ is Lord."

The earliest known Christian hymn book is a collection of songs known as the Odes of Solomon. Compiled in the late first century, this collection of forty-one psalms celebrates song as the best way to achieve salvation and communion with God. As Ode 16 has it:

My love is the Lord;
Hence I will sing unto him.
For I am strengthened by his praises,
And I have faith in him.
I will open my mouth,
And his spirit will speak through me.
The glory of the Lord and his beauty,
The work of his hands,
And the labor of his fingers;
For the multitude of his mercies,
And the strength of his Word.

Historians often puzzle over Christianity's rapid spread through the ancient world. Perhaps the explanation lies in simple hymns sung with love and heard with wonder. ■

members of the earliest Christian community there. However, when the emperor Claudius expelled the Jews from the capital in A.D. 49 (because of riots caused by "Chrestus," says the Roman historian Suetonius, though some historians think he simply guessed this), the couple moved their business to Corinth. They provided Paul with far more than a job. He lived with them in Corinth, and they later became founding members of the church across the Aegean at Ephesus, principal city in the province of Asia. Later still, they would encounter Paul at Rome, where it's probable they met their deaths as Christian martyrs.

But that lay some fifteen years ahead, and for now Paul could work for his livelihood and work for the gospel in the unpromising city of Corinth. It was a place of fevered activity night and day. The mainland of Greece was connected to the massive peninsula in the south, known as the Peloponnese, by a three-mile-wide isthmus that separates the Gulfs of Corinth and Saronicos. By running through the two gulfs, sea traffic could avoid the onerous and dangerous passage around the Peloponnese, but the isthmus stood in the way. The obvious solution was a canal, and as far back as the sixth century B.C., there had been talk of building one. It had never happened, however, and for thirteen hundred years, freight and small ships were portaged over the isthmus on huge flatcars whose wheels ran in ruts that served as rails, great gangs of

Corinth, leveled by the Romans two centuries before, had become the cosmopolitan center of trade and wealth. What New York was in the twentieth century, Corinth was in the first.

men and animals pushing and dragging them. Presiding over all this, and the attendant activity it produced, was Corinth.

It was a major port, chief city of the Peloponnese, and capital of the province of Achaia. It had a history that reached back nearly a thousand years before Paul. It had become renowned for its wealth and licentiousness in the days of classical Greece, but as the Romans began supplanting the Greek empire, it led a rebellion against Rome in 146 B.C. The Roman response was to level the whole place, except for the temple of Apollo, and sell the entire population into slavery. The site remained vacant for a century, until Julius Caesar recreated it as a Roman colony. Now, as the commerce of the eastern Mediterranean grew, Corinth grew with it, its limits constantly expanding, its old habits rapidly reviving. By Paul's day, it had become as New York was at the turn of the twentieth century, Dallas in the 1970s, or Shanghai at the turn of the twenty-first. Every known language of the Roman and much of the Persian world could be heard on its streets, and people made money as they never had before. Paul by now had known a great many cities—Tarsus, Jerusalem, Damascus, Antioch, Philippi, Thessalonica, Athens—but never had he experienced anything like this. He began, as usual, in the synagogue, encountering the usual response—genuine interest at first, followed by fierce opposition. Paul's rebuttal seems equally fierce.

"Your blood be on your own heads!" he cried. "From now on I go with a perfectly clear conscience to the Gentiles" (Acts 18:6 JBP).

That was easily spoken, but the prospect of how to actually approach this great, swirling, raucous human zoo seems to have daunted him. "Then one night," Luke reports, "the Lord spoke to Paul in a vision. 'Do not be afraid, but go on speaking and let no one silence you, for I myself am with you and no man shall lift a finger to harm you. There are many in this city who belong to me'" (Acts 18:9–10 JBP). However improbable this must have sounded to him, Paul dug in. To his undoubted astonishment, he discovered that Corinth, far from indifferent to God, was wholly receptive to religious ideas. The Corinthians would flock to his message in numbers far greater than those of any other city, meanwhile creating problems that were greater still.

Over the next eighteen months, Paul's work prospered as it never had before. First, it turned out that his failure at the Corinthian synagogue was not complete. Crispus, the synagogue president, became Christian, as did another senior synagogue official named Sosthenes. So did Titus Julius, a convert to Judaism, whose house became a Christian meeting place. To the house of Titus and to other house churches in Corinth flocked a polyglot array representing all classes of Corinthian society. There were people like Erastus, the city treasurer and a notable philanthropist, whose subsequent political career does not seem to have been impeded by his Christian commitment.[7] There were Stephanas and his

Initially daunted by this raucous human zoo, Paul discovered to his astonishment that Corinth, far from being indifferent to God, was wholly receptive.

whole family, whom Paul described as "the first fruits of Achaia." There was a professional secretary called Tertius, a slave named Achaias, freedmen, and probable former slaves like Fortunatus and Quartus; and there were Lucius, Jason, and Sosipater, otherwise unidentified. From Cenchreae, the port at the eastern end of the Corinthian isthmus, came Phoebe, who became a deaconess. Finally there were "Chloe's people." Chloe ran a business out of Ephesus, which frequently took her or her employees to Corinth. Like Lydia at Philippi and Priscilla in Corinth, Chloe was a businesswoman who became Paul's zealous helper.

This success, however, did not meet with universal enthusiasm. The people at the synagogue, having lost two of their foremost elders in Crispus and Sosthenes, as well as the wealthy convert Titus, and beholding the progress that Paul was making at every social level, brought a charge against him. He was not advocating

---

7. In 1929 archaeologists uncovered a pavement slab in Old Corinth with the inscription (as rendered by F. F. Bruce): "Erastus, in consideration of his aedileship, laid this pavement at his own expense." The title *aedile*, meaning, roughly, curator of public works, was a dignity conferred by the city. The pavement was Erastus's way of saying thank you. There is a strong possibility this is the same Erastus referred to three times in the New Testament (Acts 19:22; Rom. 16:23; 2 Tim. 4:20).

Judaism, they said; he was preaching a new religion. This would be illegal. The case came before Lucius Junius Gallio, the new governor of Achaia, a man with top-drawer credentials at Rome. (He came from an old Spanish family, and was the nephew of Lucius Annaeus Seneca, tutor of the future emperor Nero.) The new governor listened to the evidence, deemed the whole thing a theological dispute among Jews, and threw the case out. How could he, a Roman, be expected to settle a Jewish ecclesiastical dispute? he asked. The plaintiffs relieved their resentment by beating up

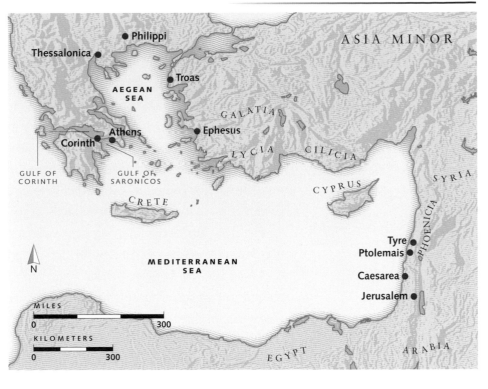

Sosthenes in front of the courthouse. But Gallio's decision, as it happened, was indeed fortunate for Paul. Had it gone the other way, it would have rendered his entire ministry illegal everywhere in the empire.[8]

Satisfied that the church in Corinth was established, Paul decided to move on. That it was firmly established he probably doubted, since the social and moral instability inherent in the whole city was almost bound to cause problems in the church. However, he had to get back to Jerusalem (for reasons undisclosed in either the Acts or his letters), so he set out for Ephesus, the big port on the west coast of modern Turkey. With him came Priscilla and Aquila, to open another branch of their tent business there and take complete charge of the Ephesus mission. After preaching briefly in the synagogue, Paul took the next available boat for Caesarea.[9] Before leaving Corinth, however, he had cut his hair short, evidence, say some historians, that he was heading back to Judea in fulfillment of a vow.

After landing in Caesarea, Paul went to Jerusalem, paid his respects to the church there, then spent a period of time in Antioch. Beyond that bare-bones account, the events of these visits are not reported. However, with the legalist movement emerging from the Christian community at Antioch, there must have been significant discussions, if not heated confrontations. One thing is definitely known. Paul returned to his missions persuaded that his Gentile converts must make

8. Since Gallio's appointment to Achaia can be dated from Roman records to July of A.D. 51 (50 is possible, though less likely), and since his term at Corinth was very brief, this provides the only close-to-firm date in Paul's whole ministry from his conversion on the road to Damascus to his execution in Rome. All the other dates are deductions from this one. That accounts for the calendrical uncertainty that characterizes all his biographies.

9. From Ephesus, before leaving for Jerusalem, Paul sent a letter back to the church at Corinth, a letter which, if it had been preserved, would doubtless have added another book to the New Testament. But no copy of it has ever been found. His next letter, known as First Corinthians, was in fact the second.

some meaningful gesture of friendship toward their brother Christians in Jerusalem, probably by then impoverished through their abortive attempt at communal living. What was needed was a Jerusalem Fund, a gift of money showing genuine concern that would keep Jew and Gentile together in the faith. That must be a top priority. So Paul revisited his churches in Galatia, then took the road west to Ephesus where much news awaited him, most of it bad.

Reports reaching Ephesus, many of them from Chloe's people, described scenes of utter bedlam at Corinth. Sexual promiscuity of every kind was rampant, the faithful (so-called) were suing each other in the pagan courts, some were eating meals in the pagan temples, fights over the food had broken out at the Last Supper observation, and the congregations had divided into various parties, some claiming loyalty to Paul, some to Peter, some to a man named Apollos, whom Paul had never met. Worst of all, some were claiming themselves more spiritually advanced than others because, they said, they were in direct contact with Jesus through the Holy Spirit.

Little if any of this was being done furtively or quietly. The Corinthians did nothing quietly. They had even sent Paul a letter. Should they eat meat that had been offered to idols? And since they were no longer under the Law, that is, since all the rules had been set aside, what should they do about marriage and sex? They were eagerly awaiting his advice.

Priscilla and Aquila hastened to bring Paul up-to-date on the mysterious Apollos. This man, they said, had an unusual background. He came from Alexandria and had become familiar with the teaching of John the Baptist and also of Jesus. He was a Jew, well versed in the Scriptures, a commercial traveler, and a superb speaker. He had turned up as a guest preacher in the Ephesus synagogue. Curiously, while he knew a great deal about Jesus, he did not know of Jesus' rite of baptism. When they had shown him how the prophecies of the

Bedlam reigned among the Christians in Corinth. Sexual promiscuity was rampant, the faithful were suing each other in the pagan courts, and the congregations had split into warring camps.

Jewish Bible had been wholly fulfilled in the person of Jesus Christ, Apollos had responded with undisguised joy. His work had taken him from Ephesus to Corinth, and they had given him a letter introducing him to the Christian community there. At Corinth, they were sure, he would do nothing but good.

As events turned out, they were absolutely right. Apollos became one of Paul's most effective lieutenants. "On his arrival he proved a source of great strength to those who had believed through grace," writes Luke in the Acts, "for by his powerful arguments he publicly refuted the Jews, quoting from the Scriptures to prove that Jesus is Christ" (18:27–28). The rivalry to Paul suggested by the competing Apollos party at Corinth never became a reality. "I have planted; Apollos watered," Paul would later write. "But God gave the increase" (1 Cor. 3:6 KJV). Years later, Martin Luther would contend, and many others would agree, that Apollos was in fact the unknown author of the remarkable Epistle to the Hebrews. (See sidebar page 124.)

Paul's response to the crisis at Corinth was the letter known to history as the First Epistle to the Corinthians, not his greatest, but undoubtedly the most quoted of all his writings. In it, he addresses the reports he was hearing about them and the issues raised in their letter. There must be no such thing as parties in the church, he warns. They were not baptized into Paul or Apollos or Cephas. (Paul always

In his first letter to the Corinthians, Paul addressed their appalling stories of sexual profligacy. 'As a Christian, I may do anything, but I must not be a slave of anything.'

calls Peter by his Aramaic name.) Paul was not crucified for them, nor was Apollos, nor Cephas. It was Christ who died for them, and all were baptized into Christ.

He then turned to the appalling stories of sexual profligacy. A case of incest was actually being condoned, something even pagans wouldn't tolerate. These scandals should leave them "in mourning," yet they were actually "puffed up" about themselves, he observed. Didn't they realize a thing like this could poison the entire community? Drunks, thieves, idolaters, extortionists should be shunned by the whole group. As for their notion that liberty from the Law entitles them to every form of license, this was ludicrous. "As a Christian I *may* do anything, but that does not mean that everything is good for me. I may do everything, but I must not be a slave of anything" (1 Cor. 6:12).

They should therefore "avoid sexual looseness like the plague" (1 Cor. 6:18). "It is a good principle for a man to have no physical contact with women. Nevertheless, because casual liaisons are so prevalent, let every man have his own wife and every woman her own husband. The husband should give his wife what is due her as his wife, and the wife should be as fair to her husband. The wife has no longer full rights over her own person, but shares them with her husband. In the same way the husband shares his personal rights with his wife. Do not cheat each other of normal sexual intercourse, unless of course you both decide to abstain temporarily to make special opportunity for prayer. But afterward, you should resume relations as before, or you will expose yourself to the obvious temptations of Satan" (1 Cor. 7:1–5 JBP).[10]

But as for this business of keeping rules versus having faith, there was another way of looking at that whole question. We should pray, said Paul, for

10. Paul's prescript for married life, in which wife and husband are portrayed as something like equal partners, would seem self-evident to the twenty-first-century Western World. It must be viewed, however, by the standards of the world in which Paul wrote it, a world in which the father of a family virtually owned his wife and children as his private property. In that world, the equality of husband and wife would have come as shocking, radical, revolutionary, and culturally dangerous.

God to bestow upon us "spiritual gifts," in particular one gift that surpasses all the others, the gift of "love."[11]

"If I were to speak with the eloquence of men and of angels," writes Paul, "but have no love, I become no more than blaring brass or crashing cymbal. If I have the gift of foretelling the future and hold in my mind not only all human knowledge but the very secrets of God, and if I also have that absolute faith which can move mountains, but have no love, I amount to nothing at all. If I dispose of all that I possess, yes, even if I give my own body to be burned, but have no love, I achieve precisely nothing."

Then he defines love, the quality that would become the highest of the Christian virtues. Love is patient; it tries to be constructive; it is not possessive; it does not try to impress, nor cherish inflated ideas of its own importance. It has good manners, doesn't seek its own advantage, doesn't gloat over other people's

'For in this life we have three lasting qualities—faith, hope and love,' wrote Paul to the misbehaving Christians of this squalid port city. 'But the greatest of these is love.'

faults, and rejoices in the truth. There is no limit to its endurance, no end to its trust, no fading of its hope, and it never falters. Other cherished qualities will become unnecessary. A gift of prophecy will mean nothing when all is fulfilled. So will knowledge when all is known.

In fact, we are now like children; we have not spiritually matured. "When I was a little child I talked and felt and thought like a little child. But now I am a man I have done away with childish things." At present we look at only the reflection of reality as in a mirror, he says, but the day will come when we see it face to face. "For in this life we have three lasting qualities—faith, hope, and love. But the greatest of these is love" (1 Cor. 13:11–13 JBP).

That description of love would descend through the centuries, memorized by children, studied by saints, framed on schoolroom walls, living room walls, faculty room walls, boardroom walls, quoted over and over again by bishops, ward politicians, Hindu gurus, and atheistic communists, providing aphorisms in every language, and challenging translators throughout the ages to create a rendering adequate to its meaning. Yet, it began as Paul's admonition to a

---

11. By the twenty-first century, the English word "love" was applied so widely to so many varied human emotions that it had virtually lost all meaning. The British literary scholar C. S. Lewis, in *The Four Loves*, distinguished four qualities, all called "love." He noted that the Greeks had a different word for each. First came *storge* (pronounced stor'/ga), meaning simply affection, the warm feeling we might have for a revered old aunt, or a loyal pet; then *philia* or comradeship, the one-for-all, all-for-one fellowship that might bind a military unit or a baseball team; then *eros*, the romantic love between a man and a woman (which Lewis distinguishes from *venus*, a purely sexual desire that he does not classify as love at all), and finally *agape* (aga'/pay), which is the highest, since it is wholly disinterested love that simply desires what is best for the beloved. Agape enables one to love those who are not naturally lovable—lepers, criminals, enemies, the sulky, the superior and the sneering. Since it is often unsupported by fine feelings, it is sometimes scorned by sentimentalists as unworthy. In his famous thirteenth chapter of First Corinthians, Paul is writing about agape. The King James Version of the Bible translates it as "charity," a word (from the Latin *caritas*) that later came to apply only to money or time given the needy.

bunch of misbehaving Christians in a rather squalid port city of the first-century eastern Mediterranean.

Paul dealt summarily and specifically with the way the Lord's Supper should be observed (see sidebar below) and provided a picture of the Christian community that would become the permanent basis for its understanding of itself. The Christians were not an institution, not an organization. Rather, they were like a human body, composed of thousands of individual parts, all different from one another, but all working together in common purpose (1 Cor. 12:4–31).

Finally, Paul broaches the issues raised by those called the "spirit people," and here the patient tone of the letter changes into one of acid sarcasm. Since their baptism came, so they said, from the Holy Spirit, they assumed a superiority over others. "Who makes you different from anybody else," he demands, "and

Paul lays down rules for the Lord's Supper

Christians at Corinth were often dismayingly greedy— even drunk—in their early Communion observances

THE CONDUCT of Paul's converts at Corinth left a great deal to be desired, and he did not hesitate to tell them so by letter, after reports of their wanton conduct reached him over at Ephesus. Drunkenness, brawling, whoring, homosexuality, even incest—there seemed no end to the list. But what was particularly disgusting was their behavior at the Lord's Supper, the observance that Jesus had enjoined upon his disciples at his last dinner with them before he went to trial and the cross.

"When you meet together," Paul wrote in his first letter to Corinthians (11:17–22 RSV), "is it not the Lord's supper that you eat?"

He had heard dismaying accounts. "For in eating each one goes ahead with his own meal, and one is hungry and another is drunk. Do you not have houses to eat and drink in? Or do you despise the church of God and humiliate those who have nothing? What shall I say to you? Should I *commend* you in this?

"No I will not! For I received from the Lord what I also delivered to you, that the Lord Jesus on the night that he was betrayed took bread, and when he had given thanks he broke it, and said: 'This is my body which is for you. Do this in remembrance of me.'

"In the same way also the cup, after supper, saying: 'This cup is the new covenant in my blood. Do this, as often as you drink it, in remembrance of me. For as often as you eat this bread and drink the cup, you proclaim the Lord's death until he comes.'"

Paul then urges them to consider what they're doing. "Whoever therefore eats the bread or drinks the cup of the Lord in an unworthy manner will be guilty of profaning the body and blood of the Lord.

"Let a man examine himself, and so eat of the bread and drink of the cup. For anyone who eats and drinks without discerning the body eats and drinks judgment upon himself. That is why many of you are weak and ill, and some have died."

This matter of self-examination is important, says Paul. "If we were closely to examine ourselves beforehand, we should avoid the judgment of God. But when God does judge us, he disciplines us as his own sons, that we may not be involved in the general condemnation of the world.

"So then, my brethren, when you come together to eat, wait your proper turn. If a man is really hungry let him satisfy his appetite at home. Don't let your communion be God's judgment upon you" (1 Cor. 11:33–34 JBP).

First-century Christians appear to have regarded this "breaking of bread" as more than merely a memorial to Jesus. It was something Jesus had specifically commanded them to do (Matt. 26:26–28; Mark 14:22–24; Luke 22:19–21), and which Paul directly identifies with "the body and blood of the Lord." They spoke of this special observance as a "commemoration," and "offering," a "thanksgiving." It was "the body and blood of Christ," a "proclamation," a "communion"

what have you got that was not given to you? And if anything has been given to you, why boast of it as if you had achieved it yourself?"

He taunts them for living in comfort while he and his helpers suffered every manner of deprivation. "Oh I know you are rich and flourishing," he writes. "You've been living like kings, haven't you, while we've been away? I would to God you were really kings in God's sight so that we might reign with you. I sometimes think that God means us, the messengers, to appear last in the procession of mankind, like men who are to die in the arena.

"For indeed we are made a public spectacle before the angels of heaven and the eyes of men. We are looked upon as fools for Christ's sake, but you are wise in the Christian faith. We are considered weak, but you are become strong; you have found honor, we little but contempt. Up to this very hour we are hungry

(with Christ and his people), a "participation," an invocation of the Holy Spirit, an acceptance of forgiveness, an act of dedication.

Thus, Clement of Rome, writing to Christians again quarreling in Corinth about 95, draws parallels between the Christian "offerings" of bread and wine and the sacrifices made by the priests in the temple at Jerusalem. Ignatius of Antioch, writing to the Ephesians some fifteen years later, describes the breaking of bread as "a remedy bestowing immortality, an antidote preventing death and giving life in Jesus Christ forever." The *Didache*, a manual for Christian living and church practice that most historians believe was composed about 125, though it has parts that were written in the first century, describes the breaking of bread as "that which is holy," and speaks of the bread and wine as "spiritual food and drink."

The question of what actually happens in the elements or in the believer by doing this did not arise until much later. Cyprian of Carthage, in the mid-third century, was concerned about sacraments performed by schismatics. Ambrose of Milan, in the late-fourth century, talked generally about a "change" in the bread and wine. Augustine of Hippo, North Africa, formally analyzed the notion of "sacrament" some years later. Theological arguments over "the real presence of Christ" arose in the ninth and eleventh centuries. In the thirteenth century, Thomas Aquinas gave the scientific (for his time) explanation for change in the elements.

But ordinary Christians, whether in the first century or the twenty-first, were more interested in taking part in it than explaining it. They thereby shared the attitude of one Christian in the sixteenth:

'Twas God the Word that spake it,
He took the bread and brake it;
And what the Word did make it
That I believe, and take it.

That Christian was Elizabeth I, Queen of England. ■

Not as well known as the city's synagogue, the remains of a building in Capernaum called Peter's House or the domus ecclesiae *(church house) tell an ancient story. The house appears to have been converted for use as a church by first-century Christians. In addition to graffiti referring to Jesus as Lord, Christ, Most High and God, there are inscriptions clearly relating to celebrations of the Lord's Supper in the building.*

and thirsty, ill-clad, knocked about and homeless. We still have to work for our living by manual labor. Men curse us, but we return a blessing. They make our lives miserable, but we take it patiently. They ruin our reputations but we go on trying to win them for God. We are the world's rubbish, the scum of the earth, yes up to this very day.

"I do not write these things merely to make you feel uncomfortable, but that you may realize facts, as my dear children" (1 Cor. 4:14 JBP). As it would turn out, observes Jerome Murphy-O'Connor, Paul made them very uncomfortable

Whether Christ rose from the dead didn't matter, said the legalists. Wrong, thundered Paul. 'If Christ did not rise, your faith is futile and your sins have never been forgiven.'

indeed, and he would suffer severely for this. For the legalist faction was about to descend on Corinth, and the "spirit people" would wholeheartedly join them in a concerted effort to discredit Paul and root out the seeds that he had planted and Apollos was so diligently watering.

However, the "spirit people" gave Paul occasion to write another immortal passage in his letter to Corinth. Whether Christ actually rose from the dead didn't really matter, they said. Our bodies are only illusory anyway. What mattered was our spirit. Wrong, thundered Paul. Especially in view of the testimony of so many witnesses to the Resurrection still living, altogether wrong.

> For if the dead do not rise, neither did Christ rise, and if Christ did not rise your faith is futile and your sins have never been forgiven. Moreover those who have died believing in Christ are utterly dead and gone. Truly if our hope in Christ were limited to this life only we should, of all mankind, be the most pitied. But the glorious fact is that Christ *was* raised from the dead. He has become the very first to rise of all those who sleep the sleep of death (1 Cor. 15:16–20 JBP).

Death came into the world through one man (Adam), and all the descendants of Adam die, Paul writes. But another man, Jesus, defeated death. All those who believe in him shall be made alive. Had they not noticed? A seed does not really come to life until it is buried in the ground as though dead. When it rises, God gives it a new body. Just so, our bodies are "sown" rotting in corruption, but raised beyond the reach of corruption.

> So listen, and I will tell you a secret. We shall not all die, but suddenly, in the twinkling of an eye, every one of us will be changed as the last trumpet sounds! For the trumpet will sound and the dead shall be raised beyond the reach of corruption, and we shall be changed. For this perishable nature of ours must be wrapped in imperishability, these bodies which are mortal must be wrapped in immortality. Then the scripture will come true: "Death is swallowed up in victory." (1 Cor. 15:51–54 JBP)

With that, Paul faces the specter of death itself in fierce defiance. "Death," he demands, "where is your sting? Grave, where is your victory? Thanks be to God who gives us the victory through our Lord Jesus Christ."

Paul dispatched his letter to Corinth, then waited for a report from Titus, who was already over there with Apollos trying to bring order out of the mess. It wasn't long in coming and it wasn't all bad, nor good either. While the more blatant misconduct had apparently been corrected, and the individual accused of incest had been ousted from the community (Paul in fact now recommended he be forgiven and restored), and while the "party"

Defending the legitimacy of his ministry to the church at Corinth, Paul lists his tribulations on behalf of the faith. "I have worked much harder, been in prison more frequently, been flogged more severely, and been exposed to death again and again. Five times I received from the Jews the forty lashes minus one. Three times I was beaten with rods, once I was stoned, three times I was shipwrecked. . . . I have been in danger from rivers, bandits, friend, and foe . . . known hunger and thirst . . . been cold and naked. . . . So, who is weak and I am not weak?"

factionalism was no longer mentioned, something else, even more serious, had arisen. The legalist faction had been well received by many—especially, speculates Murphy-O'Connor, by the "spirit people." The only thing they had in common with the legalists was their loathing of Paul, but that was enough to create a coalition that split the church.

Paul's answer came in his Second Letter to the Corinthians, a document so divided

in its tone that some historians think two letters have been conflated.[12] If he must boast in order to establish his qualifications, says Paul, then boast he will, though it is a silly business. In so doing he inventories his experiences as an apostle of Christ:

> Are they Hebrews? So am I. Are they Israelites? So am I. Are they descendants of Abraham? So am I. Are they ministers of Christ? I have more claim to this title than they. This is a silly game but look at this list: I have worked harder than any of them. I have served more prison sentences. I have been beaten times without number. I have faced death again and again. I have been beaten the regulation thirty-nine stripes by the Jews five times. I have been beaten with rods three times. I have been stoned once. I have been shipwrecked three times. I have been twenty-four hours in the open sea.
>
> In my travels I have been in constant danger from rivers, from bandits, from my own countrymen, and from pagans. I have faced danger in city streets, danger in the desert, danger on the high seas, danger among false Christians. I have known drudgery, exhaustion, many sleepless nights, hunger and thirst, fasting, cold, and exposure.
>
> Apart from all external trials, I have the daily burden of responsibility for all the churches. Do you think anyone is weak without my feeling his weakness? Does anyone have his faith upset without my burning with indignation?
>
> Oh, if I am going to boast, let me boast of the things that have shown up my weakness! The God and Father of our Lord Jesus, he who is blessed forever, knows that I speak the simple truth. (2 Cor. 11:22–31 JBP)

That Paul's view eventually triumphed over that of the legalist movement is evidenced best by subsequent history, since Christianity followed him, not them. In fact, says F. F. Bruce, as it turns out they made less headway at Corinth than they did in the other cities. But what finally doomed Judaistic Christianity, observes historian Paul Johnson in *History of Christianity*, was not Paul's mission, but the coming disaster at Jerusalem, which would all but terminate the influence of Judaistic legalism and force the Christians to center themselves elsewhere.

Paul, meanwhile, returned to Ephesus. Priscilla and Aquila had done well there, and he arrived back from Jerusalem to find a thriving church already

That Paul's view eventually triumphed over that of the legalists is evidenced by subsequent history. Christianity followed him, not them.

established, which met in their house. Excavations at Ephesus have uncovered seven two-story houses perhaps much like theirs, belonging to the well-to-do, though by no means the most opulent in the city.

Ephesus lay at the mouth of the Cayster River, on Turkish maps the Kucuk Menderes. By the twenty-first century, the city would exist only as a ruin, yet one of the most complete ruins left from the ancient world. In its heyday, its artificial harbor had to be dredged constantly to keep it navigable and rid it of the sediment deposited by the Cayster. As the Roman empire fell, the dredging stopped and Ephesus declined rapidly. By A.D. 1090 it had become a small town; by the

---

12. Two passages in 2 Corinthians, both acid in tone, sharply contrast with the rest of the letter. The first runs from 6:14 to 7:1, the second from 10:1 to the end of the letter. Some historians, though by no means all, suggest these may have come from another letter of Paul's somehow incorporated into this one.

fourteenth century it was deserted; by the twenty-first century the harbor was a marsh while the site of the city lay eight miles from the sea. In Paul's day the harbor made Ephesus the western terminus of the major road across Asia Minor to the Cilician Gates, more than five hundred zigzagging mountainous miles to the east. The road brought the city great prosperity, enabling it to build, among other things, an outdoor theater accommodating more than twenty-five thousand people. Much of Ephesus survives as an archaeological treasure trove. Rome took over Ephesus late in the second century B.C. and made it the capital of the province of Asia.

By then the Greeks had been settled in the place for nearly a thousand years and had built the original temple to Artemis (called Diana by the Romans) whose numerous breasts proclaimed her a mother-goddess, protectress of wildlife and nature. She appealed to a popular piety, influencing politics, education,

Paul's reception at the Ephesus synagogue was unusually congenial—it took three months before he was expelled. In that time he made the city his missionary base for the region.

business and culture, and was in no sense a sex symbol. An earlier temple was destroyed by an arsonist in 356 B.C. on the night, so it was said, that Alexander the Great was born.[13] The magnificent temple that replaced the original was one of the Seven Wonders of the Ancient World. Nearly three times the size of the Parthenon in Athens, the building was 375 feet long and 180 feet wide. Its columns, variously estimated at 106 to 127 in number, stood in a double row around it, about forty feet high, a spectacle that drew thousands of travelers to the city and therefore represented a significant source of its income. Antipater of Sidon, writing in the early second century B.C., describes the temple as "mounting to the clouds." He adds: "Lo, apart from Olympus the sun never looked on anything so grand."[14]

Paul's reception in the Ephesus synagogue was unusually congenial—it took three months before he was expelled. By that time he had arranged to use the facilities of a private tutorial school run by a man named Tyrannus, about whom nothing else is known. At the same time he established Ephesus as the missionary base for the whole area. One region was particularly fruitful. An assistant named Epaphras opened missions in three towns of the Lycos Valley, about one hundred miles east of Ephesus, at Hierapolis, Laodicea, and Colossae. The second would be preserved for posterity as the seventh of the seven churches named in the Book of Revelation (3:14), while a letter addressed

13. The original temple of Diana was burned by an arsonist who did it, he explained, to preserve his name throughout history. Not to cheat him of his sought-after reward, his name was Herostratus, sometimes rendered Erostratus.

14. "Few temples held such an important place in the history of religion as the Temple of Artemis in Ephesus," writes historian Henri-Paul Eydoux in his book *In search of Lost Worlds* "An inviolable temple was ideal for the storage of money and it became a veritable bank. Furthermore, it had its own resources: taxes from the citizens and port dues. It thus constituted a veritable state under the authority of a high priest."

(1) The Grand Theater at Ephesus, where Paul's teaching provoked a riot of the city's silversmiths who saw him as jeopardizing their idol-manufacturing trade, was initially built by the emperor Claudius only a few years before Paul came there. It was expanded under successive emperors for the next half century until it achieved a final seating capacity of twenty-five thousand. (2) The Marble Road, the city's main street, which in its heyday was lined with shops and bustled with trade, crosses the foreground of the photo, the pillars of its once lavish buildings standing as monuments to what once was. (3) Decorative pilasters that flanked the entrance to Ephesus's great buildings line the deserted street like sentinels. (4) The Celsus Library, one of the city's most magnificent buildings, preserves the grandeur of an illustrious past. (5) A footprint in the paving stone, first-century insignia of a brothel, remains as a reminder that the sins of the flesh are as old as mankind.

Ephesus

A living museum of the Christian past

The city of Ephesus, capital of the Roman province of Asia and one of the major centers of the eastern Roman empire, survives in the twenty-first century as a magnificent ghost town in stone and marble, about eight miles from the Aegean Sea that once gave it its chief function and livelihood.

Ephesus is on the Cayster River, which Roman engineers dredged for its last few miles, then widened into a lake at the site of the city, making it one of the best harbors in western Asia Minor. It served as terminal point of the Roman road that ran eastward to Tarsus and Antioch, then south around the eastern Mediterranean to Jerusalem and Egypt.

As Rome declined, however, the cost of continued dredging of the Cayster could not be borne, and silt reduced the city's harbor to a swamp, diverting traffic to other ports in what is now western Turkey. But this, in turn, had a curious effect. A city that had no purpose was not worth besieging and conquering, so the waves of warfare and redevelopment that demolished so many ancient sites left Ephesus alone.

Consequently, Ephesus became an archaeological treasure-trove, with the ruins of centuries of early civilization still preserved in what remains of its once-teeming streets and buildings.

The magnificent pillars of the towering Temple of Artemis, for instance, stand now where they did in Paul's day, quietly commemorating the goddess who was called Diana by the Romans. The sale of her silver statuettes furnished a principal source of income for the city's silversmiths, who set off a riot to protest Paul's luring their customers away from paganism. The great theater in which that demonstration occurred, said to seat twenty-five thousand people, is still there.

For centuries after the city's final abandonment in the late Middle Ages, its only inhabitants were wolves, who built their dens in the shelter of its once proud buildings. By the twentieth century, however, Ephesus found a new source of human activity—archaeologists and then tourists, the latter wandering down the paving stones that the Romans had laid more than two millennia before. ■

to the third, Colossae, would become another book in the New Testament.

Though it consists of only four short chapters, the epistle to the Colossians became theologically pivotal. Paul wrote it in response to ideas that had gained currency among the Christians there, ideas that Paul sought to counter. Christ is the image of God, he writes (Col. 1:15). All wisdom and knowledge are concentrated in him (Col. 1:16–18) and through him made available to his people (Col. 1:21–22). He is the sole mediator between God and man (Col. 1:19–20). Through Christ, all things were created (Col. 1:16), and through the cross he vanquished all the principalities and powers of the world (Col. 1:20).

Paul was rewarded at Ephesus with what seems a repetition of the Pentecost experience of the apostles in Jerusalem. He found there a dozen "disciples" of Jesus, all of them, like Apollos, baptized by John in the Jordan, but none baptized in the name of Christ, nor receiving the Holy Spirit. Paul baptized them

Converts to Christianity would not be needing the silver statues to the goddess Artemis. How, the silversmiths demanded, should the industry respond to this menace?

and immediately they began "speaking in tongues" and prophesying.

Another incident at Ephesus proved equally edifying and mildly comic. The seven sons of a man named Sceva, who was identified as "a Jewish high priest," wandered the country as traveling exorcists, driving devils out of the possessed. Hearing about Paul, they decided to add his name to their incantations (Acts 19:13). "I exorcise you by Jesus whom Paul proclaims," one of them pronounced over a local madman. The devil, speaking through the man, retorted, "Jesus I know, and Paul I know, but who are you?" Whereupon the possessed individual flew at the seven like a wild beast, tearing the clothes off their backs and wounding them as they fled in terror. The story spread quickly through a city that teemed with magicians. Many of them on hearing this burned their books of magic and other paraphernalia that were worth, Luke notes in passing, about fifty thousand drachmas.[15]

All this success, fruitful as it was for Paul and the Christians, was not viewed at all positively by the businessmen of Ephesus. What about Artemis, the goddess who kept the city's silver fabrication trade flourishing? The silver statuettes of her were sold all over the empire, eagerly sought by visiting devotees, a triumph of the city's artisans. Every convert to Christianity was another customer lost, declared Demetrius, president of the local silversmiths' guild. No Christian would allow one in his house. How should the industry respond to this menace?

He sounded as though he were addressing a protest rally, and he soon was. He had assembled the whole industry—owners, managers, artisans, workers—in

---

15. The twenty-first-century value of fifty-thousand drachmas is not an easy calculation. It would fall somewhere between U.S. $23,000 and $69,000, the lower figure being more likely.

the Ephesus theater. Would they stand idly by while these interlopers wrecked the city's economy? Others flocked into the theater wondering what all the fuss was about. The rally was turning into an unruly mob. A chant began and was everywhere taken up: "Great is Artemis of the Ephesians! Great is Artemis of the Ephesians!" Two Macedonian Christians, in town to help Paul, were seized by the crowd and dragged into the theater.

Paul, hastening as always to exploit such a splendid opportunity to preach the word, was intent on getting into the theater too, until civic officials—with whom, for a change, he was on good terms—persuaded him to stay away because his life would certainly be in danger. Meanwhile, the town clerk addressed the mob. Rome, he warned, would not take kindly to this exhibition. Rome disliked mob rule, and conduct like this could easily cause it to withdraw the special privileges of independence that the city had always enjoyed. These people, after all, had committed no sacrilege against the goddess. They did not threaten her. If the silversmiths had a case against these Christians, then the proper place to bring it was to the courts, not here. With that the crowd gradually dispersed. Luke, the sole source of the story, drops it there, and reports that Paul soon after left on a trip to Macedonia that would take him briefly back to Corinth.

Most historians, however, are not content to drop it there. Paul spent between two and three years in Ephesus, and they are satisfied that he spent some of it in jail. While neither a charge nor a trial is anywhere reported, there are clues in his letters. He reports figuratively "fighting with beasts" at Ephesus (1 Cor. 15:32). He speaks of enduring "a mortal peril" in the province of Asia (2 Cor. 1:8–10). He mentions "many adversaries" at Ephesus (1 Cor. 16:9) without naming them. Soon after the silversmith incident, notes F. F. Bruce, the governor of Asia, Marcus Junius Silanus, was recalled and murdered at the instigation of Agrippina, the emperor Nero's mother. A new administration, much less sympathetic to Paul, may have heard and accepted the silversmiths' case and put Paul in jail.

However Paul's last recorded visit to Ephesus may have ended, his experience there by no means ended the city's Christian history. The city was to play a key role in the events that lay ahead. It was to Ephesus a few years after Paul's departure, for example, that tradition records the arrival of the apostle John Zebedee, brother of the executed James and author of the Fourth Gospel of the New Testament, and it was at Ephesus that John as an old man, or perhaps through a disciple, produced that gospel. It's also generally assumed that John was "the beloved disciple" to whom the dying Jesus in one of his last words from the cross entrusted the care of his mother (John 19:26–27).

John is believed to have been exiled by the emperor Domitian to the island of Patmos in the Aegean where he wrote the book of Revelation. Then, under

Statues of the goddess Artemis at Ephesus were subtitled "Polymastros," referring to her multiple breasts, which were not in fact breasts, but rather bull testicles.

The cosmopolitan citizens of Ephesus, devoted to their local craftsmen's images of the goddess Artemis, are outraged by the Christians erosion of idol worship. Appealing to both the honor of the goddess and the artisans' ledger balance, a silversmith named Demetrius whips a crowd into murderous frenzy, seizing two of Paul's traveling companions. Only with difficulty is Paul himself restrained from confronting the vigilantes. A smooth-talking city bureaucrat saves the disciples from serious harm.

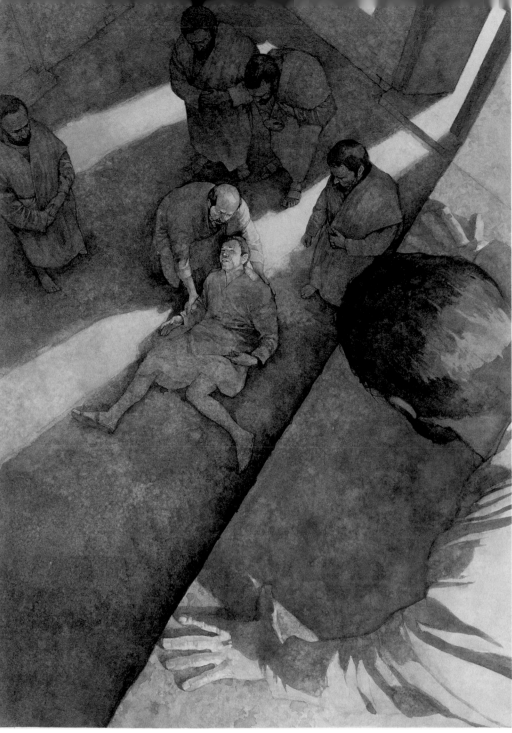

Though the youthful Eutychus would not be the last Christian to doze off during a long-winded sermon, his experience is unique for having been recorded in the New Testament. As Paul preaches on past midnight, Eutychus falls asleep on a window seat and tumbles out, plunging three stories to his death. Rushing down to his side, Paul follows the example of Elijah, stretching himself out on the young man and resuscitating him. Paul then walks back upstairs to continue his discourse, saying, "Don't be alarmed. He's alive."

HARLIN

Domitian's successor Nerva, he returned to Ephesus about A.D. 97 as a very old man for the writing of the Fourth Gospel. There too he is believed to have instructed the young Christian Polycarp, who in turn had a pupil named Irenaeus, both of whom would play pivotal roles as Christian evangelists in the years immediately ahead, as the next volume will describe.

Finally, four hundred years after Paul's visit, Ephesus would add a dark page to Christian history as the site of the so-called "Robber Council," where clerics from Alexandria collided violently in theological dispute with those from Constantinople, whose patriarch was beaten up by monks when the council dissolved into a riot. He died of injuries three days later. The council was later repudiated.

Paul's trip to Macedonia and Achaia had a clear objective, namely the Jerusalem Fund. He had urged it upon his converts in his earlier letters; now came the time to collect it. After meeting with the usual generosity from the relatively poor churches at Philippi and Thessalonica, he expected even greater sums from prosperous Corinth. He was bitterly disappointed, and found instead that the "spirit people" and the legalist faction were raising questions as to his honesty while jeering at his unimpressive preaching style. (Murphy-O'Connor speculates that it was in response to this slander that Paul wrote the furious final three chapters of 2 Corinthians and that they were in fact a third and final letter in his own defense.)

With the fund assembled—no record exists of its final amount—Paul booked passage by sea to Syria. He was warned against this: His enemies now really meant business and were plotting to do away with him at sea. So he changed plans, went back through Macedonia, and then crossed to Troas, the port from which he had first set sail for Europe nearly ten years before. He addressed the congregation there at length one warm evening. At such length, in fact, that a young man named Eutychus, sitting on the ledge of an open window, fell asleep and plunged three stories to what seemed his death. Paul rushed from the room, took the young man in his arms, and pronounced him alive and well. So he was. Paul went back upstairs and finished his sermon. What Eutychus did is not reported.

From Troas, Paul continued south by sea, bypassed Ephesus, and put in at the port of Miletus. The elders of the church at Ephesus had traveled there by land to meet him. Luke in the Acts records his final farewell to them. They will never see him again, he says. The Holy Spirit had urged him to take this voyage, but warned him he would be persecuted and imprisoned in every city. What concerned him more, however, was the certainty they would now be attacked by "savage wolves" who would seek to rip them apart. Keep alert, he says. Hold fast the message of Christ he had given them. Thus he commended them to God, knelt with them and prayed. "All of them were in tears," reports Luke, "and throwing their arms around his neck they kissed him affectionately . . . and went with him down to the boat" (Acts 20:36–38 JBP).

With that, Paul of Tarsus, like his Lord some thirty-two years before, steadfastly set his face toward Jerusalem. ■

Like Jesus, Paul recognized that his return to Jerusalem would bring the end of his ministry and his life. On his way, he gathers the elders from the now-thriving church at Ephesus to give them his final blessing. After prayers he boards his ship and leaves behind his weeping flock.

HARLIN

CHAPTER 6

The long journey home

Paul's determination to face his enemies sets off a riot in Jerusalem, and sees him through trial and storm to his final reward

I t was no doubt the Agabus incident that proved the clincher—proved, in short, that Paul the Apostle was headed for certain imprisonment, if not death, unless someone could dissuade him from going on to Jerusalem. No one could. Again and again, as he moved toward the Holy City, faithful people, those whose fondness for him was self-evident, had kept telling him: Don't go. He ignored their warnings.

But now, here came Agabus—dear, odd, but seemingly infallible Agabus, acclaimed as a prophet, the man who had years earlier at Antioch, accurately prophesied the great famine of the forties.

This time, the aging Agabus had traveled all the way from Judea to Caesarea, boldly showing up at the home of Philip the evangelist, with whom Paul was staying after his poignant farewell to the Ephesian Christians at Miletus. Agabus was determined to make Paul see what he was about to walk into if he went on to Jerusalem. And make it clear Agabus did, borrowing Paul's belt, tying it around his own wrists, and uttering a prediction that chilled the gathering of Christians who witnessed it.

The Holy Spirit, Agabus said, thrusting his bound hands into the air, had made it plain to him: The Jews at Jerusalem would tie Paul up in the same way and would deliver him into the hands of the Gentiles. Those who saw this demonstration were deeply moved, weeping in dismay as they begged Paul not to go up to Jerusalem.

Agabus, of course, did not need to be a prophet to foresee the outcome he had portrayed so vividly. By now, Paul had enemies everywhere. The Jews detested him as a complete turncoat. He had joined the other side, with dire consequences to congregations all over Achaia, Macedonia, and Asia Minor. For their part, some Christians opposed him because he seemed to be blatantly undermining the ancient Law, in favor of what he called "grace." Even the Romans were growing weary of him, because everywhere he went, he seemed to cause major trouble.

Of all this he was entirely aware, Paul told the dismayed assembly. But he was also aware that it was the voice of God himself, of the Holy Spirit, that clearly spelled out his duty. He must walk into the cauldron at Jerusalem. Yes, he agreed, he would certainly be persecuted, and might be imprisoned or even put to death. But he would go anyway. That was the will of God, and it was, therefore, a necessity. Some of the disciples from Caesarea joined Paul's band of missionaries as they set out on foot for the approximately sixty-mile trek to the Holy City.

Whatever his outward assurances to the others, Paul could not have avoided his moments of doubt. Even patient, tireless, clinically objective Luke had warned him against it. Did the impulse to go really come from God? Or was God, speaking through the others, actually warning him not to go? Or was God testing him? Or was God preparing Paul so that he could stand fast when the inevitable end came, as so many times it had threatened and as one day must? Something else: It was in Jerusalem that Paul had dealt so harshly with so many Christians, where he had stood by approvingly as Stephen was martyred. Perhaps it was only just that Paul would follow Stephen to the same end.

The warning expressed by this inscription lies behind the riot that led to Paul's imprisonment, to his various trials, and to his captive journey to Rome. Posted at several places in the outer court of the Temple, the inscription forbids Gentiles to enter the inner sanctuary on pain of death. Paul was wrongfully accused of bringing Gentiles into the sacred place.

If he had enemies among the Christians at Jerusalem, as he had good reason to believe, they were far from evident when he arrived. His appearance was an occasion for celebration. Everyone seemed delighted to see him. After resting up overnight, he and those with him paid a visit to James and the church elders and brought them up-to-date on his work among the Gentiles.

The elders were deeply impressed, but they were also cautious. The Jews in Jerusalem, they knew, had heard all kinds of stories about Paul—that he urged his followers to forsake Moses, that he forbade them from circumcising their children or observing the old customs. Though these accusations were false, they were bound to cause trouble. So the elders offered a plan. In their community were four devout Jewish Christians who had taken Nazirite vows, meaning that they had publicly consecrated themselves to God under the Law and were bound to ascetic discipline and strict regulations regarding ceremonial purity. Paul, the elders said, should join these men, paying for their Temple sacrifices and participating in the Jewish purification rituals himself. By doing this in public, he would refute those from the Christian legalist faction who were campaigning wholeheartedly against him.

Paul, recognizing the proposal's wisdom, agreed, and went into the Temple with the men for the seven-day purification ceremonies. He and the four had almost completed the week of rituals when a group of Jewish pilgrims from Asia spotted Paul in the Temple. They were outraged. They began shouting: "Men of Israel, help! This is the man who is teaching men everywhere against the people and the Law and this place." Worse still, Paul had also brought Greeks into the Temple and thereby "defiled this holy place" (Acts 21:28 RSV).

This was a serious charge. Inscriptions on stone slabs within the Temple carried a public notice in both Hebrew and Greek that anyone caught aiding or abetting the admission of a Gentile to the inner Temple would be put to death—even Jews, even Romans.[1] Paul was both, but that wouldn't stop him from being dealt with in the strongest possible manner if what the Jewish pilgrims said was true. The whole Temple was soon in an uproar. A crowd assembled around Paul, seized him, and dragged him outside, shutting the gates behind them. Mob psychology was at work, emotions were high, and Paul's life was in danger.

But from the Antonia Tower, overlooking the Temple, Claudius Lysias, the tribune of the Roman cohort of Jerusalem, spotted the turmoil and quickly summoned some soldiers and several centurions. They forced their way through the crowd, separating Paul from his attackers. Paul's assailants became enraged and began shouting at the tribune. How could the Romans interfere with them? They were just doing their duty. Wasn't it their responsibility to safeguard the purity of the Temple? "Away with him! Away with him!" shouted the crowd. The uproar made it impossible for Lysias to determine what was going on. So he ordered Paul brought to the barracks by his men, who dragged him away, carrying him bodily, to protect him from what had by now become a lynch mob.

As he had done before, Paul seized control of the situation. He spoke a few polite words to the tribune in Greek. Surprised, Lysias voiced his own suspicion—that Paul was that known Egyptian troublemaker who had recently led thousands of men out of Jerusalem, bent on revolution. Paul brushed all that

1. The wording on the stone slabs at the approaches to the Temple was unreserved: "Let no Gentile enter within the balustrade and enclosure surrounding the sanctuary. Whoever is caught will be personally responsible for his consequent death." One of these slabs still existed in the twenty-first century. Paul fell afoul of this proscription, according to St. Luke, because some of the Temple hangers-on had seen him on the city streets in the company of Trophimus, an Ephesian, and had assumed that Paul took that Gentile into the Temple.

PAUL ON OBSESSIONS AND COMPULSIONS

"So I find it to be a law that when I want to do right, evil lies close at hand. For I delight in the law of God, in my inmost self, but I see in my members another law at war with the law of my mind and making me captive to the law of sin which dwells in my members. Wretched man that I am! Who will deliver me from this body of death? Thanks be to God through Jesus Christ our Lord!"

Romans 7:21–25 RSV

The four towers of the Antonia fortress loom over the northeast colonnade of the Temple courtyard in this model (right). Within the fortress, the Roman cohort had direct access to the Temple precincts for the purpose of quelling any disturbances there—such as the one that broke out about Paul. Pavement from the fortress (below) still bears the etchings of game boards used by soldiers to while away their time.

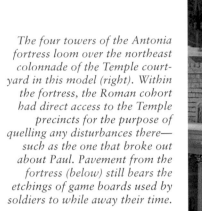

aside, saying that he was no Egyptian but a Jew from Tarsus and asking that he be allowed to address the crowd. Lysias, not knowing what else to do, cleared a space for Paul on the steps of the barracks and told him to go ahead.

Standing before the mob, Paul raised his hand. Those who had been about to kill him fell silent. He began to speak, not in Greek but in Hebrew, a touch they didn't expect. Few Hellenistic Jews knew Hebrew. He sketched the outlines of his life: born a Jew, raised and educated in the strict Jewish traditions by the respected teacher Gamaliel, persecuted the Christians in Jerusalem and elsewhere. Those in the crowd relaxed somewhat. He was, after all, one of their own, they began to believe, not some foreign agent provocateur.

They listened quietly as he described his experience on the road to Damascus: the bright light from heaven falling on him, the voice asking him, "Why do you persecute me?" and then the declaration, "I am Jesus whom you are persecuting." Paying close attention, the mob listened to Paul talk of his blindness, how other members of his party led him into Damascus, his encounter with the devout Jew Ananias, "highly respected by all the Jews who lived there," how Ananias spoke and Paul's sight was restored. It was at Ananias's suggestion that Paul was baptized. Then, he told his attentive audience, he returned to Jerusalem and entered the Temple—the very one in which he had just been assaulted—to pray.

So far, so good. Lysias was pleased. The situation had been easily resolved after all. Just by letting the man speak to his fellow Jews, he had defused a potential explosion and restored order. Paul, however, was still speaking.

Yes, he prayed in the Temple, Paul continued. And what he heard as he prayed was the voice of God. Flee from Jerusalem, that voice had said, because the city's inhabitants would not accept his testimony. Paul then argued with God. Why should the Jews reject him? "They themselves know that in every synagogue I imprisoned and beat those who believed in thee. And when the blood of Stephen . . . was shed, I also was standing by and approving, and keeping the garments of those who killed him." And to that, God had replied: "Depart, for I will send you far away to the Gentiles."

This met with a roar of fury. There it was again. The hated Gentiles! The mob began to push forward, some yelling, some shrieking, some waving their arms wildly, some taking off their cloaks and swinging them in the air, some pitching handfuls of dirt and shouting. Death, they cried. Death to this man. Quickly, Lysias's men hustled Paul into the barracks and shut the gates behind them.

Standing before the mob, Paul raised his hand. Those who had been about to kill him fell silent. He began to speak not in Greek but in Hebrew, a touch they didn't expect.

Greatly troubled by all that had occurred, and determined to get to the bottom of it, Lysias gave his usual order: Find out what this is all about by beating the prisoner until he talks. The men tied him up and were about to proceed when Paul directed a monumental question to one of the centurions: "Is it lawful for you to scourge a man who is a Roman citizen, and uncondemned?"

It was not lawful, of course, not at all lawful, and the centurion knew that if Paul actually was a Roman, and was illegally scourged, the centurion would be held to blame. Lysias, the tribune, was also deeply concerned. He had bought his own citizenship for a large sum, he told Paul. Paul replied, proudly, that he had been born a Roman citizen. Lysias immediately released him from his bonds, as the Law required.

Roman or not, the Paul problem was far from solved. The following day, Lysias called for an assembly of the Sanhedrin, the supreme council and highest Jewish court in Jerusalem. He then had Paul taken in front of the men. What, they demanded of Paul, was all this controversy about?

Standing before this august body, Paul began by identifying himself with them. "Brethren," he said, looking directly at each of them as his eyes swept the room, "I have lived before God in all good conscience up to this day."

The implication was not lost on them. He served God, not the Sanhedrin, and he was satisfied that he had done as God wished him to do. This was not the way an accused suspect was supposed to address the distinguished council. The high priest, Ananias, deeply offended, ordered those nearest him to strike Paul on the mouth, but before they could act, Paul exploded. "God shall strike you, you whitewashed wall! Are you sitting to judge me according to the Law, and yet contrary to the Law you ordered me to be struck?"

Shocked, those who had been about to hit Paul told him that he was addressing the high priest—a fact of which Paul was unaware. He apologized.

FREY

After rescuing Paul from an enraged mob at the Temple, Roman soldiers arrest him, hoping to remove the cause of the riot. Almost immediately, however, Paul takes advantage of his arrest, using it as an opportunity to speak to the throng and try to convert them.

"I did not know, brethren, that he was the high priest, for it is written, 'You shall not speak evil of a ruler of your people.'" (Ananias was known for having a quick, vicious temper—later, when the Jewish rebels waged war against Rome, they would discover Ananias hiding in an aqueduct and eagerly kill him.)

Paul sensed on the faces of the council a deep division in the way they regarded Ananias. Some were doubtless offended to see Paul bark at him so sharply; others failed to disguise their quiet satisfaction. Paul also realized that some members of the Sanhedrin were Sadducees and the others were Pharisees. The Sadducees did not believe in "resurrection, nor angel, nor spirit," while the Pharisees acknowledged them all.

That was all the opening Paul needed. Amid the clamor and confusion, he cried out: "I am a Pharisee, a son of Pharisees; with respect to the hope and the

This man Paul . . . whose mere presence had started a riot yesterday, seemed now to be provoking another one among the members of the highest court in Jerusalem.

resurrection of the dead I am on trial!" Though he was indeed a Pharisee, there was more to the matter than that, of course—Paul had been hauled before the Sanhedrin because of the great commotion his connection with the Christians had caused. As a Christian, he believed in resurrection, and it was true that he was on trial precisely because of his beliefs. Recognizing a potential attack on their own theology, some of the Pharisees sided with Paul, saying, "We find nothing wrong in this man. What if a spirit or an angel spoke to him?" Soon the two sides were brawling with one another.

The bewildered Lysias could only look on. This man Paul, a Roman, whose mere presence had started a riot yesterday, seemed now to be provoking another one among the members of the highest court in Jerusalem. Fearing that Paul might be killed—and that he, Lysias, would be held responsible—he sent soldiers into the midst of the tumult. They successfully extracted Paul and brought him back to the Antonia fortress. There, Paul had another experience that Luke describes as a direct communication from God. "Take courage," was the message, "for as you have testified about me at Jerusalem, so you must bear witness also at Rome."

Meanwhile, Paul's presence remained a thorn in the side of the Jewish establishment. Words were spoken into the appropriate ears, and soon a plot was hatched, involving more than forty men. Those in on the scheme vowed that they would neither eat nor drink until they had killed Paul. With the chief priests and elders in full agreement that Paul should die, the conspirators told the council to summon Paul before them again. But this time, the plotters swore, Paul would not live to face the Sanhedrin.

In uneasy Jerusalem, such a secret would leak beyond those sworn to carry it out. A nephew of Paul's, the son of his sister, happened to be in the right place at the right time and heard the details. Alarmed, he went straight to Paul in the

PAUL ON HIS OWN STANDING

"For I am the least of the Apostles, unfit to be called an apostle, because I persecuted the church of God. But by the grace of God I am what I am, and his grace toward me was not in vain. On the contrary, I worked harder than any of them, though it was not I, but the grace of God which is with me."

I Cor. 15:9–10 RSV

barracks and reported what he had learned. Paul sent him up to Lysias with his story, and the tribune realized that he must act, once again, to prevent this troublemaker Paul from being killed on his watch.

Lysias summoned two centurions and ordered them to organize a party of two hundred soldiers, seventy horsemen, and two hundred spearmen, and to bring them all together about nine o'clock that night, along with a horse for Paul. He also wrote a letter to be carried to the governor Felix, putting himself in the best possible light as he related what happened: "I found that he was accused

A physician writes history

Though long disputed, Luke's ancient details prove to be true

Who is the most read historian of the ancient world? the learned professor asks his class. Tacitus perhaps? Suetonius? Herodotus? All wrong, he's afraid. The most read and probably most reliable recorder of ancient history was a man known as Luke, the probable author of the Third Gospel of the New Testament and its sequel, the Acts of the Apostles.

Sir William Ramsay, a late-nineteenth-century archaeologist, started out his career convinced that the Acts of the Apostles had been produced in the middle of the second century, a hundred years after the events it purported to describe. On the basis of his archaeological discoveries, however, he was gradually compelled to reverse his views. "Luke's history," he wrote, "is unsurpassed in respect to its trustworthiness," and "Luke is a historian of the first rank" who "should be placed along with the very greatest."

Ramsay's view of Luke was considered close to preposterous at the time. Luke's critics of the then-scholarly establishment held that Luke frequently gives the wrong titles for imperial officials, the wrong dates, and the wrong places. That is, he was inventing the Acts of the Apostles as he composed it.

For example, they said, Luke mistakenly identifies Sergius Paulus as proconsul of Cyprus. A bad guess, they said. Cyprus was governed by an imperial legate, not a proconsul. Then in 1889, Ramsay noted an inscription found at Soli on Cyprus. It refers to "the proconsulship of Paulus." In another passage, Luke calls the authorities in Thessalonica "politarchs." Another bad guess, said the critics. There was no such thing as a "politarchy." Then, in the twentieth century, Thessalonian coins were found bearing the inscription "politarch."

These and other unexpected accuracies turned Luke's reputation from that of polemical flak for Paul into that of a dependable historian.

Something else helped. Luke's narrative of Paul's shipwreck provides unparalleled descriptions of sailing conditions and techniques, all of which square with ancient records. Moreover, his description of the hurricane-force wind that dooms the ship corresponds exactly with that of modern-day sailing yachtsmen who, following the south coast of Crete, are occasionally hit with the same fierce winds that sweep down from the island's seven-thousand-foot mountains.

Paul refers to Luke as "the most dear physician" (Col. 4:14), prompting Luke's critics to ask: Yes, but do his writings betray any unusual interest in medical evidence? They do indeed, replied Luke's defenders. People aren't just "sick" in Luke. Simon's mother-in-law is suffering from a "high fever" (Luke 4:38), not just "a fever." A man is "full of leprosy" (Luke 5:12), he doesn't just have "leprosy," as in Mark and Matthew.

Of the six miracles described uniquely by Luke, five are miracles of healing. One final observation: Mark (5:25–33) notes that a woman, who had hemorrhaged for twelve years, had suffered at the hands of doctors. Luke (8:43–48), doubtless out of professional scruples, delicately omits that detail.

So picturesque were Luke's portrayals of the cities of Asia Minor that some critics accused him of cribbing from an ancient travel brochure. Likewise, his descriptions of Paul's trials show an astonishing familiarity with Roman legal procedure. Luke himself acknowledges, in the prologue to his gospel, his attention to accuracy of detail. "I have followed all things carefully from the beginning," he writes. And so apparently he did.

One thing, however, Luke did not record, notably what became of him after he reached Rome. The last reference to Luke comes from Paul who, under arrest in Rome, writes, "Only Luke is with me" (2 Tim. 4:11). His Acts of the Apostles ends in mid-story. A late-second-century account asserts that Luke, "filled with the Holy Ghost," died at the age of seventy-four in Bithynia, the Roman province south of the Black Sea. ■

PAUL ON HARD TIMES

"We are afflicted in every way, but not crushed; perplexed, but not driven to despair; persecuted, but not forsaken; struck down, but not destroyed."

2 Cor. 4:8–9 RSV

about questions of their law, but charged with nothing deserving death or imprisonment. And when it was disclosed to me that there would be a plot against the man, I sent him to you at once." The soldiers brought the horse for Paul and in the darkness spirited him from the fortress. Once they were out of danger most of the escort returned to Jerusalem, while the horsemen charged on with him to Caesarea, delivering Paul and the letter to the governor.

This ended Paul's last visit to Jerusalem, and Luke's account of it in the Acts of the Apostles leaves curiously vague the outcome of the Jerusalem Fund, which Paul had so diligently collected in his missions. Luke makes a single reference to it, that Paul came to Jerusalem "to bring alms to my nation and offerings" (24:17). But as to its actual delivery and the response to it, there is no word. Historians offer several explanations for this—that the fund was essentially a peace offering by the Gentile Christians to the Jerusalem church, and since Luke tends to minimize this conflict, he could not account for the need of a peace offering. Or that relations had grown so strained that the offering had been rejected by the Jerusalem church, a rupture Luke did not want to report. More likely, other historians reply, the fund was delivered and accepted gratefully, but its significance was simply overwhelmed by the other events, which Luke describes in detail.

At Caesarea, the provincial capital of Judea, the governor Felix had gained the reputation as a powerful and savvy politician—one whose harsh administration helped spark the Jewish rebellion some eight years later. He was certainly not about to rush into any situation without examining it thoroughly for whatever benefit it might hold for himself. He put Paul under guard at Herod's palace, waiting patiently for the Jewish officials to arrive from Jerusalem and level their accusations against the man.[2]

The Jerusalem delegation, which included Ananias and some elders, along with a spokesman named Tertullus, arrived five days later and met with Felix to outline their grievances. Felix summoned Paul. Tertullus, who had been selected for the task precisely because of his public relations skills, delivered an elaborate and flattering introduction in which he praised Felix's wonderful government and expressed deep gratitude on behalf of all his subjects. On the other hand, he described Paul as a "pestilent fellow, an agitator among all the Jews . . . and a ringleader of the sect of the Nazarenes. He even tried to profane the Temple, but we seized him." The others who had come from Jerusalem nodded in agreement and assured Felix that what Tertullus alleged was true.

Paul, called to speak in his own defense, proved to be Tertullus's equal in laying out his case. He did so cheerfully, he told Felix, "realizing that for many years, you have been judge over this nation." And he refuted Tertullus forcefully. Rather than being a "pestilent agitator," he said, he had merely gone up to worship at Jerusalem, and no one had found him disputing with anyone or

---

2. Herod's palace at Caesarea, known as Herod's Praetorium, in which Paul was at first imprisoned, had been the home of Pontius Pilate and of Herod Agrippa, who died there.

stirring up the crowds, not in the Temple or synagogues and not in the city itself. Nowhere, in fact. So why was he charged with anything?

Moreover, Paul continued, although he was indeed a follower of the "sect," there was nothing wrong with that. "I worship the God of our fathers, believing everything laid down by the Law or written in the prophets, having a hope in God which these people themselves accept, that there will be a resurrection of both the just and unjust." He always took pains to maintain, he said, "a clear conscience toward God and toward men."

As for Tertullus's claim that Paul had profaned the Temple, Paul waived it aside. He had merely come to the Temple to bring alms and offerings, when some agitators raised false charges against him. As Roman law required, those men should be present and offer their own evidence, if he had done anything wrong, he said.

Felix quickly realized that he was in the midst of an impossibly intricate religious squabble, and that the further he could distance himself from it the

Retelling the Passion stories a few years after Jesus' death had to be done just right. You couldn't leave anything out—not the rooster, not the dice, not Judas's kiss nor the crown of thorns.

better. If he turned Paul loose, the Jewish officials would be upset; if he handed Paul over to the Sanhedrin he would violate Roman law—it was clear to him that Paul was a Roman citizen, with all rights to the law's protection. As he had done when Paul arrived, he decided to wait. These things often sorted themselves out if allowed to sit long enough, he reasoned. He told the Jewish officials that he would make his decision later.

Besides, for Felix there was another, more congenial, aspect to the case. Paul was well spoken and well dressed. There must be some money in his family, or perhaps among these Christians. If he played his cards right, he might be offered a substantial bribe to release Paul, and Felix had no problem at all accepting bribes. So he ordered Paul kept in custody. But the arrangement was more like house arrest than confinement behind bars. Paul was to be well treated, and his friends could visit him freely and take care of him.

Moreover, Felix was frankly intrigued by Paul, whom he found to be a very interesting fellow. Felix had made a point of learning as much as he could about what was called "the Way," the sect to which Paul belonged. Now here was a leader of that sect, an obviously intelligent and quick-witted man, who might provide him with greater insight into this movement and its implications. So after a few days, Felix summoned Paul to meet with him and his wife, Drusilla, herself a Jewess. Luke records that Paul spoke to the couple about his faith in Christ Jesus, and "argued about justice and self-control and future judgment." Because there was nothing but trouble in any of those topics for Felix, he became alarmed and sent Paul away again.

This situation dragged on for two years, with Paul held in loose confinement in Caesarea. He spent the time well, writing letters to the churches he had started—letters that would eventually be included in the New Testament. There is a sense, therefore, in which the Christians down through history owe Felix an ironic debt.

What is usually recognized as the greatest of those letters was the one Paul wrote to the city he had long wished to visit and was now about to. It was, of course, Rome. He appears to have been conscious of the fact he was now addressing a letter to people in the imperial capital, and he took much greater care than usual with the style and language. It would appear as the sixth book in the New Testament, the first of the twenty-one letters included therein.

The Epistle to the Romans has other idiosyncrasies. It is the only letter Paul wrote as a theological treatise; his other letters are addressed to specific problems in the churches. (This assumes, as do most scholars, that Paul was not the author of the Epistle to the Hebrews, which is also a treatise.) It's also the letter in which Paul addresses most directly the question that most beset him. "To Paul, brought up under the rigid Jewish law," writes the British author and translator J. B. Phillips in *The New Testament in Modern English*, "God was pre-eminently the God of Righteousness, i.e., of moral perfection. In these days when the majority of

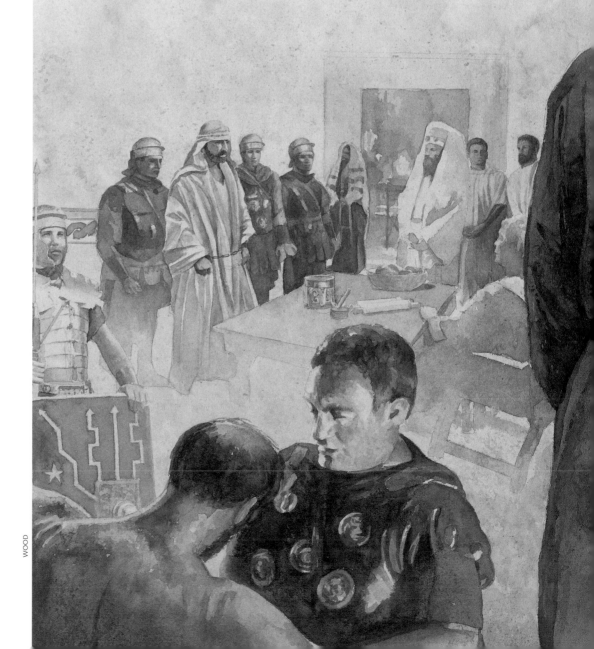

WOOD

people assume God to be a vague easy-going Benevolence it is difficult to appreciate the force of Paul's problem, or the wonder of its solution."

To Paul, God is eternally aflame with beauty, truth, and goodness, so that sin must die instantly in his presence, much as certain germs die instantly if the sun touches them. One solution to this, says Paul, is the Law, either the Law as codified and revealed to the Jews or the universal moral law of human conscience. But man habitually violates these laws, and laws as such can do nothing to remove man's guilt. We are, therefore, lost.

In this letter, says Phillips, Paul explains that the heart of the Christian gospel "is that God himself meets this deadlock by a personal visit to this world. God, as Jesus Christ, became representative man, and as such deliberately accepted the eventual consequence of evil, namely suffering and death."

Paul's eventual visit to Rome would come about not as the result of his own planning, but because of what seemed a strategic error in his conflict with the Jerusalem Jews. Toward the end of the fifties, Felix became embroiled in a political squabble with the emperor Nero

After being arrested and held in the Roman barracks in Jerusalem (bottom left), Paul was taken under armed guard to Caesarea, the provincial capital of Judea. Here he began a two-year ordeal of imprisonment and interrogation. He was summoned before Felix, the Roman governor, who questioned him in the presence of a hostile delegation from Jerusalem led by the high priest, Ananias (top left). Paul strongly denied causing trouble of any kind while in Jerusalem and, as a Roman citizen, insisted on being tried under Roman law. Uncertain as to what to do with him, Felix let Paul languish in jail. When Felix was eventually replaced, Paul was brought before the new Roman governor, Festus, and King Herod Agrippa and his wife, Bernice (this page). Speaking directly to the king, he once again forcefully, and successfully, defended his position. But having raised the issue of his Roman citizenship, he was sent to Rome for a final determination of his case.

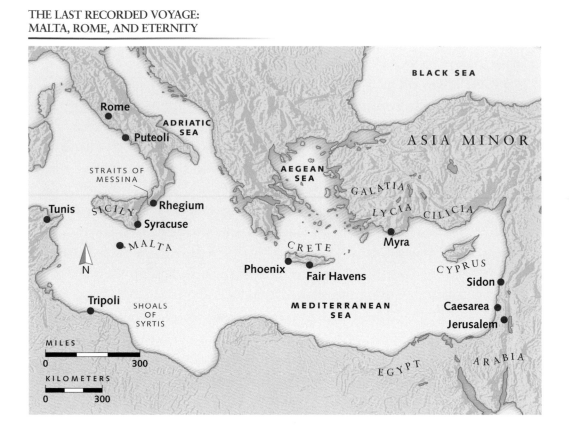

and was recalled. His successor was Porcius Festus. The Jews in Jerusalem had been waiting for such a break. They wasted no time in making the trip to Caesarea to reopen their case against Paul, and another hearing was set.

They had yet another plan. They would convince Festus to send Paul to Jerusalem, where he could stand trial in a religious court for the religious offenses of which he was accused. They did not tell Festus, however, that their plan included another little wrinkle: An ambush was all set up and ready to go, and Paul would die along the way before ever reaching Jerusalem. Festus liked the idea, as he understood it. There wasn't much evidence against Paul that he could see, and holding a man on such flimsy charges for two years wasn't a good idea. He asked Paul what he thought about it.

Paul, knowing full well where the danger lay, played the trump card of his Roman citizenship once more. If he was a wrongdoer, he said, then he should be tried and convicted. If there was nothing in the Jewish charges against him, theirs was not the court in which he should be judged. "I appeal to Caesar," he said.

Festus would be happy to oblige, to pass the whole problem on to Nero. All he needed was some kind of writ or bill to send along with the accused man—but as he explained a few days later to the visiting King Agrippa and Agrippa's wife, Bernice, the charges raised by the Jews were flimsy.

Agrippa was as curious about Paul as Felix had been, and told Festus he'd like to see the man for himself. The following day, Agrippa and Bernice "came with great pomp," Luke writes, and "entered the audience hall with the military tribunes and the prominent men of the city." Summoned before them, Paul listened as Festus outlined the matter for the distinguished gathering. Paul had appealed to Caesar, Festus said, "but I have nothing definite to write to my lord about him." Maybe the royal couple could get to the bottom of things.

Paul spoke to the dignitaries with his usual confidence and strength. He had lived his life in strict accordance with Jewish Law, he said, as a Pharisee, and he was on trial for his belief in the resurrection of the dead. He had at one time vigorously persecuted the Christians, but when he became convinced, on the Damascus road, that what they believed was true, he had joined them. "I stand here," he said, "testifying to both small and great, saying nothing but what the prophets and Moses said would come to pass: that the Christ must suffer, and that, by being the first to rise from the dead, he would proclaim light to the people and to the Gentiles."

Festus, suddenly embarrassed by having brought this strange man before the king, interrupted with a loud voice: "Paul, you are mad; your great learning is turning you mad!" But Paul addressed himself directly to the king. None of what he had said was untrue, Paul said, and Agrippa knew much of it already, because it had not happened in secret, not "in a corner." Then, looking Agrippa squarely in the eye, Paul demanded: "King Agrippa, do you believe the prophets? I know that you believe." Agrippa, amused, retorted, "In a short time you think to make me a Christian!" Paul said he prayed, indeed, that Agrippa and the rest of those within his hearing would become, whether quickly or not, "such as I am—except for these chains."

Ending the hearing, Agrippa told Festus that Paul had done nothing to deserve imprisonment or death. He could have been set free, in fact, Agrippa said, if he had not appealed to Caesar. And to Caesar, and to Rome, he would therefore go.

The sea voyage was quickly arranged. Paul would be accompanied by a Roman centurion named Julius, very likely a man with whom Paul had become

At Myra on the south coast of Asia Minor, Paul was transferred to another ship for the final leg of his journey to Rome. The port was of great antiquity, full of monuments such as this unusual necropolis (city of the dead) on the bluffs near the sea.

The rugged southern coast of Crete provides few good harbors for fishermen and even fewer for sailing vessels such as the one that carried Paul. Knowing this, the ship's captain and owner argued that the anchorage at Fair Havens was unsuitable for a winter stay. His decision to set sail from the inhospitable coastline, however, proved to be a disastrous alternative.

friendly during his long confinement. Luke would go along too, as would Aristarchus of Thessalonica. That Julius regarded Paul more as a companion than as a prisoner became obvious when the ship sailed off and put in at Sidon, and Julius allowed Paul to go ashore and visit with his Christian friends there.

The winds were stiff, and as they set sail again they had to detour around Cyprus before landing in the port of Myra, in southwestern Asia Minor. Julius then arranged for the party to board an Alexandrian ship, laden with grain and bound for Italy. The ship was among the well-organized fleet that carried passengers as well as manufactured goods such as pottery and metalware from Italy to Egypt, where it exchanged the cargo for grain and took on more passengers, and returned to Italy. With favorable weather and winds, the run from Italy to Egypt could be made in two weeks.

The return trip, however, took the grain-heavy ships against the winds, requiring them to maneuver and tack. It was not a voyage for an inexperienced captain or crew. Paul and his companions endured long periods of waiting along the coast for winds that would enable them to make progress. The captain decided to take the ship under the lee of Crete, seeking shelter from the northwesterlies, and they lost much time. When they arrived at a Cretan bay called Fair Havens, Paul—who spent his childhood in Tarsus near the sea, and was so well traveled that he would endure three shipwrecks—advised the company that because the sailing season was over, they were in danger if they continued. In fact, he said, "I perceive that the voyage will be with injury and much loss, not only of the cargo and the ship, but also of our lives."

The ship's captain and the owner were determined to set to sea anyway. Fair Havens wasn't suitable as a winter harbor. They would attempt to reach Phoenix, another harbor of Crete about forty miles away, and spend the winter there.

As they sailed out, hugging the shore, they found a gentle wind, and seemed to have made the right decision. Soon, however, a fierce blast of air swept down upon them from the land, catching the ship in all its fury. There was nothing the captain and crew could do but to give up and allow the wind to blow them where it would. On and on they blew, tossing and turning, as the wind drove the vessel ever farther out to sea and out of the shelter of the coast. Soon, dire measures became necessary. The crew dropped thick loops of cable at the ship's bow and stern, pulled them beneath the hull, and tied them above the deck, tightly undergirding the vessel.

Then came another problem. The wind and the great swells sweeping in from behind were driving the vessel directly onto the graveyards of the Mediterranean, the fearful shoals of Syrtis, a stretch of sandbanks and quicksand off the coast of Tripoli from which no ships ever escaped. The crew dropped their sails to slow their movement, and they all dumped grain to lighten the vessel. The next day they threw the ship's equipment and furniture overboard. Night and day, the great waves crashed against the frail craft, loosening its timbers, causing them to creak and groan with every heave. All aboard were soaked; nearly all were seasick, so

First-century sea voyagers never traveled light

Scout out a willing captain, strike a deal for passage, bring plenty of food, and pitch your tent on deck

Summer travel by sea in the first-century Mediterranean world was dependable and safe. But it was neither comfortable nor convenient. Nobody traveled light.

A formidable fleet of huge sailing vessels, the fabled "grain ships," plied regularly between Alexandria in Egypt and the Italian ports, laden with grain to feed the hundreds of thousands of the emperor's subjects who lived in Rome.

In addition, thousands of smaller coastal vessels worked the other ports, while the big galleys of the imperial navy, some with three or four rows of oars, patrolled the sea lanes, exterminating, promptly and inexorably, every would-be pirate.

When the Roman general Pompey brought the cities of the eastern Mediterranean, Judea and Galilee included, into the Roman fold, his first act was to rid the Mediterranean of its oldest scourge, piracy. Though the Judeans thanked Rome for little else, none could deny that it had made travel by sea fast, cheap, and popular.

But not convenient. The fact is there were no passenger vessels as such, only freighters. These had, it's true, a few cabins in their sterns for the wealthy and powerful. Everybody else more or less camped out on deck, sometimes by the hundreds.

When Paul, or anybody else, wanted to make a passage across the Aegean, Adriatic, or eastern Mediterranean, the first task was to assemble tents, bedding, mattresses, toiletries, and a week or two's food for everyone in the party. All this would then be lugged either to one of the dockside inns in the port of departure, or perhaps to the home of a friend who lived in the port city.

Next, the traveler, or his servant, must canvass the waterfront for ships' captains or owners with a vessel bound for the port to which he was headed. A financial deal was worked out, and as the day of departure neared, the party boarded. They would be assigned a position on deck to pitch their tent at night. The tent would protect the traveler from rain and some spray. If the wind was severe, however, all the travelers could expect to get soaked.

The departure time itself was subject to certain variables. Lionel Casson in his fascinating *Travel in the Ancient World*, lists some of them. Not only must the wind and weather be right, but so also must "the signs." Ominous dreams, for example, in which the dreamer saw muddy water, or a house key, or an anchor, could delay a sailing. If anyone happened to see a goat before boarding, that was bad; a black goat spelled almost

sick they began to yearn for the end. The weather grew bitterly cold. "Neither sun nor stars appeared for many a day," wrote Luke, another passenger on that voyage, "and no small tempest lay on us." Soon "all hope of our being saved was at last abandoned." Wet, afraid, cold, and hungry, they turned to Paul.

He had foreseen just this eventuality if they headed out from Crete. He had predicted the destruction of the ship and the cargo. What did he foresee now, they wondered. "I bid you to take heart," Paul encouraged them. "There will be no loss of life among you, only of the ship." He was certain of this, he told his wretched shipmates. An angel of God had appeared to him in the night and told him not to be afraid—that he, Paul, was destined to stand before Caesar, and that God would also save the lives of all who sailed with him.

For two weeks now they had been adrift, driven onward by the winds, expecting the end with every wave. But the vessel held together. The wind had shifted and they were no longer being

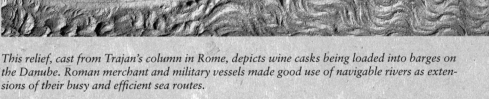

certain disaster. Wild boars were worse, as were bulls. To be gored in a nightmare by a bull made shipwreck inevitable. There were bad luck days (like Friday the thirteenth to a future generation)—a captain would have to be crazy to sail on August 24 or October 5.

When all these dangers had been somehow avoided, the vessel would sail. Headed south with the prevailing northerlies behind, from Naples or Athens to Alexandria, the trip could be made in ten days or less. Headed north, the headwinds could double the time. There were no food services, though the passengers could make use of the galleys to prepare their meals. By day, in fine weather the tents came down, and those who could afford "books" could read. Codices (leafed books), were coming in during the first Christian century, and they could be held in one hand, much more convenient than the old scrolls. Gambling was also a favored diversion, and wine drinking.

You could also watch the handling of the vessel by the crew—the huge square sail, the smaller square foresail, the relatively small tiller-bar that controlled the two huge steering oars off the stern. The size of the grain vessels was prodigious. One of them, the *Isis*, was blown off course by bad weather and wound up at Piraeus, the port of Athens, where its dimensions were recorded. It was 180 feet long, forty feet wide and measured forty-four feet from the deck to the bottom of the hold. It was said to be carrying enough grain to feed

This relief, cast from Trajan's column in Rome, depicts wine casks being loaded into barges on the Danube. Roman merchant and military vessels made good use of navigable rivers as extensions of their busy and efficient sea routes.

Athens for a year, roughly one thousand tons. It could have carried, say the records unconvincingly, up to a thousand passengers.

When the vessel approached its destination port, it would be intercepted by a many-oared towboat that would drag it over to the quay. As the gangplank went out and the passengers disembarked with all their gear, longshoremen flooded aboard to begin unloading the grain.

In the relative peace that followed the dawn of the Christian era, the efficient transportation and communication system of the empire was preserved and became a major factor in the spread of the gospel. As Roman control of the western part of the empire waned in the fifth century, however, the peaceful seas ceased to be, piracy returned, and marine technology forgot much of what it had once known. Not until the nineteenth century, Casson notes, did European shipbuilders construct a vessel capable of carrying such a cargo. In other words, it took humanity fourteen centuries to recover the ground it had lost. ∎

driven on to the Syrtis Shoals. By now they must be somewhere beyond the middle of the Mediterranean, nearing Sicily maybe, or Malta. Then, one day, some of the crew began talking about land, perhaps recognizing the sounds or smells that meant some kind of coastline must be near. They dropped their sounding lines and found their hopes rewarded. Bottom lay at twenty fathoms, one hundred and twenty feet! Then again at fifteen fathoms. They must be nearing land.

PAUL ON PREACHING

"But how are men to call upon him in whom they have not believed? And how are they to believe in him of whom they have never heard? And how are they to hear without a preacher? And how can men preach unless they are sent?"

Romans 10:14–15 RSV

But land did not mean safety, only a new and more terrible kind of danger. Land, for any ship adrift, is as likely to mean death as life. Land could mean sharp, jagged rocks, with the ship hurled against them as the mountainous waves crashed against the shore. Or reefs or sandbars on which the vessel is grounded and then smashed to pieces with the shore still a mile or more away. The crew knew that their lives were at risk, and some of them tried to get away on the ship's lifeboat, but at Paul's urging the centurion Julius and the soldiers who were with him cut the boat loose so that they could not use it.

Just before dawn, Paul addressed the passengers and crew again, telling them to eat some food, because they would need all their strength for what lay ahead. "And when he had said this," Luke writes, "he took bread, and giving thanks to God in the presence of all he broke it and began to eat." Feeling better, they tossed everything else, including all the remaining wheat, into the sea, cut loose the anchors, and hoisted the foresail to carry them to shore. Soon, as was expected, with an awful tearing of timbers, the vessel ground up onto a shoal. Crew and passengers lurched. Then the ship lay helpless, each wave crashing against it. The pounding on the rocks did what weeks at sea could not do. The ship began to break apart.

The Roman soldiers, knowing they must prevent their prisoners from escaping in the confusion, decided to kill them. No, said Julius, and he ordered everyone off the ship, to swim to shore or catch on to the flotsam and drift landward. So they did, every one of them. And as Paul had promised, all escaped alive, washing up one by one on the shores of the island of Malta.[3]

There, they received a friendly welcome from the natives, who started a bonfire to warm them up and to dry the waterlogged clothing they had been wearing for weeks. And there, another of the small, strange incidents that marked Paul's voyages and adventures occurred. Helping to build the fire, Paul gathered up a bundle of sticks and brought them toward the flames. He had also unwittingly picked up a snake. Alarmed by the fire's heat, it sprang from the bundle and attached itself to Paul's hand. When the Maltese natives saw it, they knew Paul was doomed. The snake was particularly venomous, likely the very sort of asp that Cleopatra had allowed to bite her so that she could die. "No doubt this man is a murderer," the natives said among

3. A statue of Paul stands today atop Malta, near the sites now known as St. Paul's Shoal and St. Paul's Bay. Paul L. Maier's *In the Fullness of Time* (Grand Rapids, 1991) agrees that all 276 people aboard the ship having survived such a disaster may seem incredible today, but Maier writes that a visit to the northern shore of Malta finds the shoals so near the land that "loss of life from drowning could indeed have been prevented, especially with friendly Maltese wading out to assist them."

For fourteen long days Paul's ship was driven by howling winds over the storm-tossed Mediterranean. Unable to resist telling the crew "I told you not to leave Crete," Paul then turns to comfort them, the ship's passengers, and his guards. As he predicted, none of the 276 people on board were lost. The ship had been bound for Rome, where Paul was to stand trial for his life.

themselves when they saw what happened. "Though he has escaped from the sea, justice has not allowed him to live."

Paul, stung by the bite, shook the snake into the flames. The natives waited, certain that he would "swell up or suddenly fall down dead," Luke says. But he did not. And "when they had waited a long time and saw no misfortune come to him, they changed their minds and said he was a god."

During the three months that Paul and the others stayed on Malta, he prayed and healed the father of the chief magistrate, Publius, and when the other Maltese heard about it, they brought their sick to him too, and they were cured.[4] Finally the winds were right, and Paul and the others boarded a ship that had also spent the winter on the island. Their Maltese hosts loaded them up with gifts and food and all that they needed for the voyage.

They sailed to Syracuse in Sicily, then to Rhegium, through the Straits of Messina (known to Homer as the site of the deadly rocks and whirlpool Scylla and Charybdis).[5] And on they went to Rome. When Paul landed, Christians came from miles around to greet him, and he was greatly encouraged. Paul then settled down and waited for his appeal to be heard by the emperor Nero.

Luke's account of Paul, the only contemporary history of his life that exists, does not end happily. In fact, it does not end at all. It reports Paul as waiting for his hearing, and then the whole book simply stops. The Acts of the Apostles was probably never finished. It halts abruptly at the twenty-eighth chapter. That left it to writers forty or more years later to relate what happened to Paul, Luke, and Paul's myriad of converts throughout the eastern Mediterranean, so many of them fondly named in his letters. All those later writers are in accord that Paul was martyred just outside Rome, probably in the Neronian persecution. (See chapter 8.)

However, Paul lives more in his own letters than in Luke's narrative account of him, and the letters portray a man acutely aware of the complexities of Christian life. His gentle patience with the errant Galatians contrasts sharply with his caustic contempt for the "spirit people" at Corinth. At one point, he lays down an agenda of sexual regulations for his converts in the sex-driven city of Corinth; at another, he reassures the Christians at Rome that one man's rule could be another man's license, and that the only really important thing is that whatever we do, we do it for Christ. More striking still, the same man who does not shrink from urging others to follow the example he has set for them, can also write with equal sincerity: "My own behavior baffles me. For I find myself doing what I really loathe, but not doing what I really want to do" (Rom. 7:15 JBP).

---

4. The tradition is preserved that the Publius mentioned in Acts 28:7–8 was consecrated by St. Paul and became the first bishop of Malta.

5. Scylla and Charybdis, twin dangers to ships edging along between them in the straits of Messina on the coast of Sicily, are described by Virgil in his tales of Hercules. Scylla, a massive, jagged rock named for a sea monster, threatened to become the final resting place for unlucky ships that smashed against it. Charybdis, named after another monster, was a powerful whirlpool promising an equally abrupt end for any ship approaching it too closely. The Roman poet Horace found in this a metaphor for those who, in seeking to avoid one fault, fall into another.

While such contradictions arise from Paul's letters, a much greater contradiction arises in the modern world's reaction to them. "I hold St. Paul," writes the liberal philosopher John Stuart Mill, "to have been the first great corrupter of Christianity," while theologian Paul Tillich observes: "To the man who longs for God and cannot find him, to the man who is striving for a new imperishable meaning to his life and cannot discover it—to this man Paul speaks." The dark German philosopher Friedrich Nietzsche sums up: "A god who died for our sins, redemption through faith, resurrection after death—all these are counterfeits of true Christianity for which that disastrous, wrong-headed fellow Paul must be held responsible," and a later German scholar, Adolf Deissmann, notes: "There has probably seldom been anyone at the same time hated with such fiery hatred and loved with such strong passion."

"What Jesus preached was a new birth of the human soul," writes the early British science fictionist H. G. Wells, "but what Paul preached was the ancient religion of priest and altar and propitiatory bloodshed." Says another man in similar disgust: "Christ was an Aryan. But Paul used his teaching to mobilize the underworld and to organize an earlier Bolshevism." That man's name was Adolf Hitler. "St. Paul

Paul's most touching letters
Four pastoral epistles serve as his last will and testament

For the Christian career of Paul the Apostle, spanning perhaps thirty years in the middle of the first century and powerfully influencing events in the next nineteen, we have two chief sources. One is the book called the Acts of the Apostles, probably written by his friend and associate, the physician Luke. The other is his own correspondence, letters written by himself or others on his behalf that give his own assessment of events.

Of the thirteen "Pauline epistles" in the New Testament, however, four stand apart: personal, reflective, and, in one instance, expressing finality. The game was almost over, Paul knew. Though there were problems everywhere, backsliders, turncoats, even treachery, he'd won that game, and he knew it. Or, as he himself would have hastened to add, not he, but Christ, who had worked through him.

Most historians agree that the four "pastoral epistles" were written from Rome, shortly before Paul's execution in or around A.D. 64. (Some contend they were written several years before when Paul was in prison at Ephesus, others while he awaited trial at Caesarea.) Two things distinguish them. Unlike the other nine, they are addressed to individual people. Moreover, the style is different. By then, Paul had

mellowed, writes the British historian F. F. Bruce. Historian Jerome D. Quinn describes the pastorals as Paul's last will and testament.

The probable first of the four is written to the Gentile Titus, one of Paul's earliest converts, who accompanied him to the pivotal Jerusalem conference that officially commissioned Paul as Apostle to the Gentiles. Titus served Paul all through the strife and chaos of church planting in Greece, Macedonia, and Asia Minor. Now, with this letter, Paul assigns Titus to the island of Crete, directing him to appoint clergy and setting out character standards for bishops, a passage that would be read at episcopal consecration services for centuries to come.

Advice for the conduct of all Christians follows: Old men should be temperate, serious, and wise, known for their love and patience. Old women should be reverent, not given to accusatory complaining, and not addicted to wine. Younger women should set examples for their children and be chaste, kindhearted, willing to adapt to their husbands. Young men should take life seriously, have a strict regard for truth, and not be given to affectations of speech. Slaves should serve their masters loyally, especially if their masters are Christians and therefore

would almost certainly have condemned tobacco," notes novelist Samuel Butler. "St. Paul was wrong about sex," declares Episcopalian Bishop James Pike. "No one understood Paul until [the heretic] Marcion," writes the great biblical critic Adolf von Harnack, "and he misunderstood him."[6]

Thus it was that St. Paul's nineteenth- and twentieth-century critics established the greatest contradiction of them all, a contradiction between perception and reality. In the era of modernism, Paul was popularly regarded as the pillar and founder of doctrinaire Christian authoritarianism, the man who took the "simple religion" of Jesus Christ and converted it into a morass of hair-splitting ideological and theological dogmatism. In fact, Paul of Tarsus devoted his life, from his conversion on the Damascus road, to a cause that is the precise reverse of this. More than any other first-century Christian, excepting perhaps only Jesus himself, Paul insisted, often at the peril of his very life, that each soul had a unique relationship to Christ, that a religion that consists of categorical rules means

---

6. These testimonials for and against Paul were assembled by writer and television commentator Malcolm Muggeridge and Anglican priest and author Alec Vidler, for a book they published in connection with a television documentary on Paul. The book was entitled *Paul, Envoy Extraordinary*.

brothers. Finally, all should avoid endless discussion and dissension over fine points of the Law, because these settle nothing and go nowhere.

Probably the most curious of the four is the letter addressed to Philemon. Consisting of a single twenty-five-verse chapter, it is the shortest book in the Bible. In it, Paul appeals to Philemon, one of his converts, to take back into his service a runaway slave named Onesimus who had fled to Rome, fallen in with Paul, been converted to Christianity, and given great help to Paul. Paul sends him back, accompanied by the letter, urging Philemon to receive him and offering to pay any loss Philemon sustained because of Onesimus. What Philemon did with Onesimus isn't recorded but, as one historian points out, if he had not acquiesced, the letter would certainly never have found its way into the Bible.

The Epistle to Philemon presents one other delightful historical possibility. Fifty years later, when Ignatius, bishop of Antioch, was being taken to his execution at Rome, he stopped over at Ephesus and later wrote that the bishop there, a certain Onesimus, who had been active in collecting Paul's letters, had been most gracious to him. Was it the same Onesimus? Was the onetime runaway slave, perhaps then in his twenties, now in his seventies, heading the whole Christian community? No one knows, of course, but someone had certainly preserved Paul's "covering letter" and assured it found its way into the Christian Bible.

The remaining two pastoral epistles are both addressed to Paul's assistant Timothy who, like Titus, had been with him from the beginning. To Paul,

Timothy is "my own son in the faith" and "my own dear beloved son." As in the letter to Titus, Paul sets forth the standards for Christian clergy and laity, warns against idle doctrinal disputation, and reminds the wealthy that they brought nothing into this world and will certainly take nothing out.

But more than anywhere else in his letters, Paul here foresees the end of the world. "The last times will be full of danger," he writes, in J. B. Phillips's translation, *Letters to Young Churches*, "Men will become utterly self-centered, greedy for money, full of big words. They will be proud and abusive, without any regard for what their parents taught them.

"They will be utterly lacking in gratitude, reverence, and normal human affections. They will be remorseless, scandalmongers, uncontrolled, violent, and haters of all that is good. They will be treacherous, reckless, and arrogant, loving what gives them pleasure instead of loving God. They will maintain a facade of 'religion' but their life denies its truth."

Timothy must therefore make every effort to keep his "mind sane and balanced," Paul counsels. "Go on steadily preaching the gospel and carry out to the full the commission that God gave you."

He concludes: "As for me, I feel that the last drops of my life are being poured out for God. . . . The future for me holds the crown of righteousness which the Lord, the true judge, will give to me in that day. And not, of course, only to me, but to all those who have loved what they have seen of him." ∎

'Death, where is thy sting?'

Paul of Tarsus lives on around us

The Christian foundation of American history, culture, and geography escapes the conscious awareness of many Americans. If a pollster were to ask the citizens of Minnesota, for instance, whether they could see any connection between, say, the biblical First Epistle to the Corinthians and their own state, how many, you wonder, would be able to say that the man who wrote the epistle also provided the name for their state capital city, St. Paul?

The fact is that there is probably a St. Paul's church in almost every city and town in the Western World. *The Times Atlas of the World* lists sixty-one places named either St. Paul or San Pablo, while the Library of Congress lists 742 works under the subject heading of his name.

Commercial activity, too, finds many uses for his name, either directly or through the name of some city or institution. The Manhattan telephone directory has sixteen listings under St. Paul, including three insurance companies, a film center and a book store. Chicago lists a billiard parlor, Dallas a cancer center as well as "St. Paul's Psych-Link," whatever that might be. The Santa Barbara directory lists a cleaning and laundry service; Houston a construction company; Nashville a beauty parlor; Philadelphia a credit union; Newport, Rhode Island, a furniture and appliance store; New Albany, Indiana, a hotel; and Amherst, Ohio, a beer garden—selling, perhaps, Pauli beer, made in Bremen, Germany, and brand-named after a local medieval monastery where the original brewery was located.

How Paul of Tarsus might himself have reacted to all this celebrity over all these centuries one can only imagine. He would probably have replied as he responded to the church at Corinth: "Let no man glory in man. For all things are yours, whether Paul, or Apollos, or Peter, or the world, or life, or death, or things present, or things to come. All are yours, and you are Christ's, and Christ is God's. Let a man so account of us, as of the ministers of Christ, and stewards of the mysteries of God" (1 Cor. 3:21–4:1). ■

(1) In a historic photo, St. Paul's of London, Christopher Wren's cathedral, shines through the fire and fury of the World War II Blitzkrieg. (2) Sao Paulo, greatest industrial city of South America, preserves the name of the apostle. (3) By contrast, tiny St. Paul's Island, one of the Pribilofs north of the Aleutians, honors him in Alaska. (4) The island Fortress of Peter and Paul at St. Petersburg, Russia, was built by Peter the Great to defend his new capital from attack by the Swedes. (5) The dome of the cathedral in St. Paul's, Minnesota, stands higher than the legislative building in that U.S. state capital. (6) President John F. Kennedy, in June 1963, addresses members of the German Bundestag and Bundesrat in Frankfurt's historic Paulskirche (Paul's Church). There, 150 years earlier, Germany's first Parliament had met. (7) Typical of thousands of unpretentious little St. Paul's churches around the world is St. Paul's of Windwardside at Saba in the Netherlands Antilles.

certain spiritual death, and that the way of salvation is through the grace that Christ confers on any man or woman who asks for it, so that each of his followers becomes a "new creation." As the historian F. F. Bruce put it in the title of his magnificent biography, Paul was preeminently "the apostle of the heart set free."

Perhaps, however, the greatest benefaction Paul left to the hundreds of millions of Christians who would follow him lay neither in what he taught nor in what he wrote, but in what he did. For though his letters would be diligently collected and assembled to comprise about one quarter of the New Testament, what seemed to give him the greatest joy were those he brought into the faith, his beloved converts. For it was they, men and women of every caste, of every race, and of every Mediterranean language, who bore the Word of God from man to man, woman to woman, parent to child, worker to worker, saint to emperor, moving silently, unobserved, as the leaven works in the bread, just as Jesus had said; it was they who through the grace of Christ fashioned Christianity and laid the foundations of the most powerful movement the world would ever know.

That Paul should find himself embattled on every side came as no surprise to them because they, more than anyone, understood the terrible task he must accomplish. "I am now ready to be offered," he wrote to Timothy, probably from prison in Rome, "and the time of my departure is at hand. I have fought a good fight. I have finished my course. I have kept the faith" (2 Tim. 4:7 KJV).

So indeed he had, but it would remain for a Christian writer sixteen hundred years later to portray Paul in such a way that his beloved converts of the first century would have recognized him instantly. For Paul is the undoubted model for Mr. Valiant-for-Truth, the hero figure of John Bunyan's *The Pilgrim's Progress*, which C. S. Lewis describes as "a book that astonished the whole world."

Mr. Valiant, his face slashed and scarred from a lifetime of fighting, at last receives the call to cross the river of death to the Eternal City beyond it. Drawing from Paul's First Epistle to the Corinthians, Bunyan describes the passing of Mr. Valiant and, therefore, of Paul himself.

> He called for his friends, and told them, "I am going to my Father's place. Though with great difficulty I have got this far, yet now I do not regret all the trouble I have had to arrive where I am.
> "My sword I give to him that shall succeed me in my pilgrimage, and my courage and skill to him that can get it.
> "My marks and scars I carry with me, to be a witness for me that I have fought His battles who will now be my rewarder."
> When the day that he must depart had come, many accompanied him to the riverside. As he went down into the water, he said, "Death, where is thy sting?"
> And as he went down deeper, he said, "Grave, where is thy victory?"
> So he passed over, and all the trumpets sounded for him on the other side. ∎

CHAPTER 7

The mysterious three

The Synoptic Gospels, Matthew, Mark, and Luke, are not formal histories, and they aren't legends either, but these books, along with John, have changed the world

Sometime—we don't really know when—between the death of Jesus in about A.D. 30 and the year 100, about a century after his birth, there appeared in the early Christian world four documents called the Gospels that narrated the story of his life and message. Those four Gospels—Matthew, Mark, Luke, and John, as they are traditionally known were believed from earliest times to have been inspired by the Holy Spirit, and they became the keystone of the New Testament, the part of the Christian Bible that deals with the Christian experience of Jesus Christ.

As literature, the four Gospels were like nothing that had ever been produced before. They were not like the biographies of great men that were popular reading among the educated upper classes of the Hellenistic world, books like Quintus Curtius Rufus's history of Alexander the Great, completed around 50. Nor were they a little like the *chreiae* and the *paradeigmata*, inspiring anecdotes about the deeds of famous philosophers: Diogenes with his lamp looking for an honest man, or Apollonius of Tyana wandering around the ancient world working miracles.

They were more like the books of Jewish Scripture. Their God was the God

Among the oldest fragments of the Synoptic Gospels, this papyrus particle of the twenty-first chapter of Matthew was discovered in Egypt and has been dated to the late second century. A fragment of John's Gospel, also unearthed in Egypt, considerably predates this one and is believed to have been produced between A.D. 100 and 125, while yet another fragment has been, amid great controversy, dated to the mid-first century.

of Israel, who had given his Law, his Torah, who had redeemed them from slavery, and made a covenant with them that through them, the descendants of Abraham, all nations would be blessed. But even here, the Gospels differed. They were unlike the other Jewish sacred writings because they maintained that Jesus Christ represented the fulfillment of the Torah and was himself the means of blessing for the nations. Furthermore, they carried the names of Jesus' earliest followers rather than those of Hebrew prophets or kings.

The Gospels are essentially collections of anecdotes (scholars call them pericopes), each relating an incident of something Jesus said or did: told a parable, preached a sermon, confronted an opponent, forgave a sinner, dialogued with a disciple, healed a blind man, raised a dead child, exorcised a demon. The anecdotes fall into a few categories: controversy stories, parables (the short tales that Jesus told to illustrate a point of his preaching), aphorisms, healing stories, and so forth. Although the Gospels have a rough chronological order, progressing from Jesus' birth and childhood, or his earliest ministry in Galilee, to his crucifixion and resurrection in Jerusalem, only the fourth one, John, seems concerned with time frames. The other three—Matthew, Mark, and Luke, known as the "Synoptic Gospels"—concern themselves mostly with Jesus' activities in Galilee, where he grew up, and its environs, giving the impression that Jesus ventured out of northern Israel only once, to go down to Jerusalem and die. In John's Gospel, by contrast, Jesus spends a great deal of his ministry in Judea and travels back and forth regularly between Judea and Galilee.

When we think about this selectivity on the part of the Gospel authors, and we think about all the things that Jesus must have said and done during his ministry that were obviously not recorded in the Gospels, we realize that their authors had something else in mind besides writing a detailed and orderly chronological history. In their selection of short, mostly unconnected anecdotes, the authors of the Gospels must have been more interested in trying to capture the immediacy of experiencing Jesus, not as a noble dead man who warranted a biography, but as a powerfully alive figure whose reality they wished to transmit to others by presenting examples of what he said and did, but not necessarily his entire life.

That was what Christianity was all about to the earliest Christians, as it is to Christians today: experiencing the living Jesus. To the earliest Christians, Jesus was not simply a sage or a prophet who pointed the way to God and showed people how to live. Nor was he simply someone who had achieved enlightenment and wanted to pass on his way to his followers, or a role model for imitation or a martyr who had the courage to die for a cause. He was the "Lamb of God" whose death is the sacrificial atonement for the sins of the world. He was a larger-than-life reality whom God had resurrected from the dead—he was with God, the son of God, he was God—and the whole point of being a Christian was to be part of that spiritual reality, to consume it personally, even literally, as some saw in the Lord's Supper. Thus, the stories in the Synoptic Gospels are a potent combination of realistic everyday detail—an oversize catch of fish in the Sea of Galilee, a hole cut through the roof of a village house to lower a paralytic inside for Jesus to touch and heal, a twelve year old girl raised from the dead, Jesus hungry and needing something to eat—and brief, searing confrontations with the far-larger-than-life physical presence of Jesus himself. We are at once drawn into the geographical and historical world of Jesus and immersed in it, and suspended above it in the supernatural reality of Jesus himself.

In Mark's Gospel (there is a similar version in Matthew and Luke), for example, a blind beggar, Bartimaeus, trying to attract Jesus' attention as he walks down a street in Jericho on his way to Jerusalem, shouts at him: "Jesus, Son of David, have mercy on me!" Mark continues:

> Many sternly ordered him to be quiet, but he cried out even more loudly, "Son of David, have mercy on me!" Jesus stood still and said, "Call him here. . . ." So throwing off his cloak, he sprang up and came to Jesus. Then Jesus said to him, "What do you want me to do for you?" The blind man said to him, "My teacher, let me see again." Jesus said to him, "Go; your faith has made you well" (Mark 10:48–52).[1]

The story tells of a miraculous healing, but it is also about the sheer power that emanates from Jesus, the absolute authority of the man who is more than a man—and the mercy, too, of someone who immediately takes pity on the beggar, just as he will take pity on anyone who calls his name, even the lowliest sinner.

The story of Bartimaeus thus operates on many levels. It is specific and realistic, a narrative written by someone who believed that the

As it was in New Testament times, Jericho today is a collection of neighborhoods scattered amidst the greenery of an oasis. Then it was a popular destination for the rich and famous, and boasted villas and palaces like King Herod's. But, being less than twenty miles from Jerusalem, the common folk of that city also traveled to enjoy the orchards, gardens, and springs of Jericho.

1. All biblical quotations in this chapter are from the New Revised Standard Version (NRSV).

events in it actually occurred—and might have talked to someone who witnessed them firsthand. The beggar has a name, Bartimaeus—and Mark is also careful to tell us that he is the "son of Timaeus," a translation of the Aramaic word Bartimaeus. In Mark's brief but vivid narrative, we can almost smell the narrow, dusty, fetid street in Jericho, hear the tumult of the boisterous crowd around Jesus, feel its jostling of half-washed bodies. We can sense the anxiety and the touching faith in Bartimaeus's plaintive, "My teacher, let me see again." When Jesus speaks, it is in a tone of commanding authority and utter self-confidence. (This is not the meek and gentle Jesus of sentimental Christian hymns!) Jesus knows that he has the power to make the blind see, and he knows of Bartimaeus's faith instantaneously, because he can see inside his soul.

But the story also has another plane: It tells of the believer who is always welcome in Jesus' presence, always the object of his forgiveness, despite his infirmities. Indeed, Bartimaeus's moving prayer in slightly altered form is the basis of the endlessly repeated Jesus Prayer of the Eastern Church: "Lord Jesus Christ, Son of God, have mercy on me, a sinner!"

The anecdotal, strung-together, often disconnected nature of the individual Gospel stories also served another purpose: The Gospels were almost surely written to be read aloud to a community of Christian believers, probably at worship services. Short, self-contained pericopes that could be read, then made the subject of preaching in church assemblies, made sense in the context of early Christian worship. This would also explain their focus on the immediacy of Jesus, the sense of his immanent presence, rather than on the biographical details about his family and his education and his progress toward power that a conventional Hellenistic narrative about a great man might contain. The earliest Christians were encouraged to see themselves in the people who had had those wondrous encounters with Jesus during his early ministry.

But where did these anecdotes come from? They were obviously favorite stories about Jesus that had been told and retold many times among early Christians before Matthew, Mark, and Luke wrote them down. The stories themselves undoubtedly originated among the Galileans, Samaritans, and Judeans who had seen and heard Jesus during his ministry in the Holy Land. And when those stories were retold, when Mark and Luke first heard them, there were probably older witnesses still alive who could augment the narratives. Matthew might have had his own personal recollections as one of the apostles.

The stories were retold in different ways, depending on what the tellers and listeners were interested in. That typically resulted in three different versions of the same tale: for example, neither Matthew nor Luke mentions Bartimaeus's name in their versions of the story of the blind beggar at Jericho. In fact, Matthew has two beggars in Jericho, both anonymous. There could have been many reasons for that. Two slightly different versions of the story might have been in circulation, each based on a different set of memories. Perhaps Peter, telling the story to Mark, remembered the story differently from Matthew. Or perhaps Matthew, Mark, and Luke all heard the story from different people,

CO_IER

perhaps eyewitnesses, perhaps Matthew was an eyewitness himself. According to tradition, all three Synoptic authors were living in Jerusalem at one time or other after Jesus' death: Matthew was one of the Twelve, Mark lived in Jerusalem, and Luke visited the city with Paul. They would have had plenty of opportunity to both hear stories about Jesus and talk to people who had heard Jesus preach or had seen one or more of his miracles.

Only one story in all the Gospels is not a short anecdote, or even a sequence of short anecdotes, but rather, a sustained narrative that spans several chapters. It is the story of Jesus' passion, death, and resurrection that is the climax of each. In each of the Synoptic Gospels (and in John's Gospel as well), the Passion narrative is the longest continuous section. In Mark's Gospel, for example, it takes up nearly a fourth of the narrative, dwarfing everything else. Furthermore, the Passion story is the one story in which the Synoptics are as specific about chronology and exact timing as John's Gospel. Here, the writers are not stringing discontinuous events together but giving a detailed account of the last week of Jesus' life in Jerusalem and his utter transformation after his death.

Furthermore, their three accounts of the Passion are not only similar but are virtually identical, differing only in the smallest details. All three Synoptics tell of Jesus' triumphant entry into Jerusalem, his last Passover supper with his disciples, his betrayal by the disciple Judas, his arrest at night in Gethsemane, the hearing before the Jewish Sanhedrin, Peter's denial of his master to the tune of a crowing rooster, the mob that howls for Jesus' crucifixion, the Roman prefect Pontius Pilate's interrogation of Jesus and his release of the convicted rebel Barabbas instead of Jesus, the crown of thorns and the purple cloak that the Roman soldiers make Jesus wear, the dragooning of Simon the Cyrenean on the streets of Jerusalem to help carry the cross, the two criminals crucified on either side of Jesus, the soldiers gambling for his clothes at the foot of the cross, the women who stand by him faithfully after the men flee, the tomb with its stone rolled in front of the door—which proves to be empty when those same women return early Sunday morning with their spices for anointing Jesus' corpse, and an angel tells them that he has risen. Here and there, tiny details in the accounts of the three Synoptics diverge: The cock crows at different times in the three Gospel stories during Peter's betrayal, and Luke places a second angel at Jesus' tomb when the women arrive (Matthew mentions only one angel and Mark refers simply to "a young man" who is mysteriously there). But in all, the Passion story the Synoptics tell is remarkably uniform.

Furthermore, in all three Synoptic Gospels (and also in John's Gospel), Jesus'

The Gospels consistently affirm that women were the first witnesses to the Resurrection of Jesus—a telling point, say the Gospels' defenders, since at that time the testimony of women—however many of them might corroborate a story—was considered unreliable. So if the stories were fiction, why invent non-credible witnesses? Luke states categorically, "They [the apostles] did not believe the women." Only with Peter's confirmation of the empty tomb do the disciples accept the news. And when it comes time for the disciples to relay the message to others, they pointedly omit the evidence given by the women. God may have chosen the women to believe first, but the disciples are still bound by convention—and Luke dutifully tells it as it happened.

COLLIER

death and resurrection are foreshadowed in his own predictions: "Then he began to teach them that the Son of Man must undergo great suffering . . . and be killed, and after three days rise again," writes Mark in chapter 8 of his Gospel, and in chapter 9, Mark again quotes Jesus: "For the Son of Man came not to be served but to serve, and to give his life as a ransom for many."

It seems clear that the Passion stories are not just the most important part of the Synoptic Gospels but that they are the oldest part. To the very earliest Christians—in Jerusalem, in Damascus, in Antioch just a few years after Jesus' death when the early church had just a few thousand members—retelling the story of the Crucifixion and Resurrection must have been a kind of ritual that

Retelling the Passion stories a few years after Jesus' death had to be done just right. You couldn't leave anything out—not the rooster, not the dice, not Judas's kiss nor the crown of thorns.

had to be done just right. You could not leave anything out: not the rooster, the dice, Judas's kiss, Pilate's interrogation, the mob, or the crown of thorns.

It was important that everything be remembered correctly because, as the early Christians knew, Jesus' crucifixion and resurrection lay at the center of their experience: Jesus, who was in "the form of God," had taken on "the form of a slave" (as Paul had reminded them) and had submitted to death, the cruelest of all human experiences, then been exalted to God's right hand by a resurrection that promised a similar resurrection for all into eternal life. It was a hard thing for those early Christians to take in, because crucifixion, a humiliating form of execution meted out to the worst of traitors and felons in the Roman world, was a scandal to both Jews and pagans. Jesus bore no outward signs of the messiah who was expected to restore God's kingdom; he did not die defending Jewish Law, as had the Maccabean martyrs about 150 years before his birth; and the Torah itself, in the Book of Deuteronomy, deemed anyone hanged on a tree to be "cursed." And the man who had hung there for a ghastly afternoon with nails punched into his wrists and feet bore no resemblance to the noble Hellenic philosopher who accepted his death with an epigram of resignation, or to the Greek hero who avoided death at the last moment by being transformed into a god.

Turning Jesus' ignominious death into glory, the earliest Christians reminded themselves over and over that he had shed his blood for "many" like the Suffering Servant described by the prophet Isaiah, and that he was the stone rejected by the builders who became the cornerstone, as one of the Psalms said. It is not surprising that Matthew, Mark, and Luke heard the same story, or very nearly the same story, from every witness to whom they talked. Three Passion stories made clear that Jesus was not simply a good man and wise teacher who had been accidentally executed. (That didn't happen in the Roman world, which left Hillel and other Jewish holy men who were Jesus' contemporaries

"To everyone who is able to receive what the Gospels have to offer—which is the greatest gift anyone can receive—the main thing is the life of Christ, the man Christ. . . . It is only through our living with this life that the ideas which blossom forth from it have meaning; only thus does the Gospel have meaning; only thus do we understand that it is not that the Evangelists write about Christ and his Gospel, but that Christ is the Gospel!"

Our Christ, by German philosopher Constantin Brunner (1862–1937), Translated by Graham Harrison and Michael Wex, translated by A. M. Rappaport (Assen/Maastricht, the Netherlands: Van Gorcum, 1990)

alone.) To the Synoptic authors, Jesus was the Son of God—all three used those very words—and he was killed because his bold claims to fulfill the Torah and the Jewish prophecies were regarded by both the Romans and certain Jewish leaders as a threat.

There is also a strong likelihood that one or more of the three Synoptic authors read one or more of each other's Gospels and borrowed material from it, augmenting what they had read with oral tales they had heard about Jesus or the recollections of eyewitnesses they had talked to. As we can tell from reading such first-century church fathers as Clement of Rome, even the very earliest Christians were familiar with more than one Gospel. And we also know from the discovery of a fragment of John's Gospel in Egypt dating from only thirty-five years after its generally accepted date of composition that the Gospels circulated widely, and far from their places of origin. (So did personal letters; fragments of ancient correspondence have been dug up from the Egyptian desert that were written as far away as Asia Minor and Rome). And finally, Luke tells us in the opening verses of his Gospel that during the course of his research, he not only talked to "eyewitnesses and servants of the word" but read "many" accounts of Jesus' life and teachings that had "been set down." Among those writings, it is not at all improbable that Luke consulted Mark's Gospel, Matthew's, or both.

The scene of one of the "theophanies" in which the divinity of Jesus was manifested, Mount Tabor rises spectacularly above the surrounding hills and fields of Galilee. On it Christians believe the transfiguration of Christ occurred—his body and clothes radiating with divine energy. The spirit-quickening grandeur of the mountain makes it seem a proper setting for such a profound event.

The likelihood that Luke, a careful historian, read one or more of the other Synoptic Gospels before he started writing helps explain the most puzzling feature of the Synoptic Gospels: why they all use such similar material from Jesus' life. After all, Jesus undoubtedly said and did many more things than the Gospels record. Not only are huge sections of Mark's material also in Matthew and Luke, but both Matthew and Luke follow Mark's order when using (or seeming to use) Mark's material. Often, the Greek words themselves in all three Gospels are mysteriously similar, down to the same verb form in many cases, suggesting that there is a literary relationship among them, not simply a matter of reliance on a common oral tradition or similar eyewitness accounts. The question of which Synoptic author wrote first, and which Synoptic author read which other Synoptic author, is called the Synoptic Problem.

The early Christians were not unaware of the Synoptic Problem. One church father, Augustine of Hippo in northern Africa, writing around 400, surmised that Mark had simply condensed Matthew's Gospel in writing his own shorter version of the events of Jesus' life. By the beginning of the twenty-first century, however, the majority of New Testament scholars believed that Mark's, the shortest Gospel, was actually the first to be written, with Matthew and Luke

Some scholars maintain that Matthew's and Luke's Gospels rely on a written source of Jesus' words they call 'Q.' Other scholars contend there was no such thing.

coming later. Out of that group, a majority believes that Matthew and Luke actually had copies of Mark in front of them, but they wrote their Gospels independently of each other. To account for the fifth of their Gospels that Matthew and Luke share in common but don't share with Mark—mostly sayings of Jesus together with a miracle or two—many scholars believe that there existed a written collection of Jesus' words that the scholars call "Q," from the German word *Quelle*, for source. Those scholars believe that both Matthew and Luke relied on a combination of Mark and Q in writing their Gospels, along with a good deal of material that each had separately gathered elsewhere.

Other New Testament scholars contend that there never was a Q-document— and we certainly don't have a copy of Q or any historical record telling us that such a text ever existed. They argue that Matthew used Mark's Gospel, and that Luke, writing later, used both Mark and Matthew. This theory accounts for the material that all three Synoptics have in common and also for the anecdotes that Matthew and Luke share with each other but not with Mark. Still other scholars hold a different theory: that Matthew and Mark wrote independently, drawing on common oral tradition for their material, and that Luke, the historian who prided himself on using written materials, relied on both.

The upshot is that it is impossible to prove any of these theories on the scant information we have about the actual composition of the Gospels. The Synoptic

Problem is just that: a problem likely never to be solved. In the end, we have to regard the appearance in the world of the three Gospels of Matthew, Mark, and Luke, so tantalizingly similar in subject matter yet so strikingly different in tone and details, all three written within a few years of each other, as a wonderful mystery: three striking accounts of the life, death, and resurrection of Jesus that appeared just decades after his earthly ministry ended.

We should remember that ancient writers were not like twenty-first-century college professors penning scholarly articles in their carrels, with piles of books and journal articles in front of them as their sources. It is far more likely that the authors of the Synoptic Gospels relied on a more complicated mixture of their own memories, the accounts of elderly eyewitnesses to Jesus' life and death, their observations of the Holy Land (all three had lived there, according to tradition), and the stories about Jesus that fervent early Christians had passed along to them, along with whatever written documents they had at hand that told them

Although the Gospels of Matthew, Mark and Luke are strikingly similar in content, each differs radically from the others in style and emphasis and in its portrait of Jesus.

about the risen Lord whom they revered. Those documents could have included other gospels, perhaps collections of Jesus' sayings and other now-lost writings about him, and even letters of Paul and other early Christians.

Although the Gospels of Matthew, Mark, and Luke are strikingly similar in content, each differs radically from the others in style, emphasis, and in its portrait of Jesus. Let us examine some of these similarities and differences, beginning with the Gospel of Mark. The earliest reference to Mark is a written account attributed to Papias, bishop of Hierapolis in Asia Minor around 130. Papias's document itself disappeared, but the fourth-century Christian historian, Eusebius, quoted from it in his own history of the early church.

According to Papias, Mark acted as Peter's interpreter in Rome and transcribed his preaching, taking down his Gospel at Peter's direction. This is not implausible. The fisherman Peter undoubtedly needed a translator when he preached to the early Christians of Rome, who were probably Greek-speaking Jews. (Greek was the international language of much of the Mediterranean world. It was for many their second language.) Some of the incidents in Mark's account of Jesus' ministry seem to bear the stamp of Peter's firsthand observations: a story of how Jesus healed Peter's mother-in-law of a sickness by taking her by the hand, or how Jesus once fell asleep on a pillow in Peter's fishing boat. Occasionally, Mark uses Latin words (*speculator*, meaning "executioner," for example) that suggest a Roman influence that would be natural for someone living in Rome (Mark's very name, Marcus, was one of the most popular Roman names).

Mark's Greek prose was of an uncultivated, sometimes grammatically incorrect "longshoreman" variety, with a limited vocabulary—the literary style of a

As Peter holds forth on the sayings and miracles of his Lord, Mark takes dictation. It is likely that these temporary records were made on wood tablets covered with wax. Later, the scribe would have committed these texts to the more precious medium of ink on papyrus, perhaps editing and arranging as he went.

fisherman's half-lettered companion for whom Greek was not a first language (a number of Aramaic words appear in Mark's Gospel that its author dutifully translates). Nonetheless, Mark, as the episode of the beggar Bartimaeus indicates, knew how to tell a gripping story, combining vivid dialogue with fast-paced action. He enjoyed supplying the names of his characters: Bartimaeus's or the fact that Simon the Cyrenean had two sons named Rufus and Alexander. He dotted his Gospel with precise and graphic details that are missing from the other two Synoptic accounts: the fact that Jesus was "with beasts" during a time of fasting in the desert early in his ministry or that "four" men lowered the paralytic's pallet through the roof of the house in Capernaum.

Mark's Gospel, at about 650 verses the shortest of the Synoptics, contains no account of Jesus' birth or childhood, and in its oldest surviving texts from the fourth century, it ends abruptly after the women encounter the young man at Jesus' empty tomb and learn of his Resurrection (other texts contain a few more verses in which Jesus appears after the Resurrection and instructs his disciples to preach his gospel to all nations). To Mark, Jesus' ministry in Galilee and death in Jerusalem were the central focus. He begins his story nearly as abruptly as he ends it, with Jesus' baptism by John the Baptist, a popular rustic prophet, in the Jordan River and his subsequent temptation by Satan in the desert before his ministry begins. Mark was particularly interested in Jesus' miracles. (Although his characters often address Jesus as "teacher," Mark recorded few of Jesus' teachings). He devotes a fourth of his Gospel to graphic accounts of Jesus' healings of the sick, his exorcising of demons from those tormented by Satan, and his dominion over nature: In one of his most startling miracles, he awakens from sleep in Peter's boat and calms the raging winds of a summer storm.

The subjects of those miracles—eighteen in all, more than in any other Gospel—are typically ordinary people like Bartimaeus or Peter's mother-in-law or the twelve-year-old girl raised from the dead. Lepers, demoniacs, deaf-mutes, blind men, children whom Jesus blesses, a Greek woman from Syro-Phoenicia to the north of Galilee who has a sick daughter—these plain folk are desperately in need of Jesus' help. As the story of Bartimaeus illustrates, these encounters are full of

COLLIER

In response to Jesus' "Follow me," Matthew (or Levi) is about to leave behind his lucrative tax collector's post. Would he go on to author the Gospel bearing his name? For the early church there was virtually no question. The converted publican would have had the skills, mind, and background to pen such a book, and the name of no alternative author was put forward at the time. All of which argues in favor of the disciple as author.

human emotion, both on Jesus' part and on that of those who encounter him.

But Mark is most intent on showing us that Jesus proclaims a new and divine kingdom, and is himself divine. He also aims to dramatize Jesus as the Lord of the end time. The purpose of the miracle stories seems as much to demonstrate the astonishing effect that Jesus has on other people as to show Jesus' supernatural powers. His Gospel begins with the words "The beginning of the Gospel of Jesus Christ, Son of God." And toward the end, after Jesus' death on the cross, the centurion in charge of the Crucifixion remarks, "Indeed this man was the Son of God." Even when Jesus tells an occasional parable, a short story illustrating some truth about his otherworldly kingdom, his purpose seems to be to impress his listeners rather than instruct them. Mark's Jesus is larger than life and blazing with divinity. For that reason, Mark has traditionally been depicted in Christian art accompanied by a lion.

Papias, as quoted by Eusebius, is also the earliest source of traditions about Matthew's Gospel. Papias recorded that Matthew had written the "sayings" of Jesus in the "Hebrew dialect." That ambiguous statement (Was Matthew's transcription of Jesus' "sayings" the same thing as Matthew's Gospel, and was Papias referring to the Hebrew language itself, or to the Aramaic spoken by Jews of the Holy Land during Jesus' time?) led many scholars for many centuries to believe that Matthew wrote his Gospel in either Hebrew or Aramaic, and that it was translated into Greek soon afterwards. Tradition holds that Matthew left the Holy Land before composing his Gospel, perhaps in Antioch.

But the only early text we have of Matthew's Gospel is written in Greek, and it does not seem to be a translation of an earlier Hebrew or Aramaic version. One reason for this is that the vocabulary of Matthew's Gospel is very similar to that of Mark, and Matthew not only uses nearly all of Mark's material but follows Mark's order of arranging that material most of the time, adding another fifty percent of his own. Matthew, who was clearly better educated than Mark, writes in a Greek that was cleaner and more grammatically correct than Mark's.

"*Despite the prejudices and theological preconceptions of the evangelists, they record many incidents that mere inventors would have concealed—the competition of the apostles for high places in the Kingdom, their flight after Jesus' arrest, Peter's denial, the failure of Christ to work miracles in Galilee, the references of some auditors to his possible insanity, his early uncertainty as to his mission, his confession of ignorance to the future, his moments of bitterness, his despairing cry on the cross; no one reading these scenes can doubt the reality of the figure behind them. That a few simple men should in one generation have invented so powerful and appealing a personality, so lofty an ethic, and so inspiring a vision of human brotherhood, would be a miracle far more incredible than any recorded in the Gospels. After two centuries of Higher Criticism, the outlines of the life, character, and teaching of Christ remain reasonably clear, and constitute the most fascinating creature in the history of Western man.*"

From *Caesar and Christ*, in *The Story of Civilization*, by American historian Will Durant (1885–1981)

This suggests either that Matthew had Mark's Greek text in front of him or that both authors drew on a stream of oral tradition that was preserved in Greek, not a Semitic language. This leads most modern scholars to believe that Matthew, like Mark, originally wrote his Gospel in Greek. His was certainly the most popular of all the Gospels, and it was from Matthew's Gospel—in Greek—that the earliest church fathers such as Ignatius of Antioch and Polycarp, martyred at Smyrna in Asia Minor about 156, quoted. To them and to most of the other early Christian theologians, Matthew's Gospel was the most authoritative. It commanded a status as the first book of the New Testament that it retains to this day.

Matthew's Gospel has traditionally been ascribed to the tax collector whom Jesus called to be one of the Twelve because his Gospel is the only one of the Synoptic three to give the name Matthew to the tax collector (Mark and Luke both call him Levi). This traditional ascription may not be correct, but it is certain that Matthew's Gospel, the most Jewish in flavor of the four, had an author thoroughly steeped in Jewish religiosity and learning. The very name "Matthew" is a variant of the name Mattathias, the father of the Jewish hero Judas Maccabeus, and many of the Jews of Jesus' time named their male children after the Maccabean warriors. Matthew seemed to have received an education similar to that of the Pharisees, the predecessors of the rabbis, for his Gospel, unlike Mark's, is filled with direct quotations from Jewish Scripture, some apparently translated directly from the Hebrew. He is writing as a Jew for other Jews.

Although Matthew follows Mark's story line, he nearly always shortens Mark's narratives into more concise versions—except for the story of Jesus' Passion, where Matthew's version closely tracks that of Mark, with only a few minor variations. That means that Matthew eliminates many of Mark's vivid details, and his Gospel lacks Mark's dramatic flair. Furthermore, Matthew intersperses the stories with large blocks of Jesus' teachings, such as the Sermon on the Mount, which may actually be a compilation of a number of shorter instructions by Jesus rather than a single long homily. He also presents Jesus' parables, other discourses, and miracles in clumps of three, five, and seven. Matthew is a systematizer.

That is because Matthew is not as interested in drama as he is in teaching. He is definitely working in the rabbinic tradition. And there is a kind of rabbinic goal for that teaching: Matthew wants to show us that Jesus is the Jewish Messiah, the long-awaited descendant of David whose mission is to establish God's kingdom on earth, which Matthew views as the Christian church (Matthew is the only Synoptic author to use the word "church.") That is the purpose of Matthew's frequent citations of Jewish Scripture, especially prophetic Scripture: Jesus is the fulfillment of all those messianic prophecies.

The Lord's Prayer—"thy kingdom come"—appears in Matthew's Gospel (Luke's Gospel has it, too, but in a shorter version). So do the Beatitudes, the list of the attributes of those who will inherit the kingdom. His seventeen parables,

The Gospels of Matthew and Mark record two events involving a miraculous multiplication of loaves and fishes, one in which five thousand are fed, the other four thousand. Some critics say this evidences a careless attempt to exaggerate the powers of Jesus because it's actually the same miracle. Others reply that if the story were made up, why wouldn't the author have simply eliminated one of them to make it more credible? And why are the locales different, with one in Jewish and the other in Gentile territory?

ten of them unique to him, also center on God's kingdom. He compares it to a pearl of great price, to a tiny mustard seed that grows into a great plant, to a net thrown into the sea that brings up both good and bad fish. There is an admonitory element in all of this: Jesus' followers must choose for or against the kingdom, and prepare themselves for a final judgment in which the good will be rewarded and the evil rejected.

Because Matthew has as his goal demonstrating that Jesus is Messiah and King, he begins his Gospel with a genealogy, modeled on the genealogies of the Hebrew patriarchs in the Book of Genesis that link Jesus to the royal house of David through his putative father, Joseph. But Matthew also makes it clear that Jesus' true father is God himself, and that Mary, Jesus' mother, conceived her child virginally, fulfilling the Septuagint version of a passage in the book of Isaiah predicting that a virgin would bear a son.

Matthew relates that Jesus, although he was raised in Nazareth in Galilee, was born in Bethlehem in Judea, David's own city. He tells the story of the Magi from the East who follow a great star to visit Jesus soon after his birth and give him kingly presents of gold, frankincense, and myrrh, revealing his royalty and divinity to the Gentile world, and of the jealousy of the Judean king at the time, Herod the Great, who slaughters all the baby boys in Bethlehem because he fears a possible rival, forcing Jesus' family to seek temporary sanctuary in Egypt.

A crowd gathers to sing hymns on a spot where Jesus may have preached the Sermon on the Mount to another crowd two thousand years earlier. Matthew describes the place as a mountainside, Luke as a "level place." The hillside here with the Sea of Galilee meets the descriptions of both, especially if one considers that the word used by Luke is not the usual one for plain and may indeed have meant simply even ground.

Similarly, in his narration of Jesus' ministry, Matthew uses the Torah, the Jewish Law contained in the first five books of the Hebrew Bible, to present a Jesus who is the definitive interpreter of the Torah, one of the roles of the messiah. "You are the light of the world," Jesus tells his disciples, who are to be his church. Much of what he teaches is good Jewish teaching—that his followers are to honor their father in heaven and love one another—but Jesus goes further, ultimately making enemies out of the Pharisees, the rabbis, whose values and teaching style have so much in common with his.

Jesus boldly defines himself, not only as teacher of the Torah but as fulfillment of the Torah. In fact, in Matthew's Gospel, he proclaims himself to be the very personification of the Torah—a blasphemy certain to scandalize pious Jews. Jesus is Immanuel (God with us), he is the *shekinah*, the presence of God, and he is Divine Wisdom, present at the creation of the world in the Jewish Scriptures and inspiration of prophets and wise men. Using the holiest symbols of Judaism, Matthew, a Jew himself, shockingly places Jesus at the very center of Judaism as Messiah, king, and, finally, Lord, which in Jewish theology is a substitute for the name of God himself. Because of this portrayal of Jesus as a human being who is also divine, Matthew has traditionally been depicted in art accompanied by a winged man.

The name ascribed to the third Synoptic Gospel, Lucas (in Greek, *Loukas*), is probably an abbreviation of Lucanus, a popular men's name in Hellenistic times. Tradition holds that Luke was born in Antioch and perhaps, like Matthew, wrote his Gospel in that city. Paul describes him as the "beloved physician" in his letter to the Colossians (4:14) giving rise to the customary designation of Luke as a doctor. Whatever his formal training, he was clearly an educated, cosmopolitan man, at ease in the many countries to which he traveled. He wrote in an elegant, cultivated Greek with occasional literary allusions, and he consciously adopted different styles of writing to suit his subject matter. In the manner of other classical writers, he had a patron, Theophilus, to whom he dedicated both his Gospel and the Acts of the Apostles, the first history, or partial history, of the earliest church, which follows the Gospels in the New Testament. He probably had his Gospel published for sale in the Hellenistic book market.

Although Luke's Gospel is the longest, exceeding Matthew's by about ten percent, that is not because Luke wasted words. He wrote sparely and concisely to bring his characters to life in brief sketches. His writing is crammed with action, anecdotes, and personalities (including such characters as Eutychus, a youth from Troas who dozed off during one of Paul's sermons, fell out of a third-story window, and had to be revived miraculously after landing). Luke never seems slow reading. Although it is almost certain that Luke was a Gentile, he revered Judaism and knew its Scriptures very well in their Greek Septuagint version. This was not uncommon among Gentile intellectuals, many of whom admired Judaism's monotheism and strong moral sensibility. We can imagine that Luke came to Christianity through his exposure to Judaism.

Skeptical scholars once suggested that Luke invented the imperial census in his nativity story, the event that drove Mary and Joseph from their home in Nazareth many miles south to Bethlehem just before Jesus' birth. But that, too, has received archaeological confirmation, at least as far as its procedures were concerned. During the 1970s, excavations at desert caves near the Dead Sea unearthed a letter describing the journey that an early second-century Jewish woman named Babata had taken with her husband from their hometown south of the Dead Sea to Rabbat in what is now Jordan, to comply with a census order. The letter uses exactly the same Greek word—*apographestai*, "to be registered"—that Luke used in his Gospel. Such censuses and property registrations that took years to complete were an annoying administrative feature of the Roman world, and arduous journeys for those obliged to register were common.

One of the eyewitnesses with whom Luke might have talked was Mary

The three Synoptics give various names to the site of Christ's casting out of demons into a herd of swine. One of the candidates is the cliff near Kursi (above). All have been discounted because they are not directly on the Sea of Galilee, into which the pigs are said to have rushed and drowned. However, none of the evangelists specifically puts the "steep bank" immediately adjacent to the lake. And indeed all the sites have precipices and a legitimate historical potential to be the location of the exorcism.

herself, who, according to tradition, lived in Jerusalem for many years after Jesus' death and whom Luke could have met while accompanying Paul on his journey there. Luke, like Matthew, includes the story of Jesus' birth in his Gospel, but it is a very different story, focusing on Mary and Jesus' early family life (Luke is the one who informs us that John the Baptist was Jesus' cousin). His informant on these matters could well have been Mary, and we can imagine the long conversations the two might have had together on Jerusalem evenings.

Luke went so far as to make Mary the heroine of the first two chapters in his Gospel, telling the story largely from her point of view: her encounter with the angel Gabriel in which she agreed to Jesus' conception; her visit to her cousin Elizabeth, the Baptist's mother; her giving birth to Jesus in a stable; her taking him to the Temple in Jerusalem to be circumcised and later, presented; her trip again to the Temple with a large extended family when Jesus was twelve. Luke's is the only Synoptic Gospel in which Mary speaks.

Those two opening chapters are also the most Jewish in Luke's narrative; their style echoes that of the Jewish scriptures, and they depict scene after scene of Jewish family piety. Indeed, Mary is a personification of the people of Israel, awaiting their deliverance and finally receiving it in Jesus; in her long prayer in those chapters, the *Magnificat*, she carols: "He has helped his servant Israel in remembrance of his mercy."

Luke "the historian" is shown with Paul (on the right) and Mary the mother of Jesus. Luke's interview with Mary probably occurred when he was in Jerusalem with Paul. This would have provided him with the nativity and childhood narratives for his Gospel. The scrolls of other records of Jesus' deeds and sayings are examined in the presence of another potential firsthand witness, a shepherd.

COLLIER

Luke was more than a historian, however; he was a supremely gifted storyteller. His Gospel is the sole source of Jesus' most affecting parables: the prodigal son, the good Samaritan, the rich man who went to hell because he refused to feed the beggar Lazarus. Luke also told of moving, real-life encounters with Jesus that are to be found in no other Gospel: the penitent woman who washes Jesus' feet with her tears and wipes them dry with her hair; the short-statured Zacchaeus, who climbs a sycamore tree to get a good look at Jesus; the "good thief" on the cross next to Jesus who begs to be let into his kingdom when he dies; the two sojourners who mourn Jesus' death but encounter him after the Resurrection sharing supper with them at Emmaus. The theme of these stories is always God's infinite mercy and Jesus' infinite sympathy for the poor, the helpless, the sick, the sinners, and the bereaved.

Luke had a wry sense of irony and humor, too. It is hard not to smile when he tells us that Pilate tried to palm off the responsibility for Jesus' trial onto Herod Antipas, the sly and ambitious son of Herod the Great: "When Herod saw Jesus he was very glad, for . . . he was hoping to see him perform some miracle." Luke empathized strongly with women, and his Gospel offers vivid glimpses of many of Jesus' female followers besides Mary: the penitent woman, a widow at Nain whose dead son Jesus raised, the sisters Martha and Mary who fed Jesus at their house. So skilled were Luke's word-portraits of the huge cast of characters in his Gospel that he was thought to be a painter as well as a physician.

More than Mark and Matthew, Luke's Gospel focuses attention on Jerusalem, where Jesus is shown as an infant, a child, and the man filled with the Holy Spirit who must inexorably go there and die. Jesus' sacrificial death not far from the Temple to bring deliverance to Israel is the climax of the narrative. For that reason, Luke has been traditionally depicted in art accompanied by an ox, a victim of sacrifice. ∎

An undependable liberal

Honest John Robinson, the bishop who appalled the conservatives, makes a well-documented case that no academic has answered for a much earlier and more credible New Testament

John A. T. Robinson, the late-twentieth-century Anglican bishop of Woolwich in England, was without doubt an ecclesiastical maverick. A biblical scholar, a Cambridge University chaplain, and a devout socialist, he became a darling of liberal theology in the 1960s when he published a book called *Honest to God*. The book, said popular reviewers, abandoned the old dogmas of Christianity and launched forth on a new view that man should no longer seek the Deity "out there," but within himself. Celebrated in the media, the book became an international best-seller.

On whether *Honest to God* actually did all these things, less superficial readers later cast grave doubts, as did the bishop himself, who, nevertheless, became thereafter known as "Honest

John Robinson." What there could be no doubt about was his next bombshell, this one a book on the dating of the New Testament. But it leaned in a very different theological direction, and, therefore, received almost no media attention. So the bombshell never went off. All it did was persuade academe that Honest John was not a dependable liberal.

At the dawn of the twenty-first century, though Bishop Robinson was now dead, the time bomb was still ticking, while conventional biblical academics tiptoed uneasily around it. For should its assertions ever gain reputability, it would force them to scrap most late-twentieth-century scholarship.

He called his new book simply *Redating the New Testament*, and in it he delivered an unfashionable answer

Bishop John A. T. Robinson

to a question that had puzzled biblically knowledgeable laymen for years. Since not a single book in the New Testament makes any reference to the fact that Jerusalem and its Temple were demolished by the Romans in A.D. 70, is it not probable that all the books of the New Testament were written before that date? The most plausible explanation for this staggering omission, surely, is that the event itself had not yet happened, and all the books therefore predate A.D. 70.

The response of biblical academe seemed always to come down to a "Tut, tut." Practically the whole body of biblical scholarship is agreed, came the answer, that the books of the New Testament were written between roughly A.D. 55 and 100. There was monumental evidence to support this, it was said. That evidence, however monumental, was rarely if ever produced.

The point, of course, directly affects the credibility of the books, since the closer are their dates of origin to the events they describe, the

more probable it is that they are the accounts of firsthand witnesses, not some reminiscence of what those witnesses passed on to others in a succeeding generation. It's the difference between, "I saw . . ." and "So-and-So once told me he saw. . . ."

The bishop tackles this phenomenon of scholarly unanimity in the opening pages of *Redating*. True, he says, the whole body of biblical scholarship puts the dates at roughly A.D. 55 to 100. But then, back in 1850 the whole body of biblical scholarship put the dates at A.D. 50 to 170. By 1900 the body was putting the dates at A.D. 50 to 140, and by 1950 at A.D. 50 to 125.

"One takes heart as one watches the way in which established positions can suddenly, or subtly, come to be seen as the precarious constructions they are. What seemed to be firm datings based on scientific evidence are revealed to rest on deductions from deductions. . . . Question some of the inbuilt assumptions and the entire edifice looks much less secure."

Question, therefore, the bishop did—the dating of St. Paul's Epistles, of the Gospels, of the Acts of the Apostles, and of Revelation and the dating also of certain other early Christian writings, in particular the *Didache*, a manual of Christian morality traditionally assumed to have appeared around the end of the first century.

He also questioned the explanations of "the oddest fact" that there is no mention of the fall of Jerusalem anywhere in these works. He notes immediately that he isn't the first scholar to call attention to this curious phenomenon. James Moffatt describes Jerusalem's fall as "epoch-making."

Scholar C. F. D. Moule wonders why, if the books were all written after A.D. 70, that the Christians didn't make more out of it. He writes: "It is hard to believe that a Judaistic type of Christianity . . . would not have made capital out of this signal evidence that they, and not non-Christian Judaism, were the true Israel."

The scholar Bo Reicke observes: "An amazing example of uncritical dogmatism in New Testament studies is the belief that the Synoptic Gospels should be dated after The Jewish War of 66–70 because they contain prophecies *ex eventu* (arising out of the event, or made after the event) of the destruction of Jerusalem by the Romans in the year 70." He observes that the conclusion seems to have been spontaneously drawn. Because Jesus prophesied the city's fall, and modern people know that predictions of this sort are not possible, the account of his prophecy must have been written after 70. Such is the reasoning.

It would be like concluding, says a British journalist quoted by the bishop, that Winston Churchill's warnings back in 1934 of the impending Second World War must have actually been made after 1939, because that's when the war started.

Moreover, Jesus' prophecy for the Temple and city goes notably unfulfilled as reported. If the account had been written after the event, why would these inaccuracies not have been amended? Or again, what of Jesus' assertion that "some here will not taste death until the Kingdom of God has come" (Matt. 16:28; Mark 9:1; Luke 9:27)? If this had not been written for sixty or so years after he said it,

numerous of the hearers would definitely be dead. So why would some modification of the prophecy not have been made?

Or, as in the Epistle to the Hebrews, the entire text describes the ceremonies at the Temple in the present tense, as then going on. Ah, comes the response, this is also true of other accounts of the Temple written long after it was destroyed. The writers simply describe the rites as they had been ordained to take place.

True enough, in some instances, replies the bishop, but what about a sentence like this from the epistle's 10th chapter: "[T]hese sacrifices would surely have ceased to be offered because the worshippers, cleansed once for all, would no longer have any sense of sin." If the sacrifices had already ceased, writes the bishop, "it is hard to credit that these words would have stood without modification or comment."

In conclusion, Robinson sets out his own dates for the composition of the New Testament books, all of them predating 70. He puts the *Didache* back into the 30s, just a few years after the Crucifixion.

Curiously, as Robinson published his conclusions in Britain, similar contentions began appearing in France. The biblical scholar Jean Carmignac published *The Birth of the Synoptics*, and, soon after, Claude Tresmontant came out with *The Hebrew Christ: Language in the Age of the Gospels.* By translating the Gospels from Greek into Hebrew, Carmignac discovered enough Semitic word plays and stylistic peculiarities to conclude that Mark and Matthew had been written in Hebrew or Aramaic originally and later translated into Greek.

Using both retro-translation and archaeological methods, Tresmontant concluded that even the Greek text of the Gospel of John (which he dated to

Carmignac and Tresmontant met with a barrage of criticism from the scholarly establishment, which denounced both men for abandoning the established methods of the discipline. Their defenders replied that they were not

The symbols of the four evangelists are a recurrent theme in Christian art appearing in paintings, on Gospel Book covers, and on pulpits. At the Chartres cathedral in France they surround the image of Christ in Majesty over the Royal Portal. They are (clockwise from bottom left) the lion of Mark, the winged man of Matthew, the eagle for John, and Luke's ox.

36–40, even earlier than Robinson) was first written in Hebrew, as was Matthew, whose Greek translation dates to the late forties. Carmignac assigns (Semitic) Mark to 42–50, (Greek) Luke to ca.50–60, and the first drafts of (Semitic) Matthew, which may have been a source for Luke, to the early forties, with its final Semitic form and subsequent Greek translation to the late fifties and early sixties.

Unlike Robinson's efforts, those of

abandoning it, but trying to enlarge it through the device of retro-translation. Some scholars agreed with them; most did not.

Meanwhile, throughout the twentieth century, earlier and earlier copies of the New Testament, or parts of it, kept appearing, thereby improving its credibility. The earliest texts of the historian Tacitus's *Annals of Imperial Rome*, for instance, date back to the tenth century, though

Tacitus actually wrote this in the second. The earliest existing copy, that is, was produced eight hundred years after the original. As for the classical Greeks—Plato, Aristotle, Euripides, Aristophanes, Thucydides, Homer—

with one exception, no copies of any of their works survive from earlier than one thousand years after the originals were written. The exception is Homer, whose *Iliad* exists, in part, in a manuscript dating from five hundred years after he wrote it.

The situation with the books of the New Testament is very different. Textual discoveries during the twentieth century, rather than eroding the credibility of the New Testament recurrently strengthened

it. Papyrus manuscripts have been found that date from 130 to 200, as little as eighty years from the surmised date of composition. There are some eighty other manuscripts of the New Testament that were also written on fragile papyrus, another three thousand on parchment, which replaced papyrus in the fourth century. Altogether, scholars have more than five thousand early manuscripts of the New Testament in Greek, eight thousand in Latin, and hundreds in other languages. There is simply no other ancient document for which the archaeological and scholarly trail leading back to the original is as broad, detailed, well maintained and authenticated.

All of which opens a question: Why has the direction of scholarship been increasingly toward skepticism when the direction of the evidence had been increasingly toward validation? Why, in particular, do scholars ignore the contentions such as those of Bishop Robinson for a much earlier dating of the New Testament?

The bishop himself suggested an answer to that last question: "Each new student enters a field already marked out for him by datelines which modesty as well as sloth prompts him to accept, and having accepted, to preserve," he writes. The student, that is, takes up the dating of the New Testament in his earliest and most inexperienced years. "This has a formative effect, for good or for ill, on all his subsequent work." He adopts, that is, the assumptions of his professors and never challenges them. ■

Whether they are the product of his fascination with theater or his gradual drift into lunacy, Nero's antics draw the raucous approval of his guests. Dressed as a Roman bride, the emperor "weds" a young lothario whom, for the entertainment of his guests, he then seduces. The squalid profligacy of the imperial court and "high society" contrasts sharply with the impeccability to which Rome's small but growing Christian community aspires.

CHAPTER 8

Confrontation with the diabolical

The Christians had known persecution before, but in Nero they meet the man who gives evil a whole new meaning

During the first six decades of the first century A.D., Christians were no strangers to cruel treatment. They had in their collective lore and memory the story of Herod's massacre of the children at Bethlehem, the stoning to death of Stephen at Jerusalem, and the execution of the apostle James, son of Zebedee and brother of John. Paul had been repeatedly beaten. Finally, of course, Jesus had died by crucifixion.

Yet, in the year A.D. 64, they were to encounter cruelty on an altogether new and unimaginably evil plane. Herod the Great could at least justify his infanticidal order on the grounds of public security. A peasant movement formed around some mystically destined infant would almost certainly become political, he might have reasoned, and thousands of innocent people would, as usual, perish. Better to lose a few infants and put an end to it forthwith, he might have told himself; in any event, he did not revel in the details of the slaughter or make a point of witnessing it. Similarly, the high priest Caiaphas, who condemned Jesus, contended with some logic that it was "expedient that one man should die for the people"(John 11:50 RSV). And Pontius Pilate, though he caved in when his career was threatened, at least tried to fight for justice and gave every evidence, including washing his hands symbolically in public, of disgust at the crucifixion that was about to take place.

Now, however, the Christians met cruelty, not just as a byproduct of harsh policy or political expediency, but as cruelty for its own sake. Pain was inflicted for the sheer joy of inflicting it, as an entertainment, a crowd-pleaser, an orgy of brutality so horrific that they would identify the man who inflicted this upon them as ultimate evil incarnate. The Christians at Rome, in the little community to whom Paul, some seven years before, had addressed his famous letter, were to be the victims, and their appalling fate would strike horror in Christ's followers all over the empire.

The Christians, like everyone else in Rome, had heard unsettling stories about the emperor Nero—his ribald parties, his irrational cruelty, his grandiose public exhibitionism. They believed, too, that Rome had not always been like this. Perhaps out of idealistic reminiscence of a noble past, traditionalist Romans harkened back to a time when the city, and particularly its patrician citizens, had seemed to stand for integrity, honesty, rectitude, valor, and even, despite the Roman penchant for bloodshed, justice.

But that was the Rome of an earlier era, the Rome that, like so many ancient cities, revered a past wrapped in mythology. In the myth describing Rome's origin, twin infants, Romulus and Remus, abandoned by their parents, were suckled by wolves. Romulus killed his brother in a

This model of Rome, A.D. 72–82 (viewed from the north) shows just the western portions of the city—albeit the half with most of the public buildings.

petty quarrel and later went on to found the city. The scholar Varro (166–127 B.C.) sets that date at 753 B.C., thereafter the standard starting line for Roman history. Some seven centuries later, the city had become the capital of a vast empire.

Rome evolved out of antiquity as a republic, with at least some power vested in a senate consisting of patrician elders and a number of tribunes representing the common citizenry, the plebeians, though the aristocracy always maintained a firmly controlling hand. From about 90 to 31 B.C., the old republic endured a bloody civil war and emerged, after the dictatorship and assassination of the genius general Julius Caesar, as an imperial autocracy, with Caesar succeeded in

The storied Seven Hills upon which Rome was built (merely high points in the surrounding marshes) seem little better than hummocks or rock outcroppings today. The Palatine (center of background), for example, is unprepossessing, serving more as a backdrop for the Arch of Constantine than a point of interest in and of itself. These humble foundations certainly were no indicator of the splendor that was to be imperial Rome.

31 by his adopted nephew, the emperor Augustus. Augustus founded the empire that would ultimately recognize, but at first ferociously resist, the faith to be known as Christianity.[1]

Augustus reigned until A.D. 14, presiding over an era of unprecedented peace. Though he had been a ruthless general, he seemingly tried to sustain the perceived purity of the old republic, issuing decrees to raise the level of morality,

---

1. Among other mementos Julius and Augustus Caesar bequeathed to humanity were new names for the fifth and six months of the old Roman calendar. March (Martius), originally the first month of the year, had been named for Mars, the war god. Then came Aprilis (probably from the Latin *aperire*, to open, as did the growing season); Maius, after Maia, the goddess mother of Mercury and Jupiter; and Junius, for Juno, the chief Roman goddess. Quintilis, from the Latin for "fifth," came next, but was renamed Julius in honor of Caesar; Sextilis, Latin for "sixth," was renamed in honor of Augustus; Septem, Octo, Novem and Decem, Latin for seven, eight, nine and ten, followed in the names of the next four months (September, October, November and December); Janus, the Roman god of doors, beginnings, sunset and sunrise, whose two faces looked in opposite directions, gave his name to the eleventh month, Januarius; and Februarius (from Februa, the purifications that occur during this month), on whose fifteenth day the Romans celebrated the festival of forgiveness, was last, although by the first centuries B.C. and A.D., Januarius and Februarius had become the first and second months of the year.

In his capacity as Pontifex Maximus (chief of the council of priests), Augustus personified and stood before the gods and citizens as Rome itself. This first-century statue of the emperor has him veiled as he would have been to preside at priestly rituals such as those at the Ara Pacis—Altar of Peace (right). Commissioned by the Senate in 13 B.C. to commemorate the triumphs of Augustus in Spain and Gaul, it was reconstructed in the 1930s. The altar, now housed in a special museum, is an imposing edifice whose grand dimensions (nineteen and a half feet high by thirty-six feet square) are displayed in this view taken inside the museum that houses it.

encouraging literature and the arts, building an artificial lake[2] and an Altar of Peace[3] as well as three new aqueducts to bring water to the million or more inhabitants of the great city of Rome.

More pertinently for the Christians who would emerge in the following generation, Augustus tried to renew Rome's ancient pagan religion, rebuilding temples and reviving rites for the whole plethora of gods and goddesses. Both the Romans and Greeks viewed their deities as inhabiting a supernatural society that occasionally intervened in the lives of mortal men. Julius Caesar had declared himself a god, an innovation that may have contributed to his eventual assassination. Augustus, more cautious, allowed himself to be worshiped as a god in the East, but merely to receive sacrifices in the West. Thereafter, many of the emperors associated themselves closely with the divine and demanded that sacrifices be made to their genius or greatness, a demand that in the coming years would cost the lives of hundreds of Christians because they refused to meet it.

As gods, however, even if they were not so proclaimed until after their deaths, Augustus's immediate successors left much to be desired. Following Augustus, the dynasty began a fifty-five-year descent into depravity. Tiberius, his successor, was in his mid-years an altogether competent administrator, but according to his later chroniclers, slid as a graybeard into lechery and pederasty, setting up a lavish bordello of erotic perversion for his own entertainment, and

---

2. Augustus's artificial lake was eighteen hundred feet long and twelve hundred feet wide, big enough for opposing fleets of ships manned by slaves and criminals to conduct actual and deadly battles to entertain the Roman crowd. One of Nero's exhibitions utilized nineteen thousand men and one hundred ships.

3. Augustus dedicated his Altar of Peace (Ara Pacis) on January 30, 9 B.C., to mark the success of his tireless campaign to restore civil order throughout the empire. Its original site was in the Via Flaminia, now the Corso under Rome's Palazzo Fiano at the southwest corner of the Via in Lucina. Lost for more than one thousand years, the Roman sacrificial altar, enclosed in a screen of parian marble, carved in high relief with allegorical and ceremonial scenes, was reassembled between the sixteenth and twentieth centuries—it was completed in the 1930s—and at the dawn of the twenty-first century stood in a specially constructed building near the Tiber, close to the Mausoleum of Augustus.

sexually abusing children down to the years of infancy.

Next came Gaius, nicknamed from his childhood soldier-playing games as "Little Boots" or Caligula, who began in his early youth an incestuous relationship with his three sisters, all of whom he would later farm out as prostitutes to his bawdy friends. Caligula came to power at age twenty-four, and after two years of efficient administration, was felled by a severe illness that transformed the character of his reign. Now showing every sign of being mentally disturbed, he was rumored to have built a palace for his horse, equipping it with a staff of slaves, and to have announced plans to have the animal made consul of Rome. After three years, ten months and eight days of such behavior, a group of conspirators closed the door to keep spectators out, ran swords through his breast and genitals, and quietly burned his body.

This placed the stammering, eccentric, fifty-year-old Claudius on the imperial throne, through haphazard coincidence. The troops stationed at Rome, first in jest and then in earnest, carried him in horrified terror to their camp and

Augustus's successors left much to be desired. The dynasty began a fifty-five-year descent into depravity, starting with Tiberius, continuing through Caligula, and culminating in Nero.

proclaimed him emperor. While far less distinguished for sexual extravaganza than his predecessors, Claudius gained a reputation for sadistic cruelty.

Though some of his rulings, such as his intervention in the conflict between Jews and Alexandrians, appeared to be wise and balanced, he rarely missed an execution and took delight in watching the condemned die painfully. He also manifested unpleasant physical traits, twitching at the head, foaming at the mouth and trickling from the nose when angry, his weak knees collapsing under him when he walked.

When Claudius died in A.D. 54, Romans hoped for something better. What they got was something worse—in the eyes of some, the most sordid monster of them all—and none were to discover this more hideously than the tiny Roman community already called by the name Christian.

Lucius Domitius Ahenobarbus, known to history as Nero, was born in December of 37 in Antium.[4] He appeared just as the fledgling Jewish sect called "The Way" was encountering the rising hostility of Jewish authorities in Jerusalem.

Nero's family history, true enough, did not encourage confidence. Ancient, noble, prestigious, and highly accomplished, his family nevertheless had a reputation for ostentatious cruelty, debauchery, and sexual perversion. Gladiatorial contests staged by his grandfather became so vicious that Augustus ordered them stopped. His father rather specialized in avarice, adultery, and

---

4. Antium, thirty miles south of Rome on the coast of the Tyrrhenian Sea, and birthplace of the emperor Nero, would enter into world history nineteen centuries later under its new name, Anzio. There on January 22, 1944, forty thousand Allied troops landed in an attempt to outflank the German Gustav Line to the south, which was obstructing the Allied advance. The maneuver failed. Allied casualties were very high and it took four more months for the Allied troops to take Rome.

incest. His mother, the ambitious and wanton Agrippina, had such a varied roster of courtiers that when she announced her pregnancy, her husband, presumably considering his own licentious record, declared that any child of himself and Agrippina would become a monstrosity and a curse on the state. He was to prove correct on both counts.

Yet, as a youth of sixteen when he came to the throne, Nero inspired confidence. Fair-haired, blue-eyed, he had been tutored by the venerable Seneca, the preeminent Stoic philosopher of the day—tutored, according to the historian Dio Cassius, not only in philosophy but also in pederasty, sex with young men or boys. His perverse education notwithstanding, his mother, Agrippina, had persuaded the reigning Claudius to betroth his daughter Octavia to her son, thereby assuring him the succession.

Styling himself Nero Claudius Caesar Drusus Germanicus, he announced an impressive agenda. He would improve public order, curtail forgery, and reform the treasury. Even his enemies agree that Nero's first five years were marked with some creditable accomplishments. He forbade provincial governors from exploiting locals during gladiatorial shows, and he worked hard at his judicial duties. But most of his reforms went nowhere. He abolished indirect taxes and promptly saw direct taxes increasing. He forbade Praetorian Guardsmen from attending circuses and theaters, only to see unruly spectators, now unpoliced, spread havoc. He tried to prohibit the public killing of gladiators, but had to back down when a bloodthirsty public loudly demanded its return.

He was himself an irrepressible enter-

The career of Lucius Domitius Ahenobarbus, better known as Nero (center) the first Roman emperor to order the mass executions of Christians, was ruthlessly promoted by his mother, Agrippina (far right), granddaughter of one emperor and widow of another. Nero eventually had her murdered at the instigation of his second wife, Poppaea Sabina (below), whom Nero later also put to death.

tainer. He wrote poetry, acted in skits at the palace, and sang and danced before family and close friends. Many in the public found him fascinating and even admirable, in the way that any accomplished performer is admirable. Soon, however, his fondness for celebrity ran rampant. In his increasingly elaborate public banquets, it was said, he used the whole city as his private house.

The historian Tacitus, a highly skilled author with a keen eye for the corruption of power, describes one extravaganza of Nero's that, he writes, was typical. The festivities took place on a lake, populated with exotic birds, fish, and other animals imported for the occasion. Guests were floated out on rafts, with crews "arranged according to age and experience in vice." On one side of the lake were brothels crowded with noble ladies (doing exactly what, Tacitus does not specify); on the other, naked prostitutes tried to lure guests. As darkness descended, torches were lit, and the groves and buildings resounded with song and laughter. The emperor, dressed in drag, pretended to marry a man named Pythagoras—and then, in front of the guests, consummated the "marriage."

Even Nero's Rome, long fallen from any hint of republican rectitude, became appalled, though fascinated, by the tales of imperial conduct—his allegedly erotic relationship with his mother, Agrippina (actually consummated, writes Tacitus, though no one knows whether mother or son initiated it), and his liaison with his fourteen-year-old stepbrother Britannicus.

The Britannicus affair ended badly. Nero arranged to have him poisoned at a banquet. Not to worry, he told his guests as the youth lay writhing on the floor. It was just epilepsy. Britannicus was carried in convulsions from the room to die a tortuous death, while the dinner party cheerily continued.

His most celebrated victim was his chief sponsor and champion, Agrippina, his mother. She was doomed, it was said, by Poppaea Sabina, a friend's wife and Nero's current paramour. Poppaea urged Nero to divorce Octavia and marry her, but knew that the powerful Agrippina would prevent it. So Poppaea taunted him. He was "the mere ward" of his parent, she said, a mother's boy. This worked. Nero began avoiding his mother, encouraging her to spend time away at her distant estates, finally plotting her death.

He staged a false reconciliation

party at his summer home at Baiae,[5] fondly embraced and kissed her, then sent her home across the Bay of Naples on a craft rigged to collapse at sea and drown her. The trick failed, she landed safely, and Nero panicked. "Paralyzed with terror," writes Tacitus, he feared she would discover the stratagem, arm her slaves, and assassinate him. Acting quickly, he dispatched an assistant and three high-ranking military men to her home. They beat her with clubs and ran her through with a sword.

However disgusting, even these things Rome's nobility could reluctantly stomach, because they went on in the relative privacy of the imperial circle. What they could not endure was the persona Nero presented publicly—his habit of dressing as a common slave as he meandered through Rome's darkened streets with a handful of equally decadent cronies, drinking, visiting brothels, stealing from shops, thrashing anyone who resisted or deplored them. Fistfights were common, Nero proudly showing off his wounds the next morning.

Worse still, as his nightly revels became known, others of Rome's elite began imitating him, rendering the city on some nights virtually lawless. His advisers delicately urged restraint. Perhaps, they suggested, His Excellency could, well, cut back a little—at least, say, on the poetry readings, the singing, the acting, the

Nero sent his mother home across the Bay of Naples in a boat rigged to collapse and drown her. The trick failed, she landed safely, and Nero, panicked, had to devise another plan quickly.

lyre recitals, which were causing him to lose whatever dignity remained to him and his office. His Excellency demurred. "Too small a scale for so fine a voice," he said. So in 64 A.D., he began performing on the stage publicly, with a debut at Neapolis, Greece, before a mostly Greek audience, then in Rome at the Neronian Games. He also began entering poetry and lyre-playing contests.

Rome's gentry, if not the masses, were horrified. "It was insufferable," writes Dio Cassius, a safe century and a half later, "to hear of a Roman, a caesar and emperor, an augustus, put his name on the list of competitors, exercise his voice, practice various songs, appear with long hair and smooth chin, with robe thrown back, present himself in the lists with only one or two attendants, stare savagely at his opponents, defy his rivals with abusive words, and then bribe the overseers in the games—all this to win a prize for lyre-playing."

Behind such fulminations lay the Roman elite's historic abhorrence of decline. Still deeply ingrained in the proud city's psyche were the high virtues and noble ways celebrated by the old republic, where family fidelity was outweighed only by duty to the *civitas*, the community itself. Nero's carryings-on were not merely

---

5. The ancient town on Baiae, named for Baios, the famed ancient navigator of Odysseus who died there, was located on a hillside near the northern tip of the Bay of Naples. Julius Caesar, Gaius and Nero had summer villas there, and Claudius built one for his wife. By the twenty-first century, little of this remained, and half of Baiae lay under water.

revolting and immoral. They were un-Roman! "This thick-necked, pot-bellied emperor with skinny legs," says the historian Suetonius, "was entirely shameless in style and appearance, always had his hair set in rows of curls, and when he visited Greece, he let his hair grow long and hang down his back. He often gave audiences in an unbelted silk dressing-gown and slippers, with a scarf around his neck." The foppish dress, the passion to perform, all this was unmanly, effeminate, essentially Greek. Romans did not behave in this way.

Though their roots were in the tenements of the Transtibiris, many Jews in Rome rose to wealth and status. This tombstone in the Jewish catacombs (left) marks the grave of a wealthy matron and her grandson. It reads, in Greek: "Here rest Primitiva and her grandson Euphrenon. May their sleep be in peace." Today's narrow alleys and crowded buildings of Rome's Jewish Quarter (right) seem only a few generations and construction techniques removed from the tenements of two thousand years ago.

Not in the days of the real Rome, anyway. Not in the days, two centuries past, when the republic had conquered its great rival Carthage, the other Mediterranean superpower. Yet it was that very victory over Carthage that began the republic's gradual decline. Very slowly, recalls the historian Richard E. Smith in *The Failure of the Roman Republic*, family priorities began to weaken, loose sexual relations and divorce became common, discipline in the army slackened, women became far more influential in high places, foreign religions and mystical cults proliferated in the capital city, government spending ran wild, and public debt soared.

Perhaps the most severe indictment of the squalor and degradation that seemed to overwhelm the Imperial Rome was written in the middle of the Neronian era. "God gave them up to degrading passions," it ran. "Their women exchanged natural intercourse for unnatural, and in the same way also the men, giving up natural intercourse with women, were consumed with passion for one another. God gave them up to a debased mind and to things that should not be done. They were filled with every kind of wickedness, evil covetousness, malice. Full of envy, murder, strife, deceit, craftiness; they are gossips, slanderers, God-haters, insolent, haughty, boastful, inventors of evil, rebellious toward parents, foolish, faithless, heartless, ruthless."

The author of that denunciation was a Roman citizen and proud of it, and his stern language in that regard would have been wholly endorsed by those who revered and loved the old republic. Yet he was not from the city but from Tarsus in Asia Minor. He was Paul, the Christian apostle to the Gentiles. His words in the opening chapter of the letter he addressed to the Christian community in the capital city disclosed a distinct irony. For the Christians, who would be despised and persecuted by Roman officialdom for most of the next three hundred years, in fact stood for nearly all the virtues and principles that Rome had once enshrined.

The Roman Christians lived a modest walk from Nero's palace, in a district just across the Tiber called Transtibiris. (Twenty centuries later, the Italians would call it Trastevere.) Many of Rome's Jews lived there too, and early Christianity was in general considered a Jewish religion.

In a small square of the Jewish quarter—across the Tiber River from the real Rome—Peter gathers hearers for his words of salvation. That Peter reached Rome and was martyred there is now accepted by nearly all historians, though nothing about his activities in the capital was recorded at the time. Early on, Christian influence crossed the Tiber and made itself felt in the imperial circle.

When the first Jews reached Rome is not known. There is some evidence of their presence in 139, and more after 63 B.C., when Pompey conquered Palestine and shipped off both prisoners of war and slaves to the capital. Within four years, Cicero was complaining about "how numerous" and "how clannish" they were, and "how they can make their influence felt." By the middle of the first century, their number had risen to forty or fifty thousand, making Rome's the second largest concentration of Jews outside Judea, after Alexandria.

By Paul's day, they were served by over a dozen synagogues, where it was likely the first converts to Christianity tried to convince their fellow Jews of Jesus' messiahship. Such endeavors may in fact have occurred in the mid-thirties, for the Acts of the Apostles notes that "visitors from Rome, both Jews and proselytes" attended the Pentecost Feast.

Perhaps the first evidence of a Christian presence emerges in Roman history in the year 57 A.D. Tacitus reports that Pomponia Graecina, wife of Aulus Plautius, the conqueror of Britain, was charged with subscribing to a "foreign superstition." A family court, presided over by her husband, acquitted her. By the end of the second century, some members of her family, the *gens Pomponia*, had become Christian and were buried in one of Rome's oldest Christian catacombs, lending a degree of credence to the theory that the "foreign supersti-

The Quo Vadis Legend

In his last trial, did Peter fail? An old tale says he did, then died heroically

The final years of Peter and Paul at Rome are shrouded in uncertainties. The last historical scriptural reference to Peter has him at the Council of Jerusalem advocating Paul's mission to the Gentiles (Acts 15). The last to Paul puts him at Rome awaiting trial before the emperor (Acts 28).

That both men perished there, probably in the Neronian persecution, is accepted by most historians, and church tradition, considerably strengthened by twentieth-century archaeology, identifies the places where each died and where each is buried. In addition to that, however, is a wealth of legend and mythology, most of it appearing 150 years after the apostles died.

The best known appears in the *Acts of Peter*, a third-century work that records that, when the Neronian persecution begins, Peter leaves the city rather than face crucifixion with other Christians in the Hippodrome. As he flees south along the Appian Way, he encounters Jesus walking toward the city. "*Quo vadis, Domine?*" he asks. "Where are you going, Lord?" Jesus, in what became known as the *Quo Vadis*

Legend, replies. "To Rome, to be crucified again." Peter, once again humiliated, thinks further, turns, and goes back to the city where, at his own request, he is crucified upside down, feeling himself unworthy of being crucified in the same way as his master.

In another legend, quoted by Clement of Alexandria, Peter's wife is executed before he is. He bids her farewell, saying that he is glad that at last she is returning home. "My dear," he says, "remember the Lord."

Even within the realm of the historical, the documentation of facts is sparse. The first specific mention of Paul's fate comes in a letter from a Roman priest or presbyter named Gaius, written late in the second century. It places the tomb of St. Paul near the Ostian Gate of the city and that of Peter on Vatican Hill. Monuments were erected by the Christians at both these sites in the time of the emperor Marcus Aurelius, about A.D. 160.

The apocryphal *Acts of Paul*, written about the same time, gives the site of Paul's martyrdom as three miles

tion" was indeed Christianity.

There may have been other highly placed Christians early on. Paul, in his letter to the Romans (16:11), mentions a certain Narcissus, possibly Tiberius Claudius Narcissus, a senior government officeholder under both Tiberius and Claudius, later executed by Nero at the insistence of Agrippina. In the same chapter of his letter Paul greets "the household of Aristobulus," a name common in the family of Herod the Great.[6]

Though Gentiles joined the

down the Tiber from Rome, at a place identified as Aquae Salviae, just off the road to the port of Ostia on the Via Laurentia. He was buried, says this report, at the home of a Christian matron named Lucina, and the body was later exhumed and moved to the site identified by Gaius.

In twenty-first-century Rome there are therefore two sites commemorating St. Paul, one at his traditional place of execution, the site of the Church of the *Tre Fontane*, three fountains, which memorializes the legend that when his head fell under the sword it bounced three times; at each point a fountain of water sprang up.

The second is the place usually recognized as Paul's tomb, where Constantine erected a small memorial church early in the fourth century. This was replaced by a more substantial building late in the same century which survived for nearly fifteen hundred years before it burned down in 1823. In excavations for a third church on the site, a large, flat stone was discovered that bore the letters, *Pavlo Apostolo Mart*, "Paul Apostle and Martyr." Scholars

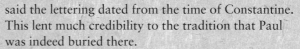

Legend or not, Peter's encounter with Jesus as the apostle attempts to escape certain death is a powerful story. "Where are you going, Lord?" the legend has him ask (in Latin, 'Quo vadis, Domine?'). "To Rome, to be crucified again," comes the reply, as Jesus walks past Peter, past the faithful Christians already crucified along the Appian Way, and to Rome. Shamed, Peter returns to the city and to his death.

said the lettering dated from the time of Constantine. This lent much credibility to the tradition that Paul was indeed buried there.

Peter is assumed to have been crucified in the Hippodrome, which stood on Vatican hill beneath the towering Caligula Obelisk, brought by the emperor Gaius Caligula from Heliopolis in Egypt. The body was buried nearby. In 1586, the Obelisk, by then crowned with a cross, was moved a short distance to St. Peter's Square, where it stands today. ■

movement too, Roman Christianity from the start reflected its Jewish origins. Hippolytus's *Apostolic Tradition*, a third-century manual of church order in Rome, describes practices patterned on Jewish rites. An anonymous fourth-century Latin commentator (whom scholars for convenience call Ambrosiaster) said the first Roman Christians embraced the faith before they saw any of the apostles, though later both Peter and Paul played key roles in the growth of the Roman Church. Catholic and Eastern Orthodox tradition claims Peter as Rome's first bishop.[7] Paul's arrival there is well documented by the Acts of the Apostles, and can be reliably dated to about 60, about three years after he wrote his letter to the faithful at Rome.

Paul's letter shows that Rome's Christians probably gathered in at least five houses, those belonging to (1) Priscilla and Aquila; (2) the family of Aristobulus; (3) the family of Narcissus; (4) a home occupied by Asyncritus, Phlegon, Hermes, Patrobas and Hermas; and (5) a home belonging to Philogus, Julia, Nereus and his sister, and Olympus. Aristobulus and Narcissus, among others, are Greek names, and so the Roman church likely included a number of converted non-Jews, though many Jews had Greek names. In his letter to Philippi, Paul writes that some members of the praitorion/praetorium (which might refer to the praetorian guard or to the headquarters of a governor in a province) were believers, and these would no doubt have met in another house church on the opposite side of the Tiber. Distinct house-churches could be a source of division, of course, and New Testament scholar Paul Minear, professor emeritus of the Yale Divinity School, discerns five possible factions, divided over ethics, rituals, and spirituality.

Many of these house churches met in the tenement buildings that crowded the narrow, winding streets of Transtibiris. Rome in the first century had much in common with urban third-world cities in the twenty-first, with population density approaching two hundred per acre. The tenement buildings (called *insulae*) were typically built around an inner courtyard, allowing light and fresh air only in the

Dated at A.D. 63, the so-called "Prie-dieu House" at Herculaneum on the Bay of Naples has tantalized archaeologists for years. The building along with the whole city was buried in ash and lava when Vesuvius erupted in A.D. 79. In one of its rooms sat this intact wooden kneeling bench, called a prie-dieu, probably used for prayer. Above it lies a mystery: Did the incision in the wall hold a cross or a shelf bracket? Whether or not the house was a place of Christian assembly, there is no doubt that house churches operated in and around Rome at exactly this time.

6. Some scholars believe that Romans 16, the chapter in which Paul greets twenty-six individuals, was originally sent to the Christians at Ephesus, because a few of the individuals were known to have lived in Ephesus, and was later attached to Paul's letter to Rome. But most disagree, observing that with the relative ease of travel on roads that led to Rome, it's not surprising that people Paul had met elsewhere lived in Rome.

In crowded Rome, much as in today's cities, "mixed use" structures such as these were common. To conserve valuable land, apartments were placed above and behind shop fronts. A replica of a first-century building was constructed at the foot of the Capitoline Hill in Rome and (right) is a model of the reconstruction. The interior view (left) shows a restored shop similar to the one in Rome but actually in the port at Ostia.

upper quarters. The apartments were one- or two-room affairs, with the interior room, the one exposed to the most light and fresh air, used for sleeping. Sometimes several unrelated families shared a common sitting room, but this would still be too small to permit entertaining. Since apartments had no kitchens, families cooked on charcoal braziers located near an opening. They used public latrines or chamber pots or the small spaces found under stairs to relieve themselves.

Small shops (called *tabernae*) were often built around the outer ring of the first floor, and the families who operated them lived in a back room behind or slightly above the shop. Some insulae had "deluxe" apartments behind the shops and facing the courtyard, apartments with servants' quarters and a room to entertain guests—or to host meetings. But even these apartments generally lacked kitchens and latrines.

Privacy was thus rare. "Not much happened in a neighborhood that would escape the eyes of the neighbors," writes social historian Wayne Meeks in *The First Urban Christians*, "News or rumor would travel rapidly; riots could flare up in a moment."

One such riot occurred in 49, when a theological disagreement over the identity of the Jewish messiah seems to have erupted into a brawl. The incident is alluded to by the Roman historian Suetonius, who says that the Jews who constantly made disturbances at the instigation of *Chrestus* were expelled from Rome, the first apparently specific reference to Christians in secular history.[8] To Roman authorities, of course, it would have appeared as a quarrel among Jews, merely an internecine religious squabble.

---

7. Historians are widely agreed on the basis of archaeological evidence and the writings of early Christians that Peter did indeed reach Rome and it is likely he would have exercised great influence because of the stature accorded him in the Gospels. That he actually held the title "bishop," however, is disputed. Even so, the term translated bishop, the Greek *episkopos*, is well attested in the New Testament, and in the Catholic and Orthodox view, Clement's letter of 90 to 100 refers to Peter as Rome's bishop.

8. Chrestus was a common name for slaves, and some historians argue that, when Suetonius reports a riot started at the "instigation of *Chrestus*," he may have been reporting a slave revolt not necessarily involving Christians. But the term *Chrestus* was likely a first-century Latin mispronunciation of the Greek *Chrestos*, the term for the Christian messiah. Early church fathers Justin, Tertullian, and Lactantius complain up into the fourth century about pagans continuing to confuse the spellings.

The monotheism of the Jews, their disciplined religious life, and their ethical ideals impressed some Romans, even among the aristocracy—impressed them enough for them to submit to circumcision and become "God-fearers," as the Jews called them. But most Romans despised the Jews as foreigners, little better than slaves, and the same stigma at first came to attach itself to Christians.

Yet Christianity soon began to represent a cross-section of society. Indeed, some of its early success was due in part to the generosity of wealthy Christians, who from the start shared their homes, fed the general community at special gatherings, and entertained travelers.

This was the role played by a couple who seem from the records to be the most well-known Christians in Rome. Priscilla (or Prisca) and Aquila are mentioned five times in the New Testament. Their tent-making business enabled them to host a Christian congregation in their home and to travel to other cities

What ever happened to the rest of the twelve apostles?

Did Andrew make it to Russia? Did Jude convert a king? The fate of these and most of the others is known only in legend and tradition

The deaths of four of Jesus' original twelve apostles can be reasonably well established by church historians. How the others died is the subject of largely unauthenticated ancient stories, some of them quite dramatic.

The first apostle to perish was, of course, Judas Iscariot, who according to Gospel accounts betrayed Jesus and then committed suicide. The next was James, the son of Zebedee, whose execution is reported in Luke's Acts of the Apostles (12:2). He was decapitated at Jerusalem on the orders of Agrippa, client king of the emperor, just before the Feast of the Passover in A.D. 44.

That Peter was crucified at Rome in the mid-sixties is generally accepted as probable, as is the death at Ephesus of the aged John Zebedee, brother of James.

The second-century North African theologian Tertullian relates that John was at one point boiled in oil, but escaped, presumably to die of old age. Much later legend has John never dying at all (as foreseen by Peter in John's Gospel 21:23), but somehow living on. One picturesque story has him buried, with the ground heaving above his grave as he continued to breathe.

The fates of the others appear almost solely in legend and pious tradition. However, some of these stories have gradually gained historical credibility,

such as the reports that Thomas founded missions in India and was martyred there in A.D. 72. (See story page 63.)

A considerable tradition surrounds the ministry of Peter's brother, Andrew. The fourth-century historian Eusebius records that Andrew led a mission to Scythia on the northwest coast of the Black Sea, an endeavor, whether factual or legendary, that eventually made him patron saint of Russia.

But the Greeks, too, preserve a devotion to St. Andrew, whom they call *Protocletus* (first called) since he was the first of the Twelve recruited. A brief biography published by the Greek Orthodox Order of Saint Andrew the Apostle tells of his founding missions in Bithynia and Pontus on the Black Sea's south coast, then another at the city of Byzantium at the Bosphorus, which links the Black to the Sea of Marmora, where the great Christian city of Constantinople would one day rise.

Andrew next led a mission to the city of Patras in southern Greece, where his preaching and healing ministry led to the conversion of the brother and wife of the Roman proconsul. The proconsul, furious at this perceived treason in his own family, ordered Andrew crucified. Andrew perished upside down on an X-shaped cross, and Patras soon became a place of Christian pilgrimage. Persuaded he had executed a

like Corinth and Ephesus. It's possible that they had a fine apartment on the first floor of an insula, with their tent-making shop facing out into the street. Since they had long acted as a patron of Paul, they were no doubt thrilled when they heard, about 60 A.D., that he had arrived in Rome to appeal to Emperor Nero the case that had been brought against him by the Jewish authorities at Jerusalem. In Rome, Paul was merely confined to house arrest. So he set up a residence, at his own expense, possibly in an apartment in one of the Transtibiris tenement houses.

In the Acts of the Apostles, Luke reports that three days after his arrival, Paul invited local Jewish leaders to hear his story. He told the gathering that he had "done nothing against our people or our customs," nor anything worthy of arrest, let alone of the death penalty. He was in Rome simply because he had been forced to the legal recourse of appealing to the emperor "even though I had no charge to bring against my nation."

very holy man, the proconsul committed suicide.

In March 357, the Roman emperor, by now Christian and living in the new imperial capital, Constantinople, the former Byzantium, ordered Andrew's bones translated (i.e., moved) there. This gave rise to a further story. St. Rule (or St. Regulus), an Irish monk, is warned by an angel to take the remains of St. Andrew to "the ends of the earth," meaning Scotland. There he moved them to a shrine that would one day be known as St. Andrew's, and by the twenty-first century would be renowned for one of the most celebrated golf courses in the world.

The tradition was strong enough to have St. Andrew made patron saint of Scotland. His cross, a white "X" lying on its side against a blue background, forms part of the British flag, the Union Jack.

The tradition that the apostle Bartholomew—known in St. John's Gospel as Nathanael[1]—also reached India and was martyred there, is regarded by many historians as spurious.

Eusebius records another story, concerning the man Matthew's Gospel calls Thaddaeus and Luke's calls Jude. In this tradition, Abgar, king of Edessa on the Persian frontier, who is stricken with an illness, hears of the fame of Jesus and writes him asking for help. Jesus sends a written reply, which Eusebius records,[2] promising to send one of his disciples to help Abgar.

Following Jesus' ascension, the apostle Thomas sends Thaddaeus to Edessa where he heals many sick people, one of them King Abgar himself, who becomes Christian. This is said to happen in the year 340 of the old Seleucid calendar, which would be A.D. 30, the approximate date of the Crucifixion, Resurrection and Ascension.

Thaddaeus, in this tradition, eventually suffers martyrdom in Persia, as do James Alphaeus (often called James the Less) and Simon the Patriot (or Zealot).

Which leaves two of the Twelve unaccounted for.

Irenaeus, writing in the second century, provides an account of the post-Resurrection career of Matthew, for whom the first Gospel in the New Testament is named. He says that Matthew became a missionary to the Hebrews. Other ancient writers describe him as a missionary to Syria, Persia, and the lands south of the Caspian. Clement of Alexandria, writing in the late-second century, reports that Matthew did not die as a martyr. Other ancient accounts are equally definite that he did, though none provides detail.

Even less is known of the apostle, Philip—not to be confused with the deacon Philip whose missionary work is described in the Acts of the Apostles. According to one ancient tradition, the apostle Philip journeyed to Scythia, on the Black Sea's north coast, and preached the gospel. At Hierapolis in Asia Minor, according to another account, he banished a serpent or dragon that was being worshiped in the temple of Mars. The creature gave off such a stench the priests of the temple captured Philip and had him crucified. Matthias, the apostle named to replace Judas, thereafter disappears from the records without a trace. ■

<hr>

1. The apostle Bartholomew, who appears in St. John's Gospel as Nathanael, was probably named Nathanael bar-Tholami (hence Bartholomew), the prefix "bar" meaning "son of."

2. Nowhere in the New Testament is Jesus Christ recorded as writing anything. However, Eusebius, writing in the fourth century, records Jesus as sending this letter to King Abgar at Edessa on the Euphrates, who had sent messengers asking Jesus to come and cure him: "Happy are you who believed in me. For it is written of me that those who have seen me will not believe in me, and that those who have not seen will believe and live. As to your request I should come to you, I must complete all that I was sent to do here, and on completing it must at once be taken up to the One who sent me. When I have been taken up I will send one of my disciples to cure your disorder and bring life to you and those with you."

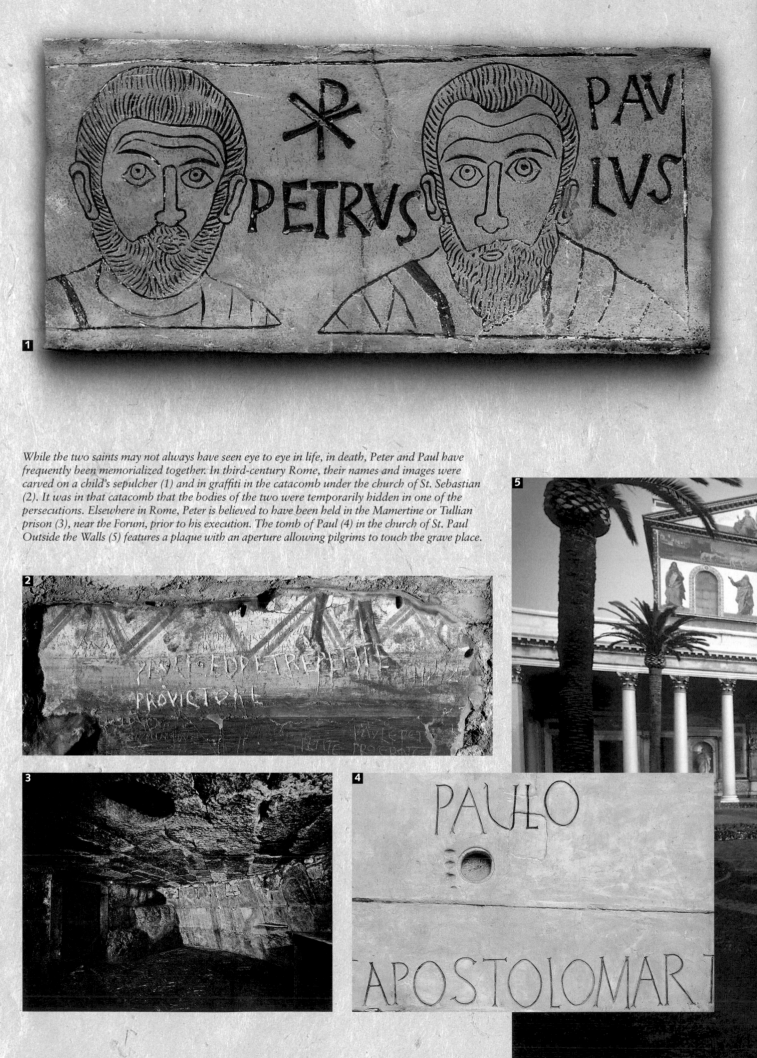

While the two saints may not always have seen eye to eye in life, in death, Peter and Paul have frequently been memorialized together. In third-century Rome, their names and images were carved on a child's sepulcher (1) and in graffiti in the catacomb under the church of St. Sebastian (2). It was in that catacomb that the bodies of the two were temporarily hidden in one of the persecutions. Elsewhere in Rome, Peter is believed to have been held in the Mamertine or Tullian prison (3), near the Forum, prior to his execution. The tomb of Paul (4) in the church of St. Paul Outside the Walls (5) features a plaque with an aperture allowing pilgrims to touch the grave place.

Peter and Paul in Rome:
Here, there and everywhere

Long after the two apostles' martyrdom under Nero, history's opinions about their final resting places differ

Tradition holds that Peter and Paul, celebrated as founders of the church in Rome, were both buried in that city following their martyrdoms. Just exactly where they died and were buried, however, has been a matter of lively debate for two millennia.

By the fourth century, when Constantine constructed the original basilicas—one for Peter on the Vatican Hill, one for Paul on the Ostian Way outside the walls—various historians had proposed a number of competing sacred sites, according to accounts of burials, exhumations and transferrals of remains.

Today's tourist in Rome is therefore able to view a multitude of historic locations of varying authenticity, some of which are pictured on these pages.

What is rarely debated, however, is Rome's claim to both of the founding apostles of Christianity. In a typical memorial inscription at the restored Christian catacombs—another possible burial site of the two—Damasus, Bishop of Rome, wrote in the late-fourth century:

Here you must know that the saints formerly dwelt, whosoever you are who ask for the names of Peter and Paul. These disciples were sent from the east, as we readily admit, but because of the merit of their blood they followed Christ through the stars and reached the ethereal bosom and the realms of the holy ones; and Rome has acquired the prior right to claim them as her citizens. ■

Monuments to Peter and Paul abound in and around Rome, witness to their continuing importance not only to the history of that city, but to Christians in general. Sometimes, however, visitors to the city may be unaware of the connection the two apostles have to certain tourist attractions. The obelisk that now stands before St. Peter's Basilica (above) would doubtless have been one of the last things that the apostle saw. It originally stood in the Vatican hippodrome—the place of his martyrdom.

His guests appeared mystified. They had heard nothing from Judea about Paul, they said, but they had heard a great deal locally about the sect he represented. These Christians were despised. Everyone spoke against them. They would like to hear what Paul thought.

And so, Luke continues, Paul met with a "great number" of Jews in his own lodging, marshaling reason, scriptural proofs, and personal testimony to convince his listeners that Jesus was the long-awaited messiah. There were questions, accusations, arguments and rebuttals. In the end, some were convinced, others not. To those who objected, Paul, who had run out of patience, delivered his parting shot: "This salvation of God has been sent to the Gentiles. They will listen!" For two years, Luke reports, Paul conducted such home meetings.

And there Luke drops the story, unresolved. What happened to Paul he doesn't say, nor does he detail the fate of any of the other Christians mentioned in his accounts. Why? No one knows, but this puzzle has given historians and theologians something to speculate about for the next two thousand years. What

'They were filled with every kind of wickedness, evil covetousness, malice,' wrote Paul of his countrymen. 'They are gossips, slanderers, God-haters, insolent, haughty, boastful. . . .'

became of Paul's hearing before Nero? Some scholars suggest that his case was simply dismissed, though that rarely happened in such circumstances. Others say Paul was acquitted, and others still, that he was found guilty and exiled to Spain.

Spain is a possibility because of some ancient evidence. Clement, spokesman for the elders at the church at Rome and recognized by Catholics as the third bishop of Rome, writing around 96, says of Paul that "to the whole world he taught righteousness, and reaching the limits of the West, he bore his witness before rulers." The limits of the Roman West would have been where Spain began. Another scenario is that Paul was, for whatever reason, set free, then went to Spain on his own, to extend his missionary endeavors. This was indeed his intent in going to Rome in the first place, or so he implies in his letter to the Romans (15:24). For the much-traveled Paul, the journey to Spain would not have represented much of a challenge. The sailing time to Spain was only about seven days.

However, accomplishing anything in Spain was a different matter. Historian Jerome Murphy-O'Connor, a Dominican priest, piecing together the evidence, concludes Paul indeed went to Spain, stayed a season and returned, his mission a failure because he couldn't speak the language. He knew Greek, not Latin. Others question that assumption. Whether Paul did or did not know Latin, they say, is itself unknown.

In any event, far more alarming news would have reached Paul, wherever he was. Word would come that Rome had suffered a truly terrible fire. Much of the city had been wiped out, countless numbers were dead, two hundred thousand were homeless. Worse still, the Roman church was in dire trouble.

The bucket-brigade efforts of Rome's firefighters (vigiles) are no match for the irresistible surge of the inferno that roars through the city in the Great Fire of A.D. 64. Citizens safely out of burning buildings succumb to the choking smoke. Ladders set to free those trapped in upper stories fail to reach high enough. The flames seem to spring up from nowhere as sparks turn the high tenements into funeral pyres for their inhabitants. Seventy percent of the great city would be destroyed. No tally of the dead survives, but hundreds of thousands were left homeless. Nero's retribution would be no less devastating for the city's Christians.

Nero was blaming the Christians for the fire. He was arresting them by the dozen; some were being put to death—by crucifixion, gruesomely, as a spectacle, as an example to the world. The first major disaster for the early Christian church was now unfolding.

Rome had had fires before, of course. In fact, fire was recognized as an ever-present menace to the entire city. Between 31 B.C. and A.D. 410, contemporary authors record no fewer than forty large fires in Rome, conflagrations in which numerous buildings and large residential districts were destroyed—an average of one destructive blaze every eleven years.

Most Romans were wholly aware that the problem was the residential architecture, if it could be called that. The tenement buildings that housed most residents soared seven stories high, stood little more than an arm's length apart, and were made of "wattle and daub" (wooden stakes, branches, and mud or clay) over a wood frame. Wattle and daub, according to the first-century Roman architect Vitruvius, should never have been invented: "For it is made to catch fire, like torches," he writes.

The satirical poet Juvenal, who was a child at the time of the blazing disaster, complained that life in urban Rome was an "endless nightmare of fire and collapsing houses." He would, he continued, "prefer to live where fires and

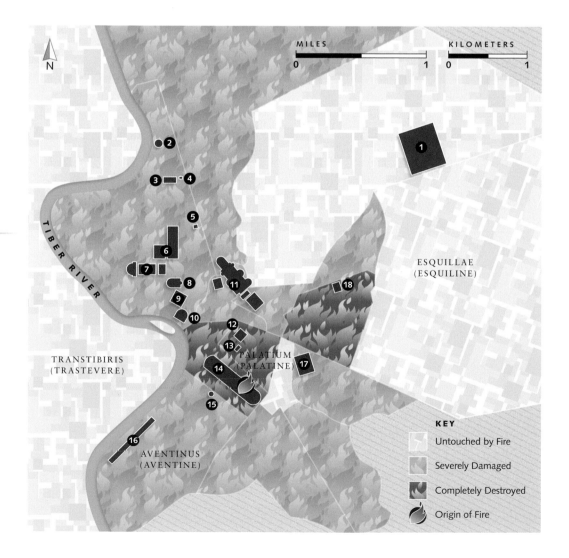

ROME'S WORST-EVER FIRE: THE TRANSTIBIRIS SURVIVES

1. Camp of the Praetorians
2. Ara Pacis Augustae
3. Solar Clock of Augustus
4. Mausoleum of Augustus
5. Arch of Claudius
6. Baths of Agrippa
7. Porticus Minuca Frumentaria
8. Theater and Crypt of Balbus
9. Portico of Octavia
10. Theater of Marcellus
11. Rome's Main Forum
12. Palace of Tiberius
13. Temple of Apollo
14. Circus Maximus
15. Temple of Diana
16. Porticus Aemilia
17. Temple of the Divine Claudius
18. Portico of Livia

midnight panics are not quite such common events. By the time the smoke is got up to your third floor apartment (and you are still asleep), your heroic downstairs neighbor is roaring for water, and shifting his bits and pieces to safety. If the alarm goes at ground-level, the last to fry will be the attic tenant, way up among the nesting pigeons with nothing but tiles between himself and the weather."

Officialdom, whether emperors or city engineers, thought the solution lay in construction codes. Laws were passed that buildings could be no taller than seventy feet and had to be separated by at least two-and-one-half feet; tenants were required to have a bucket of water on hand at all times; some rental contracts forbade renters to make an open fire; and so on. The codes were routinely ignored.

However, by the first century, fire brigades had been organized. Called *vigiles*, they consisted of seven cohorts of 560 men each. They patrolled the streets at night to discover fires that were still small. They carried buckets and axes, and their first action when encountering a fire was to form a chain of men to pass water buckets filled from the nearest reservoir. The vigiles were effective with

Rome had scores of major fires through the years. With most residences built from wooden stakes, branches and mud, the city was a torch waiting to be lit.

small fires, but they were helpless when one got out of hand. This now happened, and the fire of 64 became the worst in Rome's history.

Tacitus, who leaves the best account of the fire, says it began at the east end of the Circus Maximus, at the foot of the Palatine and Caelian Hills. "Amid the shops containing inflammable wares, the conflagration both broke out and instantly became so fierce and spread so rapidly before the wind that it seized in its grasp the entire length of the Circus."

Fed by the tinder of the circus's wooden bleachers and fanned by a brisk southeast wind, the flames roared through the circus, gathering force as they moved. Soon the whole valley between the Palatine and Aventine was one great ocean of fire, the flames climbing up hillsides and devouring the buildings and temples on their crowns. They raged through the narrow, twisting streets, engulfing the tenements and the barracks-like blocks that lined them.

Tacitus continues graphically, noting "the wailings of terror-stricken women, the feebleness of age, the helpless inexperience of childhood, the crowds who sought to save themselves or others, dragging out the infirm or waiting for them, and by their hurry in the one case, by their delay in the other, aggravating the confusion." Many people were simply overrun by the flames; some became so distraught at the loss of home and loved ones that they gave up and, even though they had a way of escape, simply let the fire sweep over them.

Then there were the ugly rumors. It was said that many who tried to stop the flames were prevented from doing so, some by men who were seeking plunder, others by men saying they were under orders to keep the fire going. Who could these be?

After five or six days, the fire, having consumed everything it could, simply sputtered out. By then it had come to the foot of the Esquiline Hill, where the buildings had been razed already so that the fire met nothing but open land and

The dramatic and final defiance of James the Just

Stand above the people and disown Christ, he's told. He stands all right, and his witness for Jesus resounds through the ages

Two years before the Great Fire at Rome and Nero's act of terror against Rome's still tiny Christian community, there occurred at Jerusalem, nominal capital of Christianity, a dramatic public death that would foreshadow the ancient city's future catastrophe.

James, brother or stepbrother of Jesus, a man revered as a model of Jewish piety and commitment to God by most Jews, whether followers of Jesus or not, was sentenced to death by an illegally constituted trial. Now an old man, he died, as had Jesus, forgiving the people who had condemned him. He was known as "the Just One."

When the failed attempt to imprison Peter drove the apostles from Jerusalem, they had named James the Just overseer, or bishop, of the Jerusalem church, which was then the founding and central authority of the new faith. James stayed behind, a center of fierce controversy, because he believed and preached Jesus as Messiah. At least one attempt may have been made on his life.

But few doubted his devotion to God. Some called him "the Man With the Callused Knees" because, as a priest, he spent whole days in the Temple, praying for the city and for its people. "He was holy from his mother's womb," reports the Christian historian Hegesippus, who wrote late in the first century, and whose work has survived in the writings of Eusebius. "He drank no wine nor strong drink, nor did he eat flesh. No razor came upon his head; he did not anoint himself with oil, and he did not use the bath."

While some Jews accepted Jesus as a prophet, some merely as a gifted teacher, and the Temple rulers denounced him as "the Great Blasphemer," James persuaded so many to become fully committed to Jesus that he alarmed the Temple authorities. "When many, even the rulers, believed," says Hegesippus, "there was a commotion among the Jews and scribes and Pharisees, who said there was a danger the whole people would be looking for Jesus as the Messiah."

(When Hegesippus uses the term "the Jews," he refers to the leadership, since everyone involved in the case, James included, was Jewish.)

The Jewish historian Josephus implies another explanation for the move to rid the Temple of the old man. James championed the cause of the poorer priests against the prosperous members of the high priestly household who ran the Temple and formed the core of the Sadducean party.

James's opponents, however, faced a legal difficulty. Though Judea at this time was formally under the rule of a Jewish king, Agrippa II, great grandson of Herod the Great, executions required the ratification of the Roman governor, whose authority superseded the king's. And the governor, as usual, was inclined to oppose anything the Temple rulers favored.

But in A.D. 62, the Roman governor Festus died in office. A successor, Albinus, was en route to Jerusalem when King Agrippa was persuaded to name a new high priest, one Ananus, whom Josephus describes as "a bold man in his temper and very insolent." Josephus notes also that Ananus was an active Sadducee, the party "who were very rigid in judging offenders, far more so than [other] Jews."

Acting in the break between the two governors' rule, Ananus called into session the Sanhedrin of the Judges, the high court of Judaism, something he had no authority to do without the governor's approval. The Sanhedrin summoned James to appear before it. Hegesippus takes up the story from there. They told the old man they knew he had great influence over the people, and they themselves recognized him as a just man. However, too many were "going astray" as regards this Jesus, and they could not let that continue.

Now Passover is coming, they said, and thousands of people would be assembled in Jerusalem. They therefore directed him to stand far above the crowd at the "pinnacle" of the Temple, to publicly repudiate Jesus, and to urge the people not to be led astray by him.

sky. But before the city could even count the toll, the fire burst forth again for another three days, consuming the more spacious districts of the city, though this time with less loss of life.

Tacitus assesses the damage: Ten of Rome's fourteen districts were destroyed, three leveled to the ground, seven left with only a few shattered, half-burnt relics of

Though this is not in the text, historians surmise that the council had reached a further conclusion. If James refused to do this, he stood condemned under a section of the Old Testament book of Deuteronomy that provides the death sentence by stoning for anyone convicted of "leading the people astray." A modification of this penalty allowed the victim to be first cast down from a great height, then be stoned if still alive.

So James knew exactly what was coming. But he also knew that they had provided him, in his last years, with a superb opportunity to bear witness to the whole assembled people on the occasion of their most sacred feast. Thus, he agreed and was taken to the pinnacle above the crowd. "Now tell them," ordered his accusers, "what is the Gate of Jesus"—meaning where Jesus was leading them. James's response rang out to the hushed crowd below:

"Why are you asking me concerning Jesus, the Son of Man? He sits in the Heaven at the right hand of the Great Power, and is about to come upon the clouds of Heaven."

The crowd became frenzied, yelling "Hosanna! Hosanna! Hosanna to the Son of David!" It was the same cry Jerusalem had heard thirty-some years before, when Jesus had entered the city on the back of a donkey, symbolizing that he came in peace.

Realizing they had bungled the job, Hegesippus recounts, Ananus's servants hurled James from the parapet. The populace must be shown, they reasoned, that this kind of defiant conduct does not pay. People rushed to the spot where he had crashed to the floor below. They found him still alive, and echoing the prayer of Jesus: "I entreat thee, Lord God our Father, forgive them, for they know not what they are doing." In response, one of his condemners took a club which was used for beating the water out of washed clothes, and bashed him to death. One version says they placed a stone on him, and bore down on it, crushing him.

Thus perished James the Just, kinsman of Christ, who emulated him in life and death. "The fruit of righteousness is sown in the peace of them that make peace," says the epistle that bears his name (James 3:18). Or, as J. B. Phillips would translate it: "The peacemakers go on quietly sowing for a harvest of righteousness."

The troublemakers, however, were about to produce a very different kind of harvest. For the moderates in the Temple, what Ananus had done was intolerable. They sent a protest to the new governor, Albinus, by now at Alexandria, who dispatched a warning to Ananus that he had acted outside the law. Hearing this, King Agrippa promptly fired the new high priest after only three months in office. Ananus became one of the first to perish in the coming catastrophe—a catastrophe that the events surrounding James's bold testimony and death had made inevitable. ■

The entrance to the Armenian Orthodox Cathedral of St. James in Jerusalem. The church is dedicated to the memory of James, the brother or stepbrother of Jesus, who was martyred in the city in A.D. 62. The dying James forgave his tormentors in words almost identical to those used by Christ. "Lord God our Father, forgive them, for they know not what they are doing."

After he lost his own residence in the fire of A.D. 64, Nero constructed his fabulous Domus Aurea (Golden House). What we see today (as here in the reconstruction of the palace's Octagonal Room) is only a feeble reflection of the original. It was reputed to have been twenty-five times larger than the Coliseum which was to occupy the site of the artificial lake adjacent to the Domus. Nero, however, was to live only four or five months in this luxury before his suicide.

houses. "It would not be easy to enter into a computation of the private mansions, the blocks of tenements, and of the temples which were lost," he writes. He specifically mentions the altar and shrine to Hercules, the Temple of Jupiter, the "various beauties of Greek art" and "the ancient and genuine historical monuments of men of genius." He concludes poignantly, "Old men will remember many things which could not be replaced."

Historian R. F. Newbold estimates that at least ten to twelve thousand tenement buildings were destroyed, plus several hundred private homes. Large sections of the city had to be rebuilt at a pace that could only sacrifice quality. Meanwhile, in the untouched areas, house and room rents skyrocketed. One of the quarters to escape unscathed was Transtibiris. The river had saved the whole district.

Since fire insurance did not exist, a wealthy family could be impoverished if its house burned down. If it had no country estate, as many did, its fate was left to the charity of friends and relatives. Wealthy families, of course, had wealthy friends and kinsmen, so they fared better than the poor. "If some millionaire's mansion is gutted," observes Juvenal sardonically, "contributions pour in while the shell is still hot." It wasn't so for the poor man.

The imperial treasury was tapped to render assistance, but those costs eventually had to be passed on to the countryside. Meanwhile, to help the homeless, Nero erected temporary buildings on the Campus Martius and in his own gardens. He opened the public buildings. He brought in food from neighboring towns and ordered that the price of grain be lowered.

Though these acts were popular, they did not stop a rumor that had begun spreading while the city still smoldered: that Nero himself had started the fire. While the flames engulfed the city, he watched the fire from the Tower of Maecenus, writes Suetonius, and was so stirred by the grandeur of the flames that he adorned himself in a tragedian costume and sang of the sack of Troy. The charge is difficult to prove. Nero was at Antium when the fire began, and he did not rush back to Rome until he heard that his house, palace, and gardens were threatened. But his return accomplished nothing: Everything he treasured went up in flames like most of the city. His palace, the Domus Transitoria, was leveled.

However, the rumors persisted. To squelch them, he encouraged everyone to appease the gods. The Sibylline Books (of oracles) were consulted; prayers were offered to Vulcanus, Ceres, and Proserpina. Matrons entreated Juno; some married women held sacred banquets and nightly vigils. Yet, as Tacitus notes, "all human efforts, all the lavish gifts of the emperor, and the propitiations of the gods, did not banish the sinister belief that the conflagration was the result of an order."

Finally, Nero conceived a plan which, he calculated, would divert the attention of the people away from himself. As Tacitus puts it, he "fastened the guilt and inflicted the most exquisite tortures on a class hated for their abominations, called Christians by the populace." This was the news that reached Paul.

The persecution of Roman Christians by Nero is remarkable for many reasons. For one, it was the first time the authorities did not identify the Christians as a Jewish religion. That may have been due to highly placed Romans like Poppaea Sabina, Nero's wife, and the actor Tigellinus, a close adviser, both of whom may have had strong Jewish sympathies—and the ear of Nero.

Then too, the persecution demonstrated that in the official view, Christianity had already become, as Tacitus puts it, "a most mischievous superstition." It had broken out in Judea but was now found "even in Rome, where all things hideous and shameful from every part of the world find their center and become popular." Christians, like Jews, tended to keep to themselves and their community; there were strange stories told about them—their agape or "love feast" which suggested sexual profligacy, their main service where they ate "the body and

Nero blamed the fire on the Christians, whom he tortured and killed in degrading ways. Some were tarred and burned to provide nighttime illumination.

blood" of their master suggested cannibalism. Many Romans believed Christians held immoral nocturnal rites and practiced black magic.[9]

Indeed, when arrests were first made, some Christians pleaded guilty, says Tacitus—although it is unclear whether he means they pleaded guilty to starting the fire (perhaps to play their part in bringing God's judgment on Rome), or simply admitted to being Christians. In any event, from those arrested early the authorities extracted the names of other Christians. These were also arrested, says Tacitus, not so much for starting the fire as for the charge of "hatred of mankind." For this, nothing less than death seemed a satisfactory punishment.

Tacitus provides a brief but devastating account of what followed: "Mockery of every sort was added to their deaths. Covered with skins of beasts, they were torn by dogs and perished, or were nailed to crosses, or were doomed to the flames and burnt, to serve as a nightly illumination." Nero held some of the

9. One of the most serious charges against Christians in Nero's Rome was the allegation that they didn't fit in. Indeed, they did not conform to the deepening decadence of the society around them. That is, they had moral rules and they followed them. "Christian ethics and their absolutised values," writes the historian Vasily Rudich, "represented the very opposite of the fashionable Neronian nihilism. This alone, if comprehended at all by the emperor and his associates (as, it seems, never happened) would have threatened the Christians with wholesale extermination" (*Political Dissidence Under Nero: The Price of Dissimulation*. London: Routledge, 1993).

Nero's penchant for spectacle was mixed with a seemingly insatiable appetite for human pain. Christians had been accused of setting the fires in an attempt to subvert the empire. Then, herded together, bound and tied to stakes, they serve as torches to illumine the gardens of the emperor's palace. Accounts of this first mass persecution horrified Christian communities all over the empire.

STIRNWEIS

executions in his own gardens, others in the Circus Maximus, and he invited the populace to come watch. Nero made a party of even this; he dressed up as a charioteer and, moving about in his chariot, mingled with the spectators.

The horror of Nero's action spread terror and consternation among Christians throughout the empire. Being hypothetically ready to die for Christ was one thing. To have it actually occurring to people was something else.

But Tacitus notes that Nero's response was so excessive that "even for criminals [i.e., the Christians] who deserved extreme and exemplary punishment there arose a feeling of compassion. For it was not, as it seemed, for the public good, but to glut one man's cruelty that they were being destroyed."

Among the Christians destroyed were Paul and Peter. We know little about why they were in Rome at the time, nor about their deaths. Tradition has it that sometime between October 66 and October 68, Paul was beheaded and Peter was crucified upside down (because he didn't feel worthy to be executed in the same manner as was his Lord).

Of course, during times of trial there are always individual failures in courage. Such was the case where some Roman Christians gave the names of their fellow worshipers to the persecuting authorities. However, these were exceptions. Adversity usually brings the church together.

Murphy-O'Connor notes another outcome: "The unfortunate long-term consequence of the episode was the creation of a sinister precedent—that the guilt of Christians could be presumed." Nero's viciousness was fortunately limited in geography and time, to one city alone for about four years. But the episode suggested to later Roman authorities that Christians were a group that needed to be watched—and punished if necessary. It was another two-and-one-half centuries before Christians would be free from such suspicions.

In one other perverse way, Nero influenced the Christians. He helped crystallize Christian thought regarding the great enemy who would arise in the last days to attack the faithful. Thus, about two-and-one-half decades later, the author of the book called Revelation, or the Apocalypse, describing the brutality of the end times, fastens on Nero, some say, as the model of ultimate Evil incarnate, the apocalyptic Beast from the Abyss.

As for Nero, in the years following the fire he became increasingly unbalanced. He did not hesitate to kill close advisers and friends if he merely suspected they were plotting against him. Finally, in early 68, governors in both Gaul and Spain rose up in rebellion, followed by generals in North Africa and Germany. Nero, paralyzed with fear, prattled on that he might win back his troops with displays of weeping. When the Senate condemned him to be flogged to death, Nero ordered his secretary to help him stab himself in the throat. The secretary obliged. Nero's last words were, "What a showman the world is losing in me."

Two years before Nero died, news had come that the Jews had broken into open rebellion in Judea. The Roman garrison in Jerusalem had been duped into surrendering, and then slaughtered. To suppress the revolt, Nero turned to an old soldier from the German and British wars. His name was Vespasian. Many said the appointment was Nero's last sane act. ∎

As Roman troops tighten their noose on Jerusalem, starvation and disease take a mounting toll, and weeping fills the streets of a city that is about to fall. Though future generations will rebuild Jerusalem, its great Temple, the heart of the Holy City and its people, will remain only in memory and story.

CHAPTER 9

Jerusalem falls, the veil vanishes

Bodies littering the streets, the looted Temple smashed, the Holy City's smoking ruins echo with cries of grief just as Jesus had foreseen forty years before

April had brought tender buds out on the trees, and white and yellow wildflowers were beginning to peep out of the cracks of the streets of Jerusalem. Yet the city was filled with the sound of weeping; women clung to each other and howled their grief as Jesus went by. Plump babies, startled by the clamor, clutched their mothers' robes and added their own fretful whimpering.

The beaten prisoner was too weak to go on. The procession came to a halt as Roman soldiers seized a man from the crowd and transferred the heavy wooden cross to his shoulders. In the momentary pause Jesus looked at the women's tear-streaked faces: "Daughters of Jerusalem, do not weep for me, but weep for yourselves and for your children," he said. "For behold, the days are coming when they will say, 'Blessed are the barren, and the wombs that never bore, and the breasts that never gave suck!' Then they will begin to say to the mountains, 'Fall on us,' and to the hills, 'Cover us.' For if they do this when the wood is green, what will they do when it is dry?"

The answer to that ominous question would unfold over the next forty years, as episodes of civil protest and intermittent violence gradually ascended into unimaginable horror. One morning in A.D. 70, a generation and more after Jesus' dire prophecy, the sun rose over Jerusalem, revealing the toppled ruin of the Temple and the city in flames. In the rubble-filled streets there was again weeping, this time the feeble tears of hopelessness, the weeping of a beaten people. Jews by the tens of thousands had died—at the hands of Romans and at the hands of fellow Jews, and many more from gnawing hunger. The streets where Jesus had walked, where he had turned to warn those who grieved for him, were now crammed with corpses. The ancient sacrificial rites of the Jewish Temple had come to an end. It was late September, hot and dry. ■

For the story of how the Jewish calamity, known to history as the Siege of Jerusalem, came about we have almost no source except Flavius Josephus, a Jewish general and a peace advocate, a prolific historian who took on the protection and the name of the Roman imperial family. Josephus is a figure of paradox, and the earnestness of his split loyalty—his love of Israel on the one hand moving him to side vehemently with Rome on the other—underscores the poignancy of these last years of Jerusalem's glory. In any event, the story that follows is his story of what happened. Historians would argue for centuries over what *really* happened, and archaeology would make a contribution, but the only surviving contemporary account was Josephus's.

The rebellion that led to this desolate morning had come on gradually, unsteadily, and beset by much dissension. For about 130 years the Jews had

The streets where Jesus had walked and delivered his dire warning were now crammed with corpses. The ancient sacrificial rites of the Jewish Temple had come to an end.

made the best of Roman domination, combating bureaucratic corruption with protest, sometimes peaceful, occasionally not. As the decade of the sixties dawned, however, Jewish resistance to the corruption of the Roman administration became more determined, the contempt of the Roman soldiery increasingly evident,[1] and the resistance of the Jewish factions opposing them increasingly rebellious. Volatile bands sprang up, variously motivated: some crusading for economic justice, some for political freedom, some for a utopian theocracy, and some, says Josephus, simply as bandits. Parents were divided against children, brother against brother, family against family. Where there was division, there was all too often bloodshed.

Many, however, especially of the ruling priestly class, viewed rebellion against

---

1. On one celebrated occasion, a trooper, routinely patrolling the Passover rites in the Temple, lowered his britches, and turned his bared behind to the crowd below. Understandably, a furious protest arose from the Jews, who saw the spectacle directed, not at them, but at God. Whatever else the incident demonstrated, it shows that the twentieth-century phenomenon known as "mooning" has ancient antecedents.

Rome as suicidal; the Romans were simply too powerful, they said, and if provoked would destroy everything Jewish in Jerusalem, including the Temple. Such appeasers were a special target of rebel ire, and risked assassination. Thus many Jews feared the rebels more than the Romans, and wished that a competent Roman governor would restore peace. Instead, the governors grew worse.

Albinus, governor from A.D. 62 to 64, began by rounding up and imprisoning the terrorist group known as the Sicarii,[2] but remaining gang members found they could gain the release of their fellows by kidnapping citizens for ransom. Albinus proved himself willing to release prisoners for bribes, and the common citizens increasingly lived in terror.

Governor Albinus, while moderately corrupt, was rectitude itself compared with his successor, Gessius Florus (A.D. 64 to 66), says Josephus. Florus shamelessly advertised his cupidity, until the outpouring of complaints to his superior, Cestius Gallus, legate of Syria, made him fear for his job. One way to keep it, he decided, was to provoke the Jews into open rebellion.

That rebellion began, not in Jerusalem, but in Caesarea, seat of the Roman government, and a fire pit of strife between Jews and local Greeks and Syrians. The war began with a real estate quarrel between a synagogue's congregation and their Greek neighbor who announced plans to turn his property into a workshop that would obstruct the synagogue entrance. The synagogue's elders paid Florus eight talents—roughly the lifetime wages of eight working men—to stop construction. Florus pocketed the money and left town.

Then one morning the Jews arrived to find another irascible Greek at the synagogue door performing a parody of Jewish worship, sacrificing birds over some sort of bowl.[3] A riot ensued. In the melee the Jewish leaders seized the scroll of the Torah and fled. They went to Florus for help, delicately reminding him of the eight talents. His response was to clap them all in jail for stealing the Torah.

Still, one riot did not constitute a rebellion, so Florus moved his attention to Jerusalem where the possibilities for deliberate mischief were much greater. Here he commandeered funds from the Temple treasury. Young Jews reacted in scorn, taking up a collection they called "pennies for the governor." To Florus, such a jeer, directed against the

---

2. The Jewish terrorist group known as the "Sicarii" were so called because they carried a sica, a short curved-blade dagger, concealed in their robes. Mingling with crowds, the Sicarii assassinated Jewish leaders who resisted revolution.

3. The bowl incident at the synagogue door was a calculated insult, writes the historian Gaalya Cornfeld in a comment on his translation of *Josephus, The Jewish War*. It probably implied that the Jews were lepers. Under Jewish Law, before a cleansed leper could return to ordinary life he must sacrifice birds.

Early in the rebellion, the Sicarii, so named for the short, curved swords they hide beneath their robes, terrorize the Judean populace, especially other Jews judged to be too accepting of the Roman occupation. But such tactics ultimately prove futile against the massive and well-organized Roman response to the uprising.

Roman governor, was execrable. In an assault foreshadowing the massive Roman attacks that would eventually bring the city down, the Jerusalem cohort of the Twelfth Legion thereupon plundered the Upper Marketplace, with orders to slay everyone who resisted.

The carnage was appalling, says Josephus, but the Jewish leaders knew that Florus was trying to provoke a full-scale war. They persuaded the people to go out and welcome the Roman cohorts, by now moving from Caesarea into Jerusalem. Under orders to ignore this demonstration, the troops snubbed the greeting and passed in silence.

The predictable occurred. At the rebuff, the people began jeering the troops. The soldiers responded by clubbing everyone in reach. Some Jews climbed up on the city walls and hurled rocks down on the soldiers below.[4] These men were trapped in the narrow confines of the city gate and found it hard to turn and retreat. In the end Florus was forced to pull back. He withdrew one of the cohorts, leaving the other to reinforce the Jerusalem garrison, stationed in the Antonia Fortress, which overlooked the Temple.

Then came the diplomatic incident that marks the outbreak of the war. Eleazar, governor of the Temple and a militant anti-Roman, decreed that no

Then came the diplomatic incident that marked the outbreak of war. Eleazar, governor of the Temple, decreed no further sacrifices would be offered for foreigners.

further sacrifices would be offered for foreigners.[5] This meant stopping offerings for Caesar, an act of defiance. Others of the high priestly party, including Eleazar's father, Ananias, feared the worst, and appealed to Agrippa II, Rome's client king in the region, for more troops to give the rebels cause to reconsider.

It didn't work. Agrippa sent two thousand Jewish soldiers into Jerusalem, but by then Jerusalem was divided. Ananias's party held the Upper City, while his son's rebels held the Temple and Lower City. After a week of fighting, Eleazar's party, joined by a number of Sicarii, drove Agrippa's forces from the Upper City into Herod's Palace. The victorious rebels also set fire to the Upper City house of the high priest Ananias, and to the Hasmonean Palace, nearby, where Agrippa II and his sister, Bernice, lived; and they torched the archive where debt records were stored, hoping to recruit the poor to the rebellion.

The rebels next seized the Antonia Fortress, and soon they were reinforced by another insurgent band, fresh from its slaughter of the Roman garrison in the Masada, the citadel high atop a mountain overlooking the Dead Sea. These were

---

4. Rocks were, and would remain, a handy weapon in Middle Eastern political process. Twenty centuries later television audiences would watch them sail across the screen on the evening news in the direction of an Israeli soldier, just as they once did to brain a Roman soldier.

5. Ancient Judaism practiced a peculiar tolerance. Though non-Jews were forbidden to enter the Temple on pain of death, there was no prohibition on making sacrifices in the Temple for foreigners and much of the Temple's furnishings were donated by Gentiles.

The rogue historian

Josephus: Scholar, turncoat—he chronicles Jerusalem's fate

Within the lavish opulence of the imperial household at Rome during the triumphant late-first-century years of the emperors Vespasian, Titus and Trajan, there labored a Jewish intellectual. He was cherished by those in authority as a scholar, a statesman and a true ally of Rome, while despised by his fellow Jews as a sleazy scoundrel and turncoat. Whether Flavius Josephus deserved either of these two reputations historians were to argue about for the next twenty centuries.

The Jewish case against Jerusalem-born Josef ben Matthias was not complicated. As the general commanding the Jewish defense of Galilee, his detractors said, he had deliberately surrendered the key city of Yodefat to the Roman forces, thereby exposing Jerusalem to siege. The Slavic edition of Josephus gives a different version of the story, notably that he contrived a suicide pact with forty of Yodefat's most valiant defenders, then engineered things so that the other thirty-eight of them perished, after which he and the thirty-ninth escaped to go over to the Romans.

Worst of all, they said, he later retired to Rome to write *The Jewish War*, a version of the Jewish struggle for independence that absolved the Romans of their bloody role in it and whitewashed his own black record as well. For these and other failings, Jews in a later age condemned him.

To some Jews, however, and to the Romans, Josephus was nothing more than a realist. Though he fought in it, he opposed the war as hopeless. He refused suicide because he believed it sinful. His history of the Jewish War was accurate, and certainly did not leave the Roman record unblemished, they said.

Finally, his other great treatise, *Antiquities*, a history of the Jewish people, did much to acquaint non-Jews with their magnificent tradition and to explain why the Jews separated themselves from Roman society. In an appendix to his history, a work he called *A Life*, which some historians recognize as the first autobiography to survive from the ancient world, Josephus proudly discloses his distinguished pedigree—his descent from the Hasmonean Jewish royal family, his own superb education in Jewish Law, how as a mere youth his advice on the Law was sought by the scholars of the Temple.

In A.D. 62, when Josephus was twenty-six, he headed a delegation to Rome to secure the release of some Jewish priests imprisoned by Nero for what Josephus calls a "trifling" offense. He succeeded in his mission by ingratiating himself with Poppaea, Nero's mistress, who became his prime connection with the imperial establishment.

Four years later, when the revolutionary movement took over Jerusalem, Josephus opposed the war as unwinnable. So did the high priests and many Pharisees. Some historians dispute this, however, contending that what made the war hopeless was the Jewish failure to first secure alliances with rebellious elements in neighboring Roman provinces and with the old Persian empire beyond the Euphrates.

His pessimism notwithstanding, the revolutionary government put Josephus in command of Galilee, widely recognized as a cauldron of radical revolutionary ferment. How well Josephus did as a general, posterity was to know only through the words of Josephus himself. (A rival account by one Justus of Tiberius, referred to by ancient authors, has not survived.) Delicately, Josephus here shifts to the third person, so

One of the few likenesses of Flavius Josephus that does not present him as an eastern potentate, this bust dates from A.D. 100.

that he tells of the brilliant strategies of Josephus, and of Josephus's daring and valor that won so much Roman admiration.

Even so, as one town after another fell to Vespasian's advancing legions, attention focused on Yodefat, the last and strongest citadel of Galilean defense. The place fell with scarcely the loss of one Roman life, after a traitorous Jewish defender revealed to the Romans that the guards on the walls were exhausted and usually asleep just before daybreak. By then, the Roman earthwork, ramped up against the city walls despite vain efforts from within to stop it, had reached almost to the height of the walls anyway. In a predawn attack, the legions broke into the city and began a methodical slaughter of its inhabitants, saving only women and children.

Josephus himself, as commander, took refuge in a concealed cave with thirty-nine other defenders. When the Romans verged on discovering their hideaway, the others deemed suicide preferable to Roman slavery. Josephus openly disagreed. God gave us life, he argued. "It is to Him that we must leave the decision whether to take it away."

To this appeal his comrades reacted in rage, some running at him with their swords. He saved himself by coming up with another plan. They would draw lots. The first man to draw would be slain by the second, and the second by the third. This ghastly process of murder unfolded therefore, writes Josephus, until there were only two men left, he and one other, "whether by providence or good fortune." (The Slavic version of *The Jewish War* says it was neither, but that Josephus had rigged the draw.) These two, having seen thirty-eight of their fellows die (and likely having helped at least one to do so), looked hard at each other, decided to forget the pact, and gave themselves up to the Romans.

Thereafter, Josephus became a close associate of the Roman general Titus and later of his father Vespasian whose ascent to the imperial throne Josephus had accurately predicted. Under Titus, Josephus became the senior Roman spokesman to the enemy. After the war, he retired to Rome, and settled down in one of the imperial apartments with a new wife to write his histories.

Since his histories cover the period of Jesus' ministry, the question arises: What does Josephus say about Jesus? The answer is one brief reference, about 135 words, known as the *Testimonium Flavianum*. It describes Jesus as "a wise man, if a man at all," identifies him as "the Anointed," meaning the Messiah, and reports that Jesus rose from the dead. To this day (i.e., the early nineties of the first century), marvels the text, Jesus' followers "have not disappeared." Most historians consider at least a portion of this reference an interpolation, something added later by a Christian editor.

Josephus offers considerably more detail on John the Baptist. He describes John's forceful preaching and his baptismal rite which, says Josephus, was not a means to have sins forgiven, but rather a consecration of the body that had already been purified by good behavior. Herod Antipas ordered John put to death as a possible revolutionary rabble rouser, says Josephus, an explanation somewhat at odds with the biblical account.[1]

It was the Christians, far more than the Jews, who preserved Josephus's writings over the centuries. Indeed, in many eighteenth or nineteenth-century households, his works stood in the bookshelf beside the Bible. Whatever his biases, he provides a distinctly non-biblical view of the world that Jesus lived in. His death, which is not recorded, occurred in Rome, perhaps as late as A.D. 120 when he would have been eighty-three years old. ■

---

1. Herod Antipas is tricked into pledging the execution of John the Baptist through the wiles of Herodias, whose marriage to Herod, John denounced.

Along with the Bible, the works of Josephus were readily available in medieval Europe. This illumination is taken from a twelfth-century Flemish edition of The Jewish War.

led by Menahem[6]—who, Josephus notes, triumphantly entered the city "in the state of a king." This spelled trouble, since Eleazar had similar aspirations.

As the attack focused now on Herod's Palace, the Roman defenders asked for terms. The Jews and Agrippa's troops were allowed to depart, while the Romans barricaded themselves in the palace's soaring towers. But they were in no state to withstand a siege, and their commandant offered a truce. His troops would surrender their arms, he said, if their lives were spared. The insurgents agreed, but as soon as the Romans laid down their arms, the rebels butchered the whole contingent. News of this perfidy and of the liquidation of two Roman garrisons, the Antonia and the Masada, trickled back to Rome. Soon the empire's fierce and methodical retribution was being planned.

The rebels, of course, could see only their recent victory, and not its eventual repercussions. Menahem captured and killed Ananias, leader of the opposition party and Eleazar's father, a feat that left him "so puffed up," says Josephus,

News of the rebels' atrocities and the liquidation of the two garrisons at Antonia and Masada trickled back to Rome. Soon the empire's fierce retribution was being planned.

"that he became barbarously cruel." Eleazar resented this pomposity, and asked why the Jews should throw off the Roman yoke in order to submit to another. As Menahem paraded to the Temple in sumptuous robes, surrounded by his entourage, the populace began pelting him—not so much in support of Eleazar as hoping, Josephus says, to halt the entire revolt. Menahem's band scattered and their leader was tortured to death.

It now fell to the legate, Cestius, to restore order. He assembled an army of thirty thousand, including the rest of the Twelfth Legion, along with two thousand men from two other legions, and marched south, approaching Jerusalem during the Feast of Tabernacles. Suddenly, out of the city poured thousands of Jews, an unruly mob, but with such fierce vigor that they caught the Roman force off guard. They claimed five hundred Roman lives, then took up a position in the hills, looking down on a highly vulnerable Roman camp. Meanwhile, Agrippa sent two of his friends on behalf of the Romans, offering pardon in return for surrender. The rebels killed one and wounded the other, then withdrew from the hilltop and returned to the city.

Here further feuding broke out, so vehemently that many rebels panicked and fled. Cestius launched one assault after another against the walls, and the people stood ready to open the gates to him. But then occurred one of the strange twists of history that baffle both reason and the historians. Cestius withdrew. He had

---

6. The father of the rebel leader Menahem, known as Judas the Galilean, was a revolutionary theologian who preached that the Jews should have no earthly ruler, only God. This was known as the "Fourth Philosophy," after those of the Pharisees, Sadducees, and Essenes. The dagger-wielding Sicarii were associated with this sect.

suffered almost no losses; he had the city under siege; he could have ended the war that day. Yet he quit. He could not assure the supply of his troops, some historians speculate. Others attribute his decision to the onset of bad weather. Josephus perceives a divine intent. God willed, he concluded, the city's total destruction as a punishment. He had abandoned his ancient sanctuary.

Fortune now favored the rebels. Under the weight of their baggage, Cestius's troops trudged northwest towards Caesarea, the rebels constantly harassing them, picking off stragglers, hurling rocks down on them as they passed through the defiles, blocking their path when they could. The mighty Twelfth abandoned

The high priests reluctantly reached a grim conclusion: They must seize leadership of the revolution rather than have it commandeered by thieves and crackpots.

their war engines, and whimpered "their mournful cries," notes Josephus, "as men use in the utmost despair." Cestius, now desperate, left a rear guard of four hundred as a decoy, while the rest of the force slipped away in the night. At daybreak, their ensigns flying, the little defense unit shouted out phony orders as though they were standing in strength. The Jews were not fooled. They slaughtered the rear guard and set out after the retreating legion. Though they didn't overtake them, they did find catapults, battering rams, and other heavy, unwieldy weapons that Cestius's men had abandoned, all of which was to prove critical in the months ahead. This treasure they carted back to Jerusalem, singing songs of triumph. The Twelfth Legion would need a long time to live down this humiliation.

In the city, the high priests reluctantly reached a grim conclusion—that they must seize leadership of the revolution rather than have it commandeered by crackpots and thieves. They resolved to prepare for war while working for peace, always hoping that the people would see reason. They moved decisively. Ex-high priest Annas was given supreme command, while the nation was divided into six military districts.

Galilee, to the north, was key. It was likely to be Rome's first target, for two reasons: Its populace was the region's most hot-headed and rebellious, and its fertile soil made it the bread basket for the arid south, the region of Judea and the capital city, Jerusalem. Three men were sent north from Jerusalem to try to maintain order in Galilee. One was Josephus, the thirty-year-old priest with no previous military experience, who would eventually become Rome's ally and the war's historian.

Josephus was a dubious choice. He had visited Rome a few years before, and what he saw there convinced him that any rebellion could not succeed. So his position was untenable from the beginning. He had to fight a war he was convinced he could not win. This dilemma brought him into instant conflict with a rebel leader who thought he could, John from Gischala in Galilee, whose band of four hundred was spoiling for a fight, whether with the Romans or with any Jews who didn't want to fight the Romans.

Such as Josephus. Hoping to be appointed in Josephus's place, John spread rumors Josephus was planning to betray the nation to Rome. Two attempts were made on Josephus's life, and for a time, control of the province seesawed between the two. John was not the only rival as would-be leader of the Jewish cause. At Jerusalem, Simon son of Gioras presented himself as champion of the needy, committed to relieving poverty. He began by relieving his own. Given a minor office in the new government, he was fired for graft, and fled to the Masada fortress. There he discovered the Sicarii, left leaderless by the death of Menahem. These joined Simon, and prepared to return in force to Jerusalem. They adopted the old name "Zealots," long the designation of those Jews who despised the Jerusalem leadership as soft. They were zealous for the faith, said Simon. Josephus saw them as brigands and rioters, zealous only for loot and booty.

Meanwhile at Rome, Nero named to command the Roman counteroffensive a proven general, Titus Flavius Vespasian, a fifty-seven-year-old frontline veteran, ex-commander of the Second Legion, credited with a major victory in the Roman invasion of Britain, who despised the prissy life of the Roman aristocracy, and was renowned for once having fallen loudly asleep during one of Nero's poetry recitations. But Nero knew his man. Vespasian had grown gray in

Coins from the period of the Jewish revolt indicate that life and commerce went on despite the warfare. This one, with Hebrew inscription, is dated about A.D. 68 and was minted by the Jewish factions.

In a last sane act, Nero gave 57-year-old veteran Titus Vespasian command of the counteroffensive. His forces numbered 60,000 and were designed to intimidate. They did.

the service and was wise and methodical. His two sons, particularly Titus, the elder, would second their father and supply youthful vigor. Both assumptions were to prove devastatingly accurate.[7]

In the spring of 67, Vespasian assembled an army at Ptolemais on the Mediterranean coast west of Galilee. He formed up the Fifteenth Legion in Syria and called in the Tenth Fretensis and the Fifth Macedonica under his son Titus from Alexandria. The disgraced Twelfth he kept in reserve. The total force, including twenty-three auxiliary cohorts, numbered sixty thousand. These marched east and set up a camp on the Galilean frontier, where they put on a fearsome display of men and armor, trumpeters and horses, banners and war engines. It was designed to intimidate and it did. Josephus's men panicked and fled, leaving him with an army too small to do battle. Taking his remaining supporters, Josephus retreated behind the walls of Tiberias on the Sea of Galilee and sent a message to Jerusalem, warning that Galilee could not sustain Vespasian's attack, and they should either send an adequate army or permit him to surrender the province.

---

7. Besides their two sons, Vespasian and his wife Flavia Domitilla had a daughter, also Domitilla. The daughter in turn had a daughter, Vespasian's granddaughter, who had the same name and who became a Christian.

Sixty thousand men at his command, the seasoned Roman general Vespasian plots his strategy against the upstart rebels in Judea. Striking first at Galilee and humbling the Jewish forces there, he brings his troops nearly to the walls of Jerusalem. His advance, however, is interrupted by a recall to Rome, where he is to be acclaimed emperor. His son, Titus, has the task of completing the brutal campaign of suppression.

Meanwhile, the Romans overran most of Galilee, first occupying its largest city, Sepphoris, and easily warding off Jewish attacks. Gabara fell on the first Roman assault; every adult male was put to death and the town burned.

Josephus in the meantime moved into the stronghold of Yodefat where the showdown battle for Galilee would occur.

As Vespasian's troops encircled the city, eliminating all hope of escape, the Jews were moved to new "deeds of gallantry," says Josephus, "for in war there is nothing like necessity to rouse the fighting spirit."

Yodefat held out for seven weeks. When Vespasian began building earthworks to assail its walls,[8] the Jews rained large rocks down on them from above. Vespasian then set up a ring of projectile-throwers, which hurled lances, rocks, and firebrands and drove the defenders off the ramparts. They retaliated in guerrilla-like raids, demolishing the earthworks and setting fire to their wooden supports. Still the earthworks rose, so Josephus built the walls higher. His messengers bypassed the Roman guards by draping themselves with sheepskins and crawling on all fours, so that at night they were taken for dogs. To bypass Vespasian's blockade, Josephus brought some supplies into the city through one of its deep flanking ravines, which Vespasian eventually discovered and blocked.

So persistent were the Jewish attacks against the earthworks, boasts Josephus, that Vespasian felt he was the one under siege. Eventually he maneuvered his war engines and a battering ram up to the city's gates. But the Jews, in a daring foray, rushed out from the town and set the engines and shelters on fire. One Jewish fighter threw a boulder down from the city wall and broke off the massive iron ram's head. He then leapt down, carried it away under the very noses of the Romans, and swiftly climbed back up the wall, to display his prize to both sides. But his triumph was short-lived. He fell headlong forward, pierced by five Roman arrows.

When the Romans finally broke down a section of the wall and began setting up gangways over the rubble, necessity once again led to inspiration. Josephus had his men bring boiling oil and pour it down on the soldiers from the ramparts that remained.[9] Roman armor was good protection against rocks and stones, but when scalding oil slipped beneath it, it became a prison of pain. As the men at the head of the gangway collapsed in agony they blocked the way of the men behind them, who could not easily retreat. Josephus's quick thinking had won him another day.

Yodefat's fall, however, came silently in the predawn darkness. A Jewish deserter advised Vespasian to slip into the city at dawn when sleep routinely overcame the exhausted sentries. This simple strategy succeeded. One morning,

---

8. The Romans had many ways of overcoming city walls. Sometimes they used huge towers, up to seventy-five feet high, that were rolled up to the wall, providing a platform from which the attackers could fire arrows down on the defenders below, then launch themselves onto the ramparts. Or they might use battering rams that were rolled up beside the wall and pound its foundational masonry to pieces until the wall collapsed. However, the ground had to be leveled and prepared for both these devices, and Josephus's use of the term "earthworks" usually refers to the construction of timber-cribbed earthen foundations.

9. Boiling oil is generally considered a medieval weapon. This, its earliest recorded use, sets it back into ancient times.

near the end of July 67, the sleeping sentries were quietly overcome by a Roman squad that stole into the city, followed by the assault force. Yodefat awoke to find the Romans rampaging through their town, killing all but women and infants, whom they enslaved. Josephus estimates that in all forty thousand Jews perished at Yodefat.

He, however, was not one of them. He leapt into a deep pit, and there discovered the opening to a cave, invisible from above, where forty leading men of the town were hiding. They hid successfully for two days, then were discovered. Vespasian

Yodefat awoke to find the Romans rampaging through the town, killing all but women and infants, whom they enslaved. An estimated forty thousand perished.

sent Josephus's friend Nicanor to offer safe conduct in return for surrender. All of which, in the eyes of Josephus's critics, was far too convenient to be convincing. They contend Josephus crassly betrayed his men and conspired with Vespasian to let the Romans in.

Josephus, of course, tells a very different story. In the cave he began to reflect on the prophetic dreams he had long had, warning of calamity for the Jews, and revealing the coming succession to the imperial throne following Nero's imminent death. Rather than accepting Vespasian's offer, he declares, he sent up a "secret prayer" of surrender to God's will. In his own eyes, he did not go to the Romans as a deserter, but as a minister of God.

So after reneging on a suicide pact (see sidebar, this chapter, pages 245–246), he surrendered to Vespasian's son Titus who, says Josephus, had been impressed with Josephus's valor, and urged his father to treat him kindly. The old man was suspicious until Josephus spoke. "Do you send me to Nero?" he asked. "Why?" Thereupon he made a prophecy. Nero and his immediate successors would soon be dead, and a new imperial line was about to begin. "You, O Vespasian, are caesar and emperor, you and this your son." Josephus was in chains, but asked,

Until the late-twentieth century, little physical evidence was available to substantiate the great battle that took place for the stronghold of Yodefat. Digs have since revealed the undistinguished hill in central Galilee to be a rich source of artifacts and architectural features—almost all bearing evidence of the destructive fury unleashed after the Roman victory there.

"Bind me now still faster, and keep me for yourself." Vespasian at first viewed this as transparent flattery. Yet it might prove true. He ordered Josephus kept in custody, but kept well, with fine clothing and food.

Vespasian now began the mop-up of Galilee, which included a naval battle on the Sea of Galilee that was disastrous to the Jews, leaving the lake stained with blood and the shores piled with corpses. Titus meanwhile took on Gischala, stronghold of rebel leader John. When he saw that his situation was desperate, John made a bargain: If Titus would let his men observe the next day's Sabbath, they would surrender the following day. That night, he and the

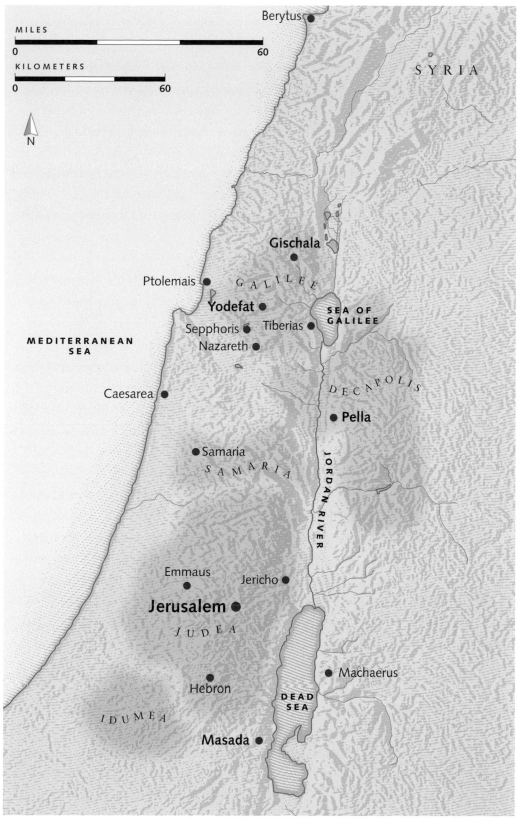

MILES

0   60

KILOMETERS

0   60

N

Berytus

SYRIA

Gischala

Ptolemais   *G A L I L E E*

Yodefat

SEA OF
GALILEE

Sepphoris   Tiberias

MEDITERRANEAN
SEA

Nazareth

D E C A P O L I S

Caesarea

Pella

Samaria

S A M A R I A

J O R D A N R I V E R

Emmaus   Jericho

Jerusalem

J U D E A

Machaerus

Hebron

DEAD
SEA

I D U M E A

Masada

town's leading citizens gathered their families and slipped away, under cover of darkness. As they fled toward Jerusalem, however, the women and children gradually fell behind. They begged their men to help them, but their pleas were ignored. The next morning, the Romans discovered they had been duped. They rushed out in pursuit of the escapees, but found only the straggling women and children, who were herded back to Gischala and probable slavery.

John made it into Jerusalem where he fueled the internecine strife that for the next three years would prove every bit as destructive and agonizing as anything threatened by the enemy. The Romans were weak, he said. His flight was merely a strategic retreat. He banded with Eleazar son of Simon, now leading the Zealots.[10] They seized the Temple, deposed the high priest, and cast lots for that office, appointing what Josephus calls a "rustic" from the countryside who knew nothing about the priesthood.

This outraged the people, and gave Annas, hitherto leader of the interim government, sufficient popular support to drive the Zealots back into the Temple's inner precinct, while Annas and the moderates secured the outer courts with a guard. Meanwhile John of Gischala joined both sides, vowing fidelity to the high priestly party, while telling the Zealots that Annas had appealed to Vespasian for help.

That spread panic among the Zealots, and they appealed to the Idumeans, a people who lived in southern Judea and had been forcibly converted to Judaism a century before, but were now ready to join any rebellion against Rome. When twenty thousand of them showed up at Jerusalem's gates the high priestly party begged them to join the moderate side. They indignantly declined, but were at a loss as to what to do next, since the moderates controlled the gate and refused them entry. That night, however, a violent storm broke, enabling some of the Zealots to open the gate to them in darkness. In poured the Idumeans, who raced through the city, killing and looting. Eighty-five hundred people died in that carnage, says Josephus, and the outer courts of the Temple were stained with blood.[11]

Not one to curry Nero's favor, Vespasian is nevertheless the man chosen by the emperor to quash the Judean rebellion of A.D. 66. This coin was minted in his honor after he had attained the "Imperial Purple" as emperor.

Eventually the Idumeans caught Annas and his senior high priestly lieutenant Jesus and slaughtered both, mocking their speeches and then throwing the bodies over the city walls without burial. "The death of Annas was the beginning of the destruction of the city," Josephus writes. The high priest was eloquent, and perhaps could have brokered a peace with the Romans. "I cannot help but think that it was because God had doomed this city to destruction, as a polluted city, and was resolved to purge his sanctuary by fire, that he cut off these great defenders."

The Zealots took part in this bloodbath with such crazed glee, then condemning the survivors after mock trials, that it was too much even for the

---

10. There are seven Eleazars in Josephus's book, *The Jewish War*, five of whom appear in this chapter. They are: Eleazar son of Ananias, who vanishes from Josephus's story at this point; Eleazar son of Simon, who now enters it as leader of the Zealots, whose ultimate fate also goes unreported; Eleazar, the father of a woman named Mary who devours her own child; Eleazar, a hero of the Jews at the Machaerus fortress, and Eleazar son of Jair, who defends to the last the fortress of Masada.

11. Since any contact with a dead body was defiling, the spectacle of corpses on the Temple Mount was unthinkable.

Idumeans, most of whom went home in disgust. This news reached the Romans, who were pleased to hear of disunity in the city, and some urged Vespasian to attack immediately while the Jews were in disarray. The seasoned general had a better idea: An attack might unite them, but if he waited they would kill each other, doing his work for him. Victory would be easier when the right time came.

But events at Rome would help delay that time for another two years. In June 68 Vespasian received word that Nero had died. Since he had been appointed by Nero, his commission lapsed, and he brought the campaign to a halt, awaiting further orders. Three more would-be emperors occupied the throne in quick succession, and Rome was in turmoil. In the summer of 69 Vespasian's legions decided that their general was the best candidate. They proclaimed him emperor, and he began to make his way from Caesarea to Rome.

By the time Vespasian reached Berytus (the future Beirut) he was already beginning to receive congratulations from many provinces. It looked as if Josephus's prophecy was being fulfilled, and Vespasian regretted the man was still in chains. He commanded that Josephus be set free, but Titus had a better idea. He asked that the chains be severed with an axe, symbolizing that a

Simon's response to the kidnapping of his wife was to attack anyone who set foot outside of Jerusalem, torturing them to death or sending them back without their hands.

prisoner had been chained unjustly. Thus Josephus was free, fully pardoned and invested with civil rights in Rome. Vespasian's family name, Flavius, became Josephus's name as well. When Vespasian reached Alexandria early in A.D. 70 he received news that he had been acclaimed emperor in Rome, and that his son Domitian was acting as ruler until he came. He sent his son Titus to finish the war at Jerusalem with the pick of his army.

In the meantime, another rebel group arrived at Jerusalem and encamped outside the walls. Simon son of Gioras had begun with a band of followers at Masada and continued to gather recruits throughout the countryside, intending to battle the other rebels and gain control of Jerusalem. He took possession of Hebron and ranged through Idumea until "there was nothing left behind Simon's army but a desert," says Josephus. Eleazar's Zealots, seeking to intimidate Simon, kidnapped his wife and demanded that he lay down his arms. Simon's response was to attack anyone who set foot outside the city, torturing them to death or sending them back into the city without their hands. These acts of raw horror worked. It was the Zealots who were intimidated, and they set Simon's wife free.

It rapidly dawned on Jerusalem's trembling citizenry that their liberators were worse than the Romans had ever been. Outside the walls, Simon killed and tortured. Within them, the followers of John of Gischala loosed a reign of terror on the populace. Sated with rape and plunder, writes Josephus, they invented new diversions: wearing women's clothes and perfume, braiding their hair and behaving as if in a brothel. (Historians warn, however, that descriptions such as this should be regarded suspiciously. They are based strictly on Josephus's account of events, and he would naturally seek to blackguard his opponents.)

Soon the remaining Idumeans had had enough of this, and drove John and his followers into the Temple. Ironically, the Idumeans now turned to the high priests' party, the people they had pounced upon first after they had gained entrance to the city. This led to an even stranger coalition. The priests, concluding anything would be better than John, proposed to bring Simon into the city and unite with him against John. This was to make things worse than ever. It was, says Josephus, as though God himself was leading them to embrace the worst possible advice.[12]

Thus in April 69 the gates were opened and Simon son of Gioras entered the city as its master and led the citizens against John, now leagued with Eleazar's Zealots, in the Temple. Though Simon had larger numbers, John's men and the Zealots had the advantage of height and from the Temple's towers were able to cast down missiles upon their assailants.

Then a new quarrel broke out. Eleazar and his Zealots, numbering about twenty-four hundred, ensconced in the Temple with John, began to resent the latter's imperious ways. They took over the Temple's inner courts and highest ground and pushed John's men out. These remained immediately under them in the Temple's outer precincts with greater numbers but caught in the middle.

While Jerusalem's efficient water cisterns ensured that the besieged city would not die of thirst, the food supplies were another matter.

Below them and occupying the city as a whole were Simon and his nervous allies, the high priestly party. The defenders were thus split three ways, and in this confusing situation John and Simon each set fires, presumably hoping to burn the other out. Instead they sealed the fate of Jerusalem. While the city's astonishingly efficient water cisterns provided it with enough water to last for years, and were virtually indestructible, its food supplies were not. What the fires did destroy were the warehouses filled with grain enough to withstand a prolonged siege.

Unlikely as it seems, in the midst of this waste and carnage the rituals of the Temple continued. Worshipers came to pray and make sacrifices, though stones and javelins rained down upon them and mixed their own blood with that of the sacrifices. Blood "stood in lakes in the holy courts themselves," writes Josephus, and common people longed for the Romans to come and

---

12. It was Matthias of the high priestly Boethus family who invited Simon to enter Jerusalem. He was to pay dearly for this mission. At the height of the siege, Simon ordered Matthias and his family executed without trial as Roman sympathizers. Matthias pleaded to be killed first. Simon refused, making him first witness the execution of his children, then die over their corpses.

free them from their supposed emancipators.

It was by now the spring of 70, and Titus with his three crack legions advanced upon Jerusalem. He sent two as pincers, the Fifth by way of Emmaus, and the Tenth by way of Jericho, and brought the Fifteenth with him. He took direct command of the Twelfth, its men now bent on avenging their humiliation and redeeming their reputation. All these were supplemented by units of two Egyptian legions, the Third known as the "Cyrenaica," and the Twenty-Second

Suddenly the Jews launched a foray against the reconnaissance party, one that nearly changed Roman history. Titus, a future emperor, found himself trapped.

"Deiotariana." Troops supplied by Rome's client kings completed the force, King Agrippa leading his men personally.

Titus advanced on Jerusalem, and made a camp about four miles north of the city. Aware of the strife going on within the walls, he picked a force of five hundred cavalrymen and set out to reconnoiter the walls for evidence of anti-rebel activity within. Suddenly the Jews launched a foray against the reconnaissance party that came narrowly near to changing the whole course of the war and of Roman history. Titus, the future emperor of Rome, found himself trapped.

Most of his squadron had stayed on the central road that led to one of the city's gates. He and a small party had veered off on a side road. Abruptly, from what was known as Jerusalem's "Women's Towers," a massive body of Jews poured forth, cutting Titus off from the main contingent, and penning him against the hedges and gardens that lined the city walls. The Jews realized that the biggest conceivable prize the Romans had to offer now lay in their grasp. Titus saw he could go neither forward nor back. He and the few men with him had either to get themselves out or, for them anyway, the war was over.

Being on a purely reconnaissance mission, he wore neither helmet nor breastplate. But signaling to his companions to follow, he plunged into the midst of his enemies, arrows flying about him, hacking them down and galloping over their bodies. Studded with arrows, two men beside him fell. But Titus and the rest escaped, back to the safety of their main party and then to the ranks of the legions.

At Mount Scopus to the north of the city he linked up with the Fifth and set up his main encampment. The Tenth took up a position on the Mount of Olives. The Jews, when they saw that the Romans were erecting fortifications, briefly forgot their differences, plunged in strength down the steep slope of the Kidron Valley, then up the other side, and took the Tenth by surprise. Its men, still engaged in building the camp, were caught without their weapons. The Jews surged about them in a disorderly pack, so disorienting the Romans that they

The life of Vespasian's son Titus was to parallel his father's. Following a successful military career that included the conquest of Jerusalem, Titus was proclaimed emperor in A.D. 79, and was a stabilizing influence on the empire until his death just twenty-six months later.

In an uncharacteristic lapse of judgment, Titus and a small Roman scouting squad venture too close to a section of Jerusalem's walls that conceals a mob of defenders. Slashing with determination at the arrows suddenly raining down on him and wearing no protective armor, Titus escapes back to the safety of a larger Roman patrol.

abandoned camp and fled.[13]

Titus soon arrived with reinforcements, and the battle raged up and down the slopes of the Kidron. Finally the Romans drove the defenders out of the valley and back into the city. Meanwhile Titus sent the Tenth to continue building their camp, while the rest of the force stood guard against further raids.

This first encounter forewarned Titus that he faced a wily and unpredictable enemy. In the long months ahead the Romans were routinely confounded by the Jews' reckless agility. Despite their crushing strength, the Romans sometimes despaired of winning the war at all.

What the Jews lacked, however, was the unity and discipline of the Legions. No sooner had the defenders withdrawn into the city than their feuds broke out again. Passover was now upon them and Eleazar cautiously admitted worshipers to the Inner Temple, his stronghold. John of Gischala used this

---

13. A Roman army camp was like a model town, with tents laid along streets that intersect at right angles, the headquarters of the commandant in the center. Just as in armies two thousand years later, men are called at a given time, form up before their centurions, who in turn salute and report to their tribunes, who then salute the commander. He gives them the day's orders and the day's password. Equipment is standard. Infantrymen wear a breastplate and helmet, with a sword on the left and a long dagger on the right. Cavalrymen carry a pike and quiver with arrows as well.

CROFUT

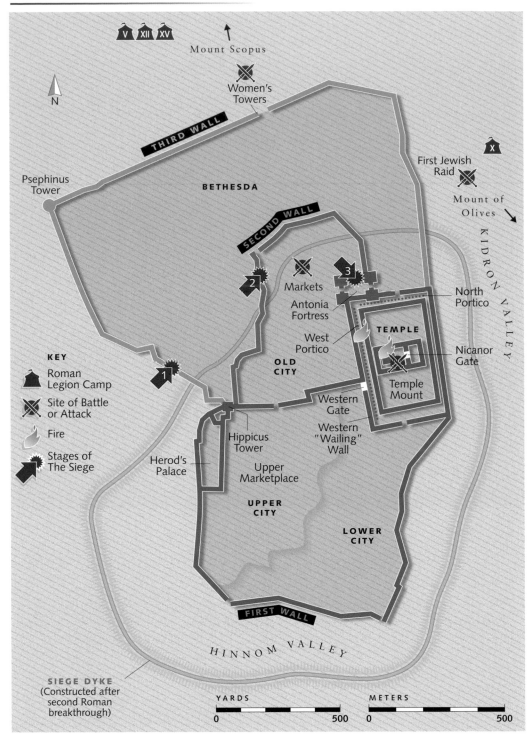

opportunity to infiltrate. Once inside, his supposedly peaceful worshipers turned out to be armed invaders. They brought forth their weapons and regained command of the Inner Temple.

Titus began clearing the land in the four miles between Mount Scopus and the northern wall of the city. This was known as the Third Wall, built thirty years before, when the Romans' client king, Agrippa I, was ruler of Judea, to enclose the sprawling new development on the city's north side. As Jewish unrest grew, the Romans ordered Agrippa to halt construction. It was therefore not considered formidable. Behind it, however, stood two more walls, very formidable indeed. (See map above.)

The Jews then staged an elaborate drama atop the New Wall, with one

A present-day view of Jerusalem (above) from Mount Scopus provides some idea of what Titus would see as he surveyed the city and monitored the advances of his troops. Looking to the south, the Temple Mount (six miles distant behind the walls, left-center) rises above the green of the Kidron Valley. The Mount of Olives, which is not shown in this photograph, would be off to the left.

group begging the Romans to come rescue them while others pretended to violently oppose them. By now wary of Jewish ploys, Titus ordered his men to stand fast. Some soldiers, however, had already advanced to the wall. When they came between gateway towers they found themselves surrounded by Jewish assailants while others pelted them from the walls. They withdrew with great difficulty, and great embarrassment. From the ramparts the Jews jeered, shouting, dancing with delight, and mocking the Romans for falling for a ruse.

While Titus arrayed his men seven deep along the northern and western sections of the wall—three lines of infantry, three of cavalry, and a row of archers in the middle—new turmoil broke out within. John's six thousand pitted themselves against Eleazar's twenty-four hundred, reducing to ashes any structures between them, while Simon's fifteen thousand ran rampant in the town below.

Riding around the walls, Titus saw it was futile to attack from the south or east, skirted as they were by deep ravines. However, where Herod's palace stood on the western edge of the city the New Wall ran out

The standards of the Tenth Fretensis (right) preceded that Legion into battle in Judea. The Fretensis had taken its name from a sea battle on the Fretum Siculum (now the Straits of Messina, separating Sicily and Italy). A standard functioned much as a totem, with figures representing significant events in a legion's history. One standard of the Fretensis displayed a boar, another a trireme (for the sea battle). The standard with the eagle signified the empire.

toward the northwest and the juncture was weak. Here Titus set men building earthworks up to the wall, under covering fire from catapults, stone-throwers, and other machines of war.

As the earthworks gradually neared completion, Titus ordered that a battering ram be brought up. This frightened the rebels into unity, and they agreed that both groups would have full access to all of Jerusalem, with Simon retaining leadership of the Upper City and John controlling the Temple and Antonia Fortress. For a time the Romans battered the wall without success. Suddenly the Jews poured out upon them, surrounded the war engines, and set the timbers on fire. Titus drove them back, killing many and taking one prisoner alive. This unfortunate he theatrically crucified in full view of the city walls.

The battering continued, with the Romans working under shelter of three enormous ironclad towers they had rolled up to the site. The towers reached twice the height of the wall. The Jews were now stymied. The towers were fireproof and too heavy to overturn, and they could not approach them without drawing a hail of arrows from the archers atop them. On the fifteenth day of the siege, May 25, the Romans breached the Third Wall (see map, below left) and poured into the northern part of the city, called Bethesda (the biblical Bethsaida). The Jews retreated behind the Second Wall, which ran in a jagged line across the city from Herod's Palace to the Antonia Fortress. John took up the defense at the Antonia, and Simon concentrated his forces at Herod's Palace, while Titus directed his battering ram at the unprotected spot on the northeastern leg of the Second Wall. Fighting continued from dawn till night, and anxiety deprived both sides of sleep.

Five days later the Second Wall was breached and Titus's forces broke into the Old City. (See map, page 263.) Josephus reports that Titus now offered the Jews an armistice. He "would preserve the city for myself, and the Temple for the city," he said, and would forbid his troops to kill prisoners or set houses on fire. Any who wanted to continue fighting would be given safe conduct outside the walls to resume the battle there, so that citizens would not be injured. He hoped, too, he said, to restore the citizens' property.

The Jews, said Josephus, took this as an indication of Roman weakness. Perhaps too they remembered the false promise of safe conduct that they had given Roman troops taking refuge in Herod's Palace four years earlier, and feared the Romans planned to even the score. The armistice was thus rejected and soon the Romans were fighting in the Old City's narrow, winding streets. Here they were at a disadvantage. The Jews knew every cranny and hiding place well but the

PHASE ONE:
TITUS BREAKS THROUGH

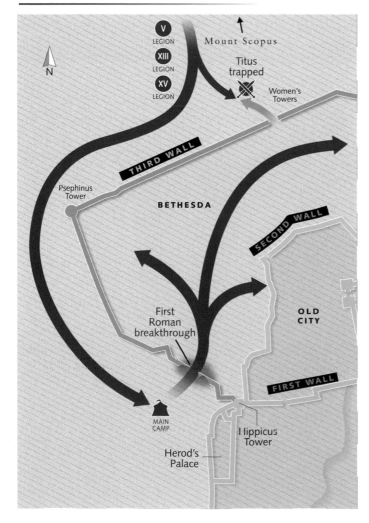

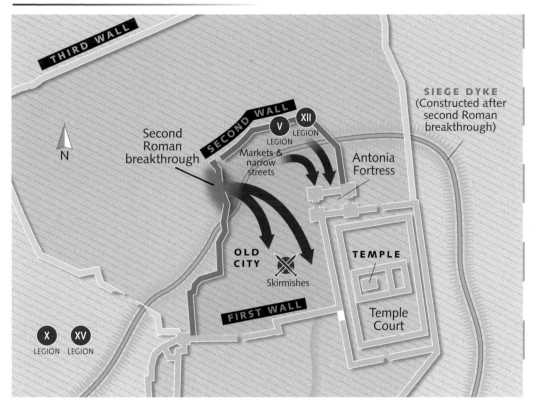

Romans knew them not at all. Getting the worst of it, the Romans tried to withdraw. But the narrow breach they had made in the wall impeded them. They finally escaped with grave difficulty, much to the exhilaration of the Jewish forces.

But another and much more formidable enemy increasingly gnawed upon the defenders' resolve. Already starvation was creeping through the city. The weak were dying. Children wept for food. Families that still had a little were looked upon with ravenous envy by neighbors who had none. Hiding it became a major imperative.

Titus briefly suspended the assault, and arranged a four-day spectacle. As the Jews watched, soldiers paraded up continuously in shining armor and glittering silver and lavish rations were poured into their hands. The troops found this interlude delightful.

The Jews, lined up on every rampart to watch, found it dismaying.

On the fifth day the Romans went back to the job. The Tenth and Fifteenth Legions addressed themselves to a point near Herod's Palace where the Second Wall met the First. The Fifth, joined by the Twelfth, took on the Antonia Fortress. At each site the Romans built two earthworks that encroached ever more closely upon the walls. But they did not do this without cost. John's followers and the Zealots constantly sprayed them with arrows from the Antonia, while Simon's followers and the Idumeans did the same from the Hippicus Tower at Herod's Palace.

Titus persevered and made good use of Josephus, who was now in the Roman ranks. Better than any, Josephus understood the mentality of those behind the walls, and rightly guessed that the high priests could clearly see nothing but ruin

Up and down the walls of Jerusalem, battles rage as the Jews attempt to repulse the juggernaut of Roman war machines—ramps, towers, catapults, and rams. More often, however, hand-to-hand skirmishes below the walls and in the streets determine the course of the war.

in the Jewish resistance. He must now therefore speak one last appeal to save his people. (Historians debate whether Josephus actually delivered this speech, or merely wrote down his thoughts in the quiet of his apartment at Rome six years later.) In Josephus's account, however, he stationed himself before the walls, close enough to be heard, far enough back to be out of range for the archers, and cried out to his countrymen.

Had they really considered what they were doing? The outcome of this insanity could well be the permanent and total destruction of the Temple and the Holy City. Did they see that they were fighting not merely the Romans but God himself? Whenever their cause was right, did not God intervene and save them?

Then he hit harder, his voice ringing out to the ramparts:

> We can produce no example wherein our fathers got any success by war, or failure when without war they committed themselves to God. . . . As for you, of the things commanded by our Lawgiver what have you done? And of the things he condemned, what have you left undone?

The response from the walls was a tirade of ridicule and execration along with showers of stones. At this Josephus seems to have broken down, pleading as had so many Jewish prophets:

> O, hard-hearted wretches that you are, cast away your weapons and take pity on your country which is already tottering to its fall. Turn and gaze at the beauty of what you are betraying: What a city! What a Temple! Who could be the first to set that Temple on fire? Who could wish that these things be no more? You inhuman creatures, you stone-hearted men! At least have pity on your families, and set before your eyes your children, wife and parents, who will gradually be consumed by either famine or war.
>
> I know that this danger extends to my own mother, my wife, and my family. Perhaps you think it is for their sakes that I offer you this advice. Then kill them, and take my own blood as well, as the price of your salvation! I am ready to die, if that could lead you to learn wisdom!

The leaders remained unmoved, but some of the people stole out of the city, and Titus allowed them to cross to freedom. John and Simon promptly declared such evacuation punishable by death, then began executing people suspected of even planning escape. Eventually they took this further by raiding the homes of the wealthy, declaring them intended evacuees, killing them and confiscating their property.

But the deepest misery of the people was hunger. As Josephus observes, it destroys the last human restraints against shame. First, families turned against each other, then strife broke out within households, husbands snatching food from wives, mothers from children. A healthy appearance became dangerous.

Those who lacked the hollow cheeks and sunken eyes were assumed to have hidden rations. They were exposed to assault, their homes to pillage. Anyone discovered to be hiding food was beaten; those with whom no food was found were subjected to grotesque torture, in the belief that they had successfully concealed it. Rebels would batter their way past locked doors and force food out of the mouths of their victims. Old men were beaten as they clung to their morsels, and women dragged away by the hair; children were swung up by their feet and slammed against the floor.

As the days wore on and the Romans could see no sign the defenders were about to yield, the Roman cruelty grew vicious. Prisoners were routinely whipped, tortured, then crucified in view of the city, the victims in a variety of poses until, says Josephus, they ran out of room for crosses, and the wood to make them, all available timber in the Jerusalem area having been cut down for the earthworks.

Still the siege troops labored on. Then another Jewish stratagem befell them. John and his men had dug a tunnel underneath the Antonia embankments,

supporting it as they went with timbers. On June 16, as the Romans brought up the war engines, John carried timber smeared with pitch and bitumen into the tunnel and set it ablaze. The tunnel collapsed with a thunderous crash followed by a burst of fire. The troops fled in panic.

Two days later Simon's men suddenly sallied forth and set fire to the framework diligently constructed by the Tenth and Fifteenth Legions. The flames spread rapidly and the Romans, seeing no way to save their work, beat a retreat to their camp, the Jews hard on their heels right up to the sentry line. Here a confused battle took place in a roil of smoke and dust. At last the Jews returned to the city, leaving the Romans wondering whether conventional weapons were of any use against such a recklessly persistent foe.

Titus pondered. He had one last weapon, he knew, that the Jews could not contend with, namely hunger. In clever stealth and by darkness, Jewish foraging parties were getting out of the city and returning with meager supplies. If these were cut off, sooner or later the defenders must yield. Quickly his tireless troops erected a five-mile-long siege dike that surrounded the entire city. Night and day they patrolled it.

Inside Jerusalem, his tactic quickly told. The final stages of starvation set in and the death toll rose rapidly. Josephus describes women and infants lying limp with exhaustion, alleys filled with corpses, and young men and children wandering the markets like shadows, collapsing wherever death overtook them. Rebels went from house to house, ravaging the possessions of the dead and dying. Some they found barely alive, slumped on the floors. These they would

Three types of Roman siege machinery were brought to bear against Jerusalem. The ballista was capable of firing not only arrows but also larger missiles such as pikes and flaming spears. The battering ram came in various sizes and designs, ranging from those hefted by soldiers to giant versions mounted on wooden pendulums. The catapult (shown here), depending on its size and design, was capable of hurling rocks as heavy as 160 pounds over distances of up to one-half mile.

CROFUT

stab through as an entertainment. To others who begged for death they would deny deliverance, leaving them to a more agonizing fate. As each died, Josephus notes, he turned his eyes toward the Temple.

Burial was impossible for such a quantity of dead, and the living were too weak to do it. However the stench was unbearable, and the rebel leaders resorted to flinging corpses over the walls and down into the ravines until these were choked with oozing bodies. There was no mourning or weeping, no sound at all, says Josephus. "Deep silence blanketed the city." Hunger deadens emotion. "With dry eyes and grinning mouths those who were slow to die watched those whose end came sooner."

Anyone who attempted to flee to the Romans met a different fate. A refugee who had found shelter among the Syrian troops was discovered picking through his excrement; he had swallowed his coins planning to recover them later. The story spread swiftly through the auxiliary forces. In a single night, Josephus reports, two thousand deserters were ripped open so that soldiers could paw through their bowels. Very few yielded such treasure; most were fleeing because they were destitute and starving.

Cover of night permits Jerusalem's defenders, trapped behind the walls, to deal with the piles of dead bodies. Those still alive are forced to throw the corpses of their families and neighbors off the walls and into the surrounding ravines, where they are left to rot.

Then Titus put his men back to work, concentrating this time only on the Antonia Fortress. The earthwork construction went slowly. The whole countryside had already been stripped of trees, and wood had to be transported eleven miles to the site. On July 20 John's forces in the Antonia made an attack against these preparations, but it was hesitant and timid. "Unlike Jews," Josephus notes. The rebels fled having accomplished nothing. Their strength and their resolve were finally fading.

The Romans too seemed desperate. Their advance parties had reached the very walls, and dug at its stones, all to no avail, they feared. Then a seeming miracle occurred. In the middle of the night the wall simply collapsed. But it was no miracle. John's tunnel had undermined it and it gave way. Only then

did the Romans discover the Jews had built a second wall behind it.

But as in many battles, the event that would prove decisive came more by luck than by generalship. It was about three in the morning. A squad of twelve men from the Fifth Legion, observing the enemy wall by night, noticed that the guard atop the Antonia looked unusually weak. The sentries were absent perhaps, or asleep. In any event, these called the standard-bearer of the Fifth, two cavalrymen and a trumpeter. They made their way silently through the ruins at the foot of the wall, scaled it, and slit the throats of the guards they found there. From the wall-top the trumpeter sounded a rallying call to the Fifth. The other guards, hearing the trumpeter, seeing a party of Romans along the wall, and observing that one of them was a standard-bearer, reached the obvious conclusion. A whole legion was now moving into the city. So they fled.

In short order this would prove true. Hearing the trumpet, Titus guessed the situation, ordered his whole force instantly to arms, and personally led his senior commanders to the site, over the wall, and into the city. By now John's force was also on hand, and charged with characteristic disregard of life directly at the assembling Roman force. It never got there. More of John's tunnel collapsed beneath them. Like the Roman earthwork and like the wall, they plunged into the pit, a melee of crushed and struggling bodies, while the legions began to form up before them. Immediately behind them stood the Temple. They knew and the Romans knew that the fall of the Temple meant the fall of the city. The crucial fight was now at hand. Josephus describes it:

Arrows and spears were useless. Both sides drew their swords and fought it out hand to hand. Hemmed in by the walls of the temple, the two sides mingled and fought at random. The din of clashing arms, shouting men and screaming wounded was so overwhelming that no individual sound was audible. The slaughter was great on both sides, the combatants trampling the fallen beneath their feet and crushing their own armor into their bodies. While those behind pushed forward those in the front ranks had no choice but to kill or be killed, retreat being impossible.

After ten hours of this—it was now one o'clock in the afternoon—the Romans withdrew into the Antonia, the rebels into the Temple. Meanwhile, from the Temple's priests came ominous news. The supply of lambs for slaughter had finally run out. The sacred sacrifice, the whole ritualistic reason for the Temple's existence, could not be made. The breakdown delivered a profound psychological and spiritual blow. Was Josephus then right? Had God abandoned his people? Titus again issued an armistice offer, Josephus and other Jews who had joined the Romans shouting it to those in the Temple. He guaranteed the sanctity of the Temple against the intrusion of any non-Jew, provided the rebels would vacate the building and finish the war outside the city. Again this was refused. Over John's jeers, some few wealthy families crossed to the Roman lines. They were resettled in the nearby town of Gophna.

Titus set his men to demolishing the Antonia to its foundations, meanwhile raising four embankments against the Temple Mount, two against the north wall and two against the west. Inside the Temple enclosure these walls were lined with magnificent many-columned porticoes with elaborately fretted wooden ceilings. The portion of the portico on the north side, at its western end, bordered the southern wall of the Antonia, and the Jews realized that the Romans could clamber onto the portico roof from their embankments. On August 12 they set this north portico on fire. Thus the first torching of the Temple, Josephus notes, was done by the Jews themselves.

Three days later, the defenders decided to use the porticoes more strategically. They stuffed the wooden ceiling of the west portico with timber, bitumen, and pitch, and then withdrew as if exhausted. Some of the Romans, observing this retreat, grabbed ladders and climbed onto the roof of the portico to give chase. When the roof was crowded with men the Jews set it on fire, and the soldiers were consumed in the flames or fell to their deaths on the pavement below.

Then, says Josephus, occurred the most appalling event of the entire siege—"an act of which there is no parallel in the annals of Greece or any other country, a horrible and unspeakable deed and one incred-ible to hear." The Jews envied those who had died before hearing of

Early one morning, the pivotal incident in the fall of Jerusalem begins as a small band of Romans, including a trumpeter, takes advantage of poor vigilance by the exhausted defenders. Easily gaining the top of a wall, the trumpeter signals a blast that sends the Jewish soldiers fleeing, brings the Roman forces to their feet, and leaves the walls finally breached.

CROFUT

it; the Romans were greatly distressed and many refused to believe it was even possible. Titus pledged to requite this abomination with the leveling of the entire city.

After witnessing relentless tides of blood and torture, what could move these hardened men to such revulsion? A woman named Mary, daughter of another Eleazar, was a member of a distinguished family, but she had long ago been plundered of all her goods. One day she realized that every possible outcome awaiting her and her infant son was evil: They would be slain by the rebels or would starve to death, and if they survived till the Romans broke through they would be sold into slavery.

She looked at the baby nursing at her breast. "Poor child, why should I keep

Four months into the siege of Jerusalem occurred the most appalling event of the entire campaign, 'a horrible and unspeakable deed and one incredible to hear.'

you alive?" she said. The child could be "an omen of vengeance for the rebels, and to the world the only tale as yet untold of Jewish misery." Soon an odor that had been long absent from Jerusalem emanated from her dwelling: that of fresh meat cooking. It attracted a band of rebels, who demanded that Mary produce her hidden food. She displayed her roasted baby, already half-devoured.

"Overcome with instant horror, they stood immobile at the sight." Mary invited them to eat as well. "Don't pretend to be more tender than a woman or more compassionate than a mother." The men left trembling, "cowards for once," and as the tale spread within and beyond the city it brought horror previously unmatched. Josephus reports the Jews as too sickened to know what to do with the woman, while some Romans simply refused to believe such a thing could happen. Josephus does not record her fate.

The climax of the war was now only days away. With the porticoes destroyed the Jews could no longer rain missiles down on the Romans, and Titus's men completed the embankments and brought up siege engines. However, after six days of pounding, the north wall of the Temple Mount stood firm. On August 28 they brought up the battering ram but this too was ineffective. Though the Romans pried out several of the enormous blocks from the foundation it still did not topple. When they attempted to climb over the wall on ladders, the Jews easily overpowered them as they stepped off on top, or simply pushed the loaded ladders backward.

On the eighth day of the Jewish month of Ab (August 28), Titus ordered that the gates of the Temple be set on fire. The silver locks and hinges melted quickly, and fire roared through the ruins of the porticoes. The Jews were stunned and retreated inside the Temple, while the Romans overran the open outer courts. All day and night the fire raged. The next day Titus ordered the flames put out and a road made through the ruins up to the north side of the Inner Temple. If possible he wanted to preserve the Temple as an architectural jewel of the empire.

Early on August 30 the Jews mustered another charge, attacking the Romans in the outer court. After three hours of fierce combat they were beaten back into the Temple. As the Romans resumed their attempts to put out the fire, the Jews renewed the attack. In this melee, one of the Romans seized a burning piece of wood and hurled it through a small window into the inner court, near the sanctuary itself. This began the Temple's destruction, Josephus writes, noting that on precisely the same day, August 30, in the year 587 B.C., the First Temple was destroyed by Nebuchadnezzar. Both events would be mourned by the Jews for the next twenty centuries.

The Jews immediately concentrated on putting out the flames, and when Titus heard the news, he rushed out and gave orders to his men to do the same. However, Josephus records, the troops driven by fury stoked the fire further, while the Jews fled from the burning courts on the north side of the Temple toward the Nicanor Gate on the east, the Romans slaughtering all they could catch, even unarmed citizens. Blood poured down the Temple steps, and the bodies of those slain at the top slid to the bottom.

Titus and his generals then strode through the Temple, past the altar of sacrifice, up the steps to the Sanctuary. They ventured down the long hall, and found the end blocked by a curtain thirty feet high. Beyond it lay the Holy of Holies. Lifting the veil they stepped into a high, square room, a place dark and silent. They found it utterly empty. (See map, below left.)

What seemed impossible had come to pass. Gentiles were standing in the final sacred, secret place, the place the high priest alone dared enter, and he only once a year in fear and trembling. Into this place rough Gentiles had walked, tracking Jewish blood on their sandals. No angel of God had stopped them.

Then someone thrust a firebrand against a wooden gate, and the entire Inner Temple began to collapse in flames. Titus and his generals escaped, as did the rebels, but thousands of unarmed men, as well as women and children, clinging to the Temple as God's last refuge for them, were hacked to death by soldiers in the smoke and confusion. Among them were looters, many of them Jews. Since all was lost anyway, why not get what you could, they reasoned, and began spiriting some of the sacred articles. Then the Romans arrived, intent on their own looting, says Josephus, "and the robbers were thrust out." The Temple Mount, everywhere enveloped in flames, seemed to be boiling over from its base; the ground could not be seen anywhere between the corpses.[14] By evening the Roman victory was complete. Soldiers brought the imperial standards into the Temple court and made sacrifices to

**PHASE THREE:
THE TEMPLE FALLS,
THE VEIL VANISHES**

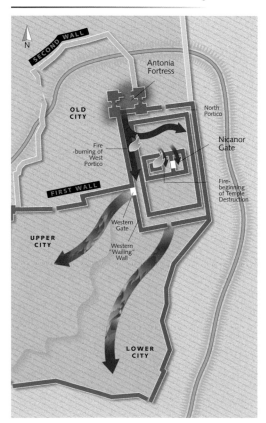

14. Though some Jewish interpreters see the Romans as tools of God's punishment, that doesn't mean they consider the Romans virtuous. Josephus, however, writing under the eye of Roman censors, is almost comically eager to exonerate his protectors. "Every one of the [Roman] soldiers was filled with reverent awe when his eye rested on the Temple," he writes, "and everyone prayed that the brigands would relent before all was lost." Considering the bloodied veterans striding through the corpse-strewn Inner Sanctuary, this is not easily believable.

CROFUT

Rebel leader John of Gischala flees for his life with members of his family through the maze of tunnels beneath Jerusalem. His attempt to escape would fail.

them, a seal of defilement on the holiest place of the Jews. Lost in the fire and the devastation was the veil of the curtain. It was gone; the Temple was gone. The old order was gone. In final flame and fury, its function had been fulfilled.

Simon and John, hiding out in the Upper City, knew they were beaten. They asked to parley with Titus. He stood, backed by his troops on the Temple Mount at its western gate. If they threw down their arms, he said, he would spare their lives. Again the rebel leaders refused. They had made a vow, they said, not to trust his word. Instead, they offered to turn over the city to him wholesale if he would guarantee their personal safety, allowing them to escape to the wilderness. Titus, aware that armed parties of rebels, at large and terrorizing the countryside, would present a continuing and probably insoluble problem, rejected this offer with contempt, and authorized his troops to sack and burn the city.[15]

At the time of the Roman siege, the rock beneath the Temple Mount and Jerusalem itself was a maze of tunnels, corridors, cisterns, water courses, pools, and sewage channels. The defenders sought refuge in all, but were invariably ferreted out by the Romans. This relatively large tunnel lies under the western wall of the Temple precincts. The system's complexity, with more of it being unearthed almost daily, has led some to speculate that the Ark of the Covenant may still lie hidden in this labyrinth.

---

15. Another general in another age, this one a Christian and commander of the losing side, would see precisely the same outcome if his defeated army were allowed to escape armed into the hills. His name was Robert E. Lee. He was urged by one of his officers not to surrender the remnant of his Confederate Army at Appomattox Courthouse, but rather to let it filter into the "wilderness." That way Lee would preserve his reputation as a general who had never surrendered. Lee refused. "The men would be without rations and under no control of officers," he said. "They would become bands of marauders. We would bring on a state of affairs it would take the country years to recover from." As "Christian men," he said, they could not even consider doing this. Some historians observe that he thereby prevented the southern United States from becoming another Balkans. For this and other reasons, Sir Winston Churchill in his *History of the English Speaking Peoples* calls Lee "one of the noblest Americans who ever lived and one of the greatest captains known to the annals of war."

As his men began the destruction of Jerusalem, the rebels fled to Herod's Palace. From here, they made their way down into the tunnels and sewers until the Romans dispersed them. Some of the priests handed over golden candlesticks, bowls, and other furnishings of the Temple in exchange for their own lives.

The Romans constructed earthworks one last time, one at Herod's Palace and another from the west of the Temple Mount. At the sound of battering the rebels abandoned the palace, and the soldiers took it without a struggle. Pouring into the Upper City they then slaughtered indiscriminately and set everything ablaze. All night long the fire spread, and as dawn rose on September 26 the entire city was in flames. Thus vanished the Temple, stone by stone, until, as Jesus Christ had once said, not one was left upon another.

Meanwhile John, with some of his lieutenants and their families, groped their way through the city's labyrinthine subterranean tunnels and passageways to make good their escape. Here they were caught by a Roman squad.

The archaeological site known as the "Burnt House" (above) bears silent witness to the fury of the destruction that the Romans visited upon Jerusalem. Excavated in the Upper City (the wealthier section), the ground floor consisted of a private mikvah or ritual bath, a small courtyard, and kitchen (shown here). More evidence of the brutality of the Roman victory (right): The bones of a woman's severed arm rest in the remains of a house of the Herodian period in Jerusalem's Upper City.

Simon on the other hand surrendered himself in a typically dramatic way. He had planned to dig a tunnel out of the city, but found the going impossible. So he robed himself in a white tunic and a regal purple cape and simply came above ground onto the Temple Mount, astonishing the soldiers there. They inquired who he was, but he refused to say, asking them to summon the officer in charge. This general immediately clapped Simon in irons.

Titus ordered that only the three great towers of Herod's Palace remain standing in order to show what strength Rome had overcome. The western part of the lower retaining wall of the Temple Mount, which would be known to history as "the Wailing Wall," was left standing, as were other parts of the retaining wall at the south and slightly east. Everything else was leveled. After awarding honors and spoils to the most valiant of his men, and assigning the Tenth Legion to garrison Jerusalem, Titus left the city a smoldering ruin. Though eager to go to Rome, he would have to wait for the spring sailing season. At Caesarea Philippi that fall he celebrated his brother's and then his father's birthdays with elaborate gladiatorial contests, killing great numbers of his Jewish prisoners of war as sport.

At home and in Judea, the Romans reveled in the victory that crushed Jerusalem. Received in Rome as a conquering hero, Titus raises his glass to toast the emperor and empire (1). To remind its subjects of the empire's might, Romans trumpeted such victories by minting coins (2), including one depicting the downcast figure of Judea Capta (Judea Captured). The Arch of Titus in Rome (3) was built by the emperor Domitian in honor of the exploits of his father (Vespasian) and brother (Titus). Reliefs on the arch celebrate such exploits as the procession into Rome of spoils taken from the Temple in Jerusalem (4).

CROFUT

At Rome he was received with joy by his father, and a triumphal procession marched through the city. Seven hundred Jewish youths had been selected for this display, chosen for their stature and physique, and marched along in fine costumes. Josephus does not disclose the eventual fate of these young men, whether they were retained as personal slaves, or perished in gladiatorial combat.

Simon and John were part of the parade as well, dragged in chains, jeered by the mob and understandably terrified. The golden candelabrum of the Temple was displayed, as well as the scroll of the Torah, in Titus's Arch of Triumph. This would remain standing for the next twenty centuries on the Forum Romanum, depicting in bas-relief the giant menorah borne over the wildly cheering crowd. The story of the war was displayed scene by scene on a series of giant floats, three or four stories high, and swathed in tapestries. On the floats other rebel

The fortress of Masada stood at the top of a mountain with sheer sides that dropped down into ravines. It had been built to be all but impervious to assault.

leaders were placed, each dramatizing the circumstances in which he was captured. These pictorial spectacles, however, caused problems. The screens proved unwieldy, swayed wildly in the wind and gravely alarmed the crowd.

At the Temple of Jupiter on the Capitol the parade came to a halt. It was the custom here during triumphal processions to execute the commander of the vanquished enemy's forces. Simon was whipped and dragged to the spot, and the announcement of his death brought exuberant acclamation. John was spared to end his life in prison.

Meanwhile, back in Palestine, two hilltop fortresses in the wilderness remained in rebel hands. The new legate of Judea, Lucilius Bassus, gathered forces first against the fortress at Machaerus. As they laboriously filled in a ravine in order to lay the siege, an unusual event won them victory in a moment. A heroic and widely admired young Jew named Eleazar had lingered outside the fortress one day after skirmishes, talking with friends up on the ramparts, when a bold soldier ran up, picked up Eleazar armor and all, and carried him back to the Roman camp. This caused such noisy lamentation from those occupying the fortress that the general formulated a plan. He had Eleazar brought to a spot in view of the rebel defenders and then set up a cross as if to crucify him. At this point those in the fortress began to shriek, and Eleazar begged his fellows to give up and save his life. They did, and Bassus allowed the unarmed band to flee in safety.

Bassus died and was succeeded by Flavius Silva, who faced the task of retaking the fortress at Masada. Eleazar son of Jair, a relative of Menahem who had led the Sicarii, was holed up here with the remnant of that rebel band. The fortress was at the top of a mountain with sheer sides that dropped down into ravines, and so was all but impervious to assault.

But not altogether impervious, Silva decided. Patiently, month after month,

Masada (above), seen here from the north, seemed impregnable in its time and it leaves that impression even to this day. The Roman troops under Flavius Silva undertook the monumental task of conquering the citadel by building a huge earthen ramp (seen at the right on the photograph above) up the west side of the mountain. The ramp itself was an outstanding engineering achievement, but moving a heavy siege tower up the steep incline was no less a feat. The outline of the Roman siege camp is visible as a rectangular space (lower right of picture above). The physical and historical mystique of Masada makes it a popular place for young Israelis to celebrate bar and bat mitzvahs (left). These coming-of-age ceremonies (for boys and girls, respectively) link the teenagers with the Jewish people whose history is powerfully symbolized by this remnant of the Masada synagogue in the wilderness.

he set the Romans to building a road up the steep slope towards the fortress. They finally reached and broke down the wall, only to find another erected behind it, this one constructed of wood and earth, to foil the battering rams with its flexibility. The Romans simply burned it.

Eleazar knew immediately that all hope was lost. They could not escape, and the Romans would not spare them. He urged his men to choose death for themselves and their loved ones rather than let their wives be raped and their children enslaved. Some protested in tears, unable to bear the thought of killing those they loved, but Eleazar continued his exhortation till all reached a peak of fervor. Men embraced their wives and children, killing them while yet clinging to their kisses. They then torched all their possessions, except the food, so the Romans would not think starvation had brought them to the deed. Ten were chosen by

Escape to Pella

The Christians survive Jerusalem's destruction—but how?

Jerusalem was a smoking ruin, the walls torn down, the Temple reduced to rubble, the great architectural achievements of Herod the Great destroyed save for the three tall towers of his palace which the Romans had preserved as a reminder of the grandeur of the city they had conquered. However, a question remained for historians ancient and modern: What had happened to Jerusalem's Christians?

One answer is provided by three ancient Christian historians—Eusebius, Hegesippus, and Epiphanius. All agreed that, warned by an angel of the devastation to come, the Christians escaped to Pella, about fifty miles northeast of Jerusalem in what the Romans called the Decapolis, the region of the ten cities on the east bank of the Jordan and the Sea of Galilee. One of the ten was Pella.

Precisely when the Christians escaped the city, whether before the war broke out in 66 or after the siege began in 70, the three do not make clear. Neither is it known whether all, or just some, of Jerusalem's Christian community left the doomed city. Some historians hold that a Christian community survived in Jerusalem right through the siege and remained in it afterward. Eusebius says that the Pella refugees returned to Jerusalem and elected Symeon, a cousin of Jesus, as bishop.

He succeeded James, the brother or stepbrother of Jesus, who had been dramatically martyred in the Temple shortly before the war broke out. (See sidebar pages 234-235.) Family leadership, in other words, was being preserved in the Jewish church, as it had been in the Jewish high priesthood.

At least one twentieth-century historian, S. G. F. Brandon of the University of Manchester, held that the escape to Pella is mere legend. The Pella Christians, he wrote, would have had to survive a general slaughter at Pella conducted by Jewish rebels the year the war broke out, and the subsequent Roman occupation, possibilities Brandon regards as highly improbable. Most other historians, however, refute his contentions and endorse the Pella escape.

Pella went on to become a substantial city with numerous churches before it began a final decline in the fifth century. By the twentieth, all that remained of it was a mound, about a thousand feet long, rising one hundred feet out of the valley of the Wadi Jirm in the foothills of the Transjordanian Plateau, three miles east of the Jordan, twenty miles south of Lake Tiberias, the biblical Sea of Galilee. ∎

Was Pella a city of refuge for Christians fleeing the destruction of Jerusalem? Certainly, as evidenced by the imposing ruins of an early Christian basilica, it would later become a prosperous Christian enclave. But the exact fate of those in the Christian church in doomed Jerusalem remains a mystery.

lot to kill the rest, and then one to kill the nine, who at last drove his sword through his own body and fell beside his family.

At dawn the Romans came up for battle, but found the site deserted and in flames. They shouted, and at the sound a woman emerged from an underground aqueduct. A relative of Eleazar, she was "more intelligent and educated than most," Josephus observes. With her was another woman, this one aged, and five little children. They had hidden themselves when the plan became clear, and were now able to explain what had happened. The Romans found it hard to believe, until they forced their way into the palace and saw the bodies of the dead. ∎

Jerusalem was gone. The smoke from the contemptuous sacrifice of a bird by an impudent Greek at Caesarea four years before had wafted southeastward to God's great city, setting sons against fathers, priests against soldiers, raining pillage and cruelty on the helpless, and finally bursting into a flame that appeared to destroy all that godly men had achieved. There had been omens for several years, Josephus recalls—an unearthly light had shone around the altar, the heavy eastern gate had mysteriously swung open unaided, at one Pentecost the priests had heard a great tumult with many voices saying, "We are leaving this place!" A great figure would arise in Israel at that time and become ruler of the world, he wrote. He identified him as Vespasian.

But Vespasian came and went, followed as emperor by Titus, followed in turn by Titus's vicious brother Domitian. Then, some 850 miles east of Domitian's Rome, across the Adriatic, across the Aegean on the Isle of Patmos, by the light of a small, smoky lamp, an old man takes up a pen with trembling hand and describes a vision.

He sees another Jerusalem. He sees it "coming down out of heaven from God, having the glory of God, its radiance like a most rare jewel, clear as crystal. It has a great, high wall, with twelve gates, and at the gates twelve angels, and on the gates the names of the twelve tribes of Israel are inscribed. . . ."

It has no Temple, "for its Temple is the Lord God the Almighty and the Lamb. And the city has no need of sun or moon to shine upon it, for the glory of God is its light, and its lamp is the Lamb. By its light shall the nations walk; and the kings of the earth shall bring their glory into it, and its gates shall never be shut by day, and there shall be no night there. Let him who hears say, 'Come,' and let him who desires, take the water of life without price."

The old man ends with a prayer. "Amen," he writes. "Even so, come, Lord Jesus!" (Book of Revelation.) ∎

HOW THE BOOKS OF THE CHRISTIAN
HISTORY PROJECT ARE PRODUCED

THE CONCEPT OF THE SERIES

The Christian History Series was conceived by TED BYFIELD, a Canadian journalist who over the years observed a notable and growing public unawareness of Christian origins, not only among fellow journalists, but also among otherwise knowledgeable Christians. Few realize the profound degree to which Christianity has shaped western culture and society—a dangerous situation, he says, since what we don't value we too easily discard. In publishing a twelve-volume history of his home province of Alberta, he developed a method by which teams of writers, illustrators, and academics could produce a multi-volume history of the Christian faith in a remarkably short time.

ASSIGNING THE WRITERS

Byfield recruited CALVIN DEMMON, a former journalistic colleague and Monterey, California, columnist and editor, to help him direct, edit, and write the nine chapters in the first volume and those in the volumes to follow. After lining up some eighteen writers, mostly journalists, from across the United States and Canada, they assigned five to do one chapter apiece in the first volume, Byfield and Demmon writing the other four chapters themselves. Together they planned the subject matter of each chapter and the content of the twenty-three sidebar stories running with the chapters.

RESEARCHING THE SUBJECT MATTER

MOIRA CALDER, a graduate statistician-turned-history-researcher who directed the research work for the Alberta series, now performs the same function for the Christian History books, heading a team of about a dozen freelance readers. She takes the schematic for each volume, decides on the basis of academic advice which books and source materials will be required by the writers, assigns researchers to the source books, and instructs them on what sort of information the writers will require. From the books, her researchers summarize interesting material for the writers. It is fed into a data bank and sent to the writers but also stored for future use in producing videos and history curricula for Christian schools.

DESIGNING THE BOOKS

The volumes are designed by DENTON PENDERGAST, formerly of Victoria, B.C., and Ottawa, now on the staff of the Christian History Project. A graphic designer for some thirty years, he saw the central challenge of the Christian History series as deriving from the essential purpose of the books— which is to inform rather than merely entertain. Denton hopes his integration of illustration, photography, maps, and text into a cohesive whole will engage browsers and turn them into avid readers of the series.

ILLUSTRATING THE BOOK

JACK KEASCHUK, who directed production on the Alberta history series and then moved to the Christian History series, is as illustrations editor responsible for the pictorial content of the series. He traveled through the United States in 1999, assembling a group of fifteen top-line illustrating artists to provide realistic representations of the events being described in the chapters. As the content of each chapter becomes known, Keaschuk develops the illustration concepts in consultation with the editors and the artists. In most cases a single artist is assigned to illustrate each chapter. He also lines up photographs from those parts of the world where the events take place, consulting people like Micha Ashkenazi of Israel Pilgrims Travel in Jerusalem, who assisted in relating locations in the first-century city with their remnants in the Jerusalem of today.

THE WRITERS

The book opens with the Pentecost experience. BYFIELD wrote the initial copy for Chapter 1 which reviews the ministry, trial and death of Jesus Christ as these had appeared, not to his followers but to his other contemporaries. DEMMON wrote Chapter 2, on the first steps taken by Jesus' followers in Jerusalem.

GARY THOMAS of Bellingham, Washington, author of three current Christian books and a contributor to *Christianity Today* newsmagazine, produced Chapter 3, covering the persecution of the church in Jerusalem, the expulsion of Jesus' followers, and the consequent spread of the Gospel throughout Judea, Samaria, the coastal towns and Antioch.

STEPHEN HOPKINS, director of publications at Clarkson University in Potsdam, New York, and a former executive editor of *Alberta Report*, produced Chapter 4, the first of the three chapters on Paul, describing his conversion and his first mission with Barnabas. Byfield produced the second Pauline chapter, No. 5, on Paul's ministry in Greece and Asia Minor, and Demmon produced the third and final Pauline chapter, 6, on Paul's ordeal in Jerusalem and consequent voyage to Rome, with a summation of the eternal debt of Christians to that man.

CHARLOTTE ALLEN, a Washington, D.C. journalist and author, contributor to the *Atlantic Monthly*, *Washington Post*, and *New Republic*, produced Chapter 7, on the emergence of the three Synoptic Gospels, Matthew, Mark and Luke, and the reason these books have informed and shaped the lives of Christians for two thousand years.

MARK GALLI of Wheaton, Illinois, managing editor of *Christianity Today* news magazine, produced chapter 8, on the founding of the Christian community at Rome and the horror that was inflicted upon it by the crazed emperor Nero, who blamed the little Christian congregations there for setting the fire that would destroy most of the city, then put them to hideous deaths as scapegoats for a deed for which many were blaming the emperor himself.

FREDERICA MATHEWES-GREEN of Linthicum, Maryland, columnist for *Christianity Today*, contributor to *Touchstone* magazine, author of several Christian books and commentator on National Public Radio, produced the magnificent final chapter, No. 9, on the fall of Jerusalem and the dire fulfillment of Christ's prophecy for the city.

The copy was edited by BYFIELD and DEMMON to sustain a reasonably consistent literary style throughout the book and to maintain the momentum of the Christian story as it unfolded in the thirty years that followed the Resurrection.

THE ACADEMIC CONSULTANTS

All text appearing in the series is submitted to academic consultants, each volume supervised by a two-member committee, one representing the Evangelical and one the Catholic or Orthodox traditions. These in turn refer us to specialist historians where specific subjects require it. The consultant committee on Volume 1 consisted of DR. WILLIAM S. BARKER (left), retired professor of history and vice president of academic affairs for Westminster Theological Seminary in Philadelphia, and DR. DENNIS MARTIN (right), professor of historical theology at Loyola University, Chicago. The project was also greatly encouraged by DR. MARK NOLL, professor of history at Wheaton College, Wheaton, Illinois; and DR. JAMES I. PACKER, Board of Governors Professor (theology) at Regent College in Vancouver.

PLANNING THE FUTURE VOLUMES

The planning of the time frames and individual chapter content for future volumes is under the direction of BARRETT PASHAK, a University of Alberta librarian and former chief researcher for *Alberta Report* newsmagazine. He is assisted by another librarian and history researcher, LOUISE HENEIN. In the west, says Pashak, Christian history and world history are much the same thing, so that planning the series is a matter of dividing western history into logical segments, each segment a volume, then dividing each segment into appropriate subsections, each of which becomes a chapter. The series is, of course, "people-centered." That is, we believe that individuals produce events, rather than events producing individuals, and this principle informs the planning process.

THE ILLUSTRATORS

The four illustrations for Chapter 1, including the striking picture of the crucified Jesus, are the work of GLENN HARRINGTON of Pipersville, Pennsylvania, who also works for Macmillan Books, Bantam-Doubleday-Dell and Paramount Studios.

The five illustrations in Chapter 2 showing the first ministry of Peter and including the three renderings on the martyrdom of Stephen are the work of RICHARD SPARKS of Norwalk, Connecticut, whose clients include Exxon, *Sports Illustrated*, *Time*, Doubleday and Simon and Schuster.

The six illustrations in Chapter 3 on the expansion of the Christians from Jerusalem (including the delightfully cunning Simon Magus) are by MICHAEL DUDASH of Moretown, Vermont, who also draws for Reader's Digest Books, 20th Century Fox, Universal Studios, Simon and Schuster, Random House and McGraw-Hill.

The color illustrations in Chapters 4, 5 and 6 on Paul were done by the studio of WOOD RONSAVILLE HARLIN Inc. of Annapolis, Maryland. (The names of the individual artists are appended alongside each illustration.)

GREG HARLIN (left) produced the striking illustration of Paul's conversion on the Damascus Road. MATTHEW FREY (center) depicts some of the violent scenes in Paul's ministry, including the fierce rage of the silversmiths at Ephesus and the near lynching of Paul by his angry countrymen at Jerusalem. ROB WOOD (right) did the two marine drawings, including the scene of the storm that imperiled Paul in the Mediterranean. All three are contributors to *National Geographic*, *Reader's Digest*, the *Smithsonian Magazine* and many other publications.

The six illustrations in Chapter 7 on the Synoptic Gospels, which portray some of the aspects of Jesus' ministry, are by JOHN COLLIER of Plano, Texas, who does work for the *New York Times* magazine, Viking Penguin, the A and E television network, *Atlantic Monthly*, Avon Books, and Warner Brothers.

The margin pen sketches of Paul are the work of JAMIE HOLLOWAY, a promising young illustrator from Edmonton, Alberta, whose work is familiar to Alberta advertising and government agencies.

The five illustrations in Chapter 8, detailing the debaucheries of Nero, the catastrophic fire of Rome and the brutalities inflicted on the Christian community whom Nero blamed for it are by SHANNON STIRNWEIS of New Ipswich, New Hampshire. His work has been used by the Department of the Interior, the U.S. Air Force Museum, and the Coast Guard. He was a founder of the Society of Illustrators.

The eight dramatic illustrations describing the Roman siege of Jerusalem, two battle scenes and the horrors of starvation within the city are by BOB CROFUT of Richfield, Connecticut, whose clients include Doubleday, Prentice-Hall, NBC, MGM, Ford, Reader's Digest and IBM.

THE MAP MAKERS

The twelve maps in the book were researched by LEANNE NASH, who has a master's degree in publishing and was marketing manager for Duthie Books, Vancouver. They were produced by MIKE GRANT. Trained in graphic design at Manchester, England, he now provides illustration and map services to the energy industry as Mike Grant Design.

CONTRIBUTORS TO THE SECOND EDITION

Art Director: JACK KEASCHUK

Design Director: DEAN PICKUP
Revision of the layout for this volume was effected by a newcomer to the project, DEAN PICKUP of Edmonton, a graduate of the visual communications program at Edmonton's Grant MacEwan College with a major in design and digital media. Pickup, who assisted Jack Keaschuk, has previously worked in retail promotions and video marketing.

Production Editor: REV. DAVID EDWARDS
REV. DAVID EDWARDS is an Orthodox monk of the Community of St. Silouan the Athonite. An arts graduate of the University of Manitoba, he received his theological training at Durham University in England and took his teacher training at Leeds University. After eighteen years in the Winnipeg, Manitoba, public school system, he came to Edmonton as a pastor at St. Herman's Orthodox Church.

BIBLIOGRAPHY

GENERAL

Amorth, Gabriel. *An Exorcist Tells His Story*. San Francisco: Ignatius Press, 1999.

De Burgh, William George. *The Legacy of the Ancient World*. London: Macdonald and Evans, 1924.

Dowley, Tim, ed. *Handbook to the History of Christianity*. Grand Rapids: Eerdmans, 1977.

Freedman, D. N., ed. *Anchor Bible Dictionary*. New York: Doubleday, 1992.

Hastings, James, John A. Selbie, and John C. Lambert, eds. *Dictionary of the Apostolic Church*. Edinburgh: T. and T. Clark, 1915.

Herbermann, Charles G. *The Catholic Encyclopedia*. New York: Appleton, 1907–1912.

Johnson, Paul. *A History of Christianity*. Harmondsworth, UK: Penguin, 1980.

Lewis, C. S. *The Four Loves*. London: G. Bles, 1960.

Maier, Paul L. *In the Fullness of Time: A Historian Looks at Christmas, Easter and the Early Church*. Grand Rapids, MI: Kregel Publications, 1997.

McManners, John, ed. *The Oxford Illustrated History of Christianity*. New York: Oxford University Press, 1990.

Robinson, John. *Honest to God*. London: SCM Press, ca. 1963.

Robinson, Thomas A. et al. *The Early Church: An Annotated Bibliography of Literature in English*. American Theological Library Association; Metuchen, NJ: Scarecrow Press, 1993.

The New Testament in Modern English. Trans. by J. B. Phillips. New York: Collins, 1958.

BIBLE COMMENTARY

Adamson, James B. *The Epistle of James*. Grand Rapids: Eerdmans, 1976.

Baird, William. "One against the other: Intra-church conflict in 1 Corinthians." In *The Conversation Continues: Studies in Paul and John*. Nashville: Abingdon Press, 1990: 116–169.

Barclay, John M. G. "Conflict in Thessalonica." In *Catholic Biblical Quarterly* 55, Vol. 3 (July 1993).

Barclay, William, trans. *The Letter to the Hebrews*, 2nd ed. Philadelphia: Westminster Press, 1957.

Betz, Hans Dieter. *Galatians: A Commentary on Paul's Letter to the Churches in Galatia*. Minneapolis: Fortress Press, 1979.

Blomberg, Craig L. *The Historical Reliability of the Gospels*. Downers Grove, IL: Inter-Varsity Press, 1987.

Bruce, F. F. *The Books and the Parchments: The Languages, Canon, Manuscripts, Versions, History and "Lost Books" of the Bible*. Old Tappan, NJ: Revell, 1963.
———. *The Book of the Acts*. Grand Rapids, MI: Eerdmans, 1981.
———. *The New Testament Documents: Are They Reliable?* London: Intervarsity Fellowship, 1960.

Fee, Gordon D. *The First Epistle to the Corinthians*. Grand Rapids, MI: Eerdmans, 1987.

Fortna, Robert T. Philippians: "Paul's most egocentric letter." In *The Conversation Continues: Studies in Paul and John*. Nashville: Abingdon Press, 1990: 220–233.

Gillquist, Peter E., Alan Wallerstedt, and Joseph Allen. *The Orthodox Study Bible: New Testament and Psalms, New King James Version*. Nashville: T. Nelson, 1993.

Griffith-Jones, Robin. *The Four Witnesses*. San Francisco: Harper San Francisco, 2000.

Gunther, John J. *Paul, Messenger and Exile: A Study in the Chronology of his Life and Letters*. Valley Forge, PA: Judson Press, 1972.

Guthrie, Donald. *The Apostles*. Grand Rapids, MI: Zondervan, 1975.

Kenyon, Frederic G. *The Bible and Modern Scholarship*. London: John Murray, 1948.

Lightfoot, J. B. *Biblical Essays*. New York: Macmillan, 1893.

Malherbe, Abraham J. *Paul and the Thessalonians: The Philosophic Tradition of Pastoral Care*. Philadelphia: Fortress Press, 1986.

Malina, Bruce J., and Jerome H. Neyrey. *Portraits of Paul: An Archaeology of Ancient Personality*. Louisville, KY: Westminster John Knox Press, 1996.

Marshall, I. Howard. *Luke: Historian and Theologian*. Grand Rapids, MI: Zondervan, 1971.

Munck, Rev. Johannes, William F. Albright, and C. S. Mann, trans. *The Acts of the Apostles. Anchor Bible Commentary*, Vol. 31. New York: Doubleday, 1967.

Ramsay, W. M. *Historical Commentary on the Galatians*. London: Hodder and Stoughton, 1900.

Robinson, John A. T. *Redating the New Testament*. Philadelphia: Westminster Press, 1976.

Sanders, E. P. and Margaret Davies. *Studying the Synoptic Gospels*. Philadelphia: Trinity Press International, 1989.

Streeter, Burnett Hillman. *The Four Gospels: A Study of Origins*. London: Macmillan, 1964.

Zodhiates, Spiros. *The Epistle of James and the Life of Faith*. Grand Rapids, MI: Eerdmans, 1959.

EARLY CHURCH

Adey, Lionel. *Hymns and the Christian "Myth"*. Vancouver: University of British Columbia Press, 1986.

Best, Ernest. *Paul and his Converts*. Edinburgh: T and T Clark, 1988.

Brown, Raymond E., and John P. Meier, eds. *Antioch and Rome: New Testament Cradles of Catholic Christianity*. New York: Paulist Press, 1982.

Brown, Raymond E., Karl P. Donfried, and John Reumann, eds. *Peter in the New Testament*. New York: Paulist Press, 1973.

Bruce, F. F. *New Testament History*. London: Oliphants, 1969.
———. *Paul: Apostle of the Free Spirit*. Exeter: Paternoster Press, 1977.
———. *The Pauline Circle*. Grand Rapids, MI: Paternoster Press, 1984.
———. *Peter, Stephen, James, and John: Studies in Early Non-Pauline Christianity*. Grand Rapids, MI: Eerdmans, 1979.

Bulmer-Thomas, Ivor, ed. *St. Paul: Teacher and Traveller*. Leighton Buzzard, UK: Faith Press, 1975.

Chilton, Bruce, and Craig A. Evans. *James the Just and Christian Origins*. Boston: Brill, 1999.

Church, F. Forrester, and Terrence J. Mulry. *The Macmillan Book of Earliest Christian Hymns*. New York: Macmillan, 1988.

Cullmann, Oscar. Peter: *Disciple, Apostle, Martyr*. London: SCM Press, 1962.

Di Berardino, Angelo, ed. *Encyclopedia of the Early Church*, trans. Adrian Walford. New York: Oxford University Press and Institutum Patriscum Augustinianum, 1992.

Doohan, Leonard. *Luke: The Perennial Spirituality*. Santa Fe, NM: Bear, 1985.

Duncan, George S. *St. Paul's Ephesian Ministry: A Reconstruction*. London: Hodder and Stoughton, 1929.

Eisenman, Robert. *James the Brother of Jesus*. New York: Penguin, 1997

Eusebius of Caesarea. *The History of the Church from Christ to Constantine*, trans. G. A. Williamson. New York: Dorset Press, 1965.

Foakes-Jackson, F. J. Peter: *Prince of Apostles*. London: Hodder and Stoughton, 1927.

Fortna, Robert T., and Beverly R. Gaventa, eds. *The Conversation Continues: Studies in Paul and John*. Nashville: Abingdon Press, 1990.

Frend, W. H. C. *The Early Church*. London: Hodder and Stoughton, 1971.

———. *Martyrdom and Persecution in the Early Church: A Study of a Conflict from the Maccabees to Donatus*. Oxford: Basil Blackwell, 1965.

Gonzalez, Justo L. *The Story of Christianity. Volume I: The Early Church to the Dawn of the Reformation*. San Francisco: Harper and Row, 1984.

Green, Michael. *Evangelism in the Early Church*. London: Hodder and Stoughton, 1970.

Hazlett, Ian. *Early Christianity: Origins and Evolution to AD 600*. Nashville: Abingdon Press, 1991.

Hengel, Martin, and Anna Maria Schwemer. *Paul between Damascus and Antioch: The Unknown Years*. Louisville, KY: Westminster John Knox Press, 1997.

Klausner, Joseph, with William F. Stinespring, trans. *From Jesus to Paul*. Boston: Beacon Press, 1943.

Knox, John. *Chapters in a Life of Paul*. New York: Abingdon Press, 1960.

Maier, Paul L. *In the Fullness of Time*. Grand Rapids, MI: Kregel, 1997.

McGuckin, John Anthony, comp. and trans. *At the Lighting of the Lamps: Hymns of the Ancient Church*. Harrisburg, PA: Morehouse Pub., 1997.

Meeks, Wayne A. *The First Urban Christians*. New Haven, CT: Yale University Press, 1983.

Minear, Paul S. "Singing and Suffering in Philippi." In *The Conversation Continues: Studies in Paul and John*. Nashville: Abingdon Press, 1990: 202–219.

Moraes, George Mark. *A History of Christianity in India*. Bombay: Manaktalas, 1964.

Muggeridge, Malcolm, and Alec Vidler. *Paul: Envoy Extraordinary*. London: Collins, 1972.

Murphy-O'Connor, Jerome. *Paul: A Critical Life*. Oxford: Clarendon, 1996.

Neill, Stephen. *A History of Christianity in India: The Beginnings to AD 1707*. Cambridge, UK: Cambridge University Press, 1984.

Nock, Arthur Darby. *Early Gentile Christianity and its Hellenistic Background*. New York: Harper and Row, 1964.

Painter, John. *Just James: The Brother of Jesus in History and Tradition*. Columbia: USC Press, 1997.

Patrick, William. *James, the Lord's Brother*. Edinburgh: T and T Clark, 1906.

Perkins, Pheme. *Peter: Apostle for the Whole Church*. Minneapolis: Fortress Press, 1994.

Ramsay, W. M. *St. Paul the Traveller and the Roman Citizen*. London: Hodder and Stoughton, 1846.

Ricciotti, Giuseppe. *Paul the Apostle*. Milwaukee: Bruce Pub., 1953.

Segal, Alan F. *Paul the Convert: The Apostolate and Apostasy of Saul the Pharisee*. New Haven, CT: Yale University Press, 1990.

Thomas, P. *Christians and Christianity in India and Pakistan*. London: Allen and Unwin, 1954.

Walsh, Michael. *The Triumph of the Meek: Why Christianity Succeeded*. Toronto: Fitzhenry and Whiteside, 1986.

Wink, Walter. "The hymn of the cosmic Christ." In *The Conversation Continues: Studies in Paul and John*. Nashville: Abingdon Press, 1990: 235–245.

GEOGRAPHICAL REFERENCES

Avigad, Nahman. *Discovering Jerusalem*. Nashville: Thomas Nelson, 1983.

Bahat, Dan, with Chaim T. Rubinstein, trans. *Shlomo Ketko: The Illustrated Atlas of Jerusalem*. NY: Simon and Schuster, 1990.

Coogan, Michael D. *The Oxford History of the Biblical World*. New York: Oxford University Press, 1998.

Downey, Glanville. *Ancient Antioch*. Princeton, NJ: Princeton University Press, 1963.

Eydoux, Henri-Paul, trans. Lorna Andrade. *In Search of Lost Worlds*. New York: Hamlyn, 1972.

Jeremias, Joachim. *Jerusalem in the Time of Jesus*. London: SCM Press, 1969.

Meyers, Eric M.: *Galilee through the Centuries*. Winona Lake, IA: Eisenbrauns, 1999.

Murphy-O'Connor, Jerome. *The Holy Land: From Earliest Times to 1700*, 4th ed. Oxford Archaeological Series. New York: Oxford University Press, 1998.

Shanks, Hershel and Dan P. Cole, eds.: *Archaeology and the Bible: The Best of BAR*. Washington, DC: Biblical Archaeology Society, 1990.

ROMAN EMPIRE

Bishop, John H. *Nero: The Man and the Legend*. New York: A. S. Barnes, 1965.

Bowman, Alan K., Edward Champlin and Andrew Lintott, eds. *The Augustan Empire, 43 BC–AD 69*. Cambridge Ancient History, Vol. 10. Cambridge: Cambridge University Press, 1970.

Carcopino, Jerome. *Daily Life in Ancient Rome*. Markham, UK: Penguin, 1985.

Casson, Lionel. *The Ancient Mariners*. Princeton, NJ: Princeton University Press, 1991.

———. *Travel in the Ancient World*. London: Allen and Unwin, 1974.

Dio Cassius, trans. Earnest Carey and Herbert Baldwin Foster. *Dio's Roman History*. London: Heinemann, 1914.

Durant, Will. *Caesar and Christ: A History of Roman Civilization and of Christianity from their Beginnings to AD 325*. New York: Simon and Shuster, 1935.

Goudsblom, Johan. *Fire and Civilization*. London: Penguin, 1992.

Grant, Michael. *Nero: Emperor in Revolt*. New York: American Heritage, 1970.

Griffin, Miriam T. *Nero: The End of a Dynasty*. London: Batsford, 1984.

Henderson, Bernard W. *The Life and Principate of the Emperor Nero*. London: Methuen, 1905.

Mattingly, Harold. *Roman Imperial Civilization*. London: E. Arnold, 1957.

Millar, Fergus. *The Emperor in the Roman World (31 BC–AD 337)*. London: Duckworth, 1977.

Petit, Paul, trans. James Willis. *Pax Romana*. London: Batsford, 1976.

Pike, E. Royston. *Love in Ancient Rome*. New York: Crown Pub., 1965.

Rudich, Vasily. *Political Dissidence under Nero: The Price of Dissimulation*. New York: Routledge, 1993.

Smith, R. E. *The Failure of the Roman Republic*. Cambridge, UK: Cambridge University Press, 1955.

Suetonius, Gaius Tranquillus. *The Twelve Caesars*, trans. Robert Graves. London: Allen Lane, 1957.

Tacitus, Cornelius. *Complete Works*, trans. Alfred John Church and William Jackson Brodribb. New York: The Modern Library, 1942.

Warmington, B. H. *Nero: Reality and Legend*. New York: W. W. Norton, 1969.

Wells, C. M. *The Roman Empire*. Stanford, CA: Stanford University Press, 1984.

Wilkins, Michael J. and J. P. Moreland, eds. *Jesus under Fire*. Grand Rapids, MI: Zondervan, 1995.

JUDAISM AND EARLY CHRISTIANITY

Donfried, Karl P., and Peter Richardson. *Judaism and Christianity in First-Century Rome*. Grand Rapids, MI: Eerdmans, 1998.

Dunn, James D. G. "Who Did Paul Think He Was? A Study of Jewish-Christian Relations." In *New Testament Studies* 45 (1999): 174–193.

Edersheim, Alfred. *The Life and Times of Jesus the Messiah*. Grand Rapids, MI: Eerdmans, 1980.

Fairchild, Mark R. *Paul's Pre-Christian Zealot Associations*. New Testament Studies 45 (1999): 514–532.

Matthews, Victor H. *Manners and Customs in the Bible*, rev. ed. Peabody, MA: Hendrickson Pub., 1991.

Nickelsburg, George W. E., and George W. MacRae, eds. *Christians among Jews and Gentiles*. Philadelphia: Fortress Press, 1986.

Sanders, E. P. "Jewish Association with Gentiles and Galatians 2:11–14." In *The Conversation Continues: Studies in Paul and John*. Nashville: Abingdon Press; 1990: 170–188.

Sanders, Jack T. *Schismatics, Sectarians, Dissidents, Deviants: The First One Hundred Years of Jewish-Christian Relations*. Valley Forge, PA: Trinity Press International, 1993.

JUDAISM AND JEWISH HISTORY

Hall, John F., and John W. Welch, eds. *Masada and the World of the New Testament*. Provo, UT: BYU Studies, 1997.

Josephus, Flavius. *Complete Works*, trans. William Whiston. Grand Rapids, MI: Kregel, 1978.

Josephus, Flavius. *Josephus, the Jewish War*, ed. Gaalya Cornfeld, Benjamin Mazar, and Paul L. Maier. Grand Rapids, MI: Zondervan, 1982.

Rhoads, David M. *Israel in Revolution: 6–74 CE: A Political History Based on the Writings of Josephus*. Philadelphia: Fortress Press, 1976.

Sanders, E. P. *Judaism: Practice and Belief, 63 BCE–66 CE*. Philadelphia: Trinity Press International, 1992.

Schwartz, Daniel R. *Agrippa I: The Last King of Judaea*. Tubingen: J. C. B. Mohr, 1990.

Shutt, R. J. H: *Studies in Josephus*. London: SPCK, 1961.

Smallwood, E. Mary. *Jews under Roman Rule from Pompey to Diocletian: A Study in Political Relations*. Leiden: Brill, 1981.

Thackeray, H. St. J. *Josephus: The Man and the Historian*. New York: Ktav, 1967.

Yadin, Yigael. *Masada: Herod's Fortress and the Zealots' Last Stand*. New York: Random House, 1966.

Zeitlin, Solomon. *The Rise and Fall of the Judaean State*, 2nd ed. Philadelphia: Jewish Publication Society of America, 1968.

ABBREVIATIONS

Apoc.	Apocrypha
AV	Authorized (King James) Version
JBP	J. B. Phillips Translation
LXX	Septuagint
NIV	New International Version
NRSV	New Revised Standard Version
NT	New Testament
OT	Old Testament
RSV	Revised Standard Version

PHOTOGRAPHIC CREDITS

INDEX

Don't miss any volumes of *The Christians*

In Volume Two

- Who was Jesus? In the writing of the Fourth Gospel, John, the Beloved Disciple, provides the answer.

- Polycarp and Ignatius: Two Christian leaders give their lives for the new faith.

- The Martyrs of Lyon: Stirred by the resolute faith of the Christian slave Blandina, forty-seven Christians accept death rather than deny Christ.

- Justin: A brilliant convert teaches the Christians to defend their faith, then suffers death for it himself.

- Perpetua: Loyalty to God or to her baby? This young mother had to decide.

- Tertullian: The acerbic lawyer who spoke for Christianity and died alone.

- Origen: The martyr's son who became an evangelical powerhouse.

- Proliferating gospel versions raise the cry for a Christian Bible.

  PLUS: Twenty-five other stories and more than two hundred illustrations and photographs, portraying Rome's rising determination to wipe out this new religion called Christianity, and how the Christians contended with it.

In Volume Three

- The emperor Decius launches an empire-wide persecution; thousands of Christians suffer rather than recant their faith.

- Cyprian: rich but disenchanted, seeks tranquility in the faith. Instead, God embroils him in a fight for the truth and he dies as a martyr.

- The emperor Diocletian delivers an intended knockout blow against the Christians, and discovers them indestructible.

- The tables are turned. Spurred by a vision, Constantine defeats the anti-Christian emperors, legalizes the faith, and Rome backs the Christians.

- Bishops, many bearing the scars of persecution, meet at Nicea and define what Christians believe, but their definition faces wide challenge.

  PLUS: The New Testament gradually takes shape; life and death in the catacombs; the soldier witnesses to the Prince of Peace; Christian morality becomes the basis of law; a rugged bishop brings Christ to Armenia; the mysterious origins of British Christianity.

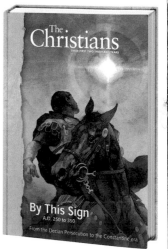

In Volume Four

- Civilization crumbles as barbarians invade the West.

- Athanasius stands firm against emperors, bishops and the world, preserving the creed Christians will recite for seventeen hundred years.

- The cut-throat Franks become the improbable founders of Christian Europe.

- How the Irish, converted by the remarkable Patrick, bring the faith to pagan Europe.

- Rome might be gone, but the convert Augustine tells of a city destined for eternity.

- The unlikely marriage of a great emperor with an ex-prostitute who had become a born-again Christian shapes Europe's destiny and the faith.

PLUS: Anthony leads an extraordinary host of men and women to the monastic solitude of the desert; Chrysostom, ancient Christianity's greatest preacher, quarrels with an empress and dies in misery; the attack and eventual defeat of the "half-human" Huns; a soldier becomes the most popular French saint ever.

The Christians
THEIR FIRST TWO THOUSAND YEARS

Darkness Descends
A.D. 350 to 565
The Fall of the Western Roman Empire

Coming in Volume Five

- The Christian attempt to convert Arabia. Where it succeeded and why it failed.

- The Arabs, an amazing people and the greatest soldiers in the world, and how Mohammed converted them to his new religion, Islam.

- How Mohammed rejected Jesus' path of love and peace and set afoot the military conquest of the world.

- Islam's astonishing simultaneous double victory over both the Roman and the Persian empires.

- The fall of Antioch and Jerusalem to Islam and how Egypt was betrayed and lost by a perfidious Christian patriarch.

- Pope Gregory the Great, whose iron pragmatism and tireless efforts would unite and save western Europe.

- The fall of Christian Spain and Islam's invasion of France, where the Muslims first encounter the Christian Franks—who stop them cold at Tours.

- The crucial battle for Constantinople, where an emperor, an innovation, and the rebellion of Christian slaves against their Muslim masters halt the Muslim attack on eastern Europe.

PLUS: The Holy Koran and how it came to be; how the desert-raised Muslims took to the sea and rapidly gained control of the whole Mediterranean.

Subsequent volumes bring the Christian story to the end of the twentieth century